Quantitative Methods
for
business decisions

Quantitative Met
for
business decisions

JON CURWIN and ROGER SLATER

Van Nostrand Reinhold (UK) Co. Ltd

First published in 1985 by
Van Nostrand Reinhold (UK) Co. Ltd,
Molly Millars Lane, Wokingham, Berkshire, England

Reprinted 1986 (twice), 1987

Typeset in Plantin 10 on 11pt by Colset Private Ltd, Singapore

Printed in Great Britain by
T. J. Press (Padstow) Ltd, Padstow, Cornwall

Library of Congress Cataloging in Publication Data

Curwin, Jon.
    Quantitative methods for business decisions.

    Includes index.
    1. Business mathematics.   2. Statistics.   I. Slater, Roger.   II. Title.
HF5691.C87   1985   519.5′024658   85-3267
ISBN 0-442-30640-7

British Library Cataloguing in Publication Data

Curwin, Jon
    Quantitative methods for business decisions.
    1. Decision-making—Mathematical models
    I. Title   II. Slater, Roger
    658.4′03   HD30.23

    ISBN 0-442-30640-7

Contents

Preface

This book is about the mathematics and statistics required for degree courses in Accountancy, Business Studies and Economics, and BTEC courses in Business Studies and Public Administration. It is concerned with the ways in which mathematics and statistics can be applied to solve business-related problems. Collectively, it is this package of mathematical and statistical skills and techniques that we refer to as **quantitative methods**.

A browse through the following pages will reveal a range of symbols, calculations, diagrams and eventually an appendix of statistical tables. What brings them all together is the need to define and solve problems. This book is about problems!

It is recognized that many students may have found mathematics a difficult subject in the past and are apprehensive about using the basic skills as part of their new first-year course. For most students, O-level mathematics would have been an entry equipment, though many would admit that their knowledge is no longer at that standard. This book makes few assumptions about previous knowledge, and develops the necessary arithmetic within the context of each topic. For those students with the advantage of A-level mathematics, they will encounter the application of skills which do seem familiar to problems which are not.

This book has been designed to cover the entire syllabus of most first year courses in quantitative methods. This includes both the mathematics and statistics. The coverage and the standard have been particularly influenced by a survey of business-related degree courses with which the authors were involved.* The approach to each topic attempts to reflect current teaching methods and trends within the disciplines.

Acknowledgements

For comments on the draft chapters we are indebted to our critical reader Mr Stanley Letchford whose diligence has considerably improved the text. We would like to thank Mr Paul Costa who translated our sketches to more meaningful illustrations. We would also like to express our thanks to Miss Carol Harris for her great help in typing and correcting the text.

---

* 'First Year Quantitative Methods on Business-related Degree Courses in England and Wales' by J. Curwin, M.E. Mortimer, G. O'Sullivan and R. Slater. *The Institute of Mathematics and its Applications*, May 1982, Volume 18.

How to use this book

The book has been arranged in seven parts, each including two, three or four chapters. These groups of chapters all develop a theme within quantitative methods.

Part	Theme
I	Quantitative information
II	Descriptive statistics
III	Mathematical methods
IV	Measuring uncertainty
V	Statistical inference
VI	Relating two or more variables
VII	Mathematical models

There is a general introduction to each part which should provide a business-related context for what follows. These introductions include ideas for supportive work which you may choose to undertake as you read the relevant chapters. This work may, for example, take the form of collecting recent data on a topic of interest and applying the described methods of analysis. Also, at the end of each part an exercise has been included for practice, revision and discussion.

As with all books of this kind, some chapters may be familiar and easily understood, and other chapters new and apparently difficult. You may, for example, understand descriptive statistics from your lecture notes but not statistical inference. **What you need to do is establish a way to use this book to your own maximum advantage**. For some, it may be a matter of using the book for supportive reading only. You will find plenty of worked examples to complement those given in lectures and seminars. For others, the book may need to provide a self-contained course in quantitative methods. You will find a description of all the methods used, exercises included at the end of chapters (except chapter 18) and selected answers (given in Appendix 7).

In working through the book, you will need to observe the following interdependencies:

(1) Chapter 4 requires Chapter 3;
(2) Chapter 10 requires Chapter 9;
(3) Chapter 11 requires Chapter 9;
(4) Chapter 12 requires Chapters 3, 4 and 11;
(5) Chapter 13 requires Chapter 12;
(6) Chapter 14 requires Chapters 11, 12 and 13;

(7) Chapter 17 requires Chapter 16;

(8) Chapter 18 requires Chapters 16 and 17.

You will see that basic descriptive statistics (Chapters 3 and 4) and an understanding of probability (Chapter 9) are fundamental. We recommend that you become fully acquainted with these chapters as you proceed through the book.

Part I
QUANTITATIVE INFORMATION

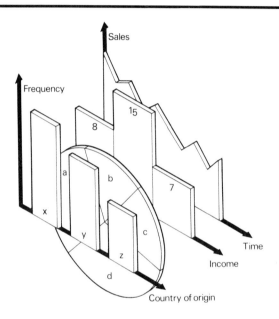

In this part we are concerned with the ways data can be collected and how such data can be effectively presented.

Mastery of the magnitude and the complexity of the world around us demands more than a verbal description. We need to understand the numbers; how many, how large and how soon. Collected together, these numbers provide our data.

Some information is available from government publications:

Annual Abstract of Statistics;
Economic Trends;
Monthly Digest of Statistics;
Regional Statistics;
Social Trends; and others.

Exercise   We suggest you visit your local library and make a list of the range of information available from these publications.

We may also require information not available from published sources.

Exercise   Make a list of the information not available to you from these publications.

Your first list is limited to information of a more general form that is of interest to government and other organizations. There will be figures on the number of people by age, by sex and by income or region. What will often be lacking is particular detail. If we want information on the attitude towards frozen foods or the preferred colour of cars we will need to collect it.

Consider, for example, employment. You will need to define what is meant by this term and who should be included: the **qualitative factors**. You may choose to include the numbers: the **quantitative factors**. A single figure, such as the total number employed in the previous year in the UK, is precise, needs little in the way of presentation, and will be easily available from published statistics. It will, however, communicate little about the nature of employment. If you investigate further you will find the numbers employed by region, by industry and a range of other factors. As you include more detail, the information will become more difficult to communicate and more difficult to present. Quantitative methods aim at the communication, presentation and analysis of numerical information. If you investigate further still you will discover that there are a number of items relevant to employment not found in the published statistics. You will find that for some issues no data have been collected in a formal way. If you want information about a particular product or particular group of individuals and it is not available, you will have to collect it. If you want to know how workers perceive their training opportunities, chances of promotion or payment of overtime working you will need to organize and implement a survey.

Exercises   1. Find out what information you can on the number of working days lost through strikes in the UK. Discuss the information not available on the number of working days lost through strikes in the UK and suggest how this might be obtained.
2. Explain how you would obtain information on the selling price of second-hand cars.

1 Data collection

Many business, social and economic questions can be assessed and evaluated more closely if some data are available upon which to base discussions and decisions. These discussions and decisions are, however, basically pointless if the data used are biased or misleading; some people would even argue that it might be better to do without such data. Managers are often faced with other people's data, so need to be able to assess if this information is likely to be biased, or if it really will be useful for their decision-making process. This is often a case of knowing which questions to ask! Even if you can ask the right questions, you also need to be able to understand the answers that you are given by the 'experts'.

Questions about the data fall into broad groups, and this chapter will consider each group, looking at the issues that may be raised. These groups are:

(a) What is the relevant population?
(b) How many people were asked and how were they selected?
(c) How was the information collected from these respondents?
(d) Who did not respond?

1.1 POPULATION

Identification of the relevant population is essential since data collection can be a costly exercise and contacting large numbers of people who could have nothing to do with the survey will only waste these valuable resources. For example, if you were concerned with the acceptability to women of a new contraceptive pill it would be pointless contacting a group of people, half of whom were men. A similar problem can arise if the group you have identified as the relevant population does not include everyone for whom the survey is relevant, since a range of views or information will be totally missed. If you were interested in why people bought foreign-built cars, but failed to contact purchasers of certain Ford models, for example, then you may fail to identify the fact that some buyers do not realize that their car is foreign-built. The term 'population' can also be used to describe all the items or organizations of interest. An audit, for example, is concerned with the correctness of financial statements. The population of interest to the auditor could be the accounting records, invoices or wage sheets. If we were concerned with job opportunities, the population could be all the local businesses or organizations employing one or more persons.

1. What is the relevant population to contact regarding a new nappy?
2. Who would be interested in a new metal paint to be sold in large quantities?

Having considered the type of people who would fall into the relevant population, the next problem is to try to identify who these people are; and perhaps even to get a list of their names and addresses. If this list can be obtained, it is called a **sampling frame**. Many surveys, particularly in market research, need a general population of adults, and make use of the Electoral Register. This contains a list of most people in the UK over 18 years old and is updated annually; of course as about 10% of the population of the UK move each year, others emigrate, some die and there is some immigration, the list cannot be 100% accurate, but it is easily available and very widely used. A study paper from the Central Statistical Office suggests that the Electoral Register is even more accurate in identifying addresses rather than people. (Houses move less frequently than people.) Other groups in the general population may appear on separate lists; for example, all those who are members of the RAC, or all those who are on a credit blacklist. These lists may not be generally available.

When a list does not exist or is not generally available, then those collecting the information may either try to compile a list, or use a method of collection which does not require a sampling frame (see next section). A method used by the Central Statistical Office to identify the population of disabled people, when a new Act of Parliament came into force, was to contact a large number of people in the general population, asking a few simple questions on whether they themselves were disabled or if they knew anyone who was, and if so who they were. This gave a fairly comprehensive list of the disabled, who could then be contacted and asked for more detailed information.

1.2 NUMBERS AND SELECTION

1.2.1 A census

One type of data collection does not require a selection procedure, and this is a census, or complete enumeration of the identified population. The best example of this type of survey is the Population Census which has been carried out in the UK once every 10 years since 1801 (with the exception of 1941 when rather more urgent matters were being dealt with). While this type of exercise should give highly detailed information and reflect data from all parts of the relevant population, it does take a long time to analyse the data and is very costly. A census is of limited use to the majority of business, social or economic applications, unless the identified population is small. For example, a census of all homes would be an expensive way of estimating the population with TV sets. In contrast, if you were representing a manufacturer who sold only to a small number of wholesalers and wanted their views on a new credit-ordering system, then a census would be a suitable method to use.

1.2.2 Selection: random and non-random

Where the relevant identified population is too large for a cost-effective census to be conducted a **sample** of that population must be selected, and individual responses generalized to represent the facts about, or the views of, the entire population. However, the method of selection will have implications for the validity of this generalization procedure: if you were to ask the next five people you see how they would vote at a general election, it is very unlikely that the answers given would be a guide to a general election result. Sampling procedures can be divided into two broad categories: those where individuals are selected by some random method prior to the collection stage, and those where the individuals are non-randomly selected at the collection stage.

Random

Random does not mean haphazard selection, but means that each member of the population has some calculable chance of being selected. There is no one in the identified population who **could not** be selected when the sample is set up. A simple random sample gives every individual an equal chance of selection. To select a random sample a list or sampling frame is required, where each member is given a number and a series of random numbers (usually generated on a computer) are used to select the individuals to take part in the survey. There is thus no human interference in the selection of the sample, and samples selected in this way will, in the long run, be representative of the population. This is the simplest form of random sampling (see below for more complex designs).

Non-random

Non-random is a catch-all for other methods of selecting the sample, where there is some judgement made in the selection procedure, and this may lead to some sections of the population being excluded from the sample, for good or bad reasons. For example, if the interviewer is asked to select who will take part in the survey and he or she has a particular aversion to men with beards, then this group may be excluded. If, then, men with beards have different views on the subject of the survey from everyone else, this view will not be represented in the results of the survey. However, a well-conducted non-random survey will produce results more quickly, and at a lower cost, than a random sample; for this reason it is often preferred for market research surveys and political opinion polls.

The most usual form of non-random sampling is the selection of a **quota sample**. In this case various characteristics of the population are noted, for example the divisions on sex, age and job type; and the sample aims to include similar proportions of people with these characteristics. This suggests that if people are representative in terms of known identifiable characteristics they will also be representative in terms of the information being sought by the survey. Having identified the proportions of each type to be included in the sample, each interviewer is then given a set number, or quota, of people with these characteristics to contact. The final selection of the individuals is left up to the interviewer. Interviewers you may have seen or met in shopping precincts are carrying out quota sample surveys.

Exercise

Apart from groups specifically avoided by a poor interviewer, which groups in the population would be excluded from such a survey?

Setting up a quota survey with a few quotas is relatively simple. The results from the Census of Population will give the proportions of men and women in the population, and also their age distribution.

Table 1.1

(i) Age distribution of population over 15 years		(ii) Sex distribution of population over 15 years	
Age (years)	Percentage	Sex	Percentage
15–20	19	Men	46
20–30	25	Women	54
30–50	26		
50 +	30		

(iii) Population (percentages)			(iv) Number for sample of 1000	
Age (years)	Men	Women	Men	Women
15–20	10	9	100	90
20–30	12	13	120	130
30–50	12	14	120	140
50 +	12	18	120	180

From the component tables of Table 1.1 we see that the general population over 15 years old consists or 46% men and 54% women, and thus our sample should also exhibit this division of sex. We can obtain similar information on the age distribution of the whole population, but this must be further analysed to show the separate age distributions of the sexes (part iii) so that we do not get the situation that all of the women in the sample are under 50 years old. Having combined the information from parts i and ii of Table 1.1 we can take each percentage of the sample size using part iii, here 1000, to find the number of each type of person to contact.

For a quota sample, it is important that the characteristics on which the quotas are based are easily identified (or at least estimated) by the interviewer, or else a lot of time will be wasted trying to identify the people who will be eligible to take part in the survey. If the number of quotas is large, some of the groups will be very small, even with an overall sample size of 1000.

1.2.3 Numbers

So far we have suggested that a census will be too costly for most subjects of business surveys, but that just asking five people would be unlikely to give a full representation of the views of the general public. The variability of the population will influence the sample size required; in the extreme case where everyone held exactly the same opinion, then it would only be necessary to ask one person. (This is a highly unlikely situation!) If everyone in the population held distinct views, then a census would be the only way to elicit the full range of views. (Again, very, very unlikely!) Sample size will also be related to how precise the results required from the survey are to be; and if the proportions are to be based on some subgroup of the sample, it is the size of these subgroups that must first be determined. Since most surveys do not aim to find out a single piece of information, but the answers to a whole range of questions, the determination of sample size can become extremely complex. It has been found that samples of about 1000 give results that are acceptable when surveying the general population.

1.2.4 More complex random samples

The simple system outlined above for a random sample will work well with a relatively small population that is concentrated geographically, but would become impractical if it were used on a national scale; you would need the complete Electoral Register for the whole of the UK and may end up visiting one person on Sark, another in the Shetlands and none in the South East. Travel costs would be phenomenal! It would not be impossible, although it would be unlikely, that the whole sample might consist of people living in Wales: this would not be too important if the people of Wales were wholly representative of all UK citizens, but on certain issues their views will tend to differ from those of, say, England, for example, in relation to charging for water supplies. To overcome these types of problem, various other sampling schemes have been developed, but they still retain the basic element of random sampling: that each member of the population has **some chance** of being selected.

Stratification
If there are distinct groups or strata within the population that can be identified **before** sample selection takes place, it will be desirable to make sure that each of these groups is represented in the final sample; thus a sample is selected from each group. The numbers from each group may be proportional to the size of the strata, but if there is a small group, it is often wise to select a rather larger proportion of this group to make sure that the variety of their views is represented. In the latter case it will be necessary to weight the results as one group is 'over-represented'.

When it is known that there are subgroups in the population, but it is not possible to identify them before sample selection, it is usual to ask a question which helps to categorize the respondent, such as 'At the last general election which party did you vote for?', and then to divide the results into groups or strata.

This is **post-stratification**. The results from these constructed strata can be weighted to provide more accurate results for the population as a whole.

Clustering
Some populations have groups which within themselves represent all of the views of the general population, for example a town, a college or a file of invoices. If this is the case, it will be much more convenient, and much more cost-effective, to select one or more of these clusters at random and then to select a sample, or carry out a census within the selected clusters.

Multi-stage designs
Even when the designs outlined above are used, there may well be problems over representativeness and costs. To overcome this, many national samples use a series of sampling stages, and at each stage select either all of the subgroups or a random sample. For a national sample in the UK, one may start by noting that the country is split into administrative regions for gas, electricity, civil defence, etc., and that each of these needs to be represented. Each region consists of a number of parliamentary constituencies, which can usually be classified on an urban–rural scale. A random sample of such constituencies may be selected for each region. Parliamentary constituencies are split into wards, and the wards into polling districts, for which the Electoral Register is available, from which a sample of individuals or addresses may be selected. This type of selection procedure will mean that all regions are represented and yet

the travelling costs will be kept to a minimum, since interviewing will be concentrated in a few, specific, polling districts. An example of a possible design is given in Table 1.2. To try to ensure that the resultant sample was fully representative, further stages could be added, or stratification could take place at some or all of the stages.

Table 1.2

Stage	Sampling unit	No selected
1	Region	12 (all)
2	Constituency	4 (samples)
3	Ward	3 (samples)
4	Polling district	2 (samples)
5	Individuals	10 (samples)

Sample size $= 12 \times 4 \times 3 \times 2 \times 10 = 2880$

Exercises

1. What form of stratification would you use for a sample of car insurance claims?
2. For which type of information would a college be a suitable cluster to use?

1.3 ASKING QUESTIONS

Having identified the relevant population for a survey, and used an appropriate method of selecting a sample of people to give the information that is required, we now need to decide exactly what questions will be used, and how these questions will be given to the people in the sample. No matter how well the first two stages of an investigation are carried out, if biased questions are used, or an interviewer incorrectly records a series of answers, the results of the survey will be worthless.

1.3.1 Questionnaire design

To be successful a questionnaire needs both a logical structure and well thought-out questions. The structure of the questionnaire should ensure that there is a flow from question to question and topic to topic, as would usually occur in a conversation. Any radical jumps between topics will tend to disorientate the respondent, and will influence the answers given. It is often suggested that a useful technique is to move from general to specific questions on any particular issue.

The Gallup organization has suggested that there are five possible objectives for a question:

(a) To find if the respondent is aware of the issue. For example:
    Do you know of any plans to build a motorway between Oxford and Birmingham?   YES/NO
    The answers that can be expected from a respondent will depend on the information already available and the source of that information (information available can vary from source to source). If the answer to the above question were 'YES' we would then need to ask further questions to ascertain the extent of the respondent's knowledge.

(b) To get general feelings on an issue. For example:
    Do you think a motorway should be built?   YES/NO

It is one thing to know whether respondents are informed about plans to build a motorway or indeed the merits of a new product but it is another to know whether they agree or disagree. In constructing such a question, the respondent can be asked to provide an answer on a **rating scale** such as:

Strongly agree	Agree	Uncertain	Disagree	Strongly disagree

A scale of this kind is less restrictive than a 'YES/NO' response and does provide rather more information.

(c) To get answers on specific parts of the issue. For example:

Do you think a motorway will affect the local environment? YES/NO

In designing a questionnaire we need to decide exactly what issues are to be included. This can be done by using a simple checklist. If environment is an issue we need then to decide whether it is the environment in general or a number of factors that make up the environment, such as noise levels and scenic beauty.

(d) To get reasons for a respondent's views. For example:

IF AGAINST:

Are you against the building of this motorway because:
  (i)   there is an adequate main road already;
  (ii) there is insufficient traffic between Oxford and Birmingham;
  (iii) the motorway would spoil beautiful countryside;
  (iv) the route would mean demolishing a house of national interest;
  (v)   other, please specify . . . .

To find the reasons for a respondent's views is going to require questions of a more complex structure. You will first need to know what his or her views are and then provide the respondent with an opportunity to give reasons why. The conditional statement 'IF AGAINST' is referred to as a **filter**. The above question is **precoded** (see below); in contrast an **open-ended** question could be used; for example:

Why are you against the motorway being built? . . . .

(e) To find how strongly these views are held. For example:

Which of the following would you be prepared to do to support your view?
  (i)   write to your local councillor;
  (ii) write to your MP;
  (iii) sign a petition;
  (iv) speak at a public enquiry;
  (v)   go on a demonstration;
  (vi) actively disrupt the work of construction.

or

How important is the Hall which would be demolished if the motorway is built?

(Place a ✔ on the grid below)

Should be saved at any cost	1	2	3	4	5	6	7	Of no importance

In many cases we would want to know not only whether something was considered good or bad but how good or how bad, and to do this we could give a series of possible attitudes or actions, or we could use a **rating scale**. A position on a rating scale provides some measure of attitude. The number of points on the rating scale will depend on the context of the question and method of analysis but in general four point and five point scales are far more common than the seven point scale shown above.

These categories reflect that much of Gallup's work is collecting information on attitudes and issues, but we could add that most surveys will also be asking questions which aim to find factual information about the respondents, their dependants or their possessions. To meet these objectives we can use either 'open' or 'precoded' questions.

An open question will allow the respondent to say whatever he or she wishes, for example:

Why did you choose to live in Kensington?

This type of question will tend to favour the articulate and educated sections of the community, as they are able to organize and express their thoughts and ideas quickly. If a respondent is finding difficulty in answering, an interviewer may be tempted to probe, or help, and unless this is done carefully, the survey may just reflect the interviewer's views. A further problem with open questions is that, since few interviews are tape recorded, the response that is recorded is that written by the interviewer, who may be forced to edit and abbreviate what is said, and again this can lead to bias. Open questions do, however, often help to put people at their ease and to make sure it is their view which they are giving, rather than one of some pre-arranged group of responses, no one of which is **exactly** their view. Further, at the early development stage of a questionnaire, open questions may be used to identify common responses.

Precoded questions give the respondent a series of possible answers, from which one may be chosen, or an alternative specified. These are particularly useful for factual questions, for example:

How many children do you have?

0   1   2   3   4   5   6   more   (circle answer)

When this type of response is used for opinion questions, some respondents will want to give a response between two of the opinions represented by the precoded answers.

Do you agree with the deployment of nuclear weapons in Britain?

Agree   ☐

Disagree   ☐

Didn't know ☐   (tick box)

Some respondents will say 'Yes, but only of a certain type' or 'No, but there is no alternative' or 'Yes, provided there is dual control of their operation'. One reaction to this type of answer is to try to expand the range of precoded answers given, but this does not necessarily solve the problem. An open question may be better. In the example given above, it may be better to ask a series of questions, building up through the objectives suggested by Gallup.

Question wording is also important in eliciting representative responses, as a biased, or leading, question will bias the answers given. Sources of bias in question design identified by the Survey Research Centre were:

(a) Two or more questions presented as one. For example:

Do you use self-service garages because they are easy to use and clean? YES/NO

Here the respondent may use the garages because they are easy to use, but feel that they are dirty and disorganized; or may find them clean but have difficulty in using the petrol pumps.

(b) Questions that contain difficult or unfamiliar words. For example:

Where do you usually shop?

The difficult word here is 'usually' since there is no clarification of its meaning. An immediate response could be 'usually shop for what?' or 'How often is usually?' People's shopping habits vary with the type of item being purchased, the day of the week the shopping is being done, and often the time of year as well.

Did you suffer from rubella as a child? YES/NO

Many people will not know what rubella is, unless the questionnaire is aimed purely at members of the medical profession; it would be much better to ask if the respondent suffered from german measles as a child. This problem will also be apparent if jargon phrases are used in questions.

(c) Questions which start with words meant to soften hardness or directness. For example:

I hope you don't mind me asking this, but are you a virgin?

In this case, the respondent is put on their guard immediately, and may want to use the opening phrase as an excuse for not answering.

Do you, like most people, feel that Britain should be represented in NATO? YES/NO

Two possible reactions to this type of leading question are

(i) to tend to agree with the statement in order to appear normal, the same as most people; or, in a few cases,

(ii) to disagree purely for the sake of disagreeing.

In either case, the response does not necessarily reflect the views held by the respondent.

(d) Questions which contain conditional or hypothetical clauses. For example:

How do you think your life would change if you had nine children?

This is a situation that few people will have considered, and so have never thought about the way in which various aspects of their life would change.

(e) Questions which contain one or more instructions to respondents. For example:

If you take your weekly income, after tax, and when you have made allowances for all of the regular bills, how much do you have left to spend or save?

This question is fairly long and this may serve to confuse the respondent, but there are also a series of instructions to follow before an answer may be given. Other problems that will arise here are that many incomes are not weekly, and most bills, for gas, electricity, loans, etc., are monthly or quarterly; many people will not make regular savings for bills, but just pay them when they become due, while others will scrupulously save a set amount each week.

Exercise   Write a series of questions seeking information on topics of your choice to illustrate the problems posed in this section.

1.3.2   Interviews

Once the respondents have been selected and the questionnaire prepared, then the two must be brought together, most frequently by an interviewer. (In a quota sample where the interviewer selects the respondents, this is the only feasible approach. The interviewer has a key role to play in a survey, where only about a third of his or her time is spent in interviewing, the rest being used for travel and locating respondents (40%), editing and clerical work (15%), and preparatory and administrative work (10%).

It is unlikely that a person could just go out and conduct successful interviews; a certain amount of training is necessary to help in recording answers correctly and, in the case of open questions, succinctly. An interviewer's attitude is also important, since if it is not neutral or unbiased, it may influence the respondent. Unbiased questions can be turned into biased ones when a bad interviewer lays stress on one of the alternatives, or 'explains' to the respondent what the question really wants to find out. This explanation, or probing, can be turned into an advantage if the interviewer is fully aware of the aims of the survey and can probe without biasing the response. Complex and intimate topics can be covered by a sympathetic interviewer.

1.3.3   Postal questionnaires

An alternative to interviewing the selected respondents is to post the questionnaire to them, with a reply-paid envelope. This method will yield a considerable saving in time and cost over an interviewer survey, and will allow time for the replies to be considered, documents consulted or a discussion of the answers with other members of the household. (This may be an advantage or disadvantage depending upon the type of survey being conducted.) Since the interviewer is not present, there is no possibility of observing the respondent or probing for more depth in the answers. The method will thus generally be more suitable for surveys looking for mostly factual answers. In general, the questionnaire should be relatively short, to maintain interest and encourage responses, but even so, postal questionnaires tend to discriminate against the less literate members of the society, and have a higher response rate from the middle classes.

1.4   NON-RESPONSE

It is almost inevitable that when surveying a human population that there will be some non-response, but the researcher's approach should aim at reducing this non-response to a minimum and to find at least some information about those who do not respond. The type of non-response and its recognition will depend upon the type of survey being conducted.

For a preselected (random) sample, some of the individuals or addresses that were selected from the sampling frame may no longer exist, e.g. demolished houses, since few sampling frames are completely up to date. Once the individuals are identified there may be no response for one or more of the following reasons:

(a) **Unsuitable for interview** — the individual may be infirm or inarticulate in English, and whilst he or she could be interviewed if special arrangements were made, this is rarely done in general surveys.

(b) **Those who have moved** — these could be traced to their new address, but this adds extra time and expense to the survey; the problem does not exist if addresses rather than names were selected from the sampling frame.

(c) **Those out at the time of call** — this will often happen but can be minimized by careful consideration of the timing of the call. Further calls can be made, at different times, to try to elicit a response, but the number of recommended recalls varies from one survey organization to another. (The government social survey recommends up to six recalls.)

(d) **Those away for the period of the survey** — in this case, recalling will not elicit a response, but it is often difficult at first to tell if someone is just out at the time of the call. A shortened form of the questionnaire could be put through the letterbox, to be posted when the respondent returns. Avoiding the summer months will tend to reduce this category of non-response.

(e) **Those who refuse to cooperate** — there is little that can be done with this group, about 5% of the population, since they will often refuse to cooperate with mandatory surveys such as the Population census, but the attitude of the interviewer may help to minimize the refusal rate.

Many surveys, particularly the national surveys of complex design, will report the number of non-respondents. In addition, non-respondents may be categorized by reason or cause to indicate whether they differ in any important way from respondents. In a quota sample, there is rarely any recording of non-response, since if one person refuses to answer the questions someone else can be selected almost immediately.

Postal questionnaires have a history of high levels of non-response, starting perhaps with the *Literary Digest* survey of 1936 which posted 10 000 000 questionnaires asking how people would vote in the forthcoming United States presidential election; they received only a 20% response rate, and also made an incorrect prediction of the result of the election. More recent surveys have had response rates of more than 90%, and this change deserves some explanation. Successful postal surveys tend to have relatively few questions, which are usually precoded and mostly factual. Inducements of money or gifts are used to encourage response, but often a well-known sponsoring organization is sufficient to encourage responses. Follow-up letters are also used to those who have not responded after three to four weeks, and in a survey of 14–20 year olds, this helped to increase the response rate from 70% after three weeks to a final figure of 93.3%.

Exercise   Why is it desirable to know something about the characteristics of non-respondents?

1.5 ALTERNATIVE METHODS

The sample survey is by far the most widely used method of original data collection for business or economic problems, but there are some adaptations of the sampling methods previously outlined which may be used, and some alternatives.

In a **panel survey** a sample, once selected, is asked a series of questions on various occasions, so that the reactions or awareness of individuals can be monitored. This method is useful in terms of assessing the effectiveness of an advertising campaign, or to monitor the general political situation provided there is not a significant dropout from the panel (known as panel mortality) and that those taking part do not become unrepresentative of the general public (known as panel conditioning).

Exercise   Suggest the types of panel conditioning that might take place in a panel asked to report on television programmes.

Longitudinal studies follow a group of people, or cohort, over a long period of time, as the name suggests, but are most suitable for studies of physical development and of sociological issues rather than business and economic problems.

Observation is again a method most suited to sociological investigations to monitor the interactions of people with each other and institutions. Where it has been used in companies, the observer has sometimes been regarded as an agent of management, and reactions have consequently been affected; however, the observer does not have to declare that he or she is observing the group of people. There is a great danger with observation that the results will become highly subjective.

Some surveys ask the respondents to keep a **diary** of the events over a short period of time, but this does rely on accurate recording of **all** of the events. The Family Expenditure Survey asks respondents to keep a diary of all purchases over a 2 week period.

1.6 CONCLUSION

Effective decision-making in business cannot be based on speculation alone and must be guided by relevant information collected by a business itself or by some other agency. Some information may be available from published sources such as the *Monthly Digest of Statistics*, the *Annual Abstract of Statistics*, *Social Trends* and *Regional Statistics*, but, in general, additional data will often be sought that are more pertinent to the subject of interest.

Sampling methods provide a cost-effective way of providing data on business, social or economic issues. However, the design and implementation of a survey are critical if representative and meaningful results are to be derived. Data of the wrong sort can lead to the same mistakes and misjudgements as no data at all.

1.7 PROBLEMS

1. Define a population for a survey of attitudes to smoking.

2. Define a population for a survey of manufacturing industry.
3. Describe how you would obtain a sampling frame for a survey of electrical goods retailers.
4. Describe how you would obtain a sampling frame for a survey of housewives.
5. What is meant by the term 'quota sampling'? Explain why the quota sampling method might be preferred to random sampling for a survey of beer drinkers.
6. Describe how you would investigate the insulation needs of housing in inner city areas. Contrast the use of a sample survey with a census inquiry.
7. State the advantages of using postal questionnaires. Give examples of when a postal questionnaire might be preferred to personal interviews.
8. Describe how you would select a sample to provide information concerning the present health of former employees of a particular industry who have been incapacitated by a common disease. Would you use postal questionnaires or interviews?
9. Produce a questionnaire to ascertain the views of students on their working conditions.
10. Construct a questionnaire to ascertain how well computers are understood by the general public.

2 Presentation of data

Collected data on social issues or business problems are likely to take a numeric form. We tend either to **count** the number of people or items with a given characteristic or to make some **measurement** concerning those people or items. In this chapter we will consider the ways of bringing together all the data from different people or different sources.

2.1 TABULATION OF DATA

The tabulation of data involves grouping together all the individually recorded values. These values could be listed as shown in Table 2.1. It is not immediately obvious from this table how much was sold, how many salesmen were involved or what were the lowest and highest sales.

Table 2.1 The number of cases of breakfast bran sold during September by Sellmore salesmen

21	50	28	39	41	25	48	35	22	36	55	47	39	27	40	37	51	51	31	23
57	37	46	42	34	32	52	42	34	46	42	26	38	35	29	42	26	45	35	56
40	26	32	43	39	27	43	39	30	36	43	40	37	45	21	38	42	50	28	37
39	45	42	46	20	35	44	26	42	25	50	32	31	54	39	46	37	51	43	35
46	34	52	31	44	49	51	36	38	38	37	47	27	49	44	33	26	44	42	39
30	38	35	24	28	38	21	41	30	34	44	25	44	34	36	35	28	34	46	32
38	22	43	35	56	36	45	32	55	27	49	28	56	19	42	39	44	39	44	25
49	32	39	47	43	38	25	28	31	37	34	30	43	50	30	22	37	46	43	40
40	30	45	36	22	31	50	35	47	49	45	29	40	31	43	39	34	55	44	36
26	47	29	38	39	49	52	38	41	23	26	54	39	33	42	25	36	48	35	42
39	42	37	35	25	43	39	31	34	30	55	38	50	37	43	37	44	29	47	31
35	31	47	35	26	34	40	42	57	21	29	36	41	24	24	46	35	43	52	38
58	39	20	31	42	30	27	38	39	27	37	42	52	38	61	28	45	37	40	31
29	42	49	36	38	25	42	48	46	48	31	56	36	43	40	54	44	32	44	26
36	34	30	33	39	35	27	51	35	37	34	31	40	50	30	34	40	51	43	47
52	48	40	47	32	46	39	24	36	60	32	20	28	36	42	37	39	31	38	40
28	55	36	40	21	52	50	37	39	35	40	36	55	45	32	25	48	30	42	59
46	37	42	51	28	40	47	41	31	30	45	40	48	39	34	36	33	38	27	34
36	32	49	46	36	37	40	37	48	28	39	51	36	30	22	47	31	40	32	37
56	24	45	37	30	50	31	27	36	33	40	49	29	35	48	37	29	53	26	50

As a first step the data could be arranged in numerical order, but this does not overcome the problem of quantity. A count of how many times a particular value occurs could be made and presented in the form of **frequency distribution**. The result of collating the data in this way is given in Table 2.2.

Table 2.2 Number of cases of breakfast bran sold during September by Sellmore salesmen

Sales	Frequency	Sales	Frequency	Sales	Frequency
19	1	33	5	47	11
20	3	34	15	48	10
21	5	35	18	49	8
22	5	36	21	50	10
23	2	37	22	51	8
24	5	38	17	52	7
25	9	39	23	53	1
26	10	40	20	54	3
27	9	41	5	55	6
28	11	42	20	56	5
29	8	43	14	57	2
30	14	44	12	58	1
31	17	45	10	59	1
32	12	46	12	60	1
				61	1
					400

If there are only a few individual values that occur, as there may well be in the answers to precoded questions on a questionnaire, then this rearrangement will be sufficient to render the data both manageable and readable. However, if there are a large number of individual values, even the rearrangement in Table 2.2 will not suffice to achieve clarity. To reduce the size of the table produced we can amalgamate certain values into groups as shown in Tables 2.3, 2.4 and 2.5.

Table 2.3

Sales	Frequency
20 or less	4
21 up to 25	26
26 up to 30	52
31 up to 35	67
36 up to 40	103
41 up to 45	61
46 up to 50	51
51 up to 55	25
56 up to 60	10
61 or more	1
	400

Table 2.4

Sales	Frequency
25 or less	30
26 up to 35	119
36 up to 45	164
46 up to 55	76
56 or more	11
	400

Table 2.5

Sales	Frequency
40 or less	252
41 or more	148
	400

The tabulations could each be argued to be technically valid, but they do not all succeed in conveying adequate information about sales. Both Tables 2.3 and 2.4 provide some information on the variation of sales, but Table 2.5 tells us very little about the pattern of sales (see Section 3.1.3).

Exercise Imagine you were a prospective employee of Sellmore and were told that your income would be totally dependent on commission from sales; which of the five tables would you prefer to be given as an indication of the performance of current salesmen?

As we have moved from Table 2.2 to any of Tables 2.3, 2.4 or 2.5 we have **lost detailed, individual information**. No longer do we know that the most successful salesman in September sold 61 units, we only know that 1 salesman sold 61 or more (Table 2.3), or that 11 salesmen sold 56 or more (Table 2.4), or that 148 salesmen sold 41 or more (Table 2.5). The loss of some detail can be worthwhile if the tables can be more easily understood and retain the basic information regarding the differences in our data. In constructing a table, we are no longer concerned with a single observation or measurement but with what is generally true. As a guide most tables are constructed with between 4 and 10 groups depending on the complexity of the data.

In collecting data we are often confronted with a multitude of measurements or counts, on different aspects or different characteristics. A survey questionnaire, for example, will ask a series of related questions. To provide marketing information we may require the detail given in Table 2.6.

Table 2.6   Numbers sold of four types of industrial trolley by region during the last financial year

| | Regions | | | | |
Mode	North	South	East	West	Total
Tug	675	60	35	20	790
Conveyor	30	490	30	20	570
Lifter	150	180	235	15	580
Mover	5	20	0	35	60
	860	750	300	90	2000

A single tabulation of the number of each model sold or sales by region would hide the regional differences between the number of models sold. If counts are made jointly with respect to two or more methods of classification, we obtain a **cross-tabulation** of the data.

2.2   VISUAL PRESENTATION

One of the most effective ways of presenting numerical information is to construct a chart or diagram. The choice depends on the type of data. As a guide we shall make one basic distinction: whether data are **discrete** or **continous**. Data are discrete if we just make a count, for example the number of people in a room or the number of cars sold last month. Data are continuous if measurement is made on a continuous scale, for example the time taken to travel to work or the yield in kilograms of a manufacturing process. There are, of course, some exceptions. Technically, money can be seen as discrete, since it changes hands in increments (pence) but is usually treated as continuous because the increments can be relatively small. Age is continuous (we all get older) but when quoted as age last birthday becomes discrete.

2.2.1   Presentation of discrete data

The counts of number of industrial trollies sold by model and region in Table 2.6 is discrete data. To make an easy comparison between regions we can present the same information as percentages (Table 2.7). It can be immediately seen that Tug accounts for 78.49% of unit sales in the North and only 8.00% of unit sales in the South. To calculate these percentages we can first find the fraction and then multiply by 100. Tug, for example, accounts for 675 sales out of the 860 achieved in northern sales region. The ratio 675 ÷ 860 = 0.7849 multiplied by 100 gives the percentage 78.49%. The original totals are often given as base figures.

Table 2.7 Percentage unit sales of four types of industrial trolley by region during the last financial year

| Model | Regions | | | |
	North	South	East	West
Tug	78.49	8.00	11.67	22.22
Conveyor	3.49	65.33	10.00	22.22
Lifter	17.44	24.00	78.33	16.67
Mover	0.58	2.67	0.00	38.89
	100.00	100.00	100.00	100.00

Pie charts

If we wish to show market shares for a product grouping (Table 2.8) or something similar, we can divide a circle into sectors, where each sector represents size. The size of each sector can be found by taking the appropriate proportion of 360° (Fig. 2.1). This type of presentation is only easily understood if a few categories are to be used.

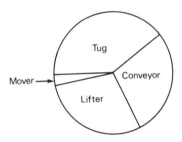

Figure 2.1

Table 2.8 Sales of four types of industrial trolley during the last financial year

Model	Sales	Proportion of total	Proportion of 360°
Tug	790	0.395	142.2
Conveyor	570	0.285	102.6
Lifter	580	0.290	104.4
Mover	60	0.030	10.8
	2000	1.000	360.0

Bar charts

The numbers sold by model or by region can be represented as vertical bars. The height of each bar is drawn in proportion to the number by using a vertical ruler scale (Fig. 2.2). We can also show the number of each model sold by region using a **component bar chart** (Fig. 2.3).

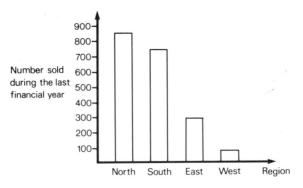

Figure 2.2   Sales of industrial trolley by region during the last financial year.

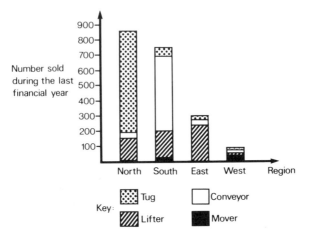

Figure 2.3   Sales of four types of industrial trolley by region during the last financial year.

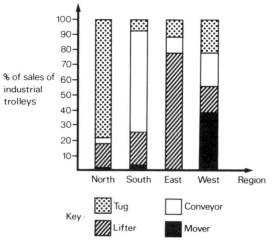

Figure 2.4   Percentage sales by region.

Once we begin to examine the composition of totals it can become difficult to see the relative size of some of the components. To combat this problem, it is often convenient to change the absolute figures into percentages, thus giving bars all of the same length and making direct comparisons possible (Fig. 2.4).

Pictogram
Bars can be replaced by appropriate pictures to show comparisons. Whilst this is more eye-catching, it is considerably less accurate and may be misleading. (In Fig. 2.5, how many does a fraction of a man represent?) Even more confusing are pictograms which use different sized figures to represent different values. An increase could be shown as an increase in height but the visual impression could be in terms of the increase of surface area or volume.

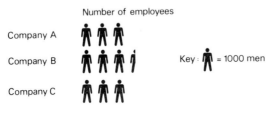

Figure 2.5

If we are making a single measurement or count, for example, presenting sales by region or turnover by company, a one-dimensional representation is generally clearer. We must try to avoid the confusion possible with the pictograms shown in Fig. 2.6. Picture A would almost certainly leave the impression of a more rapid increase in sales than picture B or picture C.

All the charts and diagrams we have considered so far are used to represent discrete data.

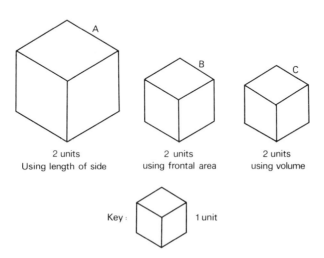

Figure 2.6   Pictogram to show a doubling of the sales of Happy Packs.

2.2.2 Presentation of continuous data

We can treat as continuous any measurement that can be represented by a line rather than just points on a line. Time and length are two good examples of continuous measurement.

Histogram

The distribution of measurement on a continuous scale is presented by means of a histogram. As an example we can use the information on income given in Table 2.9. The data presents us with two problems. Firstly, there are two open-ended groups. We do not know how low the income can be of the workers in the first group or how high the income of the workers can be in the last group. All we can do with open-ended groups of this kind is to assume reasonable lower or upper boundaries on the basis of our own knowledge of the data and the apparent distribution of the data. In this case it may be reasonable to assume a lower boundary of £100 for the first group and an upper boundary of £1000 for the last group. Whatever the decision, it is still a matter of judgement. Secondly, if we were to use bars to show the number of workers in each income group, it would appear that there were fewer in the range '£300 but less than £400' than in the range '£400 but less then £600'. However, the range has doubled in size and we need to take account of the increased chance of inclusion. To represent the distribution we plot **frequencies in proportion to area**. Income is shown as a horizontal ruler scale and frequencies as a series of blocks. These blocks are constructed with reference to a key as shown in Fig. 2.7.

Table 2.9   Income of a particular group of workers

Income	Number of workers
less than £200	10
£200 but less than £300	28
£300 but less than £400	42
£400 but less than £600	50
£600 or more	20

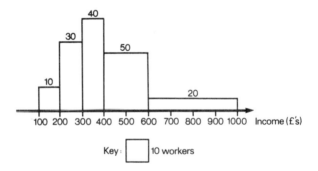

Figure 2.7   A histogram showing the distribution of income.

The key provides a standard and all blocks are constructed with reference to this. If we consider the income range '£400 and less than £600' we can note that the doubling of the standard width has had the effect of halving the height.

In practice, we choose one of the groups as our standard and scale as shown in Table 2.10.

Table 2.10   Method of constructing a histogram

Income	Frequency	Width	Scaling factor	Height of block
£100* but less than £200	10	standard	1	10
£200 but less than £300	28	standard	1	28
£300 but less than £400	42	standard	1	42
£400 but less than £600	50	2 times	$\frac{1}{2}$	25
£600 but less than £1000*	20	4 times	$\frac{1}{4}$	5

* Assumed boundary.

2.3   GRAPHICAL PRESENTATION

The way in which sales relate to advertising or the way in which sales change over time can effectively be represented by a graph. Graphically, we can show the relationship between two variables.

2.3.1   Plotting a time series

Suppose the sales of a domestic appliance over the last five years were recorded as in Table 2.11. The graph shown in Fig. 2.8 gives an immediate impression of how sales have changed over time (see Chapter 19).

Table 2.11   Sales of a domestic appliance

Year	Number Sold
1	20 000
2	26 000
3	33 800
4	43 940
5	57 122

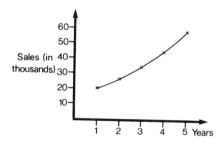

Figure 2.8

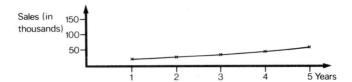

Figure 2.9

However, a change in scale can affect the impression made graphically as shown in Fig. 2.9. It is clear that the sales of this domestic appliance have increased but it is hard to judge from the graphs whether or not the increase is spectacular. In the same way, we could plot sales against advertising and seek a relationship between the two but would still lack an objective measure of this relationship (see Chapter 16). We would advise caution when interpreting any graphical representations of this kind.

2.3.2 Logarithmic graphs

If we are interested in the rate of change over time we can plot the log of values against time (Table 2.12). In this case we can see that the log values increase at a constant rate once an allowance has been made for the rounding of numbers. If we graph the log of values against time (Fig. 2.10), we get a different impression from that given in Figs. 2.8 and 2.9.

Table 2.12 The log values of sales

Year	Number sold	Log of number sold	Increase in log values
1	20 000	4.3010	
2	26 000	4.4150	0.1140
3	33 800	4.5289	0.1139
4	43 940	4.6429	0.1140
5	57 122	4.7568	0.1139

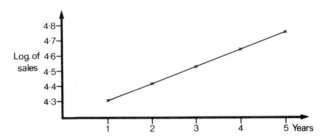

Figure 2.10

Sales can be seen to be rising, but at a **constant rate** each year. If we check the sales figure, we find the increase to be 30% each year, e.g.

$$\frac{26\ 000 - 20\ 000}{20\ 000} \times 100 = 30\%$$

Alternatively, we could antilog the increase in log values (0.1140 or 0.1139) to find the multiplication factor 1.30. To calculate the sales in the next year we multiply by 1.30, that is, increase values by 30%.

2.3.3   Lorenz curve

One particular application of the graphical method is the Lorenz curve. It is often used with income data or with wealth data to show the distribution or, more specifically, the extent to which the distribution is equal or unequal. This does not imply any value-judgement that there should be equality but only represents what is currently true. To construct a Lorenz curve each distribution needs to be arranged in order of size and then the percentages for each distribution calculated. The percentages then need to be added together to form cumulative distributions which are plotted on the graph.

Table 2.13

Group		Percentage of population		Cumulative percentage	Percentage of total wealth		Cumulative percentage
Poorest	A	50		50	10		10
	B	25	(+50)	75	20	(+10)	30
	C	10	(+75)	85	10	(+30)	40
	D	10	(+85)	95	15	(+40)	55
	E	3	(+95)	98	25	(+55)	80
Richest	F	2	(+98)	100	20	(+80)	100

Let us consider first the information given in Table 2.13. The percentage columns give a direct comparison between population and wealth. It can be seen that the poorest 50% can claim only 10% of total wealth. The cumulative percentage columns allow a continuing comparison between the two. It can also be seen that the poorest 75% of the population can claim 30% of the wealth and the poorest 85% of the population 40% and so on.

Note that in Fig. 2.11 the point representing zero population and zero wealth (point A) is joined to that representing all of the population and all of the wealth

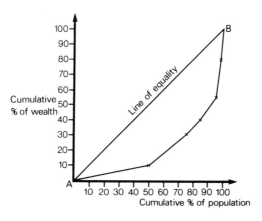

Figure 2.11   The relationship between wealth and population.

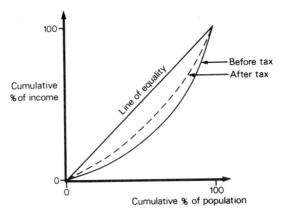

Figure 2.12   The effects of tax on the distribution of income.

(point B) to show the 'line of equality'. If the points were on this line then there would be a completely equal distribution of wealth: the further the curve is away from the straight line the less equality there is between the two distributions. The curve can also be used to show how the income distribution changes as a result of taxation. Figure 2.12 shows a progressive tax system where the post-tax income distribution is closer to equality than the pre-tax income distribution.

2.4   PROBLEMS

1. The number of faults recorded in a sample of new cars has been listed as follows:

0	0	1	3	1	0	0	2	3
1	1	0	1	0	0	4	4	1
1	2	3	0	0	1	1	4	3
0	4	2	2	1	0	0	0	3

Tabulate the number of faults in the form of a frequency distribution and construct a bar chart.

2. The mileages recorded for a sample of company vehicles during a given week yielded the following data:

138	164	150	132	144	125	149	157
146	158	140	147	136	148	152	144
168	126	138	176	163	119	154	165
146	173	142	147	135	153	140	135
161	145	135	142	150	156	145	128

(a) Using the data tabulate a grouped frequency distribution starting with '110 but under 120'.
(b) Construct a histogram from your frequency distribution.

3. The average weekly household expenditure on a particular range of products has been recorded from a sample of 20 households as follows:

£8.52	£ 7.49	£ 4.50	£ 9.28	£ 9.98
£9.10	£10.12	£13.12	£ 7.89	£ 7.90

| £7.11 | £ 5.12 | £ 8.62 | £10.59 | £14.61 |
| £9.63 | £11.12 | £15.92 | £ 5.80 | £ 8.31 |

Tabulate as a frequency distribution and construct a suitable diagram.

4. The weights used in the construction of the Retail Price Index in 1983 (see Section 5.3) have been given as follows:

Group	Weights
Food	203
Alcoholic drink	78
Tobacco	39
Housing	137
Fuel and light	69
Durable household goods	64
Clothing and footwear	74
Transport and vehicles	159
Miscellaneous goods	75
Services	63
Meals bought and consumed outside the home	39

Present this information using a bar chart and pie chart. Discuss the effectiveness of each method of presentation.

5. In a survey of housing, information on the stock of dwellings has been recorded as follows:

Housing type	Percentage
Owner occupied	53.2
Rented from local authority	31.8
Other rented	15.0

Construct a pie chart.

6. Construct a histogram from the data given in the following table:

Income (£)	Number
under 40	175
40 but under 80	229
80 but under 120	241
120 but under 200	269
200 or more	86

7. Construct a histogram from the data given in the following table:
Journey distance to and from work

Miles	Percentage
under 1	16
1 and under 3	30
3 and under 10	37
10 and under 15	7
15 and over	9

8. Construct a histogram from the information given in the following table:

Error (£)	Frequency
under −15	20
−15 but less than −10	38
−10 but less than −5	178
−5 but less than 0	580
0 but less than 10	360
10 but less than 20	114
20 or more	14

9. The sales within an industry have been recorded as follows:

Year	Quarter 1	Quarter 2	Quarter 3	Quarter 4
1	40	60	80	35
2	30	50	60	30
3	35	60	80	40
4	50	70	100	50

Graph this data and discuss the relationship between sales and time.

10. A company's advertising expenditure has been monitored for 3 years, giving the following information.

Year	Quarter 1	Quarter 2	Quarter 3	Quarter 4
1	10	15	18	20
2	14	16	19	23
3	16	18	20	25

Graph this data and write a short report describing the main features.

11. The results of a company were reported as follows:

Year	Turnover	Pre-tax Profit	Exports
1973	£ 7 572 000	£ 987 000	£ 2 900 000
1974	£ 14 651 000	£ 1 682 000	£ 6 958 000
1975	£ 17 168 000	£ 2 229 000	£ 7 580 000
1976	£ 21 024 000	£ 3 165 000	£ 9 306 000
1977	£ 25 718 000	£ 4 273 000	£10 393 000
1978	£ 37 378 000	£ 6 247 000	£18 280 000
1979	£ 53 988 000	£ 9 559 000	£28 229 000
1980	£ 79 971 000	£19 646 000	£48 770 000
1981	£122 258 000	£32 714 000	£74 410 000
1982	£183 338 000	£49 832 000	£95 029 000

(a) Graph the three sets of data against time.
(b) Graph the log values for the three sets of data against time.
(c) Comment on your graphs outlining the relative merits of those produced in parts (a) and (b).

12. Construct a Lorenz curve for the following data on income.

Income group	Percentage of people in group	Percentage of income
Poorest paid	10	5
	15	8
	20	17
	20	18
	20	20
	10	15
Highest paid	5	17

13. Construct a Lorenz curve for the following data on wealth-holding in the UK.

Group	No. of wealth holders (thousands)	Amount of wealth (£m)
Poorest	2 099	1 049.5
	3 530	7 060.0
	2 133	8 532.0
	4 414	33 105.0
	2 588	32 350.0
	1 167	20 422.5
	694	15 615.0
	1 018	38 175.0
	320	24 000.0
	94	14 100.0
Wealthiest	31	34 100.0
	18 088	228 509.0

Part I
CONCLUDING EXERCISE

On the completion of a survey the following tabulations were presented (with question wording) for questions one and two:

Q1. 'How many years have you been living in this (house/flat)? . . . .'

Number of years	Frequency
0–1	137
2–4	209
5–9	186
10–19	229
20+	205

Q2. For each item below ask 'Do you have . . .?'
(a) A fixed bath or shower with a hot water supply:

	Frequency
None	67
Shared	27
Exclusive	871
No answer	1

(b) A flush toilet inside the house:

	Frequency
None	83
Shared	30
Exclusive	850
No answer	3

(c) A kitchen separate from living rooms:

	Frequency
None	20
Shared	19
Exclusive	922
No answer	5

Report on the tabulations given using charts and diagrams when appropriate.

Describe how you would select a representative sample to provide the type of data given above.

Part II
DESCRIPTIVE STATISTICS

Quantitative methods aim at the communication, presentation and analysis of numerical information. In a market research survey, for example, we would need to summarize the attitudes, intentions and actions of all those included in our survey. In estimating the proportion of defective items from a production process we would need to examine sufficient items to obtain a representative result. In these two cases, and many others, we go beyond a single opinion or a single discovery in an attempt to ascertain what is generally true.

The following three chapters are concerned with descriptive statistics: numbers we choose to calculate to describe the available data.

Exercise Look through some business-related articles in newspapers, journals and other publications and list the descriptive statistics used.

You will probably find that most business-related data are described by a single figure such as the average. Average monthly income or the average number of hours in the working week will describe some facet of life for those persons to whom the figure or figures refer. If one considers changes over time it is likely that this information will be given in the form of an index number; you may be familiar with the Retail Price Index (see Section 5.4), for example.

3 Measures of average

A set of data, however collected, can be made more manageable by tabulation and more understandable by diagrammatic presentation as shown in Chapter 2. The differences in sales of a particular product by region can be adequately presented by the use of a bar chart or the different incomes of a particular group of workers by a histogram. These diagrams give a visible impression of something we have chosen to measure. Quantitative methods, in general, are about measurement in a succinct and effective way.

Summary figures, or statistics, are a way of describing data. Simply speaking, a statistic is any number we choose to calculate. The proportion of a population aged over 65 years is a statistic, the average weekly income for a particular group of workers is another statistic. As we shall see, the mean, median and mode are commonly used summary statistics, with each having advantages and disadvantages.

3.1 THE MEAN, MEDIAN AND MODE

3.1.1 Untabulated data

Suppose the times taken to complete a routine job were recorded as 7, 5, 6, 7 and 8 minutes. To calculate the **arithmetic mean** (from hereon referred to as the mean or average) we would first sum all the values to obtain a total and then divide this total by the number of values included. In this case the mean would be

$$\bar{x} = \frac{7 + 5 + 6 + 7 + 8}{5} = \frac{33}{5} = 6.6 \text{ minutes}$$

where $\bar{x}$ (pronounced x bar) is the symbol used to represent the mean.

As all summary statistics require some form of calculation, a shorthand has developed to describe the necessary steps. Using this shorthand, or notation the calculation of the mean would be written thus:

$$\bar{x} = \frac{\Sigma x}{n}$$

where x represents the individual values, Σ (pronounced sigma) is an instruction to sum values and n is the number of values.

The mean is used to represent the data and can be thought of as a typical value. However, there are other summary statistics that in some ways may be more representative. One alternative to the mean is the **median**, which is defined as the middle value of an ordered list. If we consider the times recorded for the completion of a routine job, rearranging them by value would give:

5, 6, 7, 7, 8 minutes

In this example, by definition, the median would be 7 (the third ordered value). If an even number of values has been recorded, 4, 5, 6, 7, 7 and 8, the median is taken to be the mean of the middle two values:

$$\text{median} = \frac{6 + 7}{2} = 6.5 \text{ minutes}$$

A third statistic used to describe what is typical from a list of values is the **mode**. This is defined as the most frequently occurring value. In our example of recorded times the mode is 7 minutes.

For this particular set of data, we can describe typical time by using the mean of 6.6 minutes, the median of 7 minutes or the mode of 7 minutes. The statistics, in this case, are fairly consistent. We can contrast these results with the statistics a rather different set of data would generate. Suppose the salaries of five salesmen over the previous 12 months were recorded as:

£6000, £6000, £6400, £6500, £10 500

The summary statistics could be given as follows:

$$\text{mean} = £7080$$
$$\text{median} = £6400$$
$$\text{mode} = £6000$$
$$\text{highest salary} = £10\ 500$$
$$\text{lowest salary} = £6000$$

Exercise

If you were thinking of joining these five salesmen and did not have access to the actual figures, which of the summary statistics would you consider the best guide to your future income?

We can note that the median has not been affected by the extreme value, £10 500 in this case. For this reason, the median is often preferred to the mean when analysing income or wealth data. There are generally a few individuals with very high levels of income or wealth and these high values tend to raise the value of the mean. In general, we would want all these statistics, as together they provide a more complete picture of the data.

Exercise

The errors in seven invoices were recorded as follows: −£120, £30, £40, −£8, −£5, £20 and £25. The use of negative and positive signs can be taken to indicate your loss and gain respectively. Calculate appropriate descriptive statistics.
(Answers: mean = −£2.57, median = £20, mode is undefined, lowest value = −£120, highest value = £40.)

3.1.2 Tabulated (ungrouped) discrete data

Suppose we had just completed a survey of 1440 new cars and wanted to describe the number of faults found. The data are clearly discrete; the number of faults taking only positive integer values. The data could be treated as untabulated (see Section 3.1.1) with the number of faults recorded for each car listed. However, it is likely that at some stage during analysis the data would be tabulated in the form of a frequency distribution as shown in Table 3.1.

Table 3.1   The number of faults recorded in a sample of new cars

Number of faults (x)	Number of cars (f)
0	410
1	430
2	290
3	180
4	110
5	20
	1440

To calculate the total number of faults we first multiply the number of faults (x) by the number of cars (f for frequency) to obtain a column of subtotals (fx). We then sum this column (Σfx) to obtain the total number of faults. To calculate the mean (Table 3.2) we divide by the number of values or observations, which is the sum of the frequencies $(n = \Sigma f)$.

Table 3.2   The calculation of the mean from a frequency distribution

x	f	fx
0	410	0
1	430	430
2	290	580
3	180	540
4	110	440
5	20	100
	1440	2090

The mean is $\bar{x} = \dfrac{2090}{1440} = 1.451$ faults

We can note that the first 410 cars contribute 0 faults to the total, the next 430 cars contribute 430 faults to the total (1 each), the next 290 cars contribute 580 faults to the total (2 each) and so on. A modified formula will remind us what we have done:

$$\bar{x} = \frac{\Sigma fx}{n}$$

The tabulation of the number of faults in new cars has ordered the set of data (the first 410 cars have 0 faults, etc.) The median, which is an order statistic, can be found if we cumulate frequencies. The **cumulative frequency** is the number of items with a given value or less. To calculate cumulative frequency we just add the next value to the running total (Table 3.3).

Table 3.3 The calculation of cumulative frequency

x	f	Cumulative frequency
0	410	410
1	430	840 = 410 + 430
2	290	1130 = 840 + 290
3	180	1310 = 1130 + 180
4	110	1420 = 1310 + 110
5	20	1440 = 1420 + 20
	1440	

To locate the median observation for listed or discrete data we can use the formula

$(n + 1)/2$

In this case the median will be the $720\frac{1}{2}$th ordered observation, i.e. it will lie between the 720th and 721st car. From the cumulative frequency it can be seen that 410 new cars have 0 (or less) faults and 840 new cars have 1 fault or less. By deduction, the 720th and 721st new cars both have 1 fault, and hence the median is 1 fault.

The mode corresponds to the highest frequency count and in this example is 1 fault.

The distribution of faults (a few new cars with a high number of faults) explains the differences between the median and the mean.

Exercise

An automatic cash dispenser allows any transaction up to the value of £30 in £5 multiples. Recent transactions have been tabulated as follows:

Value of transactions (£)	Number
5	7
10	15
15	12
20	23
25	21
30	22

Determine the mean, median and mode.
(Answers: mean = £20.10, median = £20, mode = £20.)

3.1.3 Tabulated (grouped) continuous data

If we have been presented with a frequency distribution in which the values have been grouped together, we will no longer know the exact value of each observation. However, we can still **estimate** the descriptive statistics.

Consider the income distribution given in Table 3.4. We do not know the exact weekly income of any of the workers, only the numbers with an income in a given range. We know, for example, that 28 workers have an income of between £200 but less than £300. If we assume that all the values within a group are evenly spread (the larger values tending to cancel the smaller values) then we can represent the group by its **mid-point value**. If any of the groups are open-ended we will need to assume a lower or upper boundary and then determine a mid-point value. The mid-points are then used to estimate the mean (Table 3.5).

Table 3.4 Income of a particular group of workers

Weekly income	Number of workers
less than £200	10
£200 but less than £300	28
£300 but less than £400	42
£400 but less than £600	50
£600 or more	20

Table 3.5 The estimation of the mean using mid-points

Weekly income	Mid-point (x)	Number of workers (f)	fx
£100 but less than £200	150	10	1 500
£200 but less than £300	250	28	7 000
£300 but less than £400	350	42	14 700
£400 but less than £600	500	50	25 000
£600 but less than £1000	800	20	16 000
		150	64 200

The mean is $\bar{x} = \dfrac{64\ 200}{150} = £428$

and the formula $\bar{x} = \dfrac{\Sigma fx}{n}$ where x is the value of mid-points

Exercise

Consider the following tabulations:

Sales	Frequency
20 or less	4
21 up to 25	26
26 up to 30	52
31 up to 35	67
36 up to 40	103
41 up to 45	61
46 up to 50	51
51 up to 55	25
56 up to 60	10
61 or more	1
	400

Sales	Frequency
25 or less	30
26 up to 35	119
36 up to 45	164
46 up to 55	76
56 or more	11
	400

Sales	Frequency
40 or less	252
41 or more	148
	400

For each of these tables assume an upper or lower boundary value for the open-ended groups, determine mid-point values and estimate a mean. Compare these estimated means.

(Answers: bounds of 16 and 65 give $\bar{x} = 38.225$; $\bar{x} = 38.475$; $\bar{x} = 37.38$)

We should note that the data given in the exercise are discrete (we count sales) but when grouped as above we treat in the same way as continuous data.

We can determine the median either by calculation of graphically. The first step in both cases is to find the cumulative frequencies (Table 3.6). We can note from the cumulative frequency column that 10 workers have a weekly income of less than £200, 38 workers have a weekly income of less than £300 and so on. In each case, cumulative frequency refers to the upper boundary of the corresponding income range.

Table 3.6   The determination of the median

Weekly income	Number of workers	Cumulative frequency
less than £200	10	10
£200 but less than £300	28	38
£300 but less than £400	42	80
£400 but less than £600	50	130
£600 or more	20	150

Graphical method
To find the median graphically, we plot cumulative frequency against the upper boundary of the corresponding income range and join the points with straight lines (this is the graphical representation of the assumption that values are evenly spread within groups). The resultant cumulative frequency graph or **ogive** is shown in Fig. 3.1.

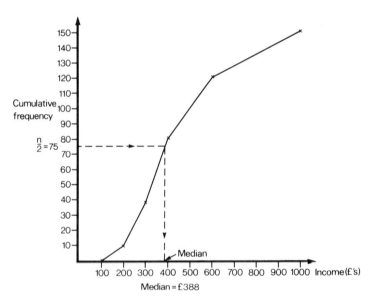

Figure 3.1

To identify the median value from grouped, continuous data we use the formula $n/2$. The corresponding observation divides the histogram into two equal areas. In this example, the median is the 75th value, which can be read from the ogive as £388.

Calculation of the median

To calculate the median, we must first locate the group that contains the 75th observation, i.e. the median group. Looking down the cumulative frequency column of Table 3.6, we can see that 38 workers have an income of less than £300 and 80 workers have an income of less than £400. The 75th worker, therefore, must have an income between £300 but less than £400. The median must be £300 plus some fraction of this interval £100. The median observation lies 37 workers inside the median group; 75 ($n/2$) minus the 38 workers whose weekly income is less than £300. There are 42 workers in the median group so the median lies 37/42th of the way through the interval. The median is equal to:

$$300 + \frac{37}{42} \times 100 = £388.10$$

In terms of a formula we can write:

$$\text{median} = l + i\left(\frac{n/2 - F}{f}\right)$$

where l is the lower boundary of the median group, i is the width of the median group, F is the cumulative frequency up to the median group and f is the frequency in the median group.

Using the figures from the example above:

$$\text{median} = 300 + 100\left(\frac{75 - 38}{42}\right)$$
$$= £388.10$$

The mode can be defined as the point of greatest density and to estimate this value we refer to the histogram shown in Fig. 3.2.

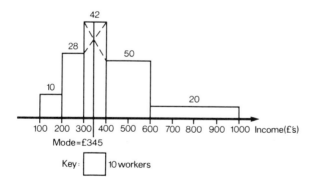

Figure 3.2

To estimate the mode, we first identify the highest block on the histogram (scaling has already taken place) and join corner points as shown above. In this example the mode is £345.

The results of a travel survey were presented as follows:

Journey distance to and from work (miles)	% of journeys
0 but under 3	46
3 but under 10	38
10 but under 20	16

Determine the mean, median and mode.
(*Hint*: we can use percentages in the same way we used frequencies to determine the mean, median and mode.)
(Answers: mean = 5.56 miles, median = 3.74 miles, mode = 2.56 miles.)

3.2 THE USE OF THE MEAN, MEDIAN AND MODE

How you choose which statistic to use from those available depends partly on the nature of the data and partly on the information you wish to convey. Suppose we wanted to describe bonuses paid by a particular company from the data given in Table 3.7. Using the methods of Section 3.1 we could calculate the mean to be £28.60, the median to be £22.50 and the mode to be £13.53. These statistics could be taken as characteristics of a skewed distribution: wrongly. A closer examination shows the frequency distribution to have two distinct humps (Fig. 3.3).

Table 3.7 Recorded bonus payments

Average weekly bonus (£)	Number of workers
0 but under 10	18
10 but under 20	30
20 but under 30	8
30 but under 30	6
40 but under 50	22
50 but under 60	12
60 but under 70	4
	100

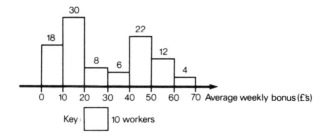

Key: ☐ 10 workers

Figure 3.3

The mean and the median are clearly not typical of the bonuses paid; 48% of workers have a bonus under £20 and 22% have a bonus of between £40 but under £50. A **bimodal distribution** (two peaks) of this sort is usually taken to indicate two separate sources of variation. In this example, if workers are firstly classified as being skilled or unskilled the more familiar distributional shapes emerge as shown in Table 3.8.

Table 3.8 Recorded bonus payments for skilled and unskilled workers

Average weekly bonus (£)	Number of workers	
	Unskilled	Skilled
0 but under 10	18	0
10 but under 20	30	0
20 but under 30	7	1
30 but under 40	3	3
40 but under 50	2	20
50 but under 60	0	12
60 but under 70	0	4
	60	40

Having isolated and controlled a major source of variation we can reasonably describe the bonus payments to skilled and unskilled workers. Essentially, the mean, median and mode can only describe the data if the data are consistent and meaningful.

Each of these statistics has particular characteristics and these are show in Figs. 3.4 and 3.5.

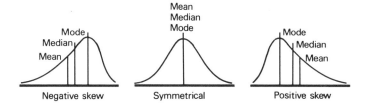

Figure 3.4 The relationship between the mean, median and mode.

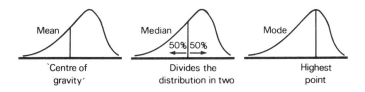

Figure 3.5 Interpretation of mean, median and mode.

Exercise Calculate the mean, median and mode for each group of workers, from the data given in Table 3.8.
(Answer: unskilled: mean £15.16, median £14, mode £13.4; skilled: mean £48.75, median £48, mode £46.8.)

3.3 WEIGHTED MEANS

Suppose that we were given a grouped frequency distribution of weekly income for a particular group of workers and in addition the average income within each of the categories. In this case we could use the set of averages rather than mid-points to calculate an overall mean. In terms of our notation we would need to write the formula as:

$$\bar{x} = \frac{\Sigma \bar{x}_i f_i}{n}$$

where $\bar{x}$ remains the overall mean, $\bar{x}_i$ is the mean in category i and f_i is the frequency in category i.

The calculation using a set of averages is shown in Table 3.9. We would note from the table, for example, that the first 10 workers have an average weekly income of £170, and together earn £1700. The overall mean is

$$\bar{x} = \frac{68\ 180}{150} = £454.53$$

The same result could have been obtained as follows:

$$\bar{x} = \left(170 \times \frac{10}{150}\right) + \left(260 \times \frac{28}{150}\right) + \left(350 \times \frac{42}{150}\right) + \left(590 \times \frac{50}{150}\right) + \left(750 \times \frac{20}{150}\right)$$
$$= £454.53$$

In terms of describing this procedure the formula can be rewritten as:

$$\bar{x} = \Sigma \left[\bar{x}_i \times \left(\frac{f_i}{n} \right) \right]$$

where f_i/n are the weighting factors.

Table 3.9   The weighting of means

Weekly income	Category average ($\bar{x}_i$)	Number of workers (f_i)	$\bar{x}_i f_i$
less than £200	£170	10	1 700
£200 but less than £300	£260	28	7 280
£300 but less than £400	£350	42	14 700
£400 but less than £600	£590	50	29 500
£600 or more	£750	20	15 000
		150	68 180

These weighting factors can be thought of as a measure of size or importance. They can be used to correct inadequacies in data or to collate results from a survey which was not completely representative.

The previous method gave a mean of £428 which underestimated the average weekly income. The extra information of group means will give a more accurate answer.

Example   Suppose that two industries, steel manufacture and mining, account for all the economic activity in a small community, and that steel manufacture traditionally accounts for 80% of employment. If 2% become unemployed from steel manufacture and 20% from mining, calculate the overall unemployment rate.

In this example, percentage unemployment from mining is going to have less impact than percentage unemployment from steel manufacture as the latter is four times larger. To average 2% and 20% to find 11% does not allow for this difference in size. To calculate the overall rate of unemployment (weighted average) we can multiply the unemployment rate in each industry by its weighting factor (f_i/n) or proportional size. The weighting factors for steel manufacture and mining are 0.80 and 0.20 respectively.

Rate of unemployment (%) = $2 \times 0.8 + 20 \times 0.2 = 5.6\%$.

The overall rate of unemployment is nearer to the 2% for steel manufacture than the 20% for mining owing to the weighting of results.

3.4 PROBLEMS

1. Which descriptive statistics would you use to describe

   (a) the most popular model of car sold each month;
   (b) house prices in a specific area;
   (c) wages of the top 10% of wage-earners;
   (d) earnings of manual workers in the UK;
   (e) journey time from Leeds to London.

2. The number of faults in a sample of new cars has been listed as follows:

0	0	1	3	1	0	0	2	3
1	1	0	1	0	0	4	4	1
1	2	3	0	0	1	1	4	3
0	4	2	2	1	0	0	0	3

   Determine the mean, median and mode.

3. The mileages recorded for a sample of company vehicles during a given week yielded the following data:

138	164	150	132	144	125	149	157
146	158	140	147	136	148	152	144
168	126	138	176	163	119	154	165
146	173	142	147	135	153	140	135
161	145	135	142	150	156	145	128

   Determine the mean, median and mode. What do these descriptive statistics tell you about the distribution of the data?

4. The average weekly household expenditure on a particular range of products has been recorded from a sample of 20 households as follows:

£8.52	£ 7.49	£ 4.50	£ 9.28	£ 9.98
£9.10	£10.12	£13.12	£ 7.89	£ 7.90
£7.11	£ 5.12	£ 8.62	£10.59	£14.61
£9.63	£11.12	£15.92	£ 5.80	£ 8.31

   (a) Determine the mean and median directly from the figures given.
   (b) Tabulate the data as a frequency distribution and estimate the mean and median from your table.
   (c) Explain any differences in your results from part (a) and part (b).

5. The number of breakdowns each day on a section of road were recorded for a sample of 250 days as follows:

Number of breakdowns	Number of days
0	100
1	70
2	45
3	20
4	10
5	5
	250

Determine the mean, median and mode. Which statistic do you think best describes this data and explain why.

6. Determine the mean, median and mode from the data given in the following table:

Income (£)	Number
Under 40	175
40 but under 80	229
80 but under 120	241
120 but under 200	269
200 or more	86

7. Determine the mean, median and mode from the data given in the following table:
   Journey distance to and from work

Miles	Percentage
under 1	16
1 and under 3	30
3 and under 10	37
10 and under 15	7
15 and over	9

8. Prepare a report identifying the main features of the following table:
   Households by size in the UK

| No. of persons | Thousands | |
	1961	1971
1	1919	3320
2	4820	5771
3	3780	3458
4	3100	3148
5	1489	1515
6 or more	1079	1106

Source: *Social Trends* **10**, page 79.
Obtain more recent data and compare with those given.

9. Determine the mean and median from the information given in the following table:

Error (£)	Frequency
under −15	20
−15 but less than −10	38
−10 but less than −5	178
−5 but less than 0	580
0 but less than 10	360
10 but less than 20	114
20 or more	15

10. Included in the following table is the average income for those in each income group:

Income (£)	Average income	Number
under 40	35	175
40 but under 80	64	229
80 but under 120	101	241
120 but under 200	158	269
200 or more	240	86

(a) Determine the mean using the average income figures given.
(b) Is the method used in part (a) as precise as working with a listing of original data?

11. A company files its sales vouchers according to their value so that they are effectively in four strata. A sample of 200 is selected and the strata means calculated.

Stratum	Number of vouchers	Sample size	Sample mean
above £1000	100	50	£1800
£800 but under £1000	200	60	£ 890
£400 but under £800	500	50	£ 560
less than £400	1000	40	£ 180
		$\overline{200}$	

Estimate the mean value and total value of the sales vouchers.

4 Measures of dispersion

In the previous chapter we were concerned with finding an average value. The mean, median and mode were calculated for various sets of data and all shown to measure some aspect of what was typical. However, we are not always interested in an average value or, indeed, average person. We may want to know how values differ. In an attitudinal survey we would be interested in the **differences of opinion**. In a comparison of countries or occupations we may be concerned with the **distribution of income**. In assessing the market for a particular product we may need to explain the **variability in sales**. This chapter is concerned with measuring the differences between values in a set of data, i.e. their variability or dispersion.

4.1 STANDARD DEVIATION

As a measure of dispersion, standard deviation is by far the most frequently used. It is a descriptive statistic and provides the basis of statistical inference (see Chapter 12). It is calculated from the differences about the mean.

4.1.1 Untabulated data

Consider, for example, the times recorded to complete a routine job; 7, 5, 6, 7 and 8 minutes. The mean for this data is 6.6 minutes. The differences about

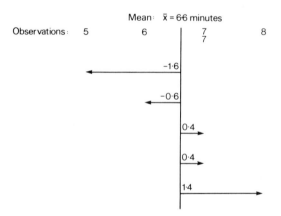

Figure 4.1   The differences about the mean.

this mean are shown diagrammatically in Fig. 4.1. To the left of the mean the differences are negative and to the right of the mean the differences are positive. The sum of these differences is zero. In terms of a physical interpretation the mean can be viewed as the centre of gravity and the observations as a number of weights which balance.

To calculate the standard deviation we:

(a) compute the mean $\bar{x}$
(b) calculate the differences from the mean $(x - \bar{x})$
(c) square these differences $(x - \bar{x})^2$
(d) sum the squared differences $\Sigma(x - \bar{x})^2$
(e) average the squared differences to find variance

$$\frac{\Sigma(x - \bar{x})^2}{n}$$

(f) square root variance to find standard deviation

$$\sqrt{\left[\frac{\Sigma(x - \bar{x})^2}{n}\right]}$$

These steps are illustrated in Table 4.1.

Table 4.1   The calculation of the standard deviation

x	$(x - \bar{x})$	$(x - \bar{x})^2$
7	0.4	0.16
5	-1.6	2.56
6	-0.6	0.36
7	0.4	0.16
8	1.4	1.96
33		5.20

where $\bar{x} = \dfrac{33}{5} = 6.6$ minutes

$$s = \sqrt{\left[\frac{\Sigma(x - \bar{x})^2}{n}\right]} = \sqrt{\left[\frac{5.20}{5}\right]} = \sqrt{1.04} = 1.02 \text{ minutes}$$

Exercises

1. The errors in seven invoices were recorded as follows: $-£120$, $£30$, $£40$, $-£8$, $-£5$, $£20$ and $£25$. Calculate the mean and standard deviation. (Answer: $\bar{x} = -£2.57$, $s = £50.66$.)

2. To check the working consistency of a new machine, the time taken to complete a specific task was recorded on five occasions. On each occasion the recorded time was 30 seconds. Calculate the mean and standard deviation. (Answer: $\bar{x} = 30$ seconds, $s = 0$ seconds.)

4.1.2   Tabulated (ungrouped) discrete data

Suppose the results of a survey were given in a tabulated form as in Table 4.2. To calculate standard deviation, we need to allow for the **frequency of occurrence**. In the first group, for example, there are 410 cars with 0 faults, so we would expect 410 differences of 0 from the mean. This requires an additional step of multiplying squared differences by frequency (see Section 3.1.2). The formula for standard deviation now becomes

$$s = \sqrt{\left[\frac{\Sigma f(x - \bar{x})^2}{n}\right]}$$

The calculations are shown in Table 4.3.

Table 4.2 The number of faults recorded in a sample of new cars

Number of faults	Number of cars
0	410
1	430
2	290
3	180
4	110
5	20

Table 4.3 Standard deviation from tabulated discrete data: The number of faults recorded in a sample of new cars

x	f	fx	$(x - \bar{x})$	$(x - \bar{x})^2$	$f(x - \bar{x})^2$
0	410	0	-1.451	2.1054	863.214
1	430	430	-0.451	0.2034	87.462
2	290	580	0.549	0.3014	87.406
3	180	540	1.549	2.3994	431.892
4	110	440	2.549	6.4974	714.714
5	20	100	3.549	12.5954	251.908
	1440	2090			2436.596

$$\bar{x} = \frac{2090}{1440} = 1.451 \text{ faults}$$

$$s = \sqrt{\left[\frac{\Sigma f(x - \bar{x})^2}{n}\right]} = \sqrt{\left[\frac{2436.596}{1440}\right]} = 1.301 \text{ faults}$$

4.1.3 Tabulated (grouped) continuous data

To calculate the standard deviation for this type of data we determine mid-points and proceed as before (see Section 4.1.2). An example is given in Table 4.4

Table 4.4 The estimation of the standard deviation using mid-points

Weekly income	Frequency (f)	Mid-point (x)	fx	$(x - \bar{x})$	$(x - \bar{x})^2$	$f(x - \bar{x})^2$
less than £200	10	150*	1 500	-278	77 284	772 840
£200 but less than £300	28	250	7 000	-178	31 684	887 152
£300 but less than £400	42	350	14 700	-78	6 084	255 528
£400 but less than £600	50	500	25 000	72	5 184	259 200
£600 or more	20	800*	16 000	372	138 384	2 767 680
	150		64 200			4 942 400

$$\bar{x} = \frac{64\ 200}{150} = £428$$

$$s = \sqrt{\left[\frac{\Sigma f(x - \bar{x})^2}{n}\right]} = \sqrt{\left[\frac{4\ 942\ 400}{150}\right]} = £181.52$$

* Assumed.

An alternative is to use a computationally easier formula. (See Section 4.6 for proof.)

$$s = \sqrt{\left[\frac{\Sigma fx^2}{n} - \left(\frac{\Sigma fx}{n}\right)^2\right]}$$

The procedure is shown in Table 4.5.

Table 4.5   The estimation of standard deviation

x	f	fx	x²	fx²
150	10	1 500	22 500	225 000
250	28	7 000	62 500	1 750 000
350	42	14 700	122 500	5 145 000
500	50	25 000	250 000	12 500 000
800	20	16 000	640 000	12 800 000
	150	64 200		32 420 000

$$s = \sqrt{\left[\frac{\Sigma fx^2}{n} - \left(\frac{\Sigma fx}{n}\right)^2\right]} = \sqrt{\left[\frac{32\,420\,000}{150} - \left(\frac{64\,200}{150}\right)^2\right]}$$
$$= £181.52$$

4.2   OTHER MEASURES OF DISPERSION

4.2.1   Range

The range is the most easily understood measure of dispersion as it is **the difference between the highest and lowest values**. If we were concerned with five recorded times of 7, 5, 6, 7 and 8 minutes the range would be 3 minutes (8 minutes – 5 minutes). It is, however, a rather crude measure, which is highly unstable as new data are added, and is naturally affected by a few extreme values. If this type of measure is to be used, it may well be better to quote the highest and lowest values rather than the difference between them. When dealing with data presented as a frequency distribution we will not always know the exact highest and lowest values, and if the groups are open-ended (e.g. 60 and more) then any values used will merely be from assumption.

4.2.2   Quartile deviation

If we are able to quote a half-way value, the median, then we can also quote quarter-way values, the quartiles. These are order statistics like the median and can be determined in the same way. Consider, for example, the income distribution and cumulative frequency given in Table 4.6. The lower quartile (referred to as Q_1), will correspond to the value one-quarter of the way through the data, the 37.5 ordered value:

$$\left(\frac{1}{4}\ n = \frac{150}{4} = 37.5\right)$$

and the upper quartile (referred to as Q_3) to the value three-quarters of the way through the data, the 112.5 ordered value

$$\left(\frac{3}{4}\ n\ =\ \frac{3}{4}\ \times\ 150\ =\ 112.5\right)$$

Table 4.6   Income distribution

Weekly income	Number of workers	Cumulative frequency
less than £200	10	10
£200 but less than £300	28	38
£300 but less than £400	42	80
£400 but less than £600	50	130
£600 or more	20	150

Graphical method
To estimate any of the order statistics graphically, we plot cumulative frequency against the values to which it refers, as shown in Fig. 4.2. The value of the lower quartile can be read from the ogive to be £298 and the value of the upper quartile to be £530.

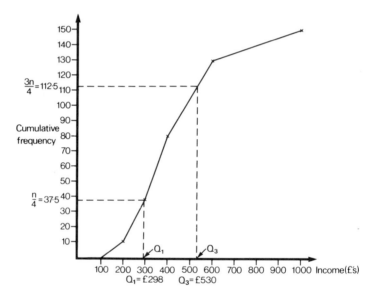

Figure 4.2

Calculation of the quartiles
We can adapt the median formula (see Section 3.1.3) as follows:

$$\text{Order value}\ =\ l\ +\ i\left(\frac{O\ -\ F}{f}\right)$$

where O is the order value of interest, l is the lower boundary of corresponding group, i is the width of this group, F is the cumulative frequency up to this group, and f is the frequency in this group.

The lower quartile will lie in the group '£200 but less than £300' and can be calculated thus:

$$Q_1 = 200 + 100\left(\frac{37.5 - 10}{28}\right) = £298.21$$

The upper quartile will lie in the group '£400 but less than £600' and can be calculated thus:

$$Q_3 = 400 + 200\left(\frac{112.5 - 80}{50}\right) = £530.00$$

The quartile deviation is the average difference between these quartiles:

$$\text{Quartile deviation} = \frac{Q_3 - Q_1}{2}$$
$$= \frac{530.00 - 298.21}{2}$$
$$= £115.90 \text{ (rounded from £115.895)}$$

4.3 VARIABILITY IN SAMPLE DATA

We would expect the results of a survey to identify differences in opinions, income and a range of other factors. The extent of these differences can be summarized by an appropriate measure of dispersion (standard deviation, quartile deviation, range). Market researchers, in particular, seek to explain differences in attitudes and actions of distinct groups within a population. It is known, for example, that the propensity to buy frozen foods varies between different groups of people. As a producer of frozen foods you might be particularly interested in those most likely to buy your products. Supermarkets of the same size can have very different turnover figures and as a manager of a supermarket you may wish to identify those factors most likely to explain the differences in turnover. A number of **clustering algorithms** have developed in recent years that seek to explain differences in sample data.

As an example, consider the following algorithm or procedure that seeks to explain the differences in the selling prices of houses:

(a) Calculate the mean and a measure of dispersion for all the observations in your sample. In this example we could calculate the average price and the range of prices (Fig. 4.3). It can be seen from the range that there is considerable variability in price relative to the average price. Normally the standard deviation would be preferred to the range as a measure of dispersion for this type of data.

(b) Decide what factors explain most of the difference (range) in price, e.g. location, house-type, number of bedrooms. If location is considered par-

$\bar{x} = £35,000$
Range = £40,000

Complete sample

Figure 4.3

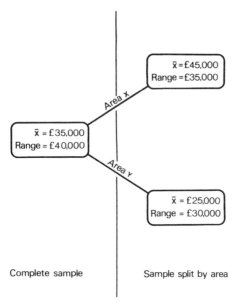

Figure 4.4

ticularly important, we can divide the sample on that basis and calculate the chosen descriptive statistics (Fig. 4.4). In this case we have chosen to segment the sample by location, areas X and Y. The smaller range within the two new groups indicates that there is less variability of house prices within areas. We could have divided the sample by some other factor and compared the reduction in the range.

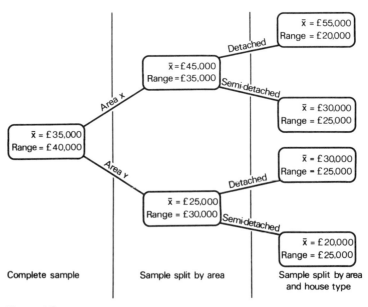

Figure 4.5

(c) Divide the new groups and again calculate the descriptive statistics. We could divide the sample a second time on the basis of house-type (Fig. 4.5).

(d) The procedure can be continued in many ways with many splitting criteria.

A more sophisticated version of this procedure is known as the automatic interactive detection (AID) technique. It has been used as a basis for market segmentation and as a guide for multiple regression (see Chapter 18).

4.4 PROBLEMS

1. Which descriptive statistics would you use to describe the differences in:

   (a) the numbers of each model of car sold each month;
   (b) house prices in a specific area;
   (c) wages of the top 10%;
   (d) earnings of manual workers in the UK;
   (e) journey time from Leeds to London.

2. The number of faults in a sample of new cars has been listed as follows:

0	0	1	3	1	0	0	2	3
1	1	0	1	0	0	4	4	1
1	2	3	0	0	1	1	4	3
0	4	2	2	1	0	0	0	3

   Determine the range, quartile deviation and standard deviation. Which of these measures of dispersion would you consider most appropriate for the data given? Explain the reasons for your choice.

3. The mileages recorded for a sample of company vehicles during a given week yielded the following data:

138	164	150	132	144	125	149	157
146	158	140	147	136	148	152	144
168	176	138	176	163	119	154	165
146	173	142	147	135	153	140	135
161	145	135	142	150	156	145	128

   Determine the range, quartile deviation and standard deviation from these figures.

4. The average weekly household expenditure on a particular range of products has been recorded from a sample of 20 households as follows:

£8.52	£ 7.49	£ 4.50	£ 9.28	£ 9.98
£9.10	£10.12	£13.12	£ 7.89	£ 7.90
£7.11	£ 5.12	£ 8.62	£10.59	£14.61
£9.63	£11.12	£15.92	£ 5.80	£ 8.31

   (a) Determine the mean and standard deviation directly from the figures given.
   (b) Tabulate the data as a frequency distribution and estimate the mean and standard deviation from your table.
   (c) Explain any differences in your results from part (a) and part (b).

5. The errors recorded in a sample of 50 invoices are as follows:

No. of errors	Frequency
0	22
1	16
2	5
3	4
4	3

Calculate the range, quartile deviation and standard deviation of the number of errors.

6. Determine the quartile deviation and standard deviation of incomes from the data given in the following table:

Income (£)	Number
under 40	175
40 but under 80	229
80 but under 120	241
120 but under 200	269
200 or more	86

7. Determine the quartile deviation and standard deviation from the data given in the following table.
   Journey distance to and from work

Miles	Percentage
under 1	16
1 and under 3	30
3 and under 10	37
10 and under 15	7
15 and over	9

8. Determine the mean and standard deviation from the data given in the following table:

Error (£)	Frequency
under −15	20
−15 but less than −10	38
−10 but less than −5	178
−5 but less than 0	580
0 but less than 10	360
10 but less than 20	114
20 or more	14

9. Given the following distribution of weekly household income:

Household income (£)	% of all households
under 30	13.7
30 but under 40	7.6
40 but under 60	11.6
60 but under 80	13.4
80 but under 100	14.2
100 but under 120	13.0

Household income (£)	% of all households
120 but under 150	12.3
150 or more	14.2

(a) calculate the mean and standard deviation;
(b) estimate the percentage of households with a weekly income below the mean;
(c) determine the median and quartile deviation;
(d) contrast the values you have determined in parts (a), (b) and (c) and comment on the skewness (if any) of the distribution.

10. You have been given the following data from a sample of 20 individuals:

Code number	Sex	Age	Employment	Amount spent weekly on alcoholic drink (£)
1	0	20	0	8.83
2	1	33	0	4.90
3	1	50	1	0.71
4	0	48	0	5.70
5	0	47	0	6.20
6	0	19	0	7.40
7	1	21	1	3.58
8	0	64	0	4.80
9	1	32	0	4.50
10	1	57	1	2.80
11	0	49	0	4.60
12	0	18	0	5.30
13	1	39	1	3.42
14	0	28	0	10.15
15	0	51	0	6.20
16	1	43	0	4.80
17	1	40	0	3.82
18	0	22	1	7.70
19	1	30	0	6.20
20	0	60	0	4.45

Sex: male 0   Age: number of years
      female 1
Employment: working   0
            not working 1

Measure and explain the variation in the amount spent weekly on alcoholic drinks with reference to the other factors given.

4.5 APPENDIX

Proof that $\sqrt{\left[\dfrac{\Sigma f(x-\bar{x})^2}{n}\right]} = \sqrt{\left[\dfrac{\Sigma fx^2}{n} - \left(\dfrac{\Sigma fx}{n}\right)^2\right]}$

$$\frac{1}{n}\Sigma f(x-\bar{x})^2 = \frac{1}{n}\Sigma f(x^2 - 2x\bar{x} + \bar{x}^2)$$

$$= \frac{1}{n}(\Sigma fx^2 - 2\bar{x}\,\Sigma fx + \bar{x}^2\,\Sigma f)$$

$$= \frac{1}{n} \left(\Sigma fx^2 - 2n\,\bar{x}^2 + n\,\bar{x}^2 \right)$$

$$= \frac{1}{n} \left(\Sigma fx^2 - n\,\bar{x}^2 \right)$$

$$= \frac{1}{n} \left[\Sigma fx^2 - n \left(\frac{\Sigma fx}{n} \right)^2 \right]$$

$$= \frac{\Sigma fx^2}{n} - \left(\frac{\Sigma fx}{n} \right)^2$$

Note: $\bar{x}$ is a constant as far as Σ is concerned; $\Sigma f = n$; $\Sigma fx = n\,\bar{x}$ since $\bar{x} = \Sigma fx/n$.

5 Index numbers

We are often concerned with changes over time, for example social or economic changes. If the change can be measured, then it can be effectively represented by an **index**. We could, for example, construct an index for the numbers unemployed in a particular population using weekly, monthly, quarterly or annual figures. In the same way, we could construct an index for the number of road accidents or the number of business studies students. The need for an index number to indicate change is even more pressing when the quantity being measured is an **aggregate** of heterogeneous quantities, e.g. the annual output of cars of all types. What they all have in common is the use of historic data.

5.1 THE INTERPRETATION OF AN INDEX NUMBER

An index is a scaling of numbers so that a start is made from a base figure of 100. In general, all the subsequent index numbers will relate to this base figure. Consider the example in Table 5.1. In this case, year 1 is the **base year**, and as an exception to our usual algebraic rules we are permitted to write year 1 = 100. The subsequent index numbers all measure the change from the base year. The index number 135 is taken to mean that there has been a 35% **increase** in the measured quantity from the base year (year 1) to year 4. Similarly, the index number 150 is taken to measure a 50% increase from the base year. To calculate a percentage increase we first find the difference between the two figures, divide by the base figure and then multiply by 100. The percentage increase from 100 to 150 can be calculated as

$$\frac{150 - 100}{100} \times 100 = 50\%$$

In the same way an increase in hourly pay from £1.80 to £2.70 is 50%:

$$\frac{2.70 - 1.80}{1.80} \times 100 = 50\%$$

One convenience of index numbers is that by starting from 100, the percentage increase from the base year is found just by subtraction. However, the differences thereafter are referred to as **percentage points**. It can be seen from Table 5.1 that there has been a 15 percentage point increase from year 4 to year 5. The percentage increase, however, is

$$\frac{150 - 135}{135} \times 100 = 11.11\%$$

There are no 'hard and fast' rules for the choice of a base year and, as shown in Table 5.2, any year can be the base year.

Table 5.1 An index

Year	Index 1
1	100
2	110
3	120
4	135
5	150

Table 5.2 Indices that all measure the same change

Year	Index 1	Index 2	Index 3	Index 4	Index 5
1	100	90.91	83.33	74.07	66.67
2	110	100.00	91.67	81.48	73.33
3	120	109.09	100.00	88.89	80.00
4	135	122.73	112.50	100.00	90.00
5	150	136.36	125.00	111.11	100.00

Each of the indices measures **the same change over time** (to two decimal places). The percentage increase from year 1 to year 2 using index 2, for example, is

$$\frac{100.00 - 90.91}{90.91} \times 100 = 10.00\%$$

To change the base year (move the 100) requires only a scaling of the index up or down. If we want index 1 to have year 2 as the base year (construct index 2), we can use the equivalence between 110 and 100 and multiply index 1 by this scaling factor 100/110.

Exercise   Scale index 2 in such a way that the base year becomes year 5 (index 5).

In terms of the mathematics, the choice of a base year really does not matter but in practice, there are a number of important considerations. As the index gets larger the same percentage change is represented by a larger difference. A change from 100 to 120 is the same as a change from 300 to 360 but the impression can be very different. If, for example, our index were used as a measure of inflation, as with the Retail Price Index, we would not want the index to move very far from 100. When, as is usually the case, an index measures the change in an aggregate of heterogeneous items, **we may need periodically to revise the items included in the index**. Suppose a manufacturer constructed a productivity index using as a measure of productivity the times taken to make the most popular products. As new products appear and established products disappear, the manufacturer would need to reconsider the basis of the index. Also, we tend to choose a typical month, quarter or year as our starting point. If we were to start an index of car sales in August, when new letter registrations are introduced, or in a month after tax cuts, the index of 1 month later would give the misleading impression of car sales falling. Index numbers are constructed to show generally what is happening and may be adjusted to allow for predictable changes at certain times of the year. Unemployment figures, for example, are adjusted each July, to allow for the number of school leavers, and the corresponding index can also be adjusted to allow for this disturbance in the general trend (for seasonal adjustment refer to Chapter 19). In practice, we may be confronted with a change of base year as shown in Table 5.3.

Table 5.3   A change of base year

Year	'Old' index	'New' index
3	120	
4	135	
5	150	100
6		115
7		125

We can use the equivalence of 150 in the 'old' index with 100 in the 'new' index at year 5. We either scale down the 'old' index using a multiplication factor of 100/150 as shown in Table 5.4 or scale up the 'new' index using 150/100 as shown in Table 5.5.

Table 5.4   Scaling-down the 'old' index

Year		'New' index
3	$120 \times 100/150 =$	80
4	$135 \times 100/150 =$	90
5		100
6		115
7		125

Table 5.5   Scaling-up the 'new' index

Year		'Old' index
3		120
4		135
5		150
6	$115 \times 150/100 =$	172.5
7	$125 \times 150/100 =$	187.5

A change in base year is often accompanied by a change in definition and the user must be aware of the effect this may have, particularly on the composition of the index (i.e. what items are included in it and the importance attached to them).

Exercises

1. The 'all items' Retail Price Index was recorded as 326.1 on 15 November 1982 and 341.9 on 15 November 1983.

   (a) Show that the percentage increase is 4.8%.
   (b) Discuss why the index number 341.9 can be misleading.

2. A company has constructed an efficiency index to monitor the performance of its major production plant. In 1981 it was decided that a new index should be started owing to the major changes in the production process. The constructed indices for the years 1979 to 1983 are given below:

Year	Existing index	New index
1979	140	
1980	155	
1981	185	100
1982		105
1983		107

(a) Calculate the percentage increase in efficiency from 1979 to 1983.
(Answer: 41.4%.)
(b) Construct another index using 1980 as the base year.
(Answer: 90.3, 100.0, 119.4, 125.3, 127.7.)
Note that no allowance has been made for changes in the methods used to construct the indices.

5.2 THE CONSTRUCTION OF INDEX NUMBERS

Index numbers are perhaps best known for measuring the change in price or prices over time. For our examples we will use the information given in Table 5.6.

Table 5.6 The prices and consumption of tea, coffee and chocolate drinks by a representative individual in a typical week

Drinks	Year 0		Year 1		Year 2	
	Price	Quantity	Price	Quantity	Price	Quantity
Tea	8	15	12	12	16	10
Coffee	15	3	17	3	18	4
Chocolate	22	1	23	3	24	5

The price can be taken as the average amount paid in pence for a cup and the quantity as the average number of cups drunk per person per week.

5.2.1 The simple price index

If we want to construct an index for the price of one item only we first calculate the ratio of the 'new' price to the base year price, the **price relative**, and then multiply by 100. In terms of a notation

$$\frac{P_n}{P_0} \times 100$$

where P_0 is the base year price
and P_n is the 'new' price.
A simple index for the price of tea, taking year 0 as the base year can be cal-

culated as in Table 5.7. The doubling of the price of tea from 8p to 16p gives a 100% increase in the index; 100 to 200. The increase from 12p to 16p is 50 percentage points or $33\frac{1}{3}\%$.

In reality we are likely to drink more than just tea. In constructing, say, an index of beverage prices, we may wish to include coffee and chocolate drinks.

Table 5.7   A simple price index

Year	Price	P_n/P_0	Simple price index
0	8	1.0	100
1	12	1.5	150
2	16	2.0	200

Exercise

Calculate a simple price index for coffee with year 0 as the base year. (Answer: 100, 113, 120.)

5.2.2   The simple aggregate price index

To include all items, we could sum the prices year by year and construct an index from this sum. If the sum of the prices in the base year is ΣP_0 and the sum of the prices in year n is ΣP_n then the simple aggregate price index is

$$\frac{\Sigma P_n}{\Sigma P_0} \times 100$$

The calculations are shown in Table 5.8.

Table 5.8   The simple aggregate price index

Drinks	P_0	P_1	P_2
Tea	8	12	16
Coffee	15	17	18
Chocolate	22	23	24
	$\Sigma P_0 = \overline{45}$	$\Sigma P_1 = \overline{52}$	$\Sigma P_2 = \overline{58}$

Year	$\Sigma P_n/\Sigma P_0$	Simple aggregate price index
0	45/45 = 1.00	100
1	52/45 = 1.15	115
2	58/45 = 1.29	129

This particular index ignores the amounts consumed of tea, coffee and chocolate drinks. In particular, the construction of this index ignores both consumption patterns and the units to which price refers. If, for example, we were given the price of tea for a pot rather than a cup, the index would be different.

5.2.3   The average price relatives index

To overcome the problem of units, we could consider price ratios of individual commodities instead of their absolute prices and treat all price movements as equally important. In many cases, the goods we wish to include will be measured in very different units. Breakfast cereal could be in price per packet, potatoes price per pound and milk price per pint bottle. As an alternative to the simple aggregate price index we can use the average price relatives index:

$$\frac{1}{k} \ \Sigma(P_n/P_0) \ \times \ 100$$

where k is the number of goods. Here the price relative, P_n/P_0, for a stated commodity will have the same value whatever the unit for which the price is quoted.

Table 5.9   The average price relatives index

Drinks	P_0	P_1	P_2	P_1/P_0	P_2/P_0
Tea	8	12	16	1.50	2.00
Coffee	15	17	18	1.13	1.20
Chocolate	22	23	24	1.05	1.09
				$\Sigma(P_1/P_0) \ = \ 3.68$	$\Sigma(P_2/P_0) \ = \ 4.29$

Year	$(1/k) \ \Sigma(P_n/P_0)$	Average price relatives index
0	1.00	100
1	(1/3) (3.68) = 1.23	123
2	(1/3) (4.29) = 1.43	143

In comparing Tables 5.9 and 5.8 we can see that the average price relatives index, in this case, shows larger increases than the simple aggregate price index. To explain this difference we could consider just one of the items, tea. The **value** of tea is low in comparison to other drinks so it has a smaller impact on the totals in Table 5.8. In contrast, the **changes** in the price of tea are larger than any of the other drinks and this makes a greater impact on the totals in Table 5.9. To construct a price index for all goods and sections of the community we need to take account of the quantities bought.

It is not a matter of comparing what is spent year by year on drinks, food, transport or housing. If prices and quantities are both allowed to **vary**, an index for the amount spent could be constructed but not an index for prices. If we want a price index we need to control quantities. In practice, we consider a **typical basket of goods** in which the quantity of goods of each kind is fixed and find how the cost of that basket has changed over time. To construct an index for the price of beverages we need the quantity information for a selected year as given in Table 5.6.

5.2.4   The Laspeyre index

This index uses the quantities bought in the base year to define the typical basket. It is referred to as a **base-weighted index** and compares the cost of this basket of goods over time. This index is calculated as

$$\frac{\Sigma P_n Q_0}{\Sigma P_0 Q_0} \ \times \ 100$$

where $\Sigma P_0 Q_0$ is the cost of the base year basket of goods in the base year and $\Sigma P_n Q_0$ is the cost of the base year basket of goods in any year (thereafter) n.

Table 5.10   The Laspeyre index

Drinks	P_0	Q_0	P_1	P_2
Tea	8	15	12	16
Coffee	15	3	17	18
Chocolate	22	1	23	24

$P_0 Q_0$	$P_1 Q_0$	$P_2 Q_0$
120	180	240
45	51	54
22	23	24
187	254	318

Year	$\Sigma P_n Q_0 / \Sigma P_0 Q_0$	Laspeyre index
0	1.00	100
1	254/187 = 1.36	136
2	318/187 = 1.70	170

It can be seen from Table 5.10 that we only require the quantities from the chosen base year (Q_0 in this case). **The index implicitly assumes that whatever the price changes, the quantities purchased will remain the same.** In terms of economic theory, no substitution is allowed to take place. Even if goods become relatively more expensive it assumes that the same quantities are bought. As a result, this index tends to **overstate** inflation.

5.2.5   The Paasche index

This index uses the quantities bought in the current year for the typical basket. This **current year weighting** compares what a basket of goods bought now (in the current year) would cost with what the same basket of goods would have cost in the base year. This index is calculated as

$$\frac{\Sigma P_n Q_n}{\Sigma P_0 Q_n} \times 100$$

where $\Sigma P_n Q_n$ is the cost of the basket of goods bought in the year n at year n prices and $\Sigma P_0 Q_n$ is the cost of the year n basket of goods at base year prices.

Table 5.11   The Paasche index

Drinks	P_0	P_1	Q_1	P_2	Q_2
Tea	8	12	12	16	10
Coffee	15	17	3	18	4
Chocolate	22	23	3	24	5

P_1Q_1	P_0Q_1	P_2Q_2	P_0Q_2
144	96	160	80
51	45	72	60
69	66	120	110
$\overline{264}$	$\overline{207}$	$\overline{352}$	$\overline{250}$

Year	$\Sigma P_n Q_n / \Sigma P_0 Q_n$	Paasche index
0	1.00	100
1	264/207 = 1.28	128
2	352/250 = 1.41	141

As the basket of goods is allowed to change year by year, the Paasche index is not strictly a price index and as such has a number of disadvantages. Firstly, the effects of substitution would mean that greater importance is placed on goods that are relatively cheaper now than they were in the base year. As a consequence, the Paasche index tends to **understate** inflation.

Secondly, the comparison between years is difficult because the index reflects both changes in price and the basket of goods. Lastly, the index requires information on the current quantities and this may be difficult or expensive to obtain.

Exercise

A small manufacturer requires quantities of barley, hops and yeast to produce a particular type of beer. Calculate the Laspeyre and Paasche price indices for 1982 and 1983 costs of production, taking 1981 as the base year, using the following information.

Inputs	Quantities bought (tons)			Price per ton (£)		
	1981	1982	1983	1981	1982	1983
Barley	1000	1500	1700	60	65	70
Hops	500	500	600	20	25	30
Yeast	100	110	110	30	60	65

(Answer: Laspeyre 114.38, 125.34; Paasche 112.88, 122.89.)

5.3 THE WEIGHTING OF INDEX NUMBERS

Weights can be considered as a measure of importance (see Section 3.3). The Laspeyre index and the Paasche index both refer to a typical basket of goods. The prices are weighted by the quantities in these baskets. In measuring a diverse range of items, it is often more convenient to use **amount spent** as a weight rather than a quantity. If we consider travel, for example, it could be more meaningful to define expenditure on public transport than the number of journeys. In the same way, we could enquire about the expenditure on meals bought and consumed outside the home rather than the number of meals and their price. Expenditure on public transport, meals outside the home and other items is **additive** since money units are homogeneous; the number of journeys, number of meals and number of shirts is not.

In constructing a base-weighted index we could use

$$\frac{\Sigma w \; P_n/P_0}{\Sigma w} \times 100$$

where P_n/P_0 are the price relatives (see Section 5.2.1) and w are the weights, each weight being the amount spent on the item in the base year.

Consider again our example from Section 5.2 (Table 5.12).

Table 5.12 Weighted price index

Goods	P_0	Q_0	w	P_1	P_1/P_0	P_2	P_2/P_0
Tea	8	15	120	12	1.50	16	2.00
Coffee	15	3	45	17	1.13	18	1.20
Chocolate	22	1	22	23	1.05	24	1.09

Goods	w	$w \times P_1/P_0$	$w \times P_2/P_0$
Tea	120	180.00	240.00
Coffee	45	50.85	54.00
Chocolate	22	23.10	23.98
	187	253.95	317.98

Year	$(\Sigma w \; P_n/P_0)/\Sigma w$	Base-weighted index
0	1.00	100
1	253.95/187 = 1.36	136
2	317.98/187 = 1.70	170

It is no coincidence that this base-weighted index is identical to the Laspeyre index of Table 5.10. The identity is proven below:

$$\text{Laspeyre index} = \frac{\Sigma P_n Q_0}{\Sigma P_0 Q_0} \times 100$$

Let the weights, w, equal the amount spent on items in the base year, e.g. $w = P_0 Q_0$:

$$\text{Laspeyre index} = \frac{\Sigma P_n Q_0}{\Sigma w} \times 100$$

If we note that $Q_0 = w/P_0$ then

$$\text{Laspeyre index} = \frac{\Sigma w \times P_n/P_0}{\Sigma w} \times 100$$

The weights only need to represent the relative order of magnitude and in practice are scaled to sum to 1000. If we were to multiply each of the weights in Table 5.12 by 1000/187, to obtain the sum of weights of 1000, the value of the index would not change. The items included in the Retail Price Index are assigned weights in this way.

Of all the indices constructed to measure economic and social change in recent times, the Retail Price Index (RPI) is probably the most prominent. It can be seen as a measure of economic or political performance and provides an accepted measure for the cost of living. Increases in wage rates have been justified in terms of the increases in the Index. Recent or anticipated changes often form the basis of a wage claim. The use of the RPI extends beyond wage bargaining. Savings and pensions, in many cases, have been **index-linked**; they increase in proportion to the Index. All forms of economic planning take some account of inflation. Economists, for example, will distinguish between **real** and **nominal** disposable income, nominal being in terms of the currency (pounds in the pocket) and real referring to the purchasing power. If the Index has doubled over a specified period, purchasing power will have halved if income remains the same.

The RPI includes a range of goods and services bought by the 'average' family. Items include rent and transport but not saving, income tax or national insurance contributions. Not every single item that this 'average' family consumes is included. The index is made up of only 350 separate items arranged into 11 broad categories. The importance of each category is indicated by a weighting as shown in Table 5.13.

Table 5.13   The weighting of the Retail Price Index

Groups	Weights*
Food	203
Alcoholic drink	78
Tobacco	39
Housing	137
Fuel and light	69
Durable household goods	64
Clothing and footwear	74
Transport and vehicles	159
Miscellaneous goods	75
Services	63
Meals bought and consumed outside the home	39
	1000

* Weights for 1983 (source: *Monthly Digest of Statistics*).

As far as the RPI is concerned, using the above weights food accounts for 20.3% of expenditure and alcoholic drink 7.8%. Once the weights are established we only require price movements to determine the new value for the index.

As an example, consider the effect on the RPI of a 10% increase in the cost of 'fuel and light'.

A 10% increase in the cost of 'fuel and light' would increase its weight from 69 to 75.9 and the sum of weights from 1000 to 1006.9. The increase in the index is therefore

$$\frac{1006.9 - 1000}{1000} \times 100 = 0.69\%$$

As 'fuel and light' accounts for 6.9% (69 out of 1000) of expenditure, a 10% increase in its cost will add just over $\frac{1}{2}$% to the index. In practice, we consider the net effect of many price movements on a month by month basis.

The typical basket of goods and services as represented in Table 5.13, will only reflect the expenditure patterns of relatively few individuals or families. Some families will tend to spend a higher proportion of their income on food, others less. In theory, it would be possible to construct an index for every individual and every household, but all these indices would have little meaning as a general measure of inflation. There are two particular groups excluded from the RPI, 'pensioner' and 'high income' households, because their spending patterns are very different. One person and two person 'pensioner' households do, in fact, have their own index.

The weights are derived from the most recent 12 months' expenditure information as available from the Family Expenditure Survey; a survey of about 11 000 households each year. In practice, the RPI is not weighted by base year or current year expenditure figures and represents a compromise between the two.

5.5 CONCLUSIONS

We have considered only the development of a price index and the ways in which we control quantities. We could produce a quantity index. The Export Volume Index or the Index of Industrial Production requires a control of prices. Index numbers are constructed to measure the change in **one** factor, either value or volume over time, and for that reason we attempt to fix all other factors. The principles of construction, of course, remain the same.

5.6 PROBLEMS

1.

Year	Index
1	100
2	115
3	120
4	125
5	130
6	145

   (a) Change the base year for this index to year 4.
   (b) Find the percentage rises from year 3 to year 4 and year 5 to year 6.

2.

Year	'Old' index	'New' index
1	100	
2	120	
3	160	
4	190	100
5		130
6		140
7		150
8		165

(a) Scale down the 'old' index for years 1 to 3.
(b) Scale up the 'new' index for years 5 to 8.
(c) Explain the reasons for being cautious when merging indices of this kind.

3.

Item	Year 0		Year 1		Year 2	
	Price	Quantity	Price	Quantity	Price	Quantity
X	£5	10	£6	15	£8	20
Y	£3	20	£4	25	£5	33
Z	£1	30	£2	40	£2	50

For the data given above:

(a) find a simple price relative for item X for years 1 and 2 with Year 0 as the base year;
(b) use the same idea, but with quantities to find the quantity relatives for item Y in years 1 and 2 with year 0 as the base year (note: quantity relative = Q_n/Q_0);
(c) find a simple aggregate price index for all items;
(d) find a Laspeyre all-items price index for years 1 and 2 with year 0 as the base year.
(e) find a Paasche all-items price index for years 1 and 2 with year 0 as the base year;
(f) find a Laspeyre all-items quantity index for years 1 and 2 with year 0 as the base year (note: here we wish to keep prices fixed, and thus the appropriate formula is:

$$[\Sigma(P_0Q_n)]/[\Sigma(P_0Q_0)] \times 100);$$

(g) find a Paasche all-items quantity index for years 1 and 2 with year 0 as the base year (note: here we are using the current year prices as the fixed weights, and thus the appropriate formula is:

$$[\Sigma(P_nQ_n)]/[\Sigma(P_nQ_0)] \times 100).$$

4.

Item	Year 0		Year 1		Year 2	
	Price	Quantity	Price	Quantity	Price	Quantity
W	£3	4	£5	5	£10	7
X	£4	3	£6	3	£15	4
Y	£4	3	£7	2	£19	2
Z	£5	2	£9	2	£25	1

Carry out questions (a) to (g) inclusive from Problem 3 using the data given above. Why do the Laspeyre and Paasche indices give such different answers for year 2 in parts (d) to (g)?

5.

	Retail price index (January 1974 = 100)	Index of basic wage rates (January 1972 = 100)
1970	73.1	78.8
1971	80.0	89.0
1972	85.7	101.3
1973	93.5	115.2
1974	108.5	138.0
1975	134.8	178.7
1976	157.1	213.2

	Retail price index (January 1974 = 100)	Index of basic wage rates (January 1972 = 100)
1977	182.0	227.3
1978	197.1	259.3
1979	223.5	298.1
1980	263.7	351.8
1981	295.0	387.5
1982	320.4	414.3

Source: *Monthly Digest of Statistics*.

    (a)   Use the *Monthly Digest of Statistics* to extend the two series given above to the current year.

    (b)   Draw comparisons between the changes in the two indices. (Hint: it would be useful to rebase one of the indices, or to find year to year percentage changes.)

6.   Use the *Monthly Digest of Statistics* to find the weights given to each group in the Retail Price Index for 1962, 1974 and the current year. Use these weights to comment on the relative importance of each group over this period.

Part II
CONCLUDING EXERCISE

A sample of 15 smokers was randomly selected in 1982 and the average amount they spent weekly on cigarettes recorded for the years 1982, 1983 and 1984.

Individual	Average amount spent weekly on cigarettes (£)		
	1982	1983	1984
1	5.20	0	0
2	6.80	7.09	8.83
3	1.52	2.40	0
4	7.09	7.48	7.56
5	5.40	5.45	5.20
6	2.40	2.50	2.08
7	4.40	0	0
8	2.29	2.66	4.88
9	6.28	6.61	5.77
10	5.92	0	2.90
11	3.77	4.88	6.04
12	3.80	0	0
13	8.11	8.11	8.21
14	5.31	5.41	0
15	4.99	5.09	5.40

Describe the amount spent on cigarettes in each of the three years using the appropriate descriptive statistics.

Construct a simple index for the average amount spent each year on cigarettes using 1982 as the base year and explain what this index measures.

Part III
MATHEMATICAL METHODS

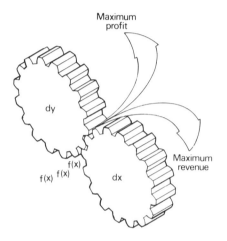

The charts and diagrams constructed and the statistics calculated in the previous chapters have been concerned with describing available data. We can also **describe** and **evaluate** a number of business, economic and social situations by the use of mathematical methods with the object of forecasting the unknown from the known. If we wish to calculate the cost of car travel we can develop a function in terms of x, the number of miles travelled. For any value of x we can compute a corresponding cost. This cost may not always be close to the true figure but does provide an estimate. How useful this estimate actually is will depend on how many factors you include in your function and how you specify these factors in your function. This function is referred to as a **model**, and mathematically we attempt to model many business activities or situations. In economics, for example, we model the market for goods with supply and demand functions. In accounting, we consider how interest rates affect investment decisions.

Exercises

1. Give examples of where equations (lines on graphs) have been used to describe some aspect of business.
2. What factors would you take into account when deciding how to invest your money?

6 Algebra and the use of equations

6.1 INTRODUCTION TO ALGEBRA

Algebra provides a systematic way to reason about unknown quantities and to manipulate their relationships in order to minimize the effort needed to solve complex problems. Although the very first use of algebra was by the Greeks, the subject was not really developed until modern times, and by the seventeenth century Descartes described it as 'that there results an art full of confusion and obscurity calculated to embarrass, instead of a science fitted to cultivate the mind.' Descartes and Fermat set about changing algebra and the results of their work give us what is now usually referred to as algebra, a system which will allow us to talk about general relationships instead of just specific ones.

Taking a simple example, if you work 40 hours per week and are paid £10 per hour, then your weekly pay is $40 \times £10 = £400$, which is a specific result. If we use a letter, say h, to represent the number of hours worked, and another letter, say p, to represent the rate of pay, then we have a general expression, hp, which represents weekly pay. (Note that we will not use an $\times$ to show that two amounts are multiplied together as this would lead to confusion when we use x to represent quantities, as we often will.) If a symbol is needed for multiplication we will use a point ($\cdot$). Having obtained an expression for weekly pay, we can now introduce other factors; for instance, the proportion of income that is taxed, say q, then qhp is taxable pay and $(1 - q)hp$ is tax-free pay; and if the tax rate is r, then the tax paid is $rqhp$ and the amount received is $hp - rqhp$ or $hp(1 - rq)$.

Example

For someone who pays tax at 30% (which gives us $r = 0.3$) on 80% of their income ($q = 0.8$) we have:

Gross pay $= hp$ $= 40 \cdot 10 = £400$
Taxable pay $= qhp$ $= (0.8) \cdot (40) \cdot (10) = £320$
Non-taxable pay $= (1 - q)hp$ $= (1 - 0.8) \cdot (40) \cdot (10) = £80$
Tax paid $= rqhp$ $= (0.3) \cdot (0.8) \cdot (40) \cdot (10) = £96$
Net pay $= hp(1 - rq)$ $= (40) \cdot (10) \cdot [1 - (0.8) \cdot (0.3)] = £304$

As well as substituting letters for quantities, as we have done above, we need to be able to manipulate expressions which are usually written as equations.

If $2x + 3y = 40$

then we may subtract $3y$ from each side, to get

$$2x + 3y - 3y = 40 - 3y$$

or

$$2x = 40 - 3y$$

Now to find x in terms of y we need to divide both sides of the equation by 2 (this is equivalent to multiplying both sides by $\frac{1}{2}$).

$$\frac{2x}{2} = \frac{(40 - 3y)}{2}$$

or

$$x = \frac{40}{2} - \frac{3y}{2} = 20 - 1.5y$$

If

$$5a + 6b = 2a - 3b$$

then to express a in terms of b, subtract $6b$ from each side

$$5a + 6b - 6b = 2a - 3b - 6b$$

or

$$5a = 2a - 9b$$

and subtract $2a$ from each side

$$5a - 2a = 2a - 9b - 2a$$
$$3a = -9b$$

and now divide both sides by 3

$$a = -3b$$

Note that because we are dealing with equations in both of the examples above, whatever is done to one side **must** also be done to the other side. With practice you will miss out many of the intermediate steps in manipulations of this type, but if in doubt, solve a problem by putting in each small step.

6.2 POWERS

When multiplying the same quantity together several times, it will be much more convenient to use powers rather than to write that quantity down each time, thus:

$$a \cdot a = a^2$$
$$a \cdot a \cdot a = a^3$$
$$a \cdot a \cdot a \cdot a = a^4, \text{ etc. (where } a \text{ is any number)}$$

Once we begin to manipulate quantities raised to powers, we can develop rules as follows:

$$a^3 \cdot a^2 = (a \cdot a \cdot a) \cdot (a \cdot a) = a^5 = a^{3+2}$$

i.e. for multiplication, we **add** the powers.

$$a^3 / a^2 = \frac{a \cdot a \cdot a}{a \cdot a} = a^1 = a^{3-2}$$

i.e. for division, we **subtract** the powers. Note also that a on its own can be written as a^1.

Another example: $a^4/a^4 = \dfrac{a \cdot a \cdot a \cdot a}{a \cdot a \cdot a \cdot a} = a^{4-4} = a^0$

Using the rule for division, we can see that any number (apart from 0) divided by itself will give a result to the power zero. In terms of the number system, any number raised to the power zero will be equal to 1.

If we have a^3/a^6, this is:

$$\dfrac{a \cdot a \cdot a}{a \cdot a \cdot a \cdot a \cdot a} \quad \text{or} \quad \dfrac{1}{a \cdot a \cdot a} \quad \text{or} \quad a^{3-6} = a^{-3} = \dfrac{1}{a^3}$$

i.e. a negative power means that we take the reciprocal value.

Since we add powers when multiplying, then:

$$a^{\frac{1}{2}} \cdot a^{\frac{1}{2}} = a^1 = a$$

and the number which multiplied by itself gives a must be the square root of a, thus:

$$a^{\frac{1}{2}} = \sqrt{a}$$

similarly $\qquad a^{\frac{1}{3}} = \sqrt[3]{a}$ — the cube root of a

similarly $\qquad a^{\frac{3}{2}} = \sqrt{a^3}$ — the square root of a cubed

If we are faced by brackets which are raised to powers, we treat them in the same way; so that

$$x(a + b) = ax + bx$$
$$(a + b)^2 = (a + b)(a + b)$$
$$= a(a + b) + b(a + b)$$
$$= a^2 + ab + ba + b^2$$

and since $ab = ba$ $\qquad = a^2 + 2ab + b^2$

$$(a - b)^2 = a^2 - 2ab + b^2$$

(Note: $a^3 + a^2$ cannot be simplified by expressing it as a to a single power.)

6.3 GRAPHS

The organization of a consistent system of representing points on a graph was a major step forward in the development of mathematics. Two straight lines placed at right angles to each other are referred to as axes (or Cartesian axes), and these divide the page into four sections or quadrants (Fig. 6.1). It is usual to refer to the horizontal axis as the x-axis and the vertical axis as the y-axis.

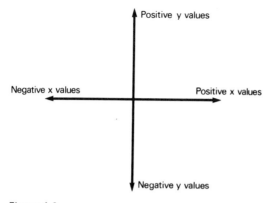

Figure 6.1

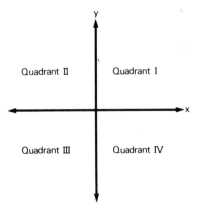

Figure 6.2

Quadrants are often numbered as in Fig. 6.2 and the majority of work in business-related areas will be in quadrant I, where we have positive values of both x and y (sometimes called the positive quadrant), with some work in quadrant IV. The reason for this is that the x-axis is often used to measure output or sales of a product and negative values would have no meaning.

Exercise

Do negative sales mean that people return goods to the factory?

With these axes we may now identify individual points by two numbers (called **coordinates**), the first of which represents the position in relation to the x-axis and the second the position in relation to the y-axis; the coordinates are usually enclosed in brackets. Thus in Fig. 6.3 the point labelled A has an x-value of 2 and a y-value of 3 and so would be quoted as (2, 3).

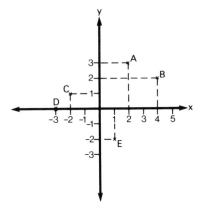

Figure 6.3

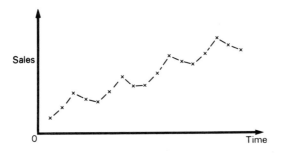

Figure 6.4

The point B is at $x = 4$, $y = 2$ and is written as $(4, 2)$. For the other points, C is $(-2, 1)$, D is $(-3, 0)$ and E is $(1, -2)$. Note that for the point D which is on the x-axis, the y-value is 0; points on the y-axis would have a zero x-value and where the axes cross, usually called the origin, the coordinates will be $(0, 0)$.

Graphs will help us in our studies since they will allow situations to be illustrated, and an illustration will often give pointers to the sort of measures and techniques that may be used in analysis. Time series graphs are frequently used, with time on the x-axis and quantities on the y-axis, as illustrated in Fig. 6.4. These graphs will help in deciding which model to use when analysing time series data (Chapter 19).

When we consider how two variables change in relation to each other, we often use a plot of points, as in Fig. 6.5, usually called a **scatter diagram**. (This will be used in considering correlation and regression in Chapters 16 and 17.)

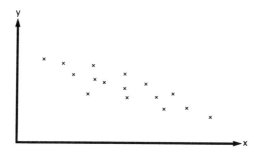

Figure 6.5

Whilst the majority of the graphs used in this course will only have two axes, i.e. two-dimensional graphs, it is possible to extend the system to deal with three measurements, as in Fig. 6.6. Here the point A would be represented by three numbers $(4, 6, 10)$ or (x, y, z). The system may be further extended but visual representation is precluded for four or more dimensions.

6.4 PROBLEMS

1. If $3a + 7b = 2a - 5b$ find a in terms of b.
2. If $2x + 3(x + 3y) = y - 4(x + 2y)$ find x in terms of y.

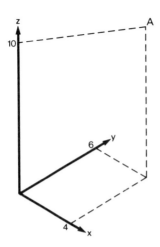

Figure 6.6

3. Simplify $a^2 \cdot a^3 \cdot a^4$.
4. Simplify a^2/a^4.
5. Simplify $a \cdot a^2 \cdot a^3/a^4$.
6. Expand $a(a + 2b)$.
7. Expand the brackets $(a + 2b)^2$.
8. Expand the brackets $(a + b)(a - b)$.
9. If $a = 4$, what is the numerical value of $a^{\frac{3}{2}}$?
10. Simplify $(a^2 + a^3)/a$.
11. On a graph, mark the following points:

   (a) $(1, 2)$
   (b) $(3, 5)$
   (c) $(5, 3)$
   (d) $(-1, 2)$
   (e) $(2, -1)$
   (f) $(-4, -2)$

12. Simplify the following expression:
$$x^2(x^2 + 4x + 3) - 3y(4y + 10) - x^4 - 4(x^3 - 10) = 3x^2 - 2y(6y + 10)$$

6.5 FUNCTIONS

A function is the specification of the relationship between a variable x and a variable y. This means that if we are given a value of x, we will also be able to find the related value of y. We will only have a function if each value of x is related to a definite value of y. If x is related to a range of values of y then we will need the methods of regression (as outlined in Chapter 17) to derive any functional relationship, and even then it is likely to be only an approximate relationship.

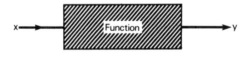

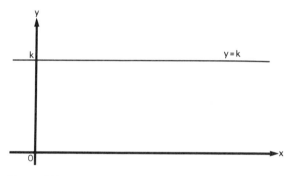

Figure 6.7

If workers are given a 10% pay rise, and the old wage is x, the new wage will be

New $x = x + 0.1x$ or $1.1x$

Note that if y is a function of x, it is often written as $y = f(x)$.

6.5.1   Constant functions

In this case, no matter what value x takes, the value of y remains the same, as shown in Fig. 6.7. The line representing $y = k$ passes through the y-axis at a value k and goes off, at least in theory, to infinity in both directions. Constant functions of this type will appear in linear programming problems (as in Chapter 20). If the values of x for which $y = k$ are limited to a particular group (known as the **domain** of the function) then we may use the following symbols:

$\quad\quad < x$ means less than x
$\quad\quad > x$ means greater than x
$\quad\quad \leqslant x$ means less than or equal to x
and $\quad \geqslant x$ means greater than or equal to x

Now if the constant function only applies between $x = 0$ and $x = 10$, then this will be as illustrated in Fig. 6.8 and is written as:

$y = k$ for $0 \leqslant x \leqslant 10$
$\quad = 0$ elsewhere

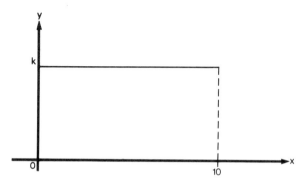

Figure 6.8

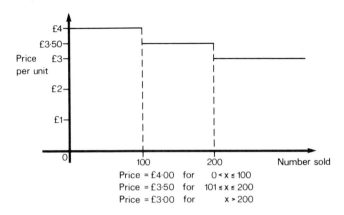

Price = £4·00 for 0 < x ≤ 100
Price = £3·50 for 101 ≤ x ≤ 200
Price = £3·00 for x > 200

Figure 6.9

We could use this idea of the domain of a function to represent graphically a price book with discounts for quantity purchase, as in Fig. 6.9.

6.5.2 Linear functions

A linear function is one that will give a straight line when we draw the graph (at least in two dimensions; it has a similar, but more complex meaning in three, four or more dimensions). This function occurs frequently when we try to apply quantitative techniques to business-related problems, and even where it does not apply exactly, it may well form a close enough approximation for the use to which we are putting it.

If the value of y is always equal to the value of x then we shall obtain a graph as in Fig. 6.10. This line will pass through the origin and will be at an angle of 45° to the x-axis, provided that both axes used the same scale. We used this function when we considered Lorenz curves. We may change the angle or slope of the line by multiplying the value of x by some constant, called a **coefficient**. Two

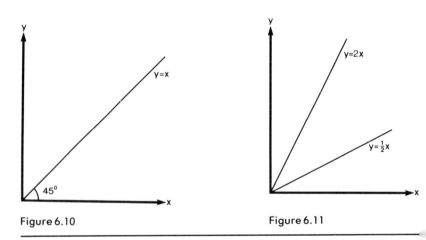

Figure 6.10   Figure 6.11

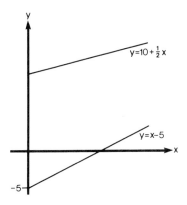

Figure 6.12

examples are given in Fig. 6.11. These functions still go through the origin; to make a function go through some other point on the y-axis, we add or subtract a constant. The point where the function crosses the y-axis is called the **inter-cept**. Two examples are given in Fig. 6.12.

The general format of a linear function is $y = a + bx$, where a and b are constants.

To draw the graph of a linear function we need to know two points which satisfy the function. If we take the function

$$y = 100 - 2x$$

then we know that the intercept on the y-axis is 100 since this is the value of y if $x = 0$. If we substitute some other, convenient, value for x, we can find another point through which the graph of the function passes. Taking $x = 10$, we have:

$$y = 100 - 2 \cdot 10 = 100 - 20 = 80$$

so the two points are (0, 100) and (10, 80). Marking these points on a pair of axes, we may join them up with a ruler to obtain a graph of the function (see Fig. 6.13).

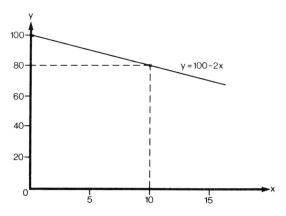

Figure 6.13

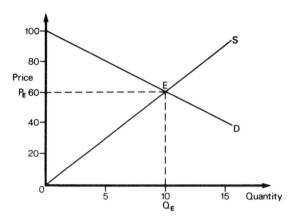

Figure 6.14

We may use two linear functions to illustrate the market situation in economics, allowing one to represent the various quantities demanded over a range of prices, and the other to represent supply conditions. Where these two functions cross is known as the equilibrium point (point E in Fig. 6.14), since at this price level the quantity demanded by the consumers is exactly equal to the amount that the suppliers are willing to produce, and thus the market is cleared. Note that we follow the tradition of economics texts and place quantity on the x-axis and price on the y-axis. Figure 6.14 might illustrate a situation in which the demand function is:

$$P = 100 - 4Q$$

and the supply function is:

$$P = 6Q$$

Since we know that the price (P_E) will be the same on both functions at the equilibrium point we can manipulate the functions to find the numerical values of P_E and Q_E:

(Demand) $\qquad\qquad P = P \qquad\qquad$ (Supply)
$$100 - 4Q = 6Q$$
$$100 = 10Q$$
$$10 = Q$$

If $Q = 10$, then

$$P = 100 - 4Q = 100 - 40 = 60$$
and $\qquad P = 6Q = 60$

thus $P_E = 60$ and $Q_E = 10$.

This system could also be used to solve pairs of linear functions which are both true at some point; these are known as **simultaneous equations** (a more general version of the demand and supply relationship above). Taking each equation in turn we may construct a graph of that function; where the two lines cross is the solution to the pair of simultaneous equations, i.e. the values of x and y for which they are both true.

If $\qquad 5x + 2y = 34$
and $\qquad x + 3y = 25$

then reading from the graph in Fig. 6.15, we find that $x = 4$ and $y = 7$ is the point of intersection of the two linear functions.

This system will work well with simple equations, but even then is somewhat time-consuming: there is a simpler method for solving simultaneous equations, which does not involve the use of graphs.

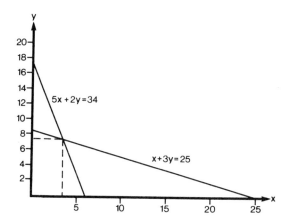

Figure 6.15

Examples

1.
$$5x + 2y = 34$$
$$x + 3y = 25$$

If we multiply each item in the second equation by 5 we have

$$5x + 15y = 125$$

and since both equations are true at the same time we may subtract one equation from the other (here, the first from the new second)

$$5x + 15y = 125$$
$$5x + 2y = 34$$
$$\overline{\qquad\qquad 13y = 91}$$

Therefore, $\qquad\qquad\qquad y = 7$

Having found the value of y, we can now substitute this into either of the original equations to find the value of x:

$$5x + 2 \cdot (7) = 34$$
$$5x + 14 = 34$$
$$5x = 20$$
$$x = 4$$

2.
$$6x + 5y = 27$$
$$7x - 4y = 2$$

Multiply the first by 4 and the second by 5

$$24x + 20y = 108$$
$$35x - 20y = 10$$

Add together $\qquad \overline{59x \qquad\quad = 118}$

87 /. Functions

Therefore, $\qquad x = 2$
substitute $\qquad 6 \cdot 2 + 5y = 27$
$$12 + 5y = 27$$
$$5y = 15$$
$$y = 3$$

and thus the solution is $x = 2$, $y = 3$.

Note that we will return to the solution of simultaneous equations by an alternative method later in this chapter.

Returning now to graphs of linear functions, we may use the method developed above to find the equation of a linear function that passes through two particular points.

Examples
1. If a linear function goes through the points $x = 2$, $y = 5$ and $x = 3$, $y = 7$ we may substitute these values into the general formula for a linear function, $y = a + bx$, to form a pair of simultaneous equations:

For (2, 5) $\qquad 5 = a + 2b$
for (3, 7) $\qquad 7 = a + 3b$

Subtract the first from the second to get

$$2 = b$$
and substitute $\qquad 5 = a + 2.2$
$$5 = a + 4$$
Therefore, $\qquad a = 1$

Now substitute the values of a and b back into the general formula.

$$y = 1 + 2x$$

2. A linear function goes through (5, 40) and (25, 20),

thus $\qquad 40 = a + 5b$
$$20 = a + 25b$$
$$\overline{}$$
$$20 = -20b$$
Therefore $\qquad b = -1$
$$40 = a - 5$$
Therefore $\qquad a = 45$
and thus $\qquad y = 45 - x$

An alternative method for finding the equation is to label the points as (x_1, y_1) and (x_2, y_2) and then substitute into

$$\frac{y_1 - y}{y_2 - y_1} = \frac{x_1 - x}{x_2 - x_1}$$

Taking the last example, we have:

$$\frac{40 - y}{20 - 40} = \frac{5 - x}{25 - 5}$$
$$\frac{40 - y}{-20} = \frac{5 - x}{20}$$

Multiplying both sides by -20 and by 20 gives:

$$20(40 - y) = -20(5 - x)$$
$$800 - 20y = -100 + 20x$$
$$900 - 20x = 20y$$
divide by 20 to give: $\qquad 45 - x = y$

6.5.3 Quadratic functions

A quadratic function has the general equation

$$y = ax^2 + bx + c$$

and once the values of a, b and c are given we have a specific function. This function will produce a curve with one bend, or change of direction. (It is usually said to have **one turning point**.) If the value assigned to the coefficient of x^2, a, is negative, then the shape in Fig. 6.16 will be produced, while if a is positive, the shape in Fig. 6.17 will result.

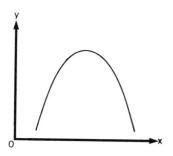

Figure 6.16   Figure 6.17

To construct the graph of a function it is necessary to produce a table of values, plot the pairs of values, and join them together.

Example   Consider the function:

$$y = x^2 - 2x + 1$$

Here we decide on a range of x values and write out each part of the function across the top of the table. We then work out each column for each value of x. Finally we add across each row to give the y-value on the right-hand side.

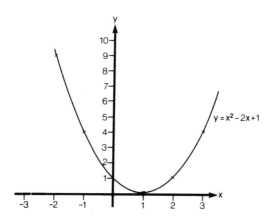

Figure 6.18

x	x^2	$-2x$	$+1$	y
-2	4	$+4$	$+1$	9
-1	1	$+2$	$+1$	4
0	0	0	$+1$	1
1	1	-2	$+1$	0
2	4	-4	$+1$	1
3	9	-6	$+1$	4

It is not always obvious at this stage for which range of values of x we should calculate the equivalent values of y; but we usually want to show where the curve changes direction and you will notice from the table above that the change in y decreases as we approach the change in direction and then increases again, so that if the changes in y are increasing as x increases, you should try lower values of x (Fig. 6.18).

Example $y = -x^2 - 2x + 1$ (Fig. 6.19).

x	$-x^2$	$-2x$	$+1$	y
-3	-9	$+6$	$+1$	-2
-2	-4	$+4$	$+1$	1
-1	-1	$+2$	$+1$	2
0	0	0	$+1$	1
1	-1	-2	$+1$	-2

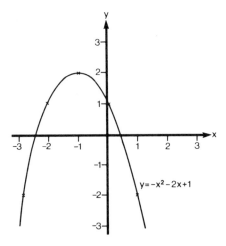

Figure 6.19

We are often interested in finding where a quadratic function crosses the x-axis; these points are known as the **roots** of the quadratic equation $ax^2 + bx + c = 0$. These roots may be found in several ways, first by constructing a graph of the function and reading off the values, as in Fig. 6.20; thus we find the roots to be -1 and $+6$.

The second way to find the roots is to equate the function to zero:

$$x^2 - 5x - 6 = 0$$

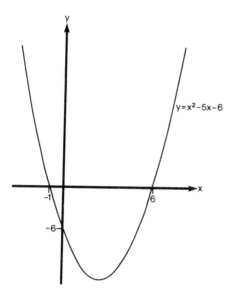

Figure 6.20

and attempt to break this down into two **factors** which are written in brackets to show which terms are grouped together. When multiplied together these factors will give us the function. Here the factors will be:

$$(x - 6)(x + 1)$$

Since
$$(x - 6)(x + 1) = 0$$
$$x(x + 1) - 6(x + 1) = 0$$
$$x^2 + x - 6x - 6 = 0$$
$$x^2 - 5x - 6 = 0$$

Now for this to be true, either the first factor equals zero or the second factor equals zero, hence

$$x - 6 = 0, \qquad \text{i.e. } x = 6$$
or $$\qquad x + 1 = 0, \qquad \text{i.e. } x = -1$$

and so the roots are -1 and $+6$. The easiest functions to break down in this way are those with just x^2 as the first term. The two numbers in the factors when multiplied together must give the third term, or constant; and the numbers when multiplied by the other x and added (allowing for signs) must give the coefficient of x (here $-6x + 1x = -5x$).

If $$\qquad x - 5x + 4 = 0$$
then $$\qquad (x - 4)(x - 1) = 0$$

and roots are $+1$ and $+4$.

The third method of finding roots is to use a formula. If $ax^2 + bx + c = 0$ then the roots are at

$$x = \frac{-b \pm \sqrt{(b^2 - 4ac)}}{2a}$$

and we substitute the appropriate values of a, b and c to find these roots.

For example $x^2 - 5x + 4 = 0$

then $a = 1$; $b = -5$; $c = +4$

roots at $x = \dfrac{-(-5) \pm \sqrt{[(-5)^2 - 4(1)(4)]}}{2(1)}$

$= \dfrac{5 \pm \sqrt{[25 - 16]}}{2} = \dfrac{5 \pm \sqrt{9}}{2} = \dfrac{5 + 3}{2}$ and $\dfrac{5 - 3}{2}$

$= \dfrac{8}{2}$ and $\dfrac{2}{2} = 4$ and 1

This method will always give the roots, **but beware** of negative values for the expression under the square root sign ($b^2 - 4ac$). If this is negative then the function is said to have **imaginary roots**, since in normal circumstances we cannot take the square root of a negative number. At this level, these imaginary roots need not concern us.

Another example: $2x^2 - 4x - 10 = 0$

$x = \dfrac{4 \pm \sqrt{(16 + 80)}}{4}$

$= \dfrac{4 \pm \sqrt{96}}{4} = \dfrac{4 \pm 9.8}{4}$

$\dfrac{13.8}{4}$ and $\dfrac{-5.8}{4}$

$= 3.45$ and -1.45

Quadratic functions are often used to represent cost equations, such as marginal cost or average cost, and sometimes profit functions. When profit is represented by a quadratic function, then we can use the idea of roots either to find the range of output for which any profit is made, or we can specify a profit level and find the range of output for which at least this profit is made.

For example, if profit $= -x^2 + 8x + 1$ where x represents output, then if the specified profit level is 8, we have:

$-x^2 + 8x + 1 = 8$

or $-x^2 + 8x - 7 = 0$

$(x - 7)(1 - x) = 0$

$x = 7$ and 1

This is illustrated in Fig. 6.21.

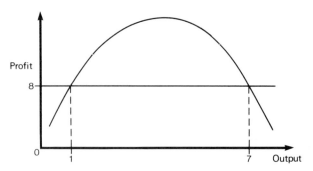

Figure 6.21

When there were two points specified on a graph we saw above how to find the equation of a linear function through these points. We will need to know three points in order to find a quadratic function through them. There are several methods of doing this, and one is given here.

Example

If a quadratic function goes through the points

$$x = 1, \qquad y = 7$$
$$x = 4, \qquad y = 4$$
$$x = 5, \qquad y = 7$$

then we may take the general equation $y = ax^2 + bx + c$ and substitute:

$(1,7)$	$7 = a(1)^2 + b(1) + c = a + b + c$	6.1
$(4,4)$	$4 = a(4)^2 + b(4) + c = 16a + 4b + c$	6.2
$(5,7)$	$7 = a(5)^2 + b(5) + c = 25a + 5b + c$	6.3

Rearranging the first equation gives $c = 7 - a - b$ and substituting this into eqn 6.2 gives

$$4 = 16a + 4b + (7 - a - b)$$
$$= 15a + 3b + 7$$

therefore, $\quad -3 = 15a + 3b$

and into eqn 6.3 gives

$$7 = 25a + 5b + (7 - a - b)$$
$$= 24a + 4b + 7$$

therefore, $\quad 0 = 24a + 4b$

We now have two simultaneous equations in two unknowns (a and b).

So, $\qquad -3 = 15a + 3b$
$$0 = 24a + 4b$$

Multiplying the first by 4 and the second by 3, gives:

$$-12 = 60a + 12b$$
$$0 = 72a + 12b$$
$$\overline{12 = 12a}$$

6.4

Therefore, $a = 1$

From eqn 6.4, we have: $\quad 0 = 72 + 12b$

Therefore, $\qquad\qquad 12b = -72$
$$b = -6$$
$$c = 7 - a - b$$
$$= 7 - 1 + 6 = 12$$

And thus the quadratic function is:

$$y = x^2 - 6x + 12$$

6.5.4 Cubics and polynomials

A cubic function has the general equation:

$$y = ax^3 + bx^2 + cx + d$$

and will have two turning points in most cases. They are often used to represent total cost functions in economics (Figs. 6.22 and 6.23). We could go on extending the range of functions by adding a term in x^4, and then one in x^5 and so on. The general name for functions of this type is **polynomials**. For most business and economic purposes we do not need to go beyond cubic functions, but for some areas, the idea that a sufficiently complex polynomial will model any situation will appear.

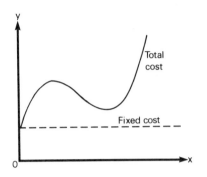

Figure 6.22

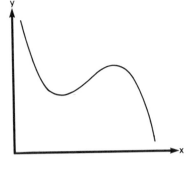

Figure 6.23

6.6.5 Exponential functions

Within mathematics, those numbers that arise in a wide variety of situations and a broad spectrum of applications (and often run to a vast number of decimal places) tend to be given a special letter. One example most people will have met is π (pi). Exponential functions make use of another such number, e (Euler's constant) which is a little over 2.7. Raising this number to a power gives the graph in Fig. 6.24, or, if the power is negative, the result is as Fig. 6.25.

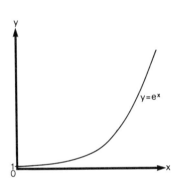

Figure 6.24

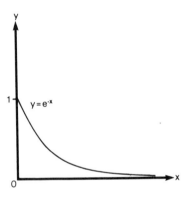

Figure 6.25

The former often appears in growth situations, and will be of use in considering money and interest (see Chapter 8). The latter may be incorporated into models of failure rates, market sizes and many probability situations (see Chapter 10).

6.6 PROBLEMS

Construct the graphs of the following functions:
1. $y = 2x$ $0 \leqslant x \leqslant 10$.
2. $y = 16 - x$ $0 \leqslant x \leqslant 12$.
3. $y = 4 + 3x$ $1 \leqslant x \leqslant 4$.

4. $x = 20 - 2y$ $0 \leqslant x \leqslant 12$.
5. $y = 10$.
6. $y = x^2 - 3x + 2$ $-2 \leqslant x \leqslant 6$.
7. $y = x^3 - 2x^2 + x - 2$ $-2 \leqslant x \leqslant 6$.

Solve the following simultaneous equations:

8. $6x + y = 22$
   $2x + 5y = 26$
9. $10a + 3b = 11$
   $12a - 7b = -8$

In the following questions D = quantity demanded, S = quantity supplied and P = price.

10. (a) A linear demand function goes through $D = 2$ if $P = 16$ and $D = 4.5$ if $P = 11$. (Note: price is a function of demand.) Find the demand function.
    (b) A linear supply function goes through $S = 13.5$ if $P = 23$ and $S = 10$ if $P = 16$. (Note: price is a function of supply.) Find the supply function.
    (c) Find the equilibrium price and quantity, i.e. the values of P and D if $S = D$.
11. (a) A linear demand function goes through $D = 4, P = 13$ and $D = 16, P = 7$. Find the demand function.
    (b) A linear supply function goes through $S = 12, P = 9$ and $S = 20, P = 11$. Find the supply function.
    (c) Find the equilibrium price and quantity.
    (d) If legislation sets a maximum price of 8, what effect will this have?

Find the roots of the following equations:

12. $x^2 - 5x - 36 = 0$.
13. $x^2 - 3x + 2 = 0$.
14. $x^2 + 12x - 28 = 0$.
15. $x^2 + 9x + 20 = 0$.
16. $2x^2 - 7x + 3 = 0$.
17. $6x^2 + 17x - 3 = 0$.
18. $x^2 - 10x + 4 = 0$.
19. $-2x^2 + 5x + 40 = 0$.
20. A quadratic demand function passes through the following points: $D = 2$ if $P = 182$; $D = 4$ if $P = 168$; and $D = 10$ if $P = 150$. (Price is a function of demand.) Find the equation of the demand function.

6.7 MATRIX ALGEBRA

Matrices are used for solving sets of simultaneous equations, and have applications in multiple regression analysis and linear programming, enabling data to be expressed in a compact form suitable for storing in an electronic digital computer. They may also be used to show how the outputs of one industry are used as inputs for another industry and thus illustrate the interrelated nature of a modern industrial state. Further applications are to Markov chains (see Chapter 9) and, with this, into manpower planning models.

A matrix is a **rectangular array** of numbers arranged in **rows** and **columns** and is characterized by its size (or **order**), written as (no. of rows × no. of columns). The whole matrix is usually referred to by a capital letter, whilst individual numbers, or **elements**, within the matrix are referred to by lower case letters, usually with a **suffix** to identify in which row and in which column they appear. Note that a matrix does not have a numerical value, it is merely a convenient way of representing an array of numbers.

If
$$A = \begin{bmatrix} 4 & 8 & 17 & 12 \\ 21 & 3 & 19 & 17 \\ 10 & 21 & 4 & 2 \end{bmatrix}$$

then the order of matrix A is (3 × 4) and the element a_{13} is the 17 since it is in the first row and the third column.

If a matrix has only one row, then it is known as a **row vector**: if it only has one column, then it is a **column vector**. e.g.

$$B = [4 \ \ 8 \ \ 7] \qquad\qquad C = \begin{bmatrix} 10 \\ 12 \\ 28 \\ 49 \\ 102 \end{bmatrix}$$

6.7.1 Addition and subtraction of matrices

To add or subtract two (or more) matrices they must be of exactly the same order (they are then said to be **conformable for addition**). When this is true, the corresponding elements in each matrix are added together (or the second is subtracted from the first), e.g.

$$A = \begin{bmatrix} 10 & 15 \\ 20 & 14 \end{bmatrix} \qquad\qquad B = \begin{bmatrix} 21 & 13 \\ 12 & 17 \end{bmatrix}$$

then $A + B = \begin{bmatrix} 10 & 15 \\ 20 & 14 \end{bmatrix} + \begin{bmatrix} 21 & 13 \\ 12 & 17 \end{bmatrix} = \begin{bmatrix} (10+21) & (15+13) \\ (20+12) & (14+17) \end{bmatrix} = \begin{bmatrix} 31 & 28 \\ 32 & 31 \end{bmatrix}$

and $A - B = \begin{bmatrix} 10 & 15 \\ 20 & 14 \end{bmatrix} - \begin{bmatrix} 21 & 13 \\ 12 & 17 \end{bmatrix} = \begin{bmatrix} (10-21) & (15-13) \\ (20-12) & (14-17) \end{bmatrix} = \begin{bmatrix} -11 & 2 \\ 8 & -3 \end{bmatrix}$

If we have:

$$\begin{bmatrix} 10 & 20 \\ 40 & 5 \end{bmatrix} - \begin{bmatrix} 10 & 20 \\ 40 & 5 \end{bmatrix} = \begin{bmatrix} 0 & 0 \\ 0 & 0 \end{bmatrix}$$

then the result is a **zero matrix** (which performs the same function as zero in ordinary arithmetic) and we see also that two matrices can only be said to be identical if each corresponding element is the same, or the subtraction of one from the other gives a zero matrix.

Addition is said to be **commutative** since $A + B = B + A$.

6.7.2 Multiplication of matrices

A matrix may be multiplied by a single number, or **scalar**, and to do this we multiply each element of the matrix by the scalar, e.g.

$$5 \times \begin{bmatrix} 4 & 8 & 3 \\ 17 & 2 & 12 \end{bmatrix} = \begin{bmatrix} 20 & 40 & 15 \\ 85 & 10 & 60 \end{bmatrix}$$

It is often convenient to reverse this argument, and take a common factor out of the matrix (cf. taking a common factor out of a bracket), to make further calculations easier, e.g.

$$\begin{bmatrix} 10 & 170 & 100 \\ 20 & 90 & 95 \\ 140 & 30 & 50 \end{bmatrix} = 10 \times \begin{bmatrix} 1 & 17 & 10 \\ 2 & 9 & 9.5 \\ 14 & 3 & 5 \end{bmatrix}$$

Where the **same** matrix is to be multiplied by a series of scalars, we have:

$$aA + bA + cA + dA = (a + b + c + d)A$$

When two matrices are to be multiplied together it is first necessary to check that the multiplication is possible, since unless the matrices are **conformable for multiplication** it will not be possible to obtain a result. To allow multiplication, the number of columns in the first matrix must be **equal** to the number of rows in the second matrix. The result of the multiplication will be a matrix with the same number of rows as the first matrix but the same number of columns as the second matrix.

Thus a (2×3) matrix multiplied by a (3×2) matrix will give a (2×2) result; whereas a (3×2) matrix multiplied by a (2×3) matrix will give a (3×3) result. It will not be possible to multiply a matrix of order (4×8) by a matrix of order (5×3). Note that even though the resultant matrix may be of the same order, multiplication is **not commutative**, since $A \cdot B \neq B \cdot A$ except in special circumstances. It is thus important to note the order in which the matrices are multiplied together.

The process of multiplication involves using a particular row from the first matrix and a particular column from the second matrix; placing the result as a single element in the result matrix, e.g.

$$A = \begin{bmatrix} 1 & 4 & 7 \\ 2 & 5 & 8 \\ 3 & 6 & 9 \end{bmatrix} \qquad B = \begin{bmatrix} 10 & 13 \\ 11 & 14 \\ 12 & 15 \end{bmatrix} \qquad A \cdot B = C$$

To find $A \cdot B$, we will work out each element separately. For example, taking the **first** row of A and the **first** column of B gives the element c_{11} in the first row and column of C, i.e.

$$\begin{bmatrix} 1 & 4 & 7 \end{bmatrix} \begin{bmatrix} 10 \\ 11 \\ 12 \end{bmatrix} = (1 \times 10) + (4 \times 11) + (7 \times 12) = 138 = c_{11}$$

Note that we have gone along the row of the first matrix and down the column of the second matrix, multiplying the corresponding elements.

To find the **second** element in the **first** row of C, we take the **first** row of the matrix A, and the **second** column of the matrix B.

$$\begin{bmatrix} 1 & 4 & 7 \end{bmatrix} \begin{bmatrix} 13 \\ 14 \\ 15 \end{bmatrix} = (1 \times 13) + (4 \times 14) + (7 \times 15) = 174 = c_{12}$$

This process continues, using the second row from A, and then the third row. In general, the mth row of A by the nth column of B gives the element c_{mn} in the mth row and nth column of C.

Exercise

Calculate the remaining elements of the matrix C.
Answer:
$$C = \begin{bmatrix} 138 & 174 \\ 171 & 216 \\ 204 & 258 \end{bmatrix}$$

Note that it is not possible to find $B \cdot A$ because the number of columns in B is not the same as the number of rows in A.

A further example:

$$\begin{bmatrix} 1 & 3 \\ 2 & 5 \end{bmatrix} \begin{bmatrix} 3 & 2 \\ 5 & 7 \end{bmatrix} = \begin{bmatrix} 18 & 23 \\ 31 & 39 \end{bmatrix}$$

$$\begin{bmatrix} 3 & 2 \\ 5 & 7 \end{bmatrix} \begin{bmatrix} 1 & 3 \\ 2 & 5 \end{bmatrix} = \begin{bmatrix} 7 & 19 \\ 19 & 50 \end{bmatrix}$$

and this again confirms that $A \cdot B \neq B \cdot A$. Since the order in which the matrices are multiplied together is crucial to the product obtained, it is useful to have a terminology to show this. In the product $A \cdot B$, A is said to be **postmultiplied** by B, whilst B is said to be **premultiplied** by A.

We have seen, above, the zero matrix which performs the same function in matrix algebra as a zero in arithmetic. We also need a matrix which will perform the function that unity (one) plays in arithmetic (e.g. $5 \times 1 = 5$).

For a matrix:

$$A \cdot ? = A$$

The matrix which performs this function is known as the **identity matrix** and consists of 1s on the diagonal from top left (a_{11}) to bottom right (a_{nn}) and 0s for all other elements. Note that all identity matrices are **square** and that the 1s are said to be on the leading or **principal diagonal**.

Thus: $\begin{bmatrix} 5 & 3 \\ 2 & 1 \end{bmatrix} \begin{bmatrix} 1 & 0 \\ 0 & 1 \end{bmatrix} = \begin{bmatrix} 5 & 3 \\ 2 & 1 \end{bmatrix}$

or $\begin{bmatrix} 6 & 8 & 10 \\ 12 & 20 & 14 \\ 2 & 75 & 3 \end{bmatrix} \begin{bmatrix} 1 & 0 & 0 \\ 0 & 1 & 0 \\ 0 & 0 & 1 \end{bmatrix} = \begin{bmatrix} 6 & 8 & 10 \\ 12 & 20 & 14 \\ 2 & 75 & 3 \end{bmatrix}$

If I is used for the identity matrix, we have: $AI = IA = A$.

6.7.3 Inverse of a matrix

As in arithmetic, division of one matrix by another is equivalent to multiplying the first matrix by the **inverse** of the second, bearing in mind that the operation is not commutative. To transfer a matrix from one side of an equation to the other, both sides are multiplied by the inverse of the matrix. The inverse of a matrix A is denoted by A^{-1}. A matrix multiplied in either order by the inverse of itself will always give the identity matrix, i.e.

$$AA^{-1} = A^{-1}A = I$$

To transfer a matrix from one side of an equation to the other, we have:

$$A \cdot B = C$$

To find B, premultiply both sides by A^{-1}:

$$A^{-1}AB = A^{-1}C$$
thus $\quad IB = A^{-1}C$
and $\quad B = A^{-1}C$

To find A, we have:

$$A \cdot B = C$$

Postmultiply both sides by B^{-1}:

$$ABB^{-1} = CB^{-1}$$
thus $\quad AI = CB^{-1}$
and $\quad A = CB^{-1}$

Finding the inverse of a matrix is only possible if the matrix is **square**, i.e. has the same number of rows as columns, and we shall initially look at the special case of a (2×2) matrix and then suggest a method for larger matrices.

(2 × 2)

If $\quad A = \begin{bmatrix} a_{11} & a_{12} \\ a_{21} & a_{22} \end{bmatrix}$

then $\quad A^{-1} = \dfrac{1}{(a_{11} \cdot a_{22}) - (a_{12} \cdot a_{21})} \begin{bmatrix} a_{22} & -a_{12} \\ -a_{21} & a_{11} \end{bmatrix}$

Putting this into words, the fraction in front of the matrix is one over the product of the two elements on the principal diagonal minus the product of the other two elements. Within the matrix the two elements on the principal diagonal change places and the other two elements change sign, e.g.

if $\quad A = \begin{bmatrix} 1 & 2 \\ 3 & 4 \end{bmatrix}$

then $\quad A^{-1} = \dfrac{1}{(1 \times 4) - (2 \times 3)} \begin{bmatrix} 4 & -2 \\ -3 & 1 \end{bmatrix} = -\dfrac{1}{2} \begin{bmatrix} 4 & -2 \\ -3 & 1 \end{bmatrix}$

or $\quad \begin{bmatrix} -2 & 1 \\ 1.5 & -0.5 \end{bmatrix}$

To check the answer we can find AA^{-1}:

$$\begin{bmatrix} 1 & 2 \\ 3 & 4 \end{bmatrix} \begin{bmatrix} -2 & 1 \\ 1.5 & -0.5 \end{bmatrix} = \begin{bmatrix} 1 & 0 \\ 0 & 1 \end{bmatrix}$$

The denominator of the fraction we calculated above is called the **determinant** of the matrix, and if this is 0 then the matrix is said to be **singular**, and does not have an inverse.

Larger matrices
To find the inverse for a matrix larger than (2×2) is a somewhat more complex procedure and may be done by using the method of **cofactors** or by **row operations**. We shall give an example of how to find the inverse for a (3×3) matrix. (For larger matrices it is probably advisable to use a computer program.)

To find an inverse using the cofactors, we must first find the determinant of the matrix, denoted by $|A|$.

If $\quad A = \begin{bmatrix} a_{11} & a_{12} & a_{13} \\ a_{21} & a_{22} & a_{23} \\ a_{31} & a_{32} & a_{33} \end{bmatrix}$

$$|A| = a_{11} \begin{vmatrix} a_{22} & a_{23} \\ a_{32} & a_{33} \end{vmatrix} - a_{21} \begin{vmatrix} a_{12} & a_{13} \\ a_{32} & a_{33} \end{vmatrix} + a_{31} \begin{vmatrix} a_{12} & a_{13} \\ a_{22} & a_{23} \end{vmatrix}$$

$$= a_{11}(a_{22}a_{33} - a_{23}a_{32}) - a_{21}(a_{12}a_{33} - a_{13}a_{32}) + a_{31}(a_{12}a_{23} - a_{13}a_{22})$$

A cofactor of an element consists of the determinant of those elements which **are not in the same row and not in the same column as that element.** Thus the cofactor of a_{11} is:

$$\begin{vmatrix} a_{22} & a_{23} \\ a_{32} & a_{33} \end{vmatrix}$$

and this can be evaluated as $(a_{22}a_{33}) - (a_{23}a_{32})$. To form the inverse matrix, each element of the initial matrix is replaced by its **signed** cofactor. (Note the signs of the cofactors replacing a_{12}, a_{21}, a_{23} and a_{32}.)

$$\begin{bmatrix} \begin{vmatrix} a_{22} & a_{23} \\ a_{23} & a_{33} \end{vmatrix} & -\begin{vmatrix} a_{21} & a_{23} \\ a_{31} & a_{33} \end{vmatrix} & \begin{vmatrix} a_{21} & a_{22} \\ a_{31} & a_{32} \end{vmatrix} \\ -\begin{vmatrix} a_{12} & a_{13} \\ a_{32} & a_{33} \end{vmatrix} & \begin{vmatrix} a_{11} & a_{13} \\ a_{31} & a_{33} \end{vmatrix} & -\begin{vmatrix} a_{11} & a_{12} \\ a_{31} & a_{32} \end{vmatrix} \\ \begin{vmatrix} a_{12} & a_{13} \\ a_{22} & a_{23} \end{vmatrix} & -\begin{vmatrix} a_{11} & a_{13} \\ a_{21} & a_{23} \end{vmatrix} & \begin{vmatrix} a_{11} & a_{12} \\ a_{21} & a_{22} \end{vmatrix} \end{bmatrix}$$

After each element of this new matrix has been evaluated, it is **transposed**; that is each column is written as a row, so that a_{12} becomes a_{21}. The resultant matrix is then multiplied by one over the determinant. This is likely to become considerably clearer as we work through an example.

Example

$$A = \begin{bmatrix} 1 & 2 & 3 \\ 1 & 3 & 5 \\ 1 & 5 & 12 \end{bmatrix}$$

then $|A| = 1 \times (3 \times 12 - 5 \times 5) - 1 \times (2 \times 12 - 3 \times 5) + 1 \times (2 \times 5 - 3 \times 3)$
$$= 11 - 9 + 1$$
$$= 3$$

Replacing elements by cofactors, we have:

$$\begin{bmatrix} \begin{vmatrix} 3 & 5 \\ 5 & 12 \end{vmatrix} & -\begin{vmatrix} 1 & 5 \\ 1 & 12 \end{vmatrix} & \begin{vmatrix} 1 & 3 \\ 1 & 5 \end{vmatrix} \\ -\begin{vmatrix} 2 & 3 \\ 5 & 12 \end{vmatrix} & \begin{vmatrix} 1 & 3 \\ 1 & 12 \end{vmatrix} & -\begin{vmatrix} 1 & 2 \\ 1 & 5 \end{vmatrix} \\ \begin{vmatrix} 2 & 3 \\ 3 & 5 \end{vmatrix} & -\begin{vmatrix} 1 & 3 \\ 1 & 5 \end{vmatrix} & \begin{vmatrix} 1 & 2 \\ 1 & 3 \end{vmatrix} \end{bmatrix}$$

$$= \begin{bmatrix} 11 & -7 & 2 \\ -9 & 9 & -3 \\ 1 & -2 & 1 \end{bmatrix}$$

Transposing this, we have:

$$\begin{bmatrix} 11 & -9 & 1 \\ -7 & 9 & -2 \\ 2 & -3 & 1 \end{bmatrix}$$

This is called the **adjunct matrix**, and A^{-1} is this matrix multiplied by the reciprocal of the determinant.

$$A^{-1} = \frac{1}{3} \begin{bmatrix} 11 & -9 & 1 \\ -7 & 9 & -2 \\ 2 & -3 & 1 \end{bmatrix}$$

Exercise   Check that $AA^{-1} = I$.

To find the inverse using row operations, we create a **partitioned matrix**, by putting an identity matrix alongside the original matrix:

$$\left[\begin{array}{ccc|ccc} 1 & 2 & 3 & 1 & 0 & 0 \\ 1 & 3 & 5 & 0 & 1 & 0 \\ 1 & 5 & 12 & 0 & 0 & 1 \end{array} \right]$$

Our objective now is to multiply and divide each row, or add and subtract rows until the matrix on the **left** of the partition is an identity. At that point, whatever is to the **right** of the partition will be the inverse of the original matrix. We already have a 1 at a_{11}, so to change the 1 at a_{21} to 0 we may subtract row 1 from row 2. (Note that we subtract corresponding elements for the **whole** row.)

$$\left[\begin{array}{ccc|ccc} 1 & 2 & 3 & 1 & 0 & 0 \\ 0 & 1 & 2 & -1 & 1 & 0 \\ 1 & 5 & 12 & 0 & 0 & 1 \end{array} \right]$$

To get 0 at a_{31}, we again subtract row 1 from row 3.

$$\left[\begin{array}{ccc|ccc} 1 & 2 & 3 & 1 & 0 & 0 \\ 0 & 1 & 2 & -1 & 1 & 0 \\ 0 & 3 & 9 & -1 & 0 & 1 \end{array} \right]$$

To get 0 at a_{12} we can subtract two times row 2 from row 1.

$$\left[\begin{array}{ccc|ccc} 1 & 0 & -1 & 3 & -2 & 0 \\ 0 & 1 & 2 & -1 & 1 & 0 \\ 0 & 3 & 9 & -1 & 0 & 1 \end{array} \right]$$

To get 0 at a_{32}, subtract three times row 2 from row 3.

$$\left[\begin{array}{ccc|ccc} 1 & 0 & -1 & 3 & -2 & 0 \\ 0 & 1 & 2 & -1 & 1 & 0 \\ 0 & 0 & 3 & 2 & -3 & 1 \end{array} \right]$$

To get 1 at a_{33}, divide row 3 by 3.

$$\left[\begin{array}{ccc|ccc} 1 & 0 & -1 & 3 & -2 & 0 \\ 0 & 1 & 2 & -1 & 1 & 0 \\ 0 & 0 & 1 & 2/3 & -1 & 1/3 \end{array} \right]$$

To get 0 at a_{13}, add row 3 to row 1.

$$\left[\begin{array}{ccc|ccc} 1 & 0 & 0 & 11/3 & -3 & 1/3 \\ 0 & 1 & 2 & -1 & 1 & 0 \\ 0 & 0 & 1 & 2/3 & -1 & 1/3 \end{array} \right]$$

To get 0 at a_{23}, subtract two times row 3 from row 2.

$$\left[\begin{array}{ccc|ccc} 1 & 0 & 0 & 11/3 & -3 & 1/3 \\ 0 & 1 & 0 & -7/3 & 3 & -2/3 \\ 0 & 0 & 1 & 2/3 & -1 & 1/3 \end{array} \right]$$

As you will see, this is the same answer that was achieved by using the cofactors method. Note also that $(A \cdot B)^{-1} = B^{-1} A^{-1}$ as you can easily prove.

6.8 PROBLEMS

$$U = \begin{bmatrix} 3 \\ 7 \\ 10 \end{bmatrix} \qquad V = \begin{bmatrix} 4 \\ 3 \\ 2 \end{bmatrix} \qquad A = \begin{bmatrix} 1 & 2 \\ 3 & 4 \end{bmatrix} \qquad B = \begin{bmatrix} 1 & 3 \\ 2 & 4 \end{bmatrix}$$

$$C = \begin{bmatrix} 1 & 2 \\ 3 & 5 \\ 7 & 8 \end{bmatrix} \qquad D = \begin{bmatrix} 4 & 3 \\ 8 & 7 \end{bmatrix} \qquad E = \begin{bmatrix} 3 & 5 & 4 \\ 7 & 9 & 3 \\ 2 & 8 & 3 \end{bmatrix}$$

$$F = \begin{bmatrix} 2 & 1 & 2 & 1 \\ 1 & 3 & 6 & 2 \\ 4 & 3 & 4 & 1 \\ 5 & 1 & 3 & 2 \end{bmatrix} \qquad G = \begin{bmatrix} 0.1 \\ 0.3 \\ 0.1 \\ 0.2 \end{bmatrix}$$

$$H = \begin{bmatrix} 4 & 8 & 1 \\ 10 & 12 & 1 \\ 8 & 3 & 1 \end{bmatrix} \qquad J = \begin{bmatrix} 2 & 1 & 8 \\ 2 & 2 & 3 \\ 2 & 4 & 1 \end{bmatrix}$$

$$L = \begin{bmatrix} -9/116 & 1/116 & 50/116 \\ -10/116 & 14/116 & 4/116 \\ 27/116 & -3/116 & -34/116 \end{bmatrix} \qquad M = \begin{bmatrix} 4 & 1 & 6 \\ 2 & 9 & 4 \\ 3 & 0 & 1 \end{bmatrix}$$

Find:

1. $U + V$
2. $5 \times V$
3. $U^1 \times V$ (where U^1 is the transpose of U).
4. $A + B$
5. $B + A$
6. $A - B$
7. $B - A$
8. $3 \times A$
9. $A \times B$
10. $B \times A$
11. $D \times I$
12. $I \times D$
13. $5 \times E$
14. $F \times G$
15. $H \times J$
16. $J \times H$
17. $L \times M$
18. $M \times L$
19. $1/10 \times F$
20. D^{-1}
21. A^{-1}
22. $A^{-1}B^{-1}$
23. $(A \cdot B)^{-1}$
24. $E \times U$
25. $M \times L \times M$
26. $G \times F$
27. E^{-1}
28. H^{-1}
29. J^{-1}

30. Compare your answers to Exercises 9, 10, 22 and 23.

6.9 SOLUTION OF SIMULTANEOUS EQUATIONS

$$7x + 4y = 80$$
$$5x + 3y = 58$$

This pair of equations may be written in matrix notation as:

$$\begin{bmatrix} 7 & 4 \\ 5 & 3 \end{bmatrix} \begin{bmatrix} x \\ y \end{bmatrix} = \begin{bmatrix} 80 \\ 58 \end{bmatrix}$$

or $\qquad A \cdot x = b$

If we premultiply by A^{-1} we have

$$A^{-1}Ax = A^{-1}b$$
or $\qquad Ix = A^{-1}b$
or $\qquad x = A^{-1}b$

The result will hold for **any** set of simultaneous equations where there are as many equations as unknowns; and thus if we premultiply the vector b by the inverse of the matrix A, we shall be able to find the values of the unknowns that satisfy the equations.

Here:
$$A^{-1} = \frac{1}{21 - 20} \begin{bmatrix} 3 & -4 \\ -5 & 7 \end{bmatrix}$$

Therefore,
$$\begin{bmatrix} x \\ y \end{bmatrix} = \begin{bmatrix} 3 & -4 \\ -5 & 7 \end{bmatrix} \begin{bmatrix} 80 \\ 58 \end{bmatrix} = \begin{bmatrix} 240 - 232 \\ -400 + 406 \end{bmatrix} = \begin{bmatrix} 8 \\ 6 \end{bmatrix}$$

Thus $x = 8$ and $y = 6$.

If we have three equations:

$$
\begin{aligned}
4x_1 + 3x_2 + x_3 &= 8 \\
2x_1 + x_2 + 4x_3 &= -4 \\
3x_1 + x_3 &= 1
\end{aligned}
$$

then it can be shown that the inverse of the A matrix is:

$$A^{-1} = \frac{1}{31} \begin{bmatrix} 1 & -3 & 11 \\ 10 & 1 & -14 \\ -3 & 9 & -2 \end{bmatrix}$$

and that the solution to the equations is:

$$\begin{bmatrix} x_1 \\ x_2 \\ x_3 \end{bmatrix} = \frac{1}{31} \begin{bmatrix} 1 & -3 & 11 \\ 10 & 1 & -14 \\ -3 & 9 & -2 \end{bmatrix} \begin{bmatrix} 8 \\ -4 \\ 1 \end{bmatrix} = \frac{1}{31} \begin{bmatrix} 31 \\ 62 \\ -62 \end{bmatrix} = \begin{bmatrix} 1 \\ 2 \\ -2 \end{bmatrix}$$

thus $x_1 = 1$, $x_2 = 2$ and $x_3 = -2$.

6.10   LEONTIEF INPUT–OUTPUT ANALYSIS

When this is applied to an economy, it is assumed that the production within the economy can be **segregated into sectors** (or **industries**) and that the outputs of these sectors can be seen as:

(a) being used by the same sector;
(b) being sold to another productive sector; or
(c) being sold to the non-productive sector which will include both households and exports.

In a complex economy, the segregation may be fairly arbitrary since many companies produce a range of products, that may fall into several sectors, but in the UK and the rest of Europe the segregation is still attempted by using a Standard Industrial Classification which gives about 40 sectors. We shall not attempt to write out a full system for 40 productive sectors (!) but will analyse a simpler model with only three productive sectors. The general results obtained would, however, apply to the larger systems.

If there are three production sectors in an economy, with outputs X_1, X_2 and X_3 of three different products, and one non-productive sector which represents final demand for the products of the productive sectors, then for the economy to be in equilibrium, the output from one industry minus the consumption of parts of that output by it or other industries must equal the level of final demand for the industry's product, i.e.

$$X_1 - a_{11}X_1 - a_{12}X_2 - a_{13}X_3 = d_1$$

where a_{11} is the proportion of output X_1 that is used in the production of X_1, a_{12} is the amount of X_1 that is used in the production of one unit of X_2, a_{13} is the amount of X_1 that is used by one unit of X_3 and d_1 is the final demand for X_1. Each constant is known as an **input–output coefficient**. For all industries, we have:

$$X_1 - a_{11}X_1 - a_{12}X_2 - a_{13}X_3 = d_1$$
$$X_2 - a_{21}X_1 - a_{22}X_2 - a_{23}X_3 = d_2$$
$$X_3 - a_{31}X_1 - a_{32}X_2 - a_{33}X_3 = d_3$$

or, rearranging, we have:

$$
\begin{array}{rcccl}
X_1(1 - a_{11}) & - & a_{12}X_2 & - & a_{13}X_3 & = d_1 \\
- a_{21}X_1 & + & (1 - a_{22})X_2 & - & a_{23}X_3 & = d_2 \\
- a_{31}X_1 & - & a_{32}X_2 & + & (1 - a_{33})X_3 & = d_3
\end{array}
$$

Thus,

$$
\begin{bmatrix}
(1 - a_{11}) & -a_{12} & -a_{13} \\
-a_{21} & (1 - a_{22}) & -a_{23} \\
-a_{31} & -a_{32} & (1 - a_{33})
\end{bmatrix}
\begin{bmatrix} X_1 \\ X_2 \\ X_3 \end{bmatrix}
=
\begin{bmatrix} d_1 \\ d_2 \\ d_3 \end{bmatrix}
$$

If a matrix A consists of all of the input–output coefficients (a_{ij}) then we have:

$$(I - A)X = D$$

When using this relationship, we often know the values in the final demand vector (D) and must know the input–output coefficients; we thus need to determine the level of output for each industry.

$$(I - A)X = D$$

Premultiplying by $(I - A)^{-1}$ gives

$$(I - A)^{-1}(I - A)X = (I - A)^{-1}D$$

thus $$IX = (I - A)^{-1}D$$

or $$X = (I - A)^{-1}D$$

Example

Consider a simplified economy which has three industrial sectors, labelled X_1, X_2 and X_3 and a final demand sector. Inter-industry sales for last year are shown in Table 6.1.

Table 6.1

Outputs from:		Inputs to: sector X_1	sector X_2	sector X_3	Final demand	Total output
	X_1	20	10	60	110	200
	X_2	40	10	50	150	250
	X_3	10	60	30	400	500
Other inputs		130	170	360		
		200	250	500		

From this table we have:

Output of X_1 = 20 + 10 + 60 + 110 = 200
Output of X_2 = 40 + 10 + 50 + 150 = 250
Output of X_3 = 10 + 60 + 30 + 400 = 500

To construct the matrix of input–output coefficients, we must rearrange these equations into the form given above, i.e.

$$X_1 - a_{11}X_1 - a_{12}X_2 - a_{13}X_3 = d_1$$

or $\quad 200 - \dfrac{20}{200}\,(200) - \dfrac{10}{250}\,(250) - \dfrac{60}{500}\,(500) = 110$

or $\quad 200\,(1 - 0.1) - 0.04\,(250) - 0.12\,(500) = 110$

thus $a_{11} = 0.1, a_{12} = 0.04, a_{13} = 0.12$
similarly $a_{21} = 40/200 = 0.2, a_{22} = 10/250 = 0.04, a_{23} = 50/500 = 0.1, a_{31} = 10/200$
$= 0.05, a_{32} = 60/250 = 0.24, a_{33} = 30/500 = 0.06$
Writing these in matrix format gives the matrix A:

$$A = \begin{bmatrix} 0.10 & 0.04 & 0.12 \\ 0.20 & 0.04 & 0.10 \\ 0.05 & 0.24 & 0.06 \end{bmatrix}$$

and $I - A$ will be:

$$\begin{bmatrix} 0.90 & -0.04 & -0.12 \\ -0.20 & 0.96 & -0.10 \\ -0.05 & -0.24 & 0.94 \end{bmatrix}$$

It can be shown that the inverse of this matrix is:

$$\frac{10}{77\,132} \begin{bmatrix} 8784 & 664 & 1192 \\ 1930 & 8400 & 1140 \\ 960 & 2180 & 8560 \end{bmatrix}$$

If we are now told that the final demand vector for the three sectors (or industries) is:

$$\begin{bmatrix} 77\,132 \\ 231\,396 \\ 385\,660 \end{bmatrix}$$

then the required outputs will be:

$$\begin{bmatrix} X_1 \\ X_2 \\ X_3 \end{bmatrix} = \frac{10}{77\,132} \begin{bmatrix} 8784 & 664 & 1192 \\ 1930 & 8400 & 1140 \\ 960 & 2180 & 8560 \end{bmatrix} \begin{bmatrix} 77\,132 \\ 231\,396 \\ 385\,660 \end{bmatrix} = \begin{bmatrix} 167\,360 \\ 328\,300 \\ 503\,000 \end{bmatrix}$$

$$X \qquad = \qquad (I - A)^{-1} \qquad\qquad D \quad = \quad X$$

The equation system can be used to show the interrelatedness of the industries within an economy and the effects if the final demand for the product of one industry changes. It was used in the UK in the early 1970s to look at the effects of a curtailment of oil supplies on the various industrial sectors. However, the difficulty with this system is not only its size for a complex economy but the implicit assumption that the input–output coefficients are constant. This is unlikely to be true as technical progress and innovation change the ways in which some industries operate. To take this into account, a new matrix of input–output coefficients must be derived every few years and this is an extremely costly process.

6.11 PROBLEMS

Solve the following sets of simultaneous equations using matrix algebra.

1. $4x + 3y = 17$
    $2x + y = 7$
2. $10x + 7y = 16$
    $3x - 2y = 13$
3. $2x - y = -5$
    $4x + 3y = 115$
4. $3x_1 + 2x_2 + x_3 = 22$
    $x_1 + 2x_2 + 3x_3 = 26$
    $2x_1 + 3x_2 + 5x_3 = 43$
5. $3x_1 - 2x_2 + 3x_3 = 38$
    $4x_1 + 2x_2 + 5x_3 = 56$
    $10x_1 - 2x_2 - 2x_3 = 2$
6. In the usual notation, find the matrices X, A and D from the following input–output data.

Outputs from:	Inputs to: sector A	sector B	Final demand	Total output ($£000$)
Product A	30	20	50	100
Product B	10	40	50	100
Other	60	40		
	$\overline{100}$	$\overline{100}$		$\overline{200}$

   (a) Indicate how X, A and D are related and verify that the relationship holds by substituting the tabulated data in your equation.
   (b) If the final demand is now changed to 120 for product A and 160 for product B what is the new total output of each product?

7. Repeat the calculation for the following input–output table.

Outputs from:	Inputs to: sector A	sector B	Final demand	Total output ($£000$)
A	50	20	130	200
B	30	60	10	100
Other	120	20		
	$\overline{200}$	$\overline{100}$		$\overline{300}$

Assume a new final demand for product A to be 270 and for product B, 378.

8.

Outputs from:	sector A	Inputs to: sector B	sector C	Final demand	Total output ($£000$)
A	10	10	20	60	100
B	20	—	10	70	100
C	20	10	10	60	100
Other	50	80	60		
	$\overline{100}$	$\overline{100}$	$\overline{100}$		$\overline{300}$

From the table above:

   (a) Find the matrix of technical coefficients.
   (b) Find $(I - A)$.

(c) Prove

$$\begin{bmatrix} 0.9 & -0.1 & -0.2 \\ -0.2 & 1 & -0.1 \\ -0.2 & -0.1 & 0.9 \end{bmatrix}^{-1} = \frac{1000}{737} \begin{bmatrix} 0.89 & 0.11 & 0.21 \\ 0.20 & 0.77 & 0.13 \\ 0.22 & 0.11 & 0.88 \end{bmatrix}$$

by multiplying out.

(d) Complete the input–output calculation to show the demand is as given in the table, i.e. calculate D from X, and A.

(e) Find the new total output if the new final D is changed to A, 7370; B, 3685; C, 1474.

9. Repeat the previous exercise on input–output.
Prove

$$\frac{1}{12} \begin{bmatrix} 8 & -2 & -2 \\ -3 & 6 & -2 \\ -1 & -3 & 9 \end{bmatrix}^{-1} = \frac{3}{74} \begin{bmatrix} 48 & 24 & 16 \\ 29 & 70 & 22 \\ 15 & 26 & 42 \end{bmatrix}$$

		Inputs to:		Final	Total output
Outputs from:	sector A	sector B	sector C	demand	(£000)
A	40	20	20	40	120
B	30	60	20	10	120
C	10	30	30	50	120
Other	40	10	50		
	$\overline{120}$	$\overline{120}$	$\overline{120}$		

New demand for A is 740; for B, 444; for C, 296.

7 The use of calculus

7.1 INTRODUCTION TO CALCULUS

Calculus developed during the seventeenth century from problems experienced by physical scientists, like Galileo, trying to describe the world. It arose from the need to give an adequate mathematical account of changes in motion, and is generally attributed to the independent work of Leibniz and Newton, although there were significant contributions from Fermat and Descartes. (Dispute over whose was the original idea arose between supporters of Leibniz and Newton, and this led to the cutting of all communication between British and European mathematicians for some years.) The problem facing the mathematicians was how to find an exact measure of the rate of motion (i.e. speed), particularly when the rate of change was not constant. Rate of change can be interpreted in two ways: the average rate of change and the instantaneous rate of change. If you consider a car travelling from Birmingham to Manchester, then its average speed (i.e. the rate of change of distance in relation to time) may be 50 miles per hour, but its speed at any particular moment may be much less (for example 5 m.p.h. in heavy traffic) or rather more (for example 70 m.p.h. on the motorway). The driver, looking at the speedometer at a particular moment, can tell his **instantaneous speed**. Now it has been argued that there can be no such thing as instantaneous speed, since speed is to do with the distance travelled, but try convincing someone who has been driving and met a wall (which was presumably stationary) that he could not be travelling at a speed at the instant the vehicle and the wall met!

The methods of calculus did not go unchallenged, and since the topic was not well presented (and perhaps not clearly understood), it formed the weakest link in the description of the physical universe proposed by the mathematicians. It

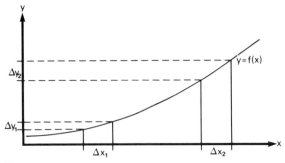

Figure 7.1

was attacked by Berkeley, who described instantaneous rates of change as: 'neither finite quantities, nor quantities infinitely small, nor yet anything' and as 'the ghosts of departed quantities. Certainly . . . he who can digest a second or third [differentiation] . . . need not, methinks, be squeamish about any point in Divinity.'

However, calculus was proving **useful** in many areas, and was becoming more clearly understood. It therefore survived these philosophical attacks.

Calculus, then, is about **instantaneous rates of change**, and is of most interest in a first year course in relation to economic concepts and applications in which mathematical modelling is relevant, including statistics.

If we take the graph of a function (as in Fig. 7.1) we can see that there is an increasing change in y ($\Delta y_1 < \Delta y_2$) for equal changes in x ($\Delta x_1 = \Delta x_2$) as we move to the right. The symbol Δ (Greek capital delta) indicates an interval in the value of a variable, e.g. Δx represents the difference between two values of x. Thus there are different rates of change in y for different values of x. To find the **average** rate of change between two values of x, we would divide the change in y by the change in x. Hence:

$$\frac{\Delta y_1}{\Delta x_1} \text{ is less than } \frac{\Delta y_2}{\Delta x_2}$$

If a small section of the graph of the function is magnified (as in Fig. 7.2), we see that the ratio $\Delta y/\Delta x$ not only measures the average rate of change of y between two values of x, but also the gradient in slope of a straight line (known as a chord) drawn between two points on the graph. As we reduce the change in x the straight line gets shorter and shorter and hence its slope or rate of change gets nearer and nearer to the slope of the curve at a single point; but if we have no change in x, then there is no change in y, although the function is still changing (cf. the car mentioned above). Now if the straight line between two points can represent the average slope of the graph between the points, is there a straight line at one point whose slope is that of the graph at that point? The answer is yes!

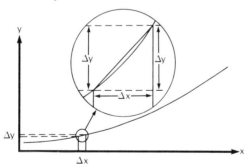

Figure 7.2

Figure 7.3 shows a straight line which touches the curve at just one point (known as a **tangent**) and the slope of this line will be the slope of the curve at the point where the two touch. Since there is only one point now in question, the slope of the curve of that point measures not the average but the instantaneous rate of change.

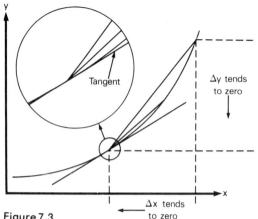

Figure 7.3

Formally, the measurement of the slope of a curve at a point is valid if the function is **continuous**, i.e. there are no gaps or jumps in the function; thus if $y = f(x)$ then both x and y are continuous variables in the relevant range or domain. The slope of the tangent at the point where it touches the function is defined as the limit of the ratio $\Delta y/\Delta x$ as Δx tends to zero.

A **limit** is a number to which the ratio gets nearer and nearer, as the **interval** Δx gets smaller. For example the ratio

$$\frac{x + \Delta x}{x}$$

will get closer and closer to 1 as the interval Δx gets smaller. Thus the limit of this expression will be 1.

Formally, the change in x is thought of as a distance, h, so that the interval Δx is from x to $x + h$. Since $y = f(x)$, the interval Δy extends from $f(x)$ to $f(x + h)$ (see Fig. 7.4).

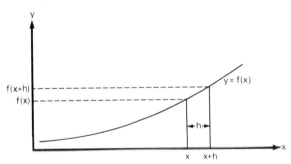

Figure 7.4

We saw above (page 109) that an average slope of a function was

$$\frac{\Delta y}{\Delta x} = \frac{y_2 - y_1}{x_2 - x_1}$$

or, in Fig. 7.4,

$$\frac{f(x + h) - f(x)}{(x + h) - x} = \frac{f(x + h) - f(x)}{h}$$

and it is this ratio, as h gets smaller and smaller, that gives the instantaneous rate of change of $f(x)$ at a single value x.

Limit of $\Delta y/\Delta x$ as $h \to 0$ is denoted by dy/dx or $f'(x)$. Here d signifies an infinitesimal change in a variable (cf. Δ which signifies finite change).

Example

If $f(x) = x^2$, then $f(x + h) = (x + h)^2 = x^2 + 2xh + h^2$

so the ratio $\Delta y/\Delta x$ is

$$\frac{(x^2 + 2xh + h^2) - x^2}{h}$$

$$= \frac{2xh + h^2}{h} = 2x + h$$

and as $h \to 0$, this gets closer and closer to $2x$.

Thus for $\qquad y = x^2$

$$\frac{dy}{dx} = 2x$$

So the rate of change of the function $y = x^2$ at $x = 2$, for example, is $2x = 2.2 = 4$. Note that the rate of change of a function is often referred to as the **gradient of the function**.

The process described above is known as **differentiation** and gives the rate of change of a function at one particular point, or gives another function from which we can find the rate of change at particular points. Looking now at the functions from the last chapter, we can find their rates of change. A **constant**, by its nature, does not change, and thus does not have a rate of change.

So if $\qquad y = k$ (a constant)

$$\frac{dy}{dx} = 0$$

The feature of a linear function was that for a given change in x, y always changes by the same amount, and thus linear functions have a constant rate of change, or slope. Thus, when we differentiate a linear function, the rate of change will be the slope b of the function.

So if $\qquad y = a + bx$

$$\frac{dy}{dx} = b$$

When we have functions with higher powers of x then we need some rule to allow us to differentiate them quickly. Such a rule does exist.

If $\qquad y = ax^n$

then $\qquad \dfrac{dy}{dx} = n \cdot a \cdot x^{n-1}$

This general rule will apply to any function or term of a function which has a constant a multiplied by x to some power n.

Thus if $\quad y = 6x^3$, then $a = 6, n = 3$

so $\qquad \dfrac{dy}{dx} = 3.6 \cdot x^{3-1} = 18x^2$

and if $\qquad y = 10x^2$

$\qquad \dfrac{dy}{dx} = 2.10 \cdot x^{2-1} = 20x^1 = 20x$

since x^1 is x. For a function consisting of several parts or terms, we differentiate each part separately and then put the results together:

If $\quad y = \qquad 6x^3 \qquad - \qquad 4x^2 \qquad + \qquad 10x \qquad - \qquad 50 \qquad + \qquad 3x^{-2}$
$\qquad\qquad a = 6, n = 3 \quad a = -4, n = 2 \quad a = 10, n = 1 \quad \text{constant} \quad a = 3, n = -2$

so $\dfrac{dy}{dx} = \quad 3.6 \cdot x^{3-1} \; + \; 2 \cdot (-4) \cdot x^{2-1} \; + \; 1.10 \cdot x^{1-1} \quad - \quad 0 \quad + (-2) \cdot 3 \cdot x^{2-1}$

$\qquad\quad = \qquad 18x^2 \qquad - \qquad 8x \qquad + \qquad 10x^0 \qquad + \qquad 0 \quad - \qquad 6x^{-3}$
$\qquad\quad = 18x^2 - 8x + 10 - 6x^{-3}$

Note that $x^0 = 1$

Certain other functions have special **derivatives**. (A derivative is the result of differentiation, also called a differential coefficient.)

For example, if $\qquad y = e^x$ (the exponential function described in Section 6.4.5)

then $\qquad\qquad \dfrac{dy}{dx} = e^x$

If $\qquad\qquad\qquad y = \log_e x$

then $\qquad\qquad \dfrac{dy}{dx} = \dfrac{1}{x}$

We will consider these functions again in Section 7.5.

7.2 ECONOMIC APPLICATIONS I

Within economics, there are several functions which are related to each other as function to derivative. For instance, the total cost (TC) represents the cost of producing a particular amount of the product; the marginal cost (MC) is the cost of producing one extra unit and so the marginal cost of a given output is the rate at which total cost is changing at that output. Thus, if we have a total cost function and differentiate it, we will find that the result is a marginal cost function. This relationship will also hold for revenue functions.

Thus if $\quad y = TC \quad$ then $\quad \dfrac{dy}{dx} = MC$

if $\qquad y = TR \quad$ then $\quad \dfrac{dy}{dx} = MR$

---

where TR is total revenue and MR is marginal revenue. For example:

if $\qquad$ TC $= 40 + 10x + 2x^2 + x^3$
then $\qquad$ MC $= \quad\ 10 + 4x + 3x^2$

(per unit change in output when output $= x$). For example:

if $\qquad$ TR $= 4x$
then $\qquad$ MR $= 4$

(per unit change in sales when sales $= x$).

We may also use the idea of averaging to find the average cost of, or revenue from, a given output. If total revenue is £100 from an output of 5, then the average revenue (AR) will be $100/5 = £20$ per unit. So if

$$TR = 100x - 10x^2$$
$$AR = \frac{1}{x}(100x - 10x^2) = \frac{100x}{x} - \frac{10x^2}{x}$$
$$= 100 - 10x$$

(per unit when x units are sold). Similarly if

$$AC = x^2 - 10x + 38$$
then $\qquad$ $TC = x(x^2 - 10x + 38)$
$$= x^3 - 10x^2 + 38x$$

If we begin with a cubic total cost function and find the marginal cost function, which will be quadratic, and the average cost function, which will also be quadratic, then graph these, we will have the typical economic diagram, as in Fig. 7.5.

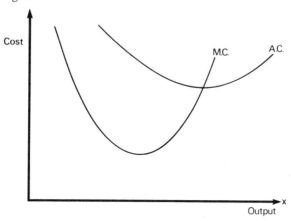

Figure 7.5

With a linear demand curve (i.e. an AR function) we will obtain the relationship in Fig. 7.6, where the marginal revenue function will also be linear, but have a slope twice that of the average revenue function.

Since if $\qquad$ AR $= a + bx$
then $\qquad$ TR $= ax + bx^2$
and $\qquad$ MR $= a + 2bx$

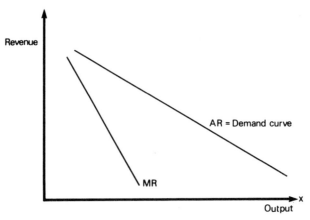

Figure 7.6

Elasticity of demand measures the responsiveness of the quantity sold to various factors: initially, the most useful of these is price elasticity (E_D).

This is defined as: $E_D = \dfrac{dq}{dp} \cdot \dfrac{p}{q}$

Example If the demand curve is $p = 100 - 5q$

then $\dfrac{dp}{dq} = -5$

and since $\dfrac{dq}{dp} = 1 \left| \dfrac{dp}{dq} \right.$

then $\dfrac{dq}{dp} = -\dfrac{1}{5}$

At a quantity of 10, the price is:

$p = 100 - 5(10) = 50$

So, elasticity is:

$E_D = \dfrac{1}{-5} \times \dfrac{50}{10} = -1$

At a quantity of 8, the price is 60 and elasticity is

$E_D = \dfrac{1}{-5} \times \dfrac{60}{8} = -1.5$

So for a linear demand function, there is a **constant** slope but a **changing** elasticity.

7.3 PROBLEMS

Differentiate each of the following functions:
1. $y = -3$
2. $y = 10x - 4$
3. $y = 4x^2$
4. $y = 4x + 3$

---

5. $y = -12x^4 + 2x^2$
6. $y = 2x$
7. $y = 15x^5 + 3x + 4x^{-2}$
8. $y = x^4 + 2x^3$
9. $p = 4q^3 + 3q^2 - 2q + 10$
10. $y = 4x^5 + 0.5x^4 - x^3 + 2x - 8$
11. $y = e^x$
12. $y = 40x^8 + 10x^3 - 30x + 2x^{-1} - 4x^{-2}$
13. $y = \dfrac{1}{x^2} + \dfrac{1}{x^3} + \dfrac{3}{x^4}$
14. If total cost is $TC = \dfrac{1}{3}x^3 - 4x^2 + 20x$

   Find the AC and MC functions.
   Graph the AC and MC functions for $0 < x < 10$.
15. If the AR function is

   $AR = 40 - 2x$

   Find the TR and MR functions.
   Graph the TR function for $0 < x < 10$.
   Graph the AR function for $0 < x < 20$.
   Graph the MR function for $0 < x < 10$ on the same graph as the AR function.
16. An oligopolist sells his product at \$950 per unit of production, and estimates his average revenue function to consist of two linear segments.
   Below 10 units, AR = 990 when production = 2
                    AR = 965 when production = 7
   Above 10 units, AR = 840 when production = 12
                    AR = 565 when production = 17
   (i) Find the equation of the average revenue function:
        (a) below 10 units of production per week;
        (b) above 10 units of production per week.
   (ii) Assuming that total revenue equals zero if production is zero, find the marginal revenue functions corresponding to the above average revenue functions.
   (iii) Sketch the average revenue and marginal revenue functions.
   (iv) Find the price elasticity of demand for:
        (a) a price rise from \$950;
        (b) a price fall from \$950.
   (v) Interpret your results.

7.4 TURNING POINTS

In Section 6.4.3 we considered quadratic functions and stated that the sign of the coefficient of x^2 determined the shape of the function. With functions that include higher powers of x the graph will have several changes of direction. We can use the method of differentiation developed above to locate both **where** these changes of direction occur and **which way** the change affects the function. This is the method of locating the **maximum** and **minimum** values of a function. By a 'maximum' value we do not necessarily mean one that is greater than all other values (a **global** maximum), it could simply be greater than all neighbouring values only (a **local** maximum). Similar definitions apply to minimum values. For the economic applications at this stage, this distinction between local and global maxima is not of great importance.

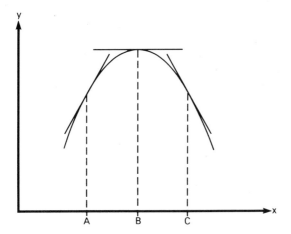

Figure 7.7

If you consider the function represented in Fig. 7.7 you can see that the slopes of the function at points A, B and C are quite different. At point A the function is increasing and thus the slope is positive. At point C the function is decreasing, and thus the slope is negative. However, at point B, it is just changing direction and is neither going up nor going down; therefore the slope is zero. Now the slope of a function can be found by differentiation.

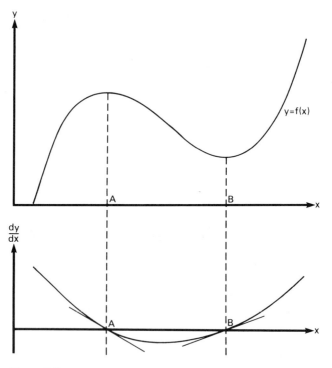

Figure 7.8

In Fig. 7.8, the first graph represents a function which has a maximum at the point A and a minimum at the point B, and the second graph shows dy/dx against x for this function. This shows that to the left of the point A there is a positive slope, but that slope is decreasing. At A there is zero slope, and so dy/dx = 0. After A the original function is decreasing and so dy/dx is negative, but when the point B is reached, where the original function begins to go up again, there will be zero slope, and dy/dx will again be 0.

To the right of point B, the original function is increasing, and hence the second graph is in the positive region.

From this we see that at both turning points the value of dy/dx = 0.

There is more information that we can gain from Fig. 7.8. Looking at the second graph we find that at the point A, the value of dy/dx is decreasing as x increases, and thus has a negative slope, while at the point B, the value of dy/dx is increasing, and thus has a positive slope. Thus, if we can find the slope of the dy/dx function, we can distinguish between maximum points like A and minimum points like B.

In effect, this means differentiating the original function a second time, and we denote this second differential by a slightly different symbol:

$$\frac{d^2y}{dx^2}$$

The process of differentiating is still the same, only it is now applied to the function dy/dx.

The rules for distinguishing a maximum from a minimum value are thus:

For a maximum, $\quad \dfrac{dy}{dx} = 0 \quad$ and $\quad \dfrac{d^2y}{dx^2} < 0$

For a minimum, $\quad \dfrac{dy}{dx} = 0 \quad$ and $\quad \dfrac{d^2y}{dx^2} > 0$

Examples

1. If $\qquad\qquad y = 2x^2 - 8x + 50$

   then $\qquad\qquad \dfrac{dy}{dx} = 4x - 8 = 0$

   therefore $4x = 8$

   and hence $\qquad\qquad x = \dfrac{8}{4} = +2$

   so the turning point is at $x = 2$.

   $\dfrac{d^2y}{dx^2} = 4$, which is **positive**, and so the turning point is a minimum.

   The value of y is

   $2(2)^2 - 8(2) + 50 = 8 - 16 + 50 = 42$

   Thus the function $y = 2x^2 - 8x + 5$ has a minimum point at (2, 42).

2. $\qquad\qquad\qquad\qquad y = \dfrac{1}{3}x^3 - 4x^2 + 15x + 10$

   then $\qquad\qquad \dfrac{dy}{dx} = x^2 - 8x + 15 = 0$

   factorizing gives $\quad (x - 3)(x - 5) = 0$

so $x = 3$ and 5 and there is a turning point for each of these values.

$$\frac{d^2y}{dx^2} = 2x - 8$$

now   at $x = 3$, $2x - 8 = 2(3) - 8 = -2$, negative (max.)

and   at $x = 5$, $2x - 8 = 2(5) - 8 = +2$, positive (min.)

also,   at $x = 3$, $y = \frac{1}{3}(3)^3 - 4(3)^2 + 15(3) + 10 = 28$

and,   at $x = 5$, $y = \frac{1}{3}(5)^3 - 4(5)^2 + 15(5) + 10 = 26.67$

Thus the function

$$y = \frac{1}{3}x^3 - 4x^2 + 15x + 10$$

has a maximum at (3, 28) and a minimum at (5, 26.67).

7.5 ECONOMIC APPLICATIONS II

The economist is often interested in finding the maximum value of certain relationships for profit, sales revenue, welfare, etc., and minimum values, particularly for cost functions. The methods developed above will allow us to specify where these turning points occur.

Examples

1. If a firm has:

$$TR = 40x - 8x^2$$

and $TC = 8 + 16x - x^2$ (x = thousands of units of product)

then its profit function (π) will be the difference between its total revenue and total cost

$$\begin{aligned} \pi &= TR - TC \\ &= (40x - 8x^2) - (8 + 16x - x^2) \\ &= 40x - 8x^2 - 8 - 16x + x^2 \\ &= -8 + 24x - 7x^2 \end{aligned}$$

If we wish to find where maximum profit occurs, we differentiate to give

$$\frac{d\pi}{dx} = 24 - 14x = 0$$

therefore $x = 24/14 = 1.714$ and $d^2\pi/dx^2 = -14$, which is negative, thus maximum.

So the firm will achieve maximum profit at an output of $x = 1.714$, and since x is measured in thousands, this is 1714 units. Profit here is 12.571. If the firm wished to maximize its sales revenue (i.e. TR), we have:

$$TR = 40x - 8x^2$$

$$\frac{dTR}{dx} = 40 - 16x = 0$$

therefore $x = 40/16 = 2.5$ and $d^2TR/dx^2 = -16$, which is negative, thus maximum.

So, maximum sales revenue will be at 2500 units, but profit here would only be 8.25.

2. If a firm's total cost function is

$$TC = 200 + 5x - 6x^2 + x^3$$

then the 200 represents fixed cost, since it does not vary with the level of output. If we remove this fixed cost, we will be left with total variable cost (TVC)

$$\text{TVC} = 5x - 6x^2 + x^3$$

and average variable cost (AVC), can be found by dividing by x:

$$\text{AVC} = 5 - 6x + x^2$$

We often want to know the output to give minimum AVC, and to find this, we differentiate:

$$\frac{d\text{AVC}}{dx} = -6 + 2x = 0$$

therefore $x = 3$

and $\dfrac{d^2\text{AVC}}{dx^2} = +2$, positive, thus minimum.

So, minimum average variable cost is at an output of 3.
(Note that although AVC is negative here, the average cost per unit will be positive because of the fixed costs.)

7.6 FURTHER NOTES

(a) If the function to be differentiated is the product of two functions, then there is a method of differentiating without having to multiply the two functions out, e.g.

$$y = (2x^2 + 10x + 5)(6x^3 + 12x^2)$$

let $\quad u = 2x^2 + 10x + 5$

and $\quad v = 6x^3 + 12x^2$

so if $\quad y = u \cdot v$

then, in general, $\dfrac{dy}{dx} = v \cdot \dfrac{du}{dx} + u \cdot \dfrac{dv}{dx}$

now if $\quad u = 2x^2 + 10x + 5$ then $\dfrac{du}{dx} = 4x + 10$

and if $\quad v = 6x^3 + 12x^2 \quad$ then $\dfrac{dv}{dx} = 18x^2 + 24x$

and $\quad \dfrac{dy}{dx} = (6x^3 + 12x^2)(4x + 10) + (2x^2 + 10x + 5)$
$$\times (18x^2 + 24x)$$
$$= 24x^4 + 60x^3 + 48x^3 + 120x^2 + 36x^4 + 48x^3 + 180x^3 + 240x^2 + 90x^2 + 120\,x$$
$$= 60x^4 + 336x^3 + 450x^2 + 120x$$

(b) If the function to be differentiated consists of one function divided by another, then the following method is appropriate:

$$y = \frac{(10x^2 + 6x + 5)}{(12x^3 + 15x^2)}$$

then let $\quad u = 10x^2 + 6x + 5$

and $\quad v = 12x^3 + 15x^2$

so, if $\quad y = \dfrac{u}{v}$

then, in general, $\dfrac{dy}{dx} = \dfrac{v \cdot \dfrac{du}{dx} - u \cdot \dfrac{dv}{dx}}{v^2}$

if $\qquad u = 10x^2 + 6x + 5$ then $\dfrac{du}{dx} = 20x + 6$

and $\qquad v = 12x^3 + 15x^2$ then $\dfrac{dv}{dx} = 36x^2 + 30x$

$\dfrac{dy}{dx} = \dfrac{(12x^3 + 15x^2)(20x + 6) - (10x^2 + 6x + 5)(36x^2 + 30x)}{(12x^3 + 15x^2)^2}$

$= \dfrac{240x^4 + 300x^3 + 72x^3 + 90x^2 - (360x^4 + 300x^3 + 216x^3 + 180x^2 + 180x^2 + 150x)}{144x^6 + 360x^5 + 225x^4}$

$= \dfrac{-120x^4 - 144x^3 - 270x^2 - 150x}{144x^6 + 360x^5 + 225x^4}$

$= \dfrac{-6x(20x^3 + 24x^2 + 45x + 25)}{x^4(144x^2 + 360x + 225)}$

Note that it is not always necessary to carry out all of the multiplications and simplifications.

(c) If the function to be differentiated is a function of another function, then the following method is appropriate:

if $\qquad y = (10x^2 + 6x)^3$

let $\qquad u = 10x^2 + 6x \qquad$ thus $\dfrac{du}{dx} = 20x + 6$

then $\qquad y = u^3 \qquad$ thus $\dfrac{dy}{du} = 3u^2$

and, in general, $\dfrac{dy}{dx} = \dfrac{dy}{du} \cdot \dfrac{du}{dx}$

$\qquad = 3u^2(20x + 6)$
$\qquad = 3(10x^2 + 6x)^2(20x + 6)$
$\qquad = 3(100x^4 + 120x^3 + 36x^2)(20x + 6)$, etc.

(d) If the function is exponential then

if $\qquad y = e^x$

$\qquad \dfrac{dy}{dx} = e^x$

if $\qquad y = e^{ax}$

$\qquad \dfrac{dy}{dx} = ae^{ax}$

e.g. $\qquad y = e^{2x} \qquad\qquad \dfrac{dy}{dx} = 2e^{2x}$

if $\qquad y = e^{(x^2 + 6)}$

let $\qquad u = x^2 + 6$ $\qquad$ and $\qquad \dfrac{du}{dx} = 2x$

so $\qquad y = e^u$

and $\qquad \dfrac{dy}{dx} = \dfrac{dy}{du} \cdot \dfrac{du}{dx}$

$\qquad\qquad = e^u \cdot 2x = 2x\, e^{(x^2+6)}$

(e) If $\qquad y = \log_e x$

then $\qquad \dfrac{dy}{dx} = \dfrac{1}{x}$

if $\qquad y = \log_e(x^3 + 2x + 3)$

then let $\qquad u = x^3 + 2x + 3$ $\qquad$ and $\qquad \dfrac{du}{dx} = 3x^2 + 2$

so $\qquad y = \log_e(u)$

and $\qquad \dfrac{dy}{dx} = \dfrac{dy}{du} \cdot \dfrac{du}{dx}$

$\qquad\qquad = \dfrac{1}{u} \cdot (3x^2 + 2)$

$\qquad\qquad = \dfrac{3x^2 + 2}{x^3 + 2x + 3}$

7.7 INTEGRATION

Differentiation has allowed us to find an expression for the rate of change of a function; what we need now is some method of reversing the process, i.e. obtaining the original function when the rate of change is known. This process is **integration**.

If $y = x^2$, we know that the rate of change is $2x$; thus if we integrate $2x$ we must get x^2. However, if $y = x^2 + 10$, the rate of change is still $2x$, and integrating will give us x^2 and **not** $x^2 + 10$. This is because the constant in the initial expression has a zero rate of change, and therefore disappears when it is differentiated. When we integrate, then, we should add a constant (c) to the expression we obtain, and we will need some further information if we are to find the specific value of this constant. For example,

if $\qquad \dfrac{dy}{dx} = 2x$

integrating gives $\quad y = x^2 + c$ and if we also know that $y = 10$ if $x = 0$ we have

$\qquad\qquad 10 = 0^2 + c$

therefore $\qquad c = 10$

hence $\qquad y = x^2 + 10$

The symbol used for integration is an 'old style' S, i.e. $\int$, and it is usual to put $\cdot dx$ after the expression to show that we are integrating with respect to x.

Thus $\qquad \int(2x)dx = x^2 + c$

As with differentiation, there is a general formula for integration.

If $\qquad\qquad y = ax^n$ (where a is a constant)

then $\qquad\qquad \int y \cdot dx = \dfrac{ax^{n+1}}{n+1} + c$

for all values of n except $n = -1$. In that special case we have

$$\int \frac{1}{x} \cdot dx = \log_e x + c$$

(cf. the derivative of $\log_e x$ on page 112). Reverting to the more usual case,

if $\qquad\qquad y = 15x^4$

$\qquad\qquad\qquad a = 15 \qquad$ and $\qquad n = 4$

so $\qquad\qquad \int y \cdot dx = \dfrac{15x^{4+1}}{4+1} + c$

$$= \frac{15x^5}{5} + c = 3x^5 + c$$

When there are several terms in the function we may treat each separately, e.g.

$$y = \quad 10x^3 \quad + \quad 6x^2 \quad - \quad 4x \quad + 10$$
$$a = 10,\, n = 3 \qquad a = 6,\, n = 2 \qquad a = -4,\, n = 1$$
$$\int y \cdot dx = \quad \frac{10x^{3+1}}{3+1} \quad + \quad \frac{6x^{2+1}}{2+1} \quad - \quad \frac{4x^{1+1}}{1+1} \quad + 10x + c$$
$$= \quad \frac{10x^4}{4} \quad + \quad \frac{6x^3}{3} \quad - \quad \frac{4x^2}{2} \quad + 10x + c$$
$$= \quad 2.5x^4 \quad + \quad 2x^3 \quad - \quad 2x^2 \quad + 10x + c$$

Note that integrating the constant, 10, gives $10x$.

Integration can be viewed as a summation process; for example, if you sum all of the marginal costs (the cost of producing one more) up to some point, then you will obtain total cost. This idea can also be used to find a sum of areas bounded by a curve between two points (known as definite integration), provided the function is positive. For example:

$$\int_2^5 (10x + 5) \cdot dx$$

means find the integral of $10x + 5$ and then find the sum of all products $(10x + 5).dx$ between the values $x = 2$ and $x = 5$.

Integrating gives the indefinite integral $5x^2 + 5x + c$.

The definite integral is usually written as

$$\left| 5x^2 + 5x \right|_2^5$$

Now evaluate this at $x = 5$, evaluate it at $x = 2$ and subtract the second from the first:

$$(5x^2 + 5x)_{(x=5)} - (5x^2 + 5x)_{(x=2)}$$
$$(125 - 25) \quad - (20 + 10)$$
$$150 \qquad - \qquad 30 \qquad\qquad = 120$$

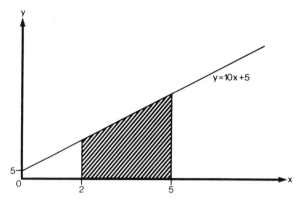

Figure 7.9

This problem is illustrated in Fig. 7.9, the shaded area being the 120 found above. Note that we did not need to include the constant c when finding the definite integral, since it would vanish when we subtract.

Within economics, the process of integration will allow us to go from marginal functions to total functions.

Thus
$$\int MR \cdot dx = TR + c$$
$$\int MC \cdot dx = TC + c$$

But with TR, there is rarely any revenue if output is zero, so in general the constant will also be zero. With TC there is a cost to the firm even if no production takes place, and so c will be non-zero and positive. It will represent fixed cost.

7.8 ECONOMIC SUMMARY

Figure 7.10 summarizes the application of calculus to simple economic models, usually of one firm or one market.

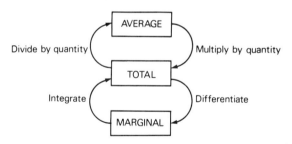

Figure 7.10

7.9 PROBLEMS

Find the maximum and/or minimum of each of the following functions, checking the second order conditions (i.e. d^2y/dx^2):

1. $y = x^2 - 5x + 14$.
2. $y = -2x^2 + 20x + 25$.
3. $y = 0.5x^2 - x + 10$.
4. $y = 5x^2 + 10x + 20$.
5. $y = 20x + 4$.
6. $y = \dfrac{1}{3} x^3 - 4x^2 + 15x + 10$.
7. $y = \dfrac{1}{3} x^3 - 11x^2 + 40x + 20$.
8. $y = 2x^3 - 15x^2 + 24x + 20$.
9. $y = \dfrac{1}{3} x^3 - 7x^2 - 120x + 10\,000$.
10. $y = -3x^3 + 24x^2 - 60x + 64$.
11. $y = \dfrac{1}{3} x^3 + 6x^2 + 13x - 10$.
12. A firm has a total revenue function $TR = 3x^2 - 25x$ and a total cost function $TC = \dfrac{1}{4} x^3 - 3x^2 + 20x + 50$. Find the output level for maximum profit, and the level of profit at this point. What price will be charged?
13. A monopolist has a demand function $P = 30 - 0.75Q$ and a total cost function $TC = 30 + 9Q + 0.3Q^2$. Find the value of Q to give maximum profits, and the profit level at this point.
14. A simple economic model has the following functions:

    $MR = 1000 - 8Q$ $\qquad$ $MC = 0.1Q^2 - 18Q + 1000$
    $TR = 0$ if $Q = 0$ $\qquad$ $TC = 0$ if $Q = 0$

    (a) Find the profit function and hence determine the level of output for maximum profit, and the level of profit.
    (b) Find also the level of output to maximize sales revenue (TR) and the level of profit at this point.
    (c) What will be the prices charged at the two outputs found above?
    (d) What will be the average cost and the marginal cost at these two outputs?
15. A company's demand function is given by $AR = 60 - 4x$ and its average variable cost by $AVC = x^2 - 5x + 30$ with fixed costs of 50. Find the level of output to give maximum profit.

Differentiate each of the following functions:

16. $y = (3x^2 + 2)(x + 3)$.
17. $y = (6x^3 + 4x^2 + 10)(2x^2 + 6x)$.
18. $y = (x^4 - 10x)(20 - 4x - x^4)$.
19. $y = \dfrac{2x}{3x - 2}$.
20. $y = \dfrac{(1 + x)}{(2x^2 + 1)}$.
21. $y = \dfrac{(3x^2 - 108)}{x + 6}$.
22. $y = (4x + 10)^4$.
23. $y = (x^2 + 2x + 1)^3$.
24. $y = (x^3 + 10)^2$.

Integrate each of the following functions with respect to x. Check your answer by differentiating the integral to obtain the original function in each case.

25. $y = 10x + 2$.
26. $y = 15x^2 + 6x + 5$.
27. $y = 0.5x^2 + 10x + 4x^{-3}$.
28. $y = 20$.

29. $y = 14x^4 + 10x^3 + 6x^2 + 5x + 3$.

30. Evaluate $\displaystyle\int_0^5 (x + 6)\cdot dx$.

31. Evaluate $\displaystyle\int_3^6 (-x^2 + 2x + 50)\cdot dx$.

32. Evaluate $\displaystyle\int_2^3 (x^3 + 6x^2 + 100)\cdot dx$.

7.10 FUNCTIONS OF MORE THAN ONE VARIABLE

The simple economic models so far discussed embody functions of only **one variable**. As we move on to consider more complex economic and business situations, we find that there are **several** factors which will affect the outcome. Where the exact relationship is unknown, it must be estimated by statistical means (see Chapter 18), but for many examples in economics an exact function can be specified. For a duopoly (two sellers), the sales of one company's product may be a function of their own price, the price charged by the competitor and the respective amounts spent on advertising. In production theory, it is the **combination** of both capital and labour which determines the amount produced and not just one factor of production; while in welfare economics we consider the combination of goods which is available to the consumer or community. For all of these situations, while we are interested in the final outcome of particular decisions, we are also interested in the individual contribution of each factor, and also in ways of making optimal decisions on each factor in order to optimize the final outcome.

Consider a function such that y is determined by x and z; for example:

$$y = 10x^2 + 6xz + 15z^2$$

We can find the rate of change of y with respect to x if we **temporarily** hold the value of z constant when differentiating. (To distinguish this from differentiation where $y = f(x)$ we now use a new symbol $\partial y/\partial x$.)

Differentiating, we have:

$$\frac{\partial y}{\partial x} = 20x + 6z$$

Note that $10x^2$ was treated as before, giving $20x$, $6xz$ was treated as $(6z)x$, giving $6z$ and $15z^2$ was treated as a constant.

We can also find the rate of change of y with respect to z by temporarily holding x constant.

Thus $\qquad \dfrac{\partial y}{\partial z} = 6x + 30z$

The process described above is known as **partial differentiation** since we are finding a rate of change while part of the function is held constant. As with the function of a single variable, each of the functions we have obtained may be differentiated again, but note the number of outcomes:

$\dfrac{\partial^2 y}{\partial x^2} = 20$, i.e. holding z constant again and differentiating $20x + 6z$.

$\dfrac{\partial^2 y}{\partial z^2} = 30$, i.e. holding x constant again and differentiating $6x + 30z$.

$\dfrac{\partial^2 y}{\partial x \, \partial z} = 6$, i.e. holding x constant and differentiating $20x + 6z$.

$\dfrac{\partial^2 y}{\partial z \, \partial x} = 6$, i.e. holding z constant and differentiating $6x + 30z$.

Note, however, that $\dfrac{\partial^2 y}{\partial x \, \partial z} = \dfrac{\partial^2 y}{\partial z \, \partial x}$ in general.

We may now use these results to find the maxima and minima for a particular function. For a **maximum**:

$$\frac{\partial y}{\partial x} = 0 \quad \text{and} \quad \frac{\partial y}{\partial z} = 0$$

$$\frac{\partial^2 y}{\partial x^2} < 0 \quad \text{and} \quad \frac{\partial^2 y}{\partial z^2} < 0$$

and
$$\left(\frac{\partial^2 y}{\partial x^2} \right) \left(\frac{\partial^2 y}{\partial z^2} \right) \geq \left(\frac{\partial^2 y}{\partial x \, \partial z} \right)^2$$

For a **minimum**:

$$\frac{\partial y}{\partial x} = 0 \quad \text{and} \quad \frac{\partial y}{\partial z} = 0$$

$$\frac{\partial^2 y}{\partial x^2} > 0 \quad \text{and} \quad \frac{\partial^2 y}{\partial z^2} > 0$$

and
$$\left(\frac{\partial^2 y}{\partial x^2} \right) \left(\frac{\partial^2 y}{\partial z^2} \right) \geq \left(\frac{\partial^2 y}{\partial x \, \partial z} \right)^2$$

Examples   1. If
$$y = 5x^2 + 4xz - 60x - 40z + 4z^2 + 1000$$

then
$$\frac{\partial y}{\partial x} = 10x + 4z - 60 = 0$$

$$\frac{\partial y}{\partial z} = 4x - 40 + 8z = 0$$

Rearranging gives:

$10x + 4z =$	60	7.1
$4x + 8z =$	40	7.2

Equation 7.1 × 2 is $20x + 8z = 120$

Subtract $16x \quad\quad = +80$

Therefore, $x = 5$

substituting gives $z = 2.5$

$$\frac{\partial^2 y}{\partial x^2} = 10, \qquad\qquad \frac{\partial^2 y}{\partial z^2} = 8; \text{ both } \textbf{positive}$$

$$\frac{\partial^2 y}{\partial x\, \partial z} = 4$$

but $\qquad \left(\dfrac{\partial^2 y}{\partial x^2}\right)\left(\dfrac{\partial^2 y}{\partial z^2}\right) = 10 \times 8 = 80 > \left(\dfrac{\partial^2 y}{\partial x\, \partial z}\right)^2 = 4^2 = 16$

Thus, the function has a **minimum** when $x = 5$ and $z = 2.5$ (the y value will be 800).

2. Consider a monopolist with two products, A and B, who wishes to maximize his total profit. The two demand functions are:

$$P_A = 80 - q_A$$
$$P_B = 50 - 2q_B$$

and the total cost function is

$$TC = 100 + 8q_A + 6q_B + 14q_A^2 + 4q_B^2 + 4q_A q_B$$

The total revenue function will consist of two parts:

$$TR_A = 80q_A - q_A^2 \quad \text{and} \quad TR_B = 50q_B - 2q_B^2$$

thus the total profit function is

$$\pi = TR_A + TR_B - TC$$
$$= -100 + 72q_A + 44q_B - 15q_A^2 - 6q_B^2 - 4q_A q_B$$

$$\frac{\partial \pi}{\partial q_A} = 72 - 30q_A - 4q_B = 0$$

$$\frac{\partial \pi}{\partial q_B} = 44 - 12q_B - 4q_A = 0$$

rearranging these equations gives:

$30q_A +$	$4q_B =$	72	7.3
$4q_A +$	$12q_B =$	44	7.4

Equation 7.3 $\times$ 3 is $\qquad 90q_A + 12q_B = 216$

Subtract $\qquad\qquad 86q_A \qquad\quad = 172$

Therefore $\qquad\qquad\qquad\quad q_A = 2$

substituting gives $\qquad\qquad\quad q_B = 3$

$$\frac{\partial^2 \pi}{\partial q_A^2} = -30, \qquad\qquad \frac{\partial^2 \pi}{\partial q_B^2} = -12; \text{ both } \textbf{negative}$$

$$\frac{\partial^2 \pi}{\partial q_A\, \partial q_B} = -4$$

but $(-30)(-12) > (-4)^2$

Thus maximum profit is where the quantity of A sold is 2, and the quantity of B sold is 3. By substitution into the profit function, we find that the level of profit

---

will be 38. The prices charged for the two products are found from the demand functions; the price of A is 78 and the price of B is 44.

7.11 MAXIMIZATION AND MINIMIZATION SUBJECT TO CONSTRAINTS

Many economics problems have **limitations upon the solution** that may be obtained: production may be limited by the available supply of raw materials or by the capacity of the current factory; cost may have to be kept to a minimum subject to certain, predetermined, output levels; or a consumer's utility maximized subject to his budget. In each of these cases, if we simply maximize or minimize the function it is unlikely that this will also satisfy the constraint and thus we need to take the constraint into consideration during the optimization process. For simple functions it may be possible to substitute the constraint into the function, but the more general method is that of **Lagrangian multipliers.**

7.11.1 Substitution

For functions of two variables, we may be able to substitute the constraint into the function. Consider the following example:

$$z = 10 + 3x - 4x^2 + 10y - 2y^2 + xy$$

to be maximized subject to the constraint that $x = 2y$.
   Substituting, we have:

$$z = 10 + 6y - 16y^2 + 10y - 2y^2 + 2y^2$$
$$= 10 + 16y - 16y^2$$

$$\frac{dz}{dy} = 16 - 32y = 0 \qquad\qquad \text{therefore } y = \tfrac{1}{2} \text{ and } x = 1$$

$$\frac{d^2z}{dy^2} = -32 \qquad\qquad \text{therefore maximum}$$

Exercise Find the values of x and y to maximize the function without the constraint. (Answer: $x = 22/31$; $y = 83/31$.)

7.11.2 Lagrangian multipliers

For more complex functions the method above will become tedious and thus we now place the constraint as part of the function we are to optimize. Again, we will work through an example:

$$z = 10x - 4x^2 + 20y - y^2 + 4xy$$

subject to $2x + 4y = 100$.

The first step is to rearrange the constraint as follows:

$$100 - 2x - 4y = 0$$

we then multiply it by a new unknown value, λ (lambda), which is the Lagrangian multiplier:

$$\lambda(100 - 2x - 4y) = 0$$

and this function is added to the function z to give a new function z^*.

Therefore $z^* = 10x - 4x^2 + 20y - y^2 + 4xy + \lambda(100 - 2x - 4y)$

This will not change the value of z since, as we have just seen, the term added is equal to 0, and it can be shown that if we find the optimum point or points of the function z^* then these will be the optimum points for the original function z subject to the constraint.

Partially differentiating z^*, we have:

$$\frac{\partial z^*}{\partial x} = 10 - 8x + 4y - 2\lambda = 0$$

$$\frac{\partial z^*}{\partial y} = 20 - 2y + 4x - 4\lambda = 0$$

and $\quad \dfrac{\partial z^*}{\partial \lambda} = 100 - 2x - 4y = 0$ (thus satisfying the constraint).

As we have seen in Chapter 6, there are several ways of solving three simultaneous equations and these will not be repeated here: solving the three equations gives

$$x = 10 \qquad y = 20 \qquad \lambda = 5$$

(We do not strictly need to know the value of λ.)

Further differentiation shows that $x = 10, y = 20$ is a maximum for the function z subject to the constraint.

$$\left(\text{Note that although } \left(\frac{\partial^2 z}{\partial x^2}\right)\left(\frac{\partial^2 z}{\partial y^2}\right) = \left(\frac{\partial^2 z}{\partial y \partial x}\right)^2 , \text{ and not 'greater than',} \right.$$

$$\left. \text{there is sufficient evidence to show a maximum.} \right)$$

A second example; consider a Cobb-Douglas production function $Q = 10 L^{\frac{1}{2}} K^{\frac{1}{2}}$ subject to the constraint that $4L + 10K = 100$, where L is the amount of labour and K is the amount of capital.

Rearranging the constraint, we have:

$$100 - 4L - 10K = 0$$
and $\quad \lambda(100 - 4L - 10K) = 0$

We thus wish to maximize the function

$$Q^* = 10L^{\frac{1}{2}} K^{\frac{1}{2}} + \lambda(100 - 4L - 10K)$$

$$\frac{\partial Q^*}{\partial L} = 5L^{-\frac{1}{2}} K^{\frac{1}{2}} - 4\lambda = 0 \tag{7.5}$$

$$\frac{\partial Q^*}{\partial K} = 5L^{\frac{1}{2}} K^{-\frac{1}{2}} - 10\lambda = 0 \tag{7.6}$$

$$\frac{\partial Q^*}{\partial \lambda} = 100 - 4L - 10K = 0 \tag{7.7}$$

Rearranging eqns 7.5 and 7.6 we have:

$$\lambda = \frac{5K^{\frac{1}{2}}}{4L^{\frac{1}{2}}} \quad \text{and} \quad \lambda = \frac{5L^{\frac{1}{2}}}{10K^{\frac{1}{2}}}$$

thus

$$\frac{5K^{\frac{1}{2}}}{4L^{\frac{1}{2}}} = \frac{5L^{\frac{1}{2}}}{10K^{\frac{1}{2}}}$$

or $\qquad 50K = 20L$

or $\qquad L = 2.5K \qquad\qquad\qquad\qquad\qquad$ 7.8

Substituting into eqn 7.6, gives

$$10K + 10K = 100$$

or $\qquad K = 5$

thus $\qquad L = 12.5 \qquad\qquad\qquad$ (from eqn 7.8)

Further partial differentiation shows this to be a maximum, and thus production (Q) is maximized subject to the constraint when $L = 12.5$ and $K = 5$. Note that the function Q itself, when unconstrained, has no maximum value.

Exercise   Check that the constraint is satisfied and find the value of Q.
(Answer: $Q = 79.06$.)

7.12 PROBLEMS

Find the first partial derivatives for each of the following:
1. $y = 10x^2 z^3$.
2. $y = 20x^3 z + 4x^2 z^2 + 15xz^3 + 20x^4 - 3z^2$.
3. $y = 40x + 20z$.
4. $y = 30x^2 z^2 + 40xz + 10$.
5. $Q = 10A^{\frac{1}{2}} B^{\frac{1}{2}}$.

Locate and identify the turning point for each of the following:
6. $y = 1000 + 18x - 1.5x^2 + 28z - 2xz - 2z^2$.
7. $y = 50 + 2x^2 - 25x + 5xz - 40z + 4z^2$.
8. $y = x^2 + xz + z^2$.
9. $y = 10x^2 + 4xz - 24x + 2z^2 - 8z$.
10. $z = 19x - 4x^2 + 16y - 2xy - 4y^2$.
11. If a firm's total costs are related to its workforce and capital equipment by the function:

$$TC = 10L^2 + 10K^2 - 25L - 50K - 5LK + 2000$$

where L = thousands of employees and K = thousands of pounds invested in capital equipment, find the combination of labour and capital to give minimum total cost. Find this cost and show that it is a minimum.

12. A monopolist has two products, X and Y, which have the following demand functions:

$$P_X = 26.2 - X$$
$$P_Y = 24 - 2Y$$

The total costs of the monopolist are given by:

$$TC = 5X^2 + XY + 3Y^2$$

Determine the amounts of X and Y the monopolist should produce to maximize profit, and the amount of profit produced.

13. A company is able to sell two products, X and Y, which have demand functions:

$$P_X = 52 - 2X$$
$$P_Y = 20 - 3Y$$

and has a total cost function

$$\text{TC} = 10 + 3X^2 + 2Y^2 + 2XY$$

    (a) Determine the profit maximizing levels of output for X and Y and the level of this profit.

    (b) If product Y were not produced, determine the production level of X to maximize profit and the level of this profit.

    (c) If product X were not produced, determine the production level of Y to maximize profit and the level of this profit.

Maximize or minimize the following functions subject to their constraints, using either substitution or the method of Lagrangian multipliers.

14. $y = 10 + 20x + 6z - 4x^2 - 2z^2$ subject to $x = 3z$.

15. $y = 4x^2 - 6x + 7z + 3z^2 + 2xz$ subject to $x = 5z$.

16. $z = 10x - x^2 + 14y - 2y^2 + xy$ subject to $2x + 3y = 100$.

17. $z = 6x - 3x^2 + 40y - 8y^2 + 5xy$ subject to $4x - 5y = 30$.

18. $z = 2xy$ subject to $x + y = 1$.

19. Maximize the production function

$$Q = 4L^{\frac{1}{2}} K^{\frac{1}{2}}$$

subject to the constraint that $3L + 5K = 200$, finding the values for L and K.

20. Find the values of L and K to maximize the production function

$$Q = 8L^{\frac{1}{4}} K^{\frac{3}{4}}$$

subject to the constraint $L + 8K = 1000$.

21. A firm's profit is given by the function

$$\pi = 600 - 3x^2 - 4x + 2xy - 5y^2 + 48y$$

where π denotes profit, x output and y advertising expenditure.

    (a) Find the profit maximizing values of x and y and hence determine the maximum profit. Confirm that second order conditions are satisfied.

    (b) If now the firm is subject to a budget constraint $2x + y = 5$ determine the new values of x and y which maximize profit.

    (c) Without further calculation determine the effect of a constraint $2x + y = 8$.

8 The time value of money

In the civilized world we have come to value money for what it can buy us now and for what it can buy us in the future. As individuals we continually decide whether to purchase items now with the aid of a loan or wait until our savings are sufficient. In making these decisions we need to consider how much the loan would cost and how long saving would take. House purchase for many is now the most important single expenditure of a lifetime involving sums many times their annual disposable income. Few would consider saving the complete amount before buying, even if they expected savings to keep abreast of inflation. In general, a deposit is saved and the rest acquired by a mortgage or an endowment policy.

The performance of a business for the most part is assessed in terms of monetary value. It may aim to provide a good service, a good product and achieve a good market share but it will still need to make and continue to make money to survive. Decisions will continually need to be made between competing projects with differing costs and differing returns over time.

In this chapter we consider what makes us save, invest and borrow in the ways we do.

8.1 COMPOUND INTEREST

An interest rate, usually quoted as a percentage, gives the gain we can expect from each £1 saved. If, for example, we were offered 10% per annum we would expect a gain of 10 pence each year for each £1 invested. If this interest were compounded, the gain would be added each time the saving were carried forward in order to compute the interest for the next period. If the interest rate were 10%, after 1 year our £1 would be worth £1.10 and after 2 years our £1 would be worth £1.21.

The sum at the end of each year can be calculated using the following formula:

$$A_t = A_0 \left(1 + \frac{r}{100}\right)^t$$

where A_0 is the initial sum invested, A_t is the sum after t years and r is the rate of interest as a percentage.

Example
What amount would an initial sum of £100 accumulate to in 8 years if it were invested at a compound interest rate of 10% per annum?
By substitution we obtain

$$A_8 = 100 \left(1 + \frac{10}{100}\right)^8 = 100 \, (1.1)^8 = 100(2.143588)$$

$$= £214.36$$

After 8 years of investment, at a compound rate of interest of 10%, the initial sum of £100 would be worth £214.36.

A proof of this formula will demonstrate the principle involved. Suppose we invest an initial sum of A_0 at an annual interest rate of $r\%$. After 1 year, this sum would be worth

$$A_1 = A_0 + \frac{r}{100} \, A_0$$

$$= A_0 \left(1 + \frac{r}{100}\right)^1$$

The term in brackets gives the annual gain of each £1. An interest rate of 10% would give a multiplicative factor of 1.1 in the first year. If the sum at the end of the first year is then carried forward for one more year, the investment of A_0 at the end of the second year would be worth

$$A_2 = A_1 + \frac{r}{100} \, A_1$$

$$= A_1 \left(1 + \frac{r}{100}\right)^1$$

We can substitute the value we already have for A_1 to obtain

$$A_2 = A_0 \left(1 + \frac{r}{100}\right)^1 \left(1 + \frac{r}{100}\right)^1$$

$$= A_0 \left(1 + \frac{r}{100}\right)^2$$

If the interest rate is 10%, then the multiplicative factor of 1.1 is used twice to obtain the value of the investment after 2 years.

Continuing in this way, we can obtain the general formula for any number of years t:

$$A_t = A_0 \left(1 + \frac{r}{100}\right)^t$$

The example has assumed that the interest is paid at the end of the year, so that the £1 invested at 10% gains 10p each year. Some investments are of this type, but many others give or charge interest every 6 months (e.g. building societies) or more frequently (e.g. interbank loans interest is charged per day). The concept of compound interest can deal with these situations provided that we can identify how many times per year interest is paid. If, for example, 5% interest is paid every 6 months, during the second 6 months we will be earning interest on more than the initial amount invested. Given an initial sum of £100, after 6 months we have £100 + £5 (interest) = £105 and after 1 year we would have £105 + £5.25 (interest) = £110.25.

Putting this idea into the formula above

$$A_1 = £100 \left(1 + \frac{0.1}{2}\right)^{2\times1} = £110.25$$

i.e. divide the annual rate of interest (10% in this case) by the number of payments each year, and multiply the power of the bracket by the same number of periods.

More generally,

$$A_t = A_0 \left(1 + \frac{r}{100 \times m}\right)^{mt}$$

where m is the number of payments per year.

8.1.1 The use of present value tables

The growth of an investment is determined by the interest rate and the time scale of the investment as we can see from the multiplicative factor:

$$\left(1 + \frac{r}{100}\right)^t$$

Any mathematical term of this kind can be tabulated to save repeated calculations. In this particular case, the tabulation takes the form of present value factors (see Appendix 6) which can be used indirectly to find a compound interest factor. These factors are the reciprocal of what is required:

$$present\ value\ factor = \frac{1}{\left(1 + \frac{r}{100}\right)^t}$$

hence

$$\left(1 + \frac{r}{100}\right)^t = \frac{1}{present\ value\ factor}$$

If we were interested in the growth over 8 years of an investment made at 10% per annum we could first find the present value factor of 0.4665 from tables and then use the reciprocal value of 2.1436 to calculate a corresponding accumulated sum.

Example

What amount would an initial sum of £150 accumulate to in 8 years if it were invested at a compound interest rate of 10% per annum?
    Using tables

$$\begin{aligned}
A_8 &= 150 \times \frac{1}{0.4665} \\
&= 150 \times 2.1436 \\
&= £321.54
\end{aligned}$$

It should be noted that the use of tables with four significant digits sometimes results in rounding errors.

8.2 DEPRECIATION

In the same way that an investment can increase by a constant percentage each year as given by the interest rate, the value of an asset can decline by a constant percentage. If we use r as the depreciation rate we can adapt the formula for compound interest to give

$$A_t = A_0 \left(1 - \frac{r}{100}\right)^t$$

where A_t becomes the book value after t years.

Example

Use the 'declining balance method' of depreciation to find the value after 3 years of an asset initially worth £20 000 and whose value declines at 15% per annum.

By substitution we obtain

$$A_3 = 20\ 000 \left(1 - \frac{15}{100}\right)^3$$
$$= 20\ 000\ (0.85)^3$$
$$= £12\ 282.50$$

A manipulation of this formula gives the following expression for the rate of depreciation.

$$r = \left(1 - \sqrt[t]{\frac{A_t}{A_0}}\right) \times 100$$

where A_0 is the original cost and A_t is the salvage (or scrap) value after t years.

Example

The cost of a particular asset is known to be £20 000 and its salvage value is estimated at £8000 after a useful life of 5 years. Determine the book value of this asset at the end of each year.

By substitution

$$r = \left(1 - \sqrt[5]{\frac{8000}{20\ 000}}\right) \times 100$$
$$= 16.74\%$$

We can now depreciate the asset at 16.74% a year.

	£
Cost	20 000.00
Depreciation year 1 (16.74% of £20 000)	3 348.00
Book value (end of year 1)	16 652.00
Depreciation year 2 (16.74% of £16 652)	2 787.54
Book value (end of year 2)	13 864.46
Depreciation year 3 (16.74% of £13 864.46)	2 320.91
Book value (end of year 3)	11 543.55
Depreciation year 4 (16.74% of £11 543.55)	1 932.39
Book value (end of year 4)	9 611.16
Depreciation year 5 (16.74% of £9611.16)	1 608.91
Book value (end of year 5)	8 002.25

It is worth noting that this procedure is unlikely to provide the scrap value exactly, due to the rounding errors. In this case, it is an accounting practice to make an adjustment in the final year depreciation to get the exact salvage value.

8.3 PRESENT VALUE

The formula for compound interest can be rearranged to allow the calculation of the amount of money required now to achieve a specific sum at some future point in time given a rate of interest:

$$A_0 = A_t \ \frac{1}{\left(1 + \dfrac{r}{100}\right)^t}$$

Example

What amount would need to be invested now to provide a sum of £242 in 2 years' time given that the market rate of interest is 10%?

By substitution we obtain

$$A_0 = 242 \times \frac{1}{\left(1 + \dfrac{10}{100}\right)^2} = 242 \times 0.826446 = £200$$

The amount required now to produce a future sum can be taken as a measure of the worth or the **present value** of that future sum. A choice between £200 now and £200 in 2 years' time would be an easy one for most people. Most would prefer the money in their pockets now. Even if the £200 were intended for a holiday in 2 years' time, it presents the owner with opportunities; one of which is to invest the sum for 2 years and gain £42. The choice between £200 now and £242 in 2 years' time, however, would be rather more difficult. If the interest rate were 10%, the present value of £242 in 2 years time would be £200. Indeed, if one were concerned only with interest rates there would be an indifference between the two choices.

Present value provides a method of comparing monies available at different points in time. As such, it presents those in business with a basis for making decisions. The calculation of the present value of future sums of money is referred to as **discounting**.

Example

You need to decide between two business opportunities. The first opportunity will pay £700 in 4 years' time and the second opportunity will pay £850 in 6 years' time. You have been advised to discount these future sums by using the interest rate of 8%.

By substitution we are able to calculate a present value for each of the future sums.

First opportunity:
$$A_0 = 700 \times \frac{1}{\left(1 + \dfrac{8}{100}\right)^4}$$
$$= 700 \times 0.7350$$
$$= £514.50$$

Second opportunity:
$$A_0 = 850 \times \frac{1}{\left(1 + \dfrac{8}{100}\right)^6}$$
$$= 850 \times 0.6302$$
$$= £535.67$$

On the basis of present value (or discounting) we would choose the second opportunity as the better business proposition. In practice, we would need to consider a range of other factors.

The present value factors of 0.7350 and 0.6302 calculated in this example could have been obtained directly from tables (see Section 8.1.1). **Look at the present value factors given in appendix 6.** We can explain the meaning of these factors in two ways. Firstly, if we invest $73\frac{1}{2}$ pence at 8% per annum it will grow to £1 in 4 years and 63 pence (0.6302) will grow to £1 in 6 years. Secondly, if the rate of interest is 8% per annum, £1 in 4 years' time is worth $73\frac{1}{2}$ pence now and £1 in 6 years' time is worth 63 pence now.

Example

A business needs to choose between two investment options. It has been decided to discount future returns at 12%. The expected revenues and initial cost are given as follows:

| | Estimated end of year revenue | |
Year	Option 1	Option 2
1	300	350
2	350	350
3	410	350
Cost in year 0	300	250

In calculating the present value from different options we generally refer to a discount rate or the rate of return on capital rather than the interest rate. These rates tend to be higher than the market interest rate and reflect the cost of capital to a particular business. Net present value (NPV) for each option is the sum of the constituent present values.

The present value factors can be obtained directly from tables or calculated using $(1 + 0.12)^{-t}$ for the years $t = 1$ to 3. In this example, the costs are immediate so therefore not discounted.

Year	Present value factors	Revenues Option 1	Option 2	Present value Option 1	Option 2
1	0.8929	300	350	267.87	312.515
2	0.7972	350	350	279.02	279.02
3	0.7118	410	350	291.838	249.13
		Present value (PV)		838.728	840.665
		Cost		− 300	− 250
		Net present value (NPV)		538.728	590.665

Although the total revenue over 3 years is slightly higher with option 1, the value now to a business is higher with option 2. A more immediate revenue presents a business with more immediate opportunities. It can be seen in this example that option 2 offers the business an extra £50 in the first year which can itself be used for additional gain, and is especially useful in maintaining cash flow.

The comparison of these two options depends crucially on the 'time value of money', that is the discount rate, the estimates given for revenue and the completeness of information.

This type of exercise looks straightforward in a textbook but presents a series of problems when it is to be used in business. Initial costs of each project to be considered will be known, but there may be extra costs involved in the future which cannot be even estimated at the start, e.g. a change in tariffs in a country to which the company exports. All further cash flow information must be estimated, since it is to come in the future, and is thus open to some doubt: if we are dealing with a new product these cash flows will be based on market research (see Chapter 1 on survey methods).

A further practical difficulty is to decide upon which discount rate to use in the calculations. This could be:

(a) the market rate of interest;
(b) the rate of return gained by the company on other projects;
(c) the average rate of return in the industry;
(d) a target rate of return set by the Board of Directors; or
(e) one of these plus a factor to allow for the 'riskiness' of the project — high risk projects being discounted at a higher rate of interest.

High risk projects are likely to be discriminated against in two ways: by the discount rate used which is likely to be high, and in the estimated cash flows which are often conservatively estimated.

All attempts to use this type of present value calculation to decide between projects make an implicit assumption that the project adopted will succeed.

Net present value is only an **aid** to management in deciding between projects, as it only considers the monetary factors, and those only as far as they are known, or can be estimated: there are many personal, social and political factors which may be highly relevant to the decision. If a company were considering moving its factory to a new site, several sites may be considered, and the net present value of each assessed for the next 5 years. However, if one site is in an area that the managing director (or spouse) dislikes intensely, then it is not likely to be chosen. The workforce may be unwilling to move far, so a site 500 miles away could present difficulties. There may be further environmental problems, which are not costed by the company, but are a cost to the community, e.g. smoke, river pollution, extra traffic on country roads.

Exercises

1. Should a company try to include environmental (or social) costs in its calculations of net present value? How could these be incorporated into the calculations?
2. Evaluate the two investment options given in the example on page 137 using a discount rate of 9%.
   (Answer: option 1, NPV = £586.42; option 2, NPV = £635.96.)
3. Suppose we are given more complete information on the two options. The business discovers that it will cost £10 a year in each of years 1 to 3 to implement option 1 and cost an additional £20 immediately to implement option 2. In addition, option 1 will have a scrap value (book value) of £30 at the end of year 3 and option 2 a scrap value of £28 at the end of year 4. Use a discount rate of 10% to evaluate these two options and comment on your analysis.
   (Answer: option 1, NPV = £567.67; option 2, NPV = £619.50.)

8.4 INCREMENTAL PAYMENTS

In Section 8.1 we considered the growth of an initial investment when subject to compound interest. Many saving schemes will involve the same sort of initial investment but will then add or subtract given amounts at regular intervals. If x is an amount added at the end of each year, then the sum receivable, S, at the end of t years is given by

$$S = A_0 \left(1 + \frac{r}{100}\right)^t + \frac{x\left(1 + \frac{r}{100}\right)^t - x}{r/100}$$

An outline proof of this particular formula is given in Section 8.7.

1. A saving scheme involves an initial investment of £100 and an additional £50 at the end of each year for the next 3 years. Calculate the receivable sum at the end of 3 years assuming that the annual rate of interest paid is 10%.

By substitution we obtain

$$S = 100 \left(1 + \frac{10}{100}\right)^3 + \frac{50 \left(1 + \frac{10}{100}\right)^3 - 50}{10/100}$$

$$= £133.10 + £165.50$$
$$= £298.60$$

The sum is in two parts, the first being the value of the initial investment (£133.10) and the second being the value of the end of year increments (£165.50).

An alternative is to calculate the growing sum year by year.

	Value of investment
Initial sum	£100
Value at the end of year 1	£110
+ increment of £50	£160
Value at the end of year 2	£176
+ increment of £50	£226
Value at the end of year 3	£248.60
+ increment of £50	£298.60

If the rate of interest or the amount added at the end of the year changed from year to year it would no longer be valid to substitute into the formula given.

In the case of regular withdrawals, we use a negative increment.

2. It has been decided to withdraw £600 at the end of each year for 5 years from an investment of £30 000 made at 8% per annum compound.

In this example, we have a negative increment of £600. By substitution we obtain:

$$S = 30\ 000 (1 + 0.08)^5 + \frac{(-600) (1 + 0.08)^5 - (-600)}{0.08}$$

$$= 44\ 079.842 - 3519.9606$$
$$= £40\ 559.881$$

8.4.1 Sinking funds

A business may wish to set aside a fixed sum of money at regular intervals to achieve a specific sum at some future point in time. This sum, known as a sinking fund, may be in anticipation of some future investment need such as the replacement of vehicles or machines.

How much would we need to set aside at the end of each of the following 5 years to accumulate £20 000, given an interest rate of 12% per annum compound?

We can substitute the following values:

S = £20 000
A_0 = 0 (no saving is being made immediately)
r = 12%
t = 5 years

to obtain

$$20\ 000 = 0 + \frac{x(1 + 0.12)^5 - x}{0.12}$$

$$20\ 000 \times 0.12 = 0.7623x$$

$$x = £3148.37$$

where x is the amount we would need to set aside at the end of each year.

8.4.2 Annuities

An annuity is an arrangement whereby a fixed sum is paid in exchange for regular amounts to be received at fixed intervals for a specified time. Such schemes are usually offered by insurance companies and are particularly attractive to retired people.

How much is it worth paying for an annuity of £1000 receivable for the next 5 years and payable at the end of each year, given interest rates of 11% per annum?

We can substitute the following values:

$S = 0$ (final value of investment)
$x = -£1000$ (a negative increment)
$r = 11\%$
$t = 5$

to obtain

$$0 = A_0(1 + 0.11)^5 + \frac{(-1000)(1 + 0.11)^5 - (-1000)}{0.11}$$

$$A_0 = 1000 \times \frac{(1 + 0.11)^5 - 1}{0.11 \times (1 + 0.11)^5}$$

$$= 1000 \times \frac{1 - \frac{1}{(1 + 0.11)^5}}{0.11}$$

$$= 1000 \times 3.69589$$

$$= £3695.89$$

where A_0 is the value of the annuity. (Note that $\dfrac{1}{(1 + 0.11)^5} = 0.5935$ from Appendix 6.)

The present value of the annuity is £3695. We could have calculated the value of the annuity by discounting each of £1000 receivable for the next 5 years by present value factors.

8.4.3 Mortgages

The most common form of mortgage is an agreement to make regular repayments in return for the initial sum borrowed. At the end of the repayment period the outstanding debt is zero.

What annual repayment at the end of each year will be required to repay a mortgage of £25 000 over 25 years if the annual rate of interest is 14%?

We can substitute the following values

$S = 0$ (final value of mortgage)
$A_0 = £25\ 000$ (a negative saving)
$r = 14\%$
$t = 25$

to obtain

$$0 = -25\ 000(1 + 0.14)^{25} + \frac{x(1 + 0.14)^{25} - x}{0.14}$$

$$x = 25\ 000 \frac{(1 + 0.14)^{25} \times 0.14}{(1 + 0.14)^{25} - 1}$$

$$= 25\ 000 \times \frac{0.14}{1 - \dfrac{1}{(1 + 0.14)^{25}}}$$

$$= 25\ 000 \times 0.1455$$

$$= 3657.46$$

where x is the annual repayment.

The multiplicative factor of 0.1455 is referred to as the **capital recovery factor** and can be found from tabulations.

8.5 REFLECTIONS ON THE ASSUMPTIONS

Throughout this chapter we have made assumptions about payments and interest, but how realistic have these been? An early assumption was that interest was paid, or money received at the end of a year — this is clearly not always the case, but the assumption was made to **simplify** the calculations (and the algebra!). For compound interest we showed how to incorporate more frequent payments, and the same principle could be applied to all of the other calculations in this chapter.

The second major assumption throughout the chapter has been that interest rates remain constant for several years — this has clearly **not** been true in the UK in the 1970s and 1980s. A few contracts do involve fixed interest rates, e.g. hire-purchase agreements, but the vast majority of business contracts have **variable** interest rates. If we try to incorporate these variable rates into our calculations of, say, net present value, then we will need to estimate or predict future interest rates. These predictions will increase the uncertainty in the figures we calculate. As we have already noted, the higher the interest or discount rate, the less likely we are to invest in projects with a long-term payoff. However, since the interest rates charged to borrowers and lenders tend to change together over time, the opportunity cost of using or borrowing money should not be much affected.

Stable conditions are also assumed in the calculations. It is taken for granted that the general political and social structure of the Western economic system will still be the same in 5 or 10 years' time. International changes may have far-reaching domestic consequences; recent examples being the floating of currency exchange rates, the oil crises of 1973 and 1978 and the debt problems of certain nations in 1983 and the consequences for the private banking system. Even a change of government may lead to drastic changes in the direction of fiscal and monetary policy.

Exercises
1. Find two more examples of sociopolitical changes which would affect the stability assumption in the calculations.
2. At certain times in the past, money lending for interest (or usury) has been regarded as morally wrong. How would you justify the practice in today's world?

8.6 PROBLEMS

1. An investment of £10 000 has been made on your behalf for the next 5 years. How much will this investment be worth if

    (a) the rate of interest is 10% per annum;

(b)   interest is paid at 7% per annum for the first £1000, 9% per annum for the next £5000 and 12% per annum for the remainder;

(c)   the rate of interest is 9% per annum but paid on a 6 monthly basis?

2.   How much would an investment of £500 accumulate to in 3 years if interest were paid at 6% per annum for the first year, 8% per annum for the second year and 12% per annum for the third year?

3.   A customer credit scheme charges interest at 2% a month compounded. Calculate the true annual rate of interest, i.e. the rate which would produce an equivalent result if interest were compounded annually.

4.   A car is bought for £5680. It loses 15% of its value immediately and 10% per annum thereafter. How much is this car worth after 3 years?

5.   A company buys a machine for £7000. If depreciation is allowed for at a rate of 16% per annum, what will be the value of the machine in 4 years' time?

6.   You are offered £400 now or £520 at the end of 5 years. You know that 8% per annum is the highest rate of interest you can get. Which offer should you accept?

7.   A firm is trying to decide between two projects which have the following cash flows:

		Year		
Project	1	2	3	4
I	£10 000	£5000	£6000	£4000
II	£12 000	£4000	£4000	£4000

If project I is discounted at 15% and project II at 20%, which project should be chosen?

8.   A company has to replace a current production process. The current process is rapidly becoming unreliable whereas demand for the product is growing. The company must choose between alternatives to replace the process.
It can buy

(a)   either a large capacity process now at a cost of £4 million, or

(b)   a medium capacity process at a cost of £2.2 million and an additional medium capacity process, also at a cost of £2.2 million, to be installed after 3 years.

The contribution to profit per year from operating the two alternatives are:

	Contribution (£m) at year end					
	1	2	3	4	5	6
Large process	2.0	2.3	2.8	2.8	2.8	2.8
2 medium processes	2.0	2.0	2.0	2.4	2.8	2.8

Assume a discount rate of 20%. Present a discounted cash flow analysis of this problem and decide between the alternatives.

Comment on other factors, not taken into account in your discounted cash flow analysis, which you think may be relevant to management's decision.

9.   You have decided to save £200 at the end of each year for the next 5 years. How much will you have at the end of the 5 years if you are paid interest of 10% per annum?

10.   You have decided to save £200 at the beginning of each year for the next 5 years. How much will you have at the end of the 5 years if you are paid interest of 10% per annum?

11.   A sum of £5000 was invested 4 years ago. At the end of each year a further £1000 was added. If the rate of interest paid was 12% per annum, how much is the investment worth now?

12. You require £4000 in 5 years' time. How much will you have to invest at the end of each year if interest charged is 15% per annum?
13. A company has borrowed £5000 to be repaid in equal end of year payments over 10 years. What will the annual repayment be if the interest charged is 15% per annum?

8.7 APPENDIX

Proof that

$$S = A_0\left(1 + \frac{r}{100}\right)^t + \frac{x\left(1 + \frac{r}{100}\right)^t - x}{\frac{r}{100}}$$

where S is the sum at the end of t years, A_0 is the initial investment and x is the amount added at the end of each year.

The value of the investment at the end of the first year is

$$S_1 = A_0\left(1 + \frac{r}{100}\right)^1 + x$$

The value at the end of the second year is

$$S_2 = \left[A_0\left(1 + \frac{r}{100}\right)^1 + x\right]\left(1 + \frac{r}{100}\right)^1 + x$$

$$= A_0\left(1 + \frac{r}{100}\right)^2 + x\left(1 + \frac{r}{100}\right)^1 + x$$

If we continue in this way, it can be shown that the value after t years is

$$S = A_0\left(1 + \frac{r}{100}\right)^t + x\left(1 + \frac{r}{100}\right)^{t-1} + x\left(1 + \frac{r}{100}\right)^{t-2} + \ldots + x$$

This can be simplified using the summation formula for a geometric progression to give

$$S = A_0\left(1 + \frac{r}{100}\right)^t + x\left[\frac{1 - \left(1 + \frac{r}{100}\right)^t}{1 - \left(1 + \frac{r}{100}\right)}\right]$$

$$= A_0\left(1 - \frac{r}{100}\right)^t + \frac{x}{r/100}\left[1 - \left(1 + \frac{r}{100}\right)^t\right]$$

$$= A_0\left(1 + \frac{r}{100}\right)^t + \frac{x\left(1 + \frac{r}{100}\right)^t - x}{r/100}$$

Part III
CONCLUDING EXERCISE

Suppose you need to commute from Birmingham to London every working day.

(a) Identify the possible modes of transport and the time involved.

(b) Establish the costs involved for each mode of transport and the timing of payment, e.g. you may be able to purchase a season ticket.

(c) Describe the social and personal factors which would be important in any decision you make.

(d) Evaluate the options available to you, and state which option you would choose and why.

Part IV
MEASURES OF UNCERTAINTY

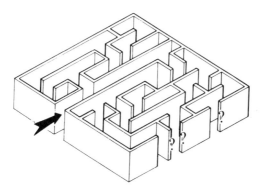

As an introduction to descriptive statistics (Part II) we said that quantitative methods aim at the communication, presentation and analysis of numerical data. As we have seen, the construction of appropriate charts and diagrams, and the calculation of various descriptive statistics is **one** important aspect of this. Quantitative methods are also about the measurement and analysis of numerical information. Consider the following.

We could collect data on the ages of members of a particular population. The distribution of age, a continuous measurement, can be presented as a histogram and described with statistics such as the average age. We could also ask of the data 'what is the life expectancy?' or 'what is the chance of an individual living 60 years?' To provide answers to these types of question will require a number of assumptions, methods of analysis and the measurement of chance (probability).

We could count the number of defective items produced by a single machine each day. The results of our survey could be presented by a bar chart, as we are dealing with discrete data, and described by a single figure such as the proportion of defectives. This provides some information about the machine, but as a production manager we might also want to know what the consequences are for a product assembled from two or more of these items or whether the results obtained show that the machine needs adjusting or are merely unrepresentative.

In this part of the book, we are concerned with the measurement of chance or probability and the relevance of random variations in a business context.

Exercises

1. List a number of events, the outcomes of which you believe are determined by chance.

2. How would you, as an individual, assess a risk of 1 million to 1? Give examples of risks you believe are 1 million to 1 or smaller.

9 Probability

Almost everyone has met, or been involved in, situations with a chance element, whether it is tossing a coin at the start of a sports match, playing cards, owning a premium bond or taking out some form of insurance. Even events which seem to have sound logical reasons for occurring may have their timing selected by chance. Other events, especially those involving large groups of people or items, often have characteristics which can be represented, or **modelled**, by some reference to probability.

Probability was first studied in relation to gambling, and many examples may still be drawn from the use of cards, dice, roulette wheels, etc., simply because these items are familiar to many people. However, it quickly became apparent that the ideas being investigated had a much wider application, initially in relation to rates to be charged for insurance of freight carried by sea.

If we consider some results from a survey, as shown in Table 9.1, we may deduce various probabilities. In Table 9.1 we see that 300 individuals responded to the survey, 160 of whom were men, and 140 were women. Thus if one individual were selected at random from the survey results, there would be 140 chances out of 300 that it was a woman.

Table 9.1

	Less than £6000	Annual Salary £6000 and less than £10 000	£10 000 or more	Total
Men	30	50	80	160
Women	50	50	40	140
	80	100	120	300

i.e. Probability (woman) $= \dfrac{140}{300}$

or P(woman) $= \dfrac{7}{15} = 0.467$

The probability that the person selected had a salary between £6000 and less than £10 000 would thus be 100/300: or $P(£6000 < £10\ 000) = 1/3 = 0.333$.

Looking again at the probabilities of selecting a man or a woman, we have

$$P(\text{man}) = \frac{160}{300} \qquad P(\text{woman}) = \frac{140}{300}$$

i.e. $P(M) + P(W) = 1$
thus $P(M) + P(\text{not } M) = 1$
or $P(M) = 1 - P(\text{not } M)$
$\qquad\qquad = 1 - 0.467 = 0.533$

In this context, the manipulation above seems very obvious, but in many cases it will be easier to find the probability of something not happening than to find the probability that it does occur. For example, if items were packed in boxes of 1000 and we wanted to find the probability that there were two or more defective items in a box, then to calculate this directly, we would need to use the following relationships:

$$P(2 \text{ or more}) = P(2) + P(3) + P(4) + \ldots + P(999) + P(1000)$$

However, if we notice that the **only alternatives** to '2 or more' are 'no defective items' or 'one defective item', then

$$P(2 \text{ or more}) = 1 - P(\text{not 2 or more})$$
$$= 1 - [P(0) + P(1)]$$

and this will usually be very much easier to evaluate.

Probabilities are often used to suggest what is likely to happen, so that if the probability of a 'head' when you toss a coin is $\frac{1}{2}$ and you toss the coin 500 times, then you would **expect** to get $\frac{1}{2} \times 500 = 250$ heads. This value is known as an expectation, but note that this does not imply that if you actually toss a coin 500 times that you will get exactly 250 heads every time. What it is suggesting is that if a coin is tossed 500 times, and that this experiment is carried out many times, then the average number of heads over **all** of the experiments will be 250. In general:

expectation = (probability) × (total number of trials)

9.1 DEFINITIONS

In each case above we have used the **classical definition** of probability, because we have counted the number of ways that a person could be selected with the characteristic that we are seeking and divided this by the number of possible results that could have been obtained. For any event, E, we have:

$$P(E) = \frac{\text{no. of ways } E \text{ can occur}}{\text{total number of outcomes}}$$

This definition is widely used when trying to assess a particular situation but it is not complete. If you consider a die, there are six different faces, and this definition would suggest that $P(5) = 1/6$. However, if the die has been weighted so that, say, 6 will appear each time it is thrown, then the probability of a 5 is zero ($P(5) = 0$) despite the fact that there is one five, and there are six faces on the die. To complete the definition, we need to add that each outcome is **equally likely**; equally likely means equally probable, and thus we have a definition of probability which uses probability in that definition, i.e. a **tautology**. Even if we are sure that the outcomes are equally likely, the definition cannot deal with situations where there are an infinite number of outcomes. Despite these comments, most people will use this definition when considering simple probability situations.

Exercises 1. In a survey of 1000 people, of which 100 were from Scotland, what is the probability when selecting one individual at random, that he or she came from Scotland?
(Answer: P(from Scotland) = 0.1.)
2. If you toss two unbiased coins, what is the probability of getting two tails?
(Answer: P(two tails) = 0.25.)

An alternative way to look at probability would be to carry out an experiment to determine the **proportion in the long run**, sometimes called the **frequency definition of probability**.

i.e. $$P(E) = \frac{\text{no. of times } E \text{ occurs}}{\text{no. of times the experiment was conducted}}$$

This would certainly overcome the problem involving the biased die given above, since we would have $P(5) = 0$ and $P(6) = 1$. One problem with this definition is assessing how long the long run is. Experiments with a theoretical, unbiased coin do not necessarily conclude that the probability of a 'head' is $\frac{1}{2}$, even after 10 million tosses, and it can be shown that this frequency definition will not necessarily ever stabilize at some particular proportion. A second problem with this definition is that it must be possible to carry out repeated trials, whereas some situations only occur once; for example, the chance of a salesman selling more than his target next March.

Exercise Toss a coin 50 times and count the number of heads that occur. Estimate the probability of a head for your coin.

Asking a series of questions may enable a researcher to find out people's **subjective probabilities** or their degree of confidence in certain events happening. This system will be useful if those questioned are in a position to assess the chances of the events under consideration, and will work for once-only situations. As with all sampling, the larger the number of the relevant population who take part in the survey, the better the result.

Exercise Who would you question to assess the chance of a company running out of stock of one of its raw materials?

The logical difficulty of defining probability is recognized by the modern trend which founds the whole probability theory on a number of **axioms** from which theorems are deduced. The axioms and theorems are formulated in terms of set theory and, avoiding details, some of them may be paraphrased as follows:

(a) The probability of an event lies in the interval $0 \leqslant P(E) \leqslant 1$ and no other values are possible.
(b) If something is certain to occur, then it has a probability of 1.
(c) If two or more different outcomes of a trial or experiment cannot happen at the same time, then the probability of one or other of these outcomes occurring is the sum of the individual probabilities

e.g. if $P(E_1) = \frac{1}{4}$, $P(E_2) = \frac{1}{2}$

and if they cannot both happen simultaneously then

$P(E_1 \text{ or } E_2) = \frac{1}{4} + \frac{1}{2} = \frac{3}{4}$

Whilst the probability of a single event will be of some interest, most practical situations involve two or more events.

9.2.1 Mutually exclusive events

Mutually exclusive events is the situation represented in (c) above, and, as we have seen, we just add the probabilities together to find the probability that one or other of the events will occur. For example, if a group of people consists of 20 single and 40 married men with 30 single and 10 married women, then, selecting a person at random we have:

$$P(\text{single man}) = \frac{20}{100}$$

$$P(\text{single woman}) = \frac{30}{100}$$

$$\text{and} \quad P(\text{single person}) = \frac{20}{100} + \frac{30}{100} = \frac{50}{100} = 0.5$$

9.2.2 Non-mutually exclusive events

Where one outcome has, or can have more than one characteristic, then these outcomes are said to be non-mutually exclusive. In this case it will not be possible simply to add the probabilities together as we did above to find the overall probability of one characteristic or another, since this would involve counting some outcomes twice. For example, if a group of people contains both men and women, and these people either agree or disagree with some proposition, then to find the probability of selecting a person who is either a man, or disagrees, will be

$$P(\text{man or disagree}) = P(\text{man}) + P(\text{disagree}) - P(\text{man and disagree})$$

Since the men who disagree appear in each of the first two probabilities, we need to subtract the probability of this group from our required probability. If, for example, there were 30 men, of whom 10 disagree with the proposition, and 70 women, of whom 40 disagree with the proposition then:

$$P(\text{man}) = \frac{30}{100} \quad P(\text{disagree}) = \frac{50}{100}$$

$$P(\text{man and disagree}) = \frac{10}{100}$$

$$\text{Therefore,} \quad P(\text{man or disagree}) = \frac{30}{100} + \frac{50}{100} - \frac{10}{100} = \frac{70}{100} = 0.7$$

9.2.3 Independent events

When one outcome is known to have no effect on another outcome, then the events are said to be **independent**. For example, if the probability of a machine breaking down is 1/10 and the probability of stoppage of raw material supplies is 1/8, then we can find the probability of the two events happening together by **multiplying** the two probabilities, because the occurrence of one of these events does not affect the probability of the other. Thus,

$$P(\text{breakdown } \textbf{and} \text{ stoppage of supplies}) = \frac{1}{10} \times \frac{1}{8} = \frac{1}{80} = 0.0125$$

9.2.4   Non-independent events

If two events are such that the outcome of one affects the probability of the outcome of the other, then the probability of the second event is said to be **dependent** on the outcome of the first. From a group of 10 people, 5 of whom are men and 5 women, the probability of selecting a man is $P(\text{man}) = 5/10 = 0.5$. If a second person is now selected from the remaining 9 people, the probabilities will depend on the outcome of the first selection.

If man first:	If woman first:
$P(\text{man}) = 4/9$	$P(\text{man}) = 5/9$
$P(\text{woman}) = 5/9$	$P(\text{woman}) = 4/9$

or $P(\text{man} \mid \text{man}) = 4/9$ $P(\text{man} \mid \text{woman}) = 5/9$

where the notation (man | man) is read as 'the probability is 4/9 of selecting a second man when a man has already been selected at the first selection'. (Note that if the second selection had been from the original group of 10 people, then the two probabilities would be independent.)

These relationships can be summarized as follows:

If events A and B are mutually exclusive, then

$$P(A \textbf{ or } B) = P(A) + P(B)$$

If events A and B are any two events, then

$$P(A \textbf{ or } B) = P(A) + P(B) - P(A \textbf{ and } B)$$

If events A and B are independent, then

$$P(A \textbf{ and } B) = P(A) \times P(B)$$

If events A and B can both occur, then

$$P(A \textbf{ and } B) = P(A) \times P(B \mid A)$$

where $P(B \mid A)$ is the probability that B occurs **given that** A has already happened.

9.3   PROBLEMS

Many of the exercises below use coins, dice and cards; this does not imply that this is the only use to which these ideas can be put, but they do provide a fairly simple mechanism for determining if you have absorbed the ideas of the previous section.
1. If you toss three fair coins what is the probability of getting three heads?
2. If you toss three fair coins what is the probability that the first is a head, the second a tail and the third a head?
3. If you toss three fair coins, what is the probability of two heads and one tail in any order?
4. How would the probabilities in Exercises 1–3 change if a biased coin were used, such that the probability of a head were 0.6?

5. If the experiment in Exercise 4 were carried out 1000 times, how many times would you expect to get the three specified outcomes?
6. When throwing an unbiased die, what is the probability of getting a 2 or a 5?
7. When throwing two dice, what is the probability of getting a 2 and a 5?
8. Is the probability in 7 changed if we specify that the 2 must be on the first die thrown? If so, what is the new probability?
9. When throwing two dice, what is the probability of getting a double?
10. When throwing two dice, what total score is most probable?
11. If a die is thrown and a coin is tossed, what is the probability of getting a 6 and a head?
12. From Exercise 11, what is the probability of getting either a 6, or a head, or both?
13. From a normal pack of 52 playing cards, consisting of four suits each of 13 cards, find the probabilities of selecting on a single draw:

    (a) a queen;
    (b) the queen of hearts;
    (c) a spade;
    (d) an ace or a king;
    (e) a red card;
    (f) a two or a club;
    (g) a black ten;
    (h) a picture card (i.e. jack, queen or king).

14. What is the probability of an ace on either or both of two selections from a pack

    (a) with replacement?
    (b) without replacement?

15. What is the probability of getting either a queen or a heart on either or both of two cards selected from a pack without replacement?
16. At a first interview, candidates are divided into three groups, with probabilities of selection for A of 0.5, B of 0.3 and C of 0.2. If a candidate is in group A he or she has a probability of 0.1 of a second interview. Candidates in group B have a probability of 0.5 of a second interview, and the probability for group C is 0.9. What is the probability of:

    (a) being selected for A and getting a second interview;
    (b) being selected for B and getting a second interview;
    (c) being selected for C and not getting a second interview;
    (d) of getting a second interview?

17. A company manufactures red and blue plastic pigs: 5% red and 10% blue are misshapen during manufacture. If the company makes equal numbers of each colour, what is the probability of selecting a misshapen pig on a random selection? How would the probability change if 60% of the pigs manufactured were blue?
18. Of 1000 people responding to a survey, 650 are men. One question asked if the respondent would agree with a particular statement, and the response is given below.

Agree	500
Disagree	450
Don't know	50
	1000

If we assume that sex and opinion are independent, find the following expected numbers:

    (a) men who agreed with the statement;
    (b) women who disagreed with the statement;
    (c) men who answered 'Don't know'.

19. Of 1000 workers in a company, 80 are classified as 'general managers', 50 are

classified as 'accountants', and 20 of these people are classified in both categories. What is the probability that a worker selected at random will perform a management function? What is the probability of selecting a manager or an accountant?

20. If 85% of managers are, or have been married, what is the probability that of four selected

(a) all four either are, or have been, married?
(b) that the first is and always has been single, but the rest are married or have been?

(You can assume that the number of managers is so large that the selections are independent.)

9.4 PROBABILITY TREES

Probability trees can be used to illustrate the combination of probabilities for a series of events which are independent or dependent. For the independent case, if the probability of outcomes A, B and C are 0.3, 0.2 and 0.5, and of outcomes X and Y are 0.6 and 0.4 then we have the situation in Fig. 9.1. As the outcomes of each event are mutually exclusive

$P(A \text{ or } B \text{ or } C) = 0.3 + 0.2 + 0.5 = 1.0$
$P(X \text{ or } Y) = 0.6 + 0.4 = 1.0$

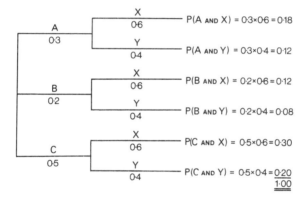

Figure 9.1

We can note that the sum of all the probabilities on the right-hand side of Fig. 9.1 is 1.00, and thus this represents all of the possible mutually exclusive outcomes. If we have three groups of people, a red team of 10 men and 10 women; a blue team of 7 men and 3 women and a yellow team of 4 men and 6 women, then using a two stage selection procedure firstly selecting a team, and then selecting an individual, the probability of selecting a woman will be dependent on which team is selected. In Fig. 9.2 the probabilities of selecting a red, blue or yellow team are respectively 0.4, 0.4 and 0.2. The probabilities of being a man or a woman were derived from the numbers in each team.

The probability tree can be combined with the idea of expectation in order to make a comparison between what actually happened and what we would expect to happen. Taking the information from Table 9.1 we have

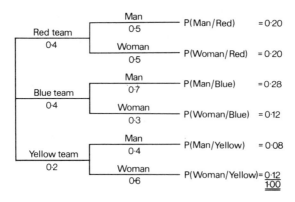

Figure 9.2

$$P(\text{man}) = \frac{160}{300}; \qquad\qquad P(\text{woman}) = \frac{140}{300};$$

$$P(\text{less than } £6000) = \frac{80}{300};$$

$$P(£6000 \text{ but less than } £10\,000) = \frac{100}{300}$$

$$P(£10\,000 \text{ or more}) = \frac{120}{300}$$

If we assume that these two factors are independent, we have the results in Table 9.2.

Table 9.2

	Annual salary		Probability	Expected number	Actual (from Table 9.1)
Man 160/300	less than £6000	80/300	0.142 22	42.67	30
	£6000 and less than £10 000	100/300	0.177 78	53.33	50
	£10 000 or more	120/300	0.213 33	64.00	80
Woman 140/300	less than £6000	80/300	0.124 44	37.33	50
	£6000 and less than £10 000	100/300	0.155 56	46.67	50
	£10 000 or more	120/300	0.186 67	56.00	40
			1.000 00	300	300

Looking down the final two columns of Table 9.2 we see that there are quite large differences between what actually happened and the expected number from the probability tree.

Suggest reasons why this might happen.

(We shall return to this problem in Chapter 15.)

9.5 BAYES' THEOREM

As we have seen in Section 9.2, when events are dependent, the probability of a subsequent event will depend on the outcome of some previous event. By using Bayes' theorem we may move from the position of **knowing** the outcome of the second event, and find the probabilities of each of the outcomes of the first event, given this extra knowledge. Consider the situation in Fig. 9.3.

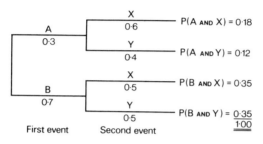

Figure 9.3

If we know that the outcome of the second event was X, then either A or B could have been outcomes of the first event. We are trying to find the probability of each of these outcomes. Since the combinations of events (A and X) and (B and X) are mutually exclusive, these two probabilities can be added together to obtain the overall probability of X occurring.

$$P(X \mid A \text{ or } B) = P(A \text{ and } X) + P(B \text{ and } X)$$
$$= 0.18 + 0.35$$
$$= 0.53$$

If A occurred first, we have that

$$P(X \mid A) = 0.6 \quad \text{and} \quad P(A) = 0.3$$

which, as we have seen, gives

$$P(A \text{ and } X) = P(A) \times P(X \mid A) = 0.18$$

$$P(A \mid X) = \frac{\text{probability, we obtained for outcome } X \text{ via outcome } A}{\text{probability, we obtained for outcome } X \text{ via any route}}$$

$$= \frac{P(A \text{ and } X)}{P(X \mid A \text{ or } B)} = \frac{P(X \mid A) \, P(A)}{P(X \mid A) + P(X \mid B)}$$

$$= \frac{0.18}{0.53} \qquad = 0.3396$$

$$\text{and} \quad P(B \mid X) = \frac{0.35}{0.53} \qquad = 0.6604$$

or more generally:

$$P(A_j \mid X) = \frac{P(X \mid A_j) \, P(A_j)}{\sum_{i=1}^{n} P(X \mid A_i) \, P(A_i)}$$

where A_j is the particular route for which the probability is required, and A_i ($i = 1$ to n) represents each of the routes to X (the known result).

From Fig. 9.3 we have that 0.3 is the probability of A before anything happens; this is known as the **prior probability** of A. Once the outcome of the second event is known to be X, then the probability that X was reached via A is 0.3396; this is known as the **posterior probability** of A. These ideas from Bayes' Theorem are often used in decision analysis and **decision theory**.

9.6 MARKOV CHAINS

A Markov chain combines the ideas of probability with the matrix presentation shown in Chapter 6. It assumes that probabilities remain **fixed** over time, but that the system that is being modelled is able to change from one **state** to another, using these fixed values as **transition probabilities**. Consider, for example, the following transition matrix:

$$P = \begin{array}{c} \\ E_1 \\ E_2 \end{array} \begin{array}{cc} E_1 & E_2 \\ \begin{bmatrix} 0.8 & 0.2 \\ 0.3 & 0.7 \end{bmatrix} \end{array}$$

This means that if the system is in some state labelled E_1, the probability of going to E_2 is 0.2. If the system is at E_2, then the probability of going to E_1 is 0.3, and the probability of remaining at E_2 is 0.7. This matrix could be represented by a **directed graph** (Fig. 9.4).

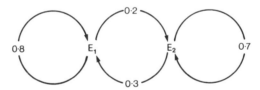

Figure 9.4

If we consider the movement from one state to another to happen at the end of some specific time period, and look at the passage of two of these periods we have the situation in Fig. 9.5.

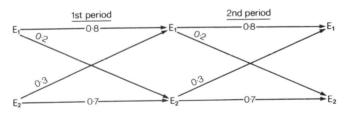

Figure 9.5

The probability of **ending** after two periods at E_1 if the system started at E_1 will be

$$P(E_1 \rightarrow E_1 \rightarrow E_1) + P(E_1 \rightarrow E_2 \rightarrow E_1) = (0.8)(0.8) + (0.2)(0.3)$$
$$= 0.70$$

Starting at E_1 and ending at E_2:

$$P(E_1 \rightarrow E_1 \rightarrow E_2) + P(E_1 \rightarrow E_2 \rightarrow E_2) = (0.8)(0.2) + (0.2)(0.7)$$
$$= 0.30$$

Starting at E_2 and ending at E_1:

$$P(E_2 \rightarrow E_1 \rightarrow E_1) + P(E_2 \rightarrow E_2 \rightarrow E_1) = (0.3)(0.8) + (0.7)(0.3)$$
$$= 0.45$$

Starting at E_2 and ending at E_2:

$$P(E_2 \rightarrow E_2 \rightarrow E_2) + P(E_2 \rightarrow E_1 \rightarrow E_2) = (0.7)(0.7) + (0.3)(0.2)$$
$$= 0.55$$

Thus the transition matrix for **two periods** will be:

$$\begin{array}{cc} & \begin{array}{cc} E_1 & E_2 \end{array} \\ \begin{array}{c} E_1 \\ E_2 \end{array} & \begin{bmatrix} 0.70 & 0.30 \\ 0.45 & 0.55 \end{bmatrix} \end{array}$$

but note that this is equal to P^2, i.e. the square of the transition matrix for one period. To find the transition matrix for four periods, we would find P^4 and so on.

The states of the system at a given instant could be an item working or not working, a company being profitable or making a loss, an individual being given a particular promotion or failing at the interview, etc. In all transition matrices, the movement over time is from the state on the left to the state above the particular column, and thus, since something must happen, the sum of any row must be equal to 1.

A state is said to be **absorbant** if it has a probability of 1 of returning to itself each time. In the matrix

$$\begin{array}{cccc} & \begin{array}{ccc} E_1 & E_2 & E_3 \end{array} \\ \begin{array}{c} E_1 \\ E_2 \\ E_3 \end{array} & \begin{bmatrix} 0.4 & 0.2 & 0.4 \\ 0.2 & 0.7 & 0.1 \\ 0 & 0 & 1 \end{bmatrix} \end{array}$$

the state E_3 is an absorbant state, since each time the system reaches state E_3 it remains there. This can again be shown by a directed graph (Fig. 9.6).

To use these transition matrices for predicting a future state, we need to know the **initial state**, which is written in the form of a **vector**. For example, if state E_1 for Fig. 9.4 were a company being profitable, and E_2 were a company not being profitable, then we would consider what would happen to a group of companies. If the group consists of 150 profitable companies and 50 non-profitable companies, the initial vector will be:

$$\begin{array}{cc} & \begin{array}{cc} E_1 & E_2 \end{array} \\ A_0 = & [150 \quad 50] \end{array}$$

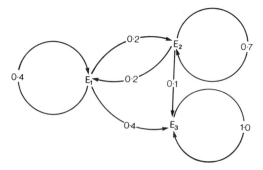

Figure 9.6

To find the situation after one time period, say 1 year, we multiply the initial state vector by the transition matrix:

$$[150 \quad 50] \begin{bmatrix} 0.8 & 0.2 \\ 0.3 & 0.7 \end{bmatrix} = [135 \quad 65] = A_1$$

A_1 now represents the situation after one time period, where we would expect 135 companies to be profitable, and 65 not to be profitable. To find the situation after two time periods, we either multiply the initial state vector by P^2

$$[150 \quad 50] \begin{bmatrix} 0.7 & 0.3 \\ 0.45 & 0.55 \end{bmatrix} = [127.5 \quad 72.5] = A_2$$

or multiply the vector A_1 by P:

$$[135 \quad 65] \begin{bmatrix} 0.8 & 0.2 \\ 0.3 & 0.7 \end{bmatrix} = [127.5 \quad 72.5] = A_2$$

Both calculations give a row vector labelled A_2, which represents the expected number of companies in each state after 2 years. Note that some of the companies that are currently profitable may not have been profitable after only 1 year.

The process given above can continue with any transition matrix for any number of time periods; however, it is likely that the probabilities within the matrix will become out of date, and thus not fixed, if a prediction into the distant future is made. Markov chains are often used in manpower planning exercises and in market predictions.

9.7 PROBLEMS

1. Two events are independent. For the first event the probabilities of each outcome are for A 0.7, for B 0.2 and for C 0.1. For the second event, the probabilities of each outcome are for X 0.2, for Y 0.5 and for Z 0.3.

   (a) Construct a probability tree to represent this situation.
   (b) What is the probability that the outcome of both events includes outcome X?

2. A group of 100 people contains 70 women. Thirty of the women and ten of the men agree with a particular management style when questioned.

(a) Construct a probability tree to illustrate this situation; hence find the probability that a randomly selected person is a man who disagrees with this management style.

(b) Given that a person agrees with the management style, what is the probability that he is a man?

3. A company has four machines; 40% of production is by machine A, 30% by machine B, 20% by machine C and 10% by machine D. 99% of the production from A has no faults, as has also 98% of production from B. Machine C produces 1% of its items defective whilst D has 3% defective. Given that an item is found to be defective, what is the probability it was produced by:

(a) Machine A;
(b) Machine B;
(c) Machine C;
(d) Machine D.

4. Items on a production line have to pass through two processes, before being subjected to a quality control check. For the first process, an item may go to work station A, B or C with probabilities 0.6, 0.3, and 0.1 respectively. For the second process items may go to work station X, Y or Z with probabilities 0.4, 0.5 and 0.1 respectively. Items may go to any pair or work stations. Work Stations X, Y and Z produce items which will pass the quality control check with probabilities 0.95, 0.98 and 0.99 respectively. Given that an item fails to pass the check, what is the probability that

(a) it passed through A and X;
(b) it passed through B and Z;
(c) it passed through C;
(d) it passed through Y?

5. Draw a directed graph to represent the following transition matrices:

(a)

$$P = \begin{array}{c} \\ E_1 \\ E_2 \end{array} \begin{array}{cc} E_1 & E_2 \\ \begin{bmatrix} 0.2 & 0.8 \\ 0.6 & 0.4 \end{bmatrix} \end{array}$$

(b)

$$P = \begin{array}{c} \\ E_1 \\ E_2 \\ E_3 \end{array} \begin{array}{ccc} E_1 & E_2 & E_3 \\ \begin{bmatrix} 0.7 & 0.2 & 0.1 \\ 0 & 0.8 & 0.2 \\ 0 & 0 & 1 \end{bmatrix} \end{array}$$

(c) What will happen eventually in the situation represented by (b) above?

6. A system has two states E_1 and E_2 with a transition matrix P.

$$P = \begin{bmatrix} 0.7 & 0.3 \\ 0.3 & 0.7 \end{bmatrix}$$

Find the two, four, eight and sixteen period transition matrices.

7. A company takes on 50 people at grade 1. The promotion system can be modelled by a transition matrix P:

$$P = \begin{array}{c} \\ \text{Grade 1} \\ \text{Grade 2} \\ \text{Grade 3} \end{array} \begin{array}{ccc} \text{Grade 1} & \text{Grade 2} & \text{Grade 3} \\ \begin{bmatrix} 0.8 & 0.2 & 0 \\ 0 & 0.85 & 0.15 \\ 0 & 0 & 1 \end{bmatrix} \end{array}$$

(a) Specify the initial state vector.
(b) Find the expected number on each grade after:
  (i) one time period;
  (ii) two time periods;
  (iii) three time periods.

Probability occasionally gives answers which do not seem to match our own guesses. For instance, if you were asked 'What is the probability of two or more people in a group of 23 having the same birthday in terms of day and month, but not necessarily year?', what would you guess the answer to be?

It is in fact more than $\frac{1}{2}$!

To build up to this answer, consider a group size of two. Whenever the first person's birthday, if all birthdays are equally likely, then the probability that they have the same birthday will be 1/365 (ignoring leap years), and that they do not 364/365. For a group of 3, given the first person's birthday, the probability that the second has a different birthday is 364/365 and that the third has a different birthday still, 363/365.

Thus P(at least 2 same) $= 1 - P$(all different)

$$= 1 - \frac{364}{365} \times \frac{363}{365} = 0.0082$$

For a group of 4, we have:

$$P(\text{at least 2 same}) = 1 - \frac{364}{365} \times \frac{363}{365} \times \frac{362}{365} = 0.01636$$

We can continue this process, to give Table 9.3.

Table 9.3

No. of people	Probability	No. of people	Probability
2	0.002 739 7	26	0.598 24
3	0.008 024 2	27	0.626 859
4	0.016 355 9	28	0.654 46
5	0.027 135 57	29	0.680 968 5
6	0.040 462 48	30	0.706 3
7	0.056 235 7	31	0.730 45
8	0.074 335	32	0.753 347 5
9	0.094 623 8	33	0.774 97
10	0.116 948	34	0.795 3
11	0.141 141 4	35	0.814 38
12	0.167 025	36	0.832 18
13	0.194 4	37	0.848 738
14	0.223	38	0.864 06
15	0.252 9	39	0.878 2
16	0.283 6	40	0.891 23
17	0.315	41	0.903 15
18	0.346 91	42	0.914
19	0.379 1	43	0.923 9
20	0.411 4	44	0.932 885
21	0.443 688	45	0.940 97
22	0.475 695	46	0.948 25
23	0.507 297	47	0.954 77
24	0.538 34	48	0.960 597
25	0.568 699 7	49	0.965 779 6

Exercises

1. When will the probability reach 1?
2. If the group are all from the same country or cultural background, what factors will increase the probabilities proposed in the model given above?

10 Discrete probability distributions

In the last chapter we discussed some of the basic ideas of probability, considering the possibility of an individual event, or the chance that certain events would happen at the same time, or in a particular sequence. If we wish to use these ideas in a business context, we need to look for probability models which are capable of representing a range of situations. A series of these have been recognized and are referred to generally as **probability distributions**. During a first year course, it would not be possible to discuss the whole range of distributions that might be used in particular cases, but several of those most frequently encountered are considered below.

10.1 UNIFORM DISTRIBUTION

We have already met this distribution in Chapter 1 when random numbers were used to select samples for interview or analysis. In a uniform distribution, each outcome is equally likely to occur. Thus in random number tables each of the digits 0, 1, 2, 3, 4, 5, 6, 7, 8, 9 should occur about the same number of times in a large sample. A histogram of this distribution is shown in Fig. 10.1. Note that this illustrates a theoretical distribution and that in an actual sample the numbers of each digit will be only approximately the same.

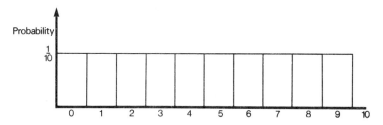

Figure 10.1

Exercise   Select a sample of 100 numbers from the random number tables and count the number of times each digit occurs. (Select a starting point in the tables and continue along the row or down the column without missing any digits.)

10.2   BINOMIAL DISTRIBUTION

In many cases the probabilities for each of a number of complex outcomes will be different, but if the individual parts of the outcome are independent, then we can model the situation. The model appropriate to outcomes with two possible independent constituents is called a binomial model. Consider the situation of items coming off the end of a production line, some of which are defective. If the proportion of defective items is 10% of the flow of items, we can regard the selection of a small sample as consisting of independent selections, and thus the probability of selecting a defective item will remain constant as P(defective) = 0.1. (Note that if there were a small, fixed number of items in total and selection were without replacement, then we would have a situation of conditional probabilities, and P(defective) would not remain constant.) Samples will be selected from production lines to monitor quality, and thus we will be interested in the number of defective items in our sample. However, the number of defectives may be related to the size of the sample and to whether or not the process is working as expected.

Exercise

Which would lead to most concern, more than 1 defective in a sample of 10, or more than 10 defectives in a sample of 100?

We shall return to this exercise to compare your impressions with the theoretical results of the appropriate probability model, but first we will consider much smaller samples.

For a sample of size 1, the probability that the item selected is defective is 0.1 and the probability that it is not defective is 0.9.

For a sample of two, for each item the probabilities are as above, but we are now interested in the sample **as a whole**. There are four possibilities:

(a)   both items are defective;
(b)   the first is defective, the second is OK;
(c)   the first is OK, the second is defective;
(d)   both items are OK.

Since the two selections are independent, we can multiply the unconditional probabilities together, thus:

(a) P(both defective)   = $(0.1)(0.1)$ = 0.01
(b) P(1st defective, 2nd OK)   = $(0.1)(0.9)$ = 0.09
(c) P(1st OK, 2nd defective)   = $(0.9)(0.1)$ = 0.09
(d) P(both OK)   = $(0.9)(0.9)$ = $\underline{0.81}$
                                                                            1.00

However, (b) and (c) both represent one defective in the sample of two, since we are not interested in the **order** in which the events occur. For a sample of two, we have:

P(2 defective)   = 0.01
P(1 defective)   = 0.18
P(no defectives)   = $\underline{0.81}$
                                      1.00

If p = probability of a defective, then $q = (1 - p)$ is the probability of a non-defective item, and we have:

$P(2 \text{ defective}) = p^2$
$P(1 \text{ defective}) = 2pq$
$P(0 \text{ defective}) = q^2$

For a sample of three, the following possibilities exist (where def. is an abbreviation for defective):

(a) 3 defective	$P(3 \text{ def.}) = (0.1)^3$		$= 0.001$
(b) 1st,2nd defective; 3rd OK	$P(1,2 \text{ def.}; 3 \text{ OK}) = (0.1)^2(0.9)$		$= 0.009$
(c) 1st,3rd defective; 2nd OK	$P(1,3 \text{ def.}; 2 \text{ OK}) = (0.1)(0.9)(0.1)$	$=$	0.009
(d) 2nd,3rd defective; 1st OK	$P(2,3 \text{ def.}; 1 \text{ OK}) = (0.9)(0.1)^2$		$= 0.009$
(e) 1st defective; 2nd,3rd OK	$P(1 \text{ def.}; 2,3 \text{ OK}) = (0.1)(0.9)^2$		$= 0.081$
(f) 2nd defective; 1st,3rd OK	$P(2 \text{ def.}; 1,3 \text{ OK}) = (0.9)(0.1)(0.9)$	$=$	0.081
(g) 3rd defective, 1st,2nd OK	$P(3 \text{ def.}; 1,2 \text{ OK}) = (0.9)^2(0.1)$		$= 0.081$
(h) all OK	$P(3 \text{ OK}) = (0.9)^3$		$= 0.729$

$\cdot \ 1.000$

Again, we can combine events, since order is not important; (b), (c) and (d) represent two defectives; (e), (f) and (g) represent one defective. Thus:

$P(3 \text{ defectives}) = 0.001 = p^3$
$P(2 \text{ defectives}) = 0.027 = 3p^2q$
$P(1 \text{ defective}) = 0.243 = 3pq^2$
$P(0 \text{ defectives}) = 0.729 = q^3$

$\overline{1.000}$

We could continue with the procedure, looking at sample sizes of four, five and so on, but a pattern is already emerging from the results given above. At the extreme, the probability that all of the items are defective is p^2 or p^3, and for a sample of size n, this will be p^n. With other outcomes, these consist of a series of possibilities, each with the **same probability**, and these are then combined. For example, in a sample of 10, the probability of 4 defectives would consist of a series of outcomes, each of which would have a probability of $(0.1)^4(0.9)^6 = p^4q^6 = 0.000\ 053\ 1$. (Note that four defective items means that there are also 6 items which are OK, since the sample size is 10.) The question that needs to be answered now is: 'How many of the outcomes from a sample of ten have four defective items?' To answer this question we will use the idea of **combinations**. The number of combinations of r defective items in a sample of n items is given by:

$$^nC_r = \binom{n}{r} = \frac{n!}{r!(n-r)!}$$

where ^nC_r and $\binom{n}{r}$ are the two most commonly used notations for combinations, and $n!$ is the **factorial** of n. This means, n times $(n-1)$ times $(n-2)$, etc., until 1 is reached.

For example:

$2! = 2 \times 1 = 2$
$3! = 3 \times 2 \times 1 = 6$
$4! = 4 \times 3 \times 2 \times 1 = 24$
$10! = 10 \times 9 \times 8 \times 7 \times 6 \times 5 \times 4 \times 3 \times 2 \times 1 = 3\ 628\ 800$

However, $0! = 1$

Note also that these factorials can be written as

$$10! = 10 \times 9 \times 8 \times 7!$$
or
$$= 10 \times 9!$$
or
$$= 10 \times 9 \times 8 \times 7 \times 6 \times 5 \times 4!$$

since this will help when calculating the number of combinations. (See Section 10.7 for an alternative method for use with small samples.) Returning now to the sample of 10, the number of ways of getting 4 defective items in a sample will be:

$$n = 10 \qquad r = 4$$

$$^{10}C_4 = \begin{pmatrix} 10 \\ 4 \end{pmatrix} = \frac{10!}{4!(10 - 4)!}$$

$$= \frac{10!}{4! \ 6!}$$

If we note the highest factorial in the denominator is 6, we have

$$\begin{pmatrix} 10 \\ 4 \end{pmatrix} = \frac{10 \times 9 \times 8 \times 7 \times 6!}{4 \times 3 \times 2 \times 1 \times 6!} = 210$$

There are 210 different ways of getting four defectives in a sample of ten, and thus the probability of this outcome is

$$P(4 \text{ defective in } 10) = 210 \, (0.1)^4 (0.9)^6$$
$$= 0.011 \ 151$$

Looking back to the probabilities of different numbers of defectives in a sample of 3, these can now be rewritten as follows:

$$P(3 \text{ defectives}) = p^3$$

$$P(2 \text{ defectives}) = \begin{pmatrix} 3 \\ 2 \end{pmatrix} p^2 q$$

$$P(1 \text{ defective}) = \begin{pmatrix} 3 \\ 1 \end{pmatrix} pq^2$$

$$P(0 \text{ defectives}) = q^3$$

The general formula for a binomial probability will be:

$$P(r \text{ items in a sample of } n) = \begin{pmatrix} n \\ r \end{pmatrix} p^r q^{n-r}$$

Example

What is the probability of more than 3 defective items in a sample of 12 items, if the probability of a defective item is 0.2?
   The required probability is:

$$P(4) + P(5) + P(6) + P(7) + P(8) + P(9) + P(10) + P(11) + P(12)$$

but this may be written as:

$$1 - [P(0) + P(1) + P(2) + P(3)]$$

which will simplify the calculation.

$$n = 12 \qquad p = 0.2 \qquad q = 1 - p = 0.8$$
$$P(0) = q^{12} = (0.8)^{12} \qquad\qquad = 0.068 \ 719 \ 5$$

$$P(1) = \binom{12}{1} p\,q^{11} = 12(0.2)(0.8)^{11} = 0.206\ 159\ 4$$

$$P(2) = \binom{12}{2} p^2\,q^{11} = 66(0.2)^2(0.8)^{10} = 0.283\ 467\ 8$$

$$P(3) = \binom{12}{3} p^3\,q^9 = 220(0.2)^3(0.8)^9 = \underline{0.236\ 223\ 2}$$
$$0.794\ 569\ 9$$

Therefore, required probability $= 1 - 0.794\ 569\ 9$
$$= 0.220\ 543\ 01$$

An alternative to this calculation would be to use tables of the cumulative binomial distribution (see Appendix 1). For example, if we require the probability of 5 or more items in a sample of 10, when $p = 0.20$, from the table we find that

$P(5 \text{ or more}) = 0.0328$

For the same sample, if the required probability were for 5 or less, then we would look up $P(6 \text{ or more}) = 0.0064$ and subtract this from 1:

$P(5 \text{ or less}) = 1 - 0.0064 = 0.9936$

Returning now to the problem of whether it is a greater matter of concern to find more than 1 defective in a sample of 10, or more than 10 defectives in a sample of 100, we see that:

for a sample of 10, $p = 0.1$, $P(2 \text{ or more}) = 0.2639$
for a sample of 100, $p = 0.1$, $P(11 \text{ or more}) = 0.4168$

Exercise   Determine these probabilities.

Thus, if the process is working as was proposed, giving 10% of items defective in some way, then the probability of finding 2 or more in a sample of 10 is very much lower than the probability of finding 11 or more in a sample of 100, i.e. in both cases finding more than the expected number in a sample. However, from the note on expectations in Chapter 9, we know that we are unlikely always to get the expected number in a particular sample selection. Even so, the small sample result would suggest more strongly that something was wrong with the process and would therefore be cause for more concern.

For a binomial distribution, the mean can be shown to be np and the variance to be npq. Thus, for a sample of size 10 with a probability $p = 0.3$, the average, or expected number, of items per sample with the characteristic will be

$np = 10 \times 0.3 = 3$

the variance will be

$npq = 10 \times 0.3 \times 0.7 = 2.1$

10.3 PROBLEMS

Evaluate the following combinations (Exercises 1–4):

1. $\binom{4}{3}$

2 $\binom{10}{6}$ and $\binom{10}{4}$

3. $\binom{20}{2}$; $\binom{20}{1}$ and $\binom{20}{0}$

4. $\binom{52}{13}$ This represents the number of different possible hands of 13 cards that could be dealt with a standard pack of playing cards.

5. Given your answer to Exercise 4, what is the probability of getting a complete suit of cards in one of the four hands dealt from a standard pack of cards?

6. A binomial model has $n = 5, p = 0.5$. Find the probabilities of each of the six possible outcomes.

7. A large population of people has 60% women and 40% men. If a random sample of 8 people is selected, find the probabilities of the following outcomes:

   (a) all women are selected;
   (b) two men are selected;
   (c) less than four men are selected.

8. What would be the probabilities if the sample size had been 10 in Exercise 7?

9. Find each of the probabilities for a binomial model with $n = 8, p = 0.1$.

10. A quality control scheme takes a sample of 10 items and checks the whole batch if more than 1 is defective. Given that the probability of a defective item is 0.05, what is the probability that the whole batch will be checked?

10.4 POISSON DISTRIBUTION

While the binomial model given above will be successful in many cases in modelling business or production situations, where the numbers involved are large and the probability of the occurrence of a characteristic is small, or where the numbers involved become infinite, then the Poisson probability model will be a better representation of the situation. The model works with the expected or average number of occurrences; if this is not given it can be found as np.

The probability model is:

$$P(x) = \frac{\lambda^x e^{-\lambda}}{x!}$$

where λ is the average number of times a characteristic occurs and x is the number of occurrences (x may be any integer from 0 to infinity). For example, if a company receives an average of three calls per 5 minute period of the working day, then we can calculate the probabilities of receiving a particular number of calls in a randomly selected 5 minute period.

The average number of calls $= \lambda = 3$

and $e^{-3} = 0.0498$

Therefore,

$$P(0 \text{ calls}) = \frac{3^0(0.0498)}{0!} = 0.0498$$

$$P(1 \text{ call}) = \frac{3^1(0.0498)}{1!} = 0.1494$$

$$P(2 \text{ calls}) = \frac{3^2(0.0498)}{2!} = 0.2241$$

$$P(3 \text{ calls}) = \frac{3^3(0.0498)}{3!} = 0.2241$$

$$P(4 \text{ calls}) = \frac{3^4(0.0498)}{4!} = 0.168\ 075$$

As you may have noticed, there is a **recursive relationship** between any two consecutive probabilities, such that:

$$P(4) = \frac{3}{4}\ P(3) = \frac{3}{4}\ (0.2241) = 0.168\ 075$$

or more generally:

$$P(N) = \frac{\lambda}{N}\ P(N - 1)$$

If the company quoted above has only four telephone lines, and calls last for at least 5 minutes, then there is a probability of:

$$P(0) + P(1) + P(2) + P(3) + P(4)$$
$$0.0498 + 0.494 + 0.2241 + 0.2241 + 0.168075 = 0.815\ 475$$

or approximately 0.815 of the switchboard being able to handle all incoming calls. Put another way, you would expect the switchboard to be sufficient for 81.5% of the time, but for callers to be unable to make the connection during 18.5% of the time. This raises the question of whether another line should be installed.

$$P(5 \text{ calls}) = \frac{3}{5}\ P(4) = 0.1008$$

The switchboard would now be in a position to handle all calls for an **extra** 10% of the time, but whether or not this is worth while would depend upon the likely extra profits that this would create, against the cost of installation and running an extra telephone line.

Again, there is an alternative to calculating all of the probabilities each time, by using tables of cumulative Poisson probabilities. For example, if the average number of faults found on a new car at its pre-delivery inspection is five, then from tables we can find that

	(a) $P(3 \text{ or more})$	= 0.8753
or	(b) $P(5 \text{ or more})$	= 0.5595
or	(c) $P(10 \text{ or more})$	= 0.0318

and, as before, these can be manipulated. From (a), we see that $1 - 0.8753 = 0.1247$ so that the probability of a car having less than three faults is 0.1247; or we would expect only 12.47% of cars that have pre-delivery inspections to have less than three faults.

For the Poisson distribution it can be shown that the mean and variance are both equal to λ.

10.5 POISSON APPROXIMATION TO THE BINOMIAL

Both distributions are discrete probability models, but for many values of λ = np the Poisson model is considerably more skewed than the binomial. However, for small values of p (less than 0.1), and large values of n, it may be easier to use a Poisson distribution. (Note that if p is very small, $(1 - p)$ will be close to 1 and hence $np(1 - p) \approx np = \lambda$ which is both the mean and the variance of the Poisson distribution.)

Example

If the probability of a fault in a piece of precision equipment is 0.0001, and each completed machine has 10 000 components, what is the probability of there being two or more faults?

(a) Using Poisson distribution:

$\lambda = np = 10\,000 \times 0.0001 = 1$

$P(0) = e^{-1} = 0.3679$

$P(1) = e^{-1} = \underline{0.3679}$

$\phantom{P(1) = e^{-1} = }0.7358$

Therefore, $P(2 \text{ or more}) = 1 - 0.7358 = 0.2642$

(b) Using binomial distribution:

$P(0) = (0.9999)^{10\,000}$ $= 0.3679$

$P(1) = 10\,000\,(0.0001)(0.9999)^{9999} = \underline{0.3679}$

$\phantom{P(1) = 10\,000\,(0.0001)(0.9999)^{9999} = }0.7358$

Therefore, $P(2 \text{ or more}) = 1 - 0.7358 = 0.2642$

Comparing these two answers, it is suggested that method (a) is very much easier to work with than method (b).

10.6 PROBLEMS

1. Find each of the Poisson probabilities from $P(0)$ to $P(6)$ of a distribution with a mean of 3.
2. For the distribution in Exercise 1, what is the probability of more than 6?
3. Find each of the Poisson probabilities from $P(0)$ to $P(4)$ of a distribution with a mean of 2.3.
4. For the distribution in Exercise 3, what is the probability of 4 or less? What is the probability of more than 4?
5. (a) Items are packed into boxes of 1000, and each item has a probability of 0.001 of having some type of fault. What is the probability that a box will contain less than three defective items?
   (b) If the company sells 100 000 boxes per year and guarantees less than three defectives per box, what is the expected number of guarantee claims?
   (c) Replacement of a box returned under the guarantee costs £150. What is the expected cost of guarantee claims?
   (d) Boxes sell at £100 but cost £60 to produce and distribute. What is the company's expected profit for sales of boxes?
6. A man has four cars for hire. The average demand on a weekday is for two cars. Assuming 312 weekdays per year, obtain the theoretical frequency distribution of the number of cars demanded during a weekday. Hence estimate to the nearest whole number, the number of days on which demand exceeds supply. (Assume demand does not surpass nine cars per day.) Would you suggest that the man buys another car?

10.7 APPENDIX

For a small sample it may be preferable to use **Pascal's triangle** to find the number of combinations, or the coefficients for each term in the binomial probability model. This begins with:

```
   1
 1   1
```

to find the next line, which will have three terms, the first and last will be 1s, the middle term will be the sum of the two terms just **above** it:

```
      1
    1   1
     (1 + 1)
  1    2    1
```

and this will apply to a sample size of two.

This process continues, to give the next line,

```
    (1 + 2)  (2 + 1)
  1    3      3    1
```

which will apply for a sample of size three. The process can continue until the desired sample size is reached.

```
                        1
                     1     1
                  1     2     1                                    2
               1     3     3     1                                 3
            1     4     6     4     1                              4
         1     5    10    10     5     1                           5
      1     6    15    20    15     6     1                        6
   1     7    21    35    35    21     7     1                     7
 1    8    28    56    70    56    28     8    1                   8
 1   9    36    84   126   126    84    36    9    1               9
1   10   45   120   210   252   210   120   45   10   1           10
1  11   55   165   330   462   462   330  165   55   11  1        11
1 12  66  220  495  792  924  792  495  220  66  12  1           12
```

Example   The number of different combinations of six defective items in samples of size 10 is the 7th term from the left in the row corresponding to sample size 10, i.e. 210.
Alternatively, the binomial coefficient

$$\binom{10}{6} = \frac{10!}{4! \, 6!} = 210$$

11 The normal distribution

When a variable is **continuous**, and its value is affected a large number of chance factors, none of which predominates, then it will frequently have a **normal distribution**. (The word 'normal' does not imply any value-judgement.) The distribution does occur frequently and is probably the most widely used statistical distribution. A normal distribution is a **symmetrical** distribution about its mean (Fig. 11.1).

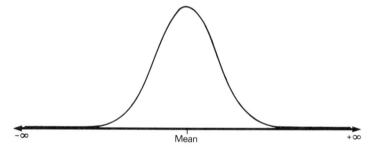

Figure 11.1   A normal distribution.

Variables having a normal distribution may be associated with production, for example the weights of jars of jam, or with human populations, for example people's height and weight, and thus clothes' sizes, or with opinions if measured on a suitable scale. These distributions are often summarized by their mean and variance (usually labelled μ and σ^2 respectively). If a variable X has a normal distribution, this may be written as $X \sim N(\mu, \sigma^2)$. Normal distributions are characterized particularly by the **areas** in various sectors of the distribution. If these areas are considered as a proportion of the total area under the distribution curve, then they may also be considered as the probabilities of obtaining a value from the distribution in that sector.

Theoretically, to find the area under the distribution curve in the sector less than some value x we should need to evaluate the integral

$$\int_{-\infty}^{x} \frac{1}{\sigma \sqrt{2\pi}} \exp\left[-\frac{(x - \mu)^2}{2\sigma^2} \right] dx$$

which equals 1 when x is infinite.

Fortunately there is an easier method of finding this area.

11.1 THE STANDARD NORMAL DISTRIBUTION

For **any** normal distribution, if the horizontal scale is measured in terms of the number of standard deviations away from the mean we may use published tables to find various required areas, and hence probabilities. This is a transformation to the standard normal distribution, which now has a mean of 0 and a standard deviation of 1.

For a value of X in a normal distribution, this transformation will be:

$$Z = \frac{X - \mu}{\sigma}$$

For example, if a variable X has a normal distribution with a mean of 100 and a standard deviation of 10, then:

if $X = 115$ $\qquad Z = \dfrac{115 - 100}{10} = 1.5$

if $X = 75$ $\qquad Z = \dfrac{75 - 100}{10} = -2.5$

if $X = 111.3$ $\qquad Z = \dfrac{111.3 - 100}{10} = 1.13$

The area excluded in the **right-hand tail** of the distribution is given in Appendix 3 and is shown in Fig. 11.2. For example, the area in the right-hand tail above $Z = 1.03$ is 0.1515. Since the total under the standard normal curve is 1, this area is also the probability of obtaining a value from the **original distribution** more than 1.03 standard deviations above the mean. Manipulating the value from the table, we see that the probability of obtaining a value below 1.03 standard deviations above the mean is:

$1 - 0.1515 = 0.8485$

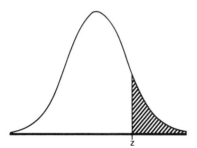

Figure 11.2

To find the probability of a value between 1 and 1.1 standard deviations above the mean, we have

area above $Z = 1$: 0.1587
area above $Z = 1.1$: 0.1357 subtract
area between $Z = 1$ and $Z = 1.1$: 0.0230

Since the standard normal distribution is symmetrical about its mean of 0, an area to the right of a positive value of Z will be identical to the area to the left of the corresponding negative value of Z. (Note that areas cannot be negative.) Thus to find the area between $Z = -1$ and $Z = +1$, we have:

area to left of $Z = -1$:   0.1587
area to right of $Z = +1$:   0.1587   add
                                         0.3174

Therefore,

area between $Z = -1$ and $Z = +1$ is $1 - 0.3174 = 0.6826$

For **any** normal distribution, 68.26% of the values will be within one standard deviation of the mean. (Hint: it is often useful to draw a sketch of the area required by a problem and compare this with Fig. 11.2.)

Exercise   What percentage of values will be within 1.96 standard deviations of the mean? (Answer: 95%.)

If a population is known to have a normal distribution, and its mean and variance are known, then we may use the tables to express facts about this population.

Example   The attendance at rock concerts at a particular stadium has a normal distribution with a mean of 15 000 and a variance of 4 000 000. The promoters are able to break even at an attendance of 12 500; what proportion of concerts will make a loss?

Mean = 15 000,   variance = 4 000 000:
standard deviation = $\sqrt{\text{variance}}$ = 2000
Therefore, $Z = \dfrac{12500 - 15000}{2000} = -1.25$

(Note that we have used two scales in Fig. 11.3, one for Z and one for the original distribution; this may help in understanding some questions.)

From tables, area to right of $Z = +1.25$
is equal to area to left of $Z = -1.25$: 0.1056
Thus, 10.56% of the concerts will make a loss.

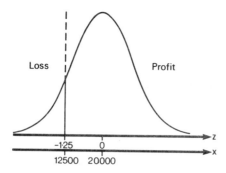

Figure 11.3

11.2 PROBLEMS

1. A normal distribution has a mean of 25 and a standard deviation of 10. Find the Z-values for each of the following X values:

   (a) 26
   (b) 35
   (c) 19
   (d) 12.35
   (e) 28.42

2. Use the tables of areas under the standard normal distribution to find the following areas:

   (a) to the right of $Z = 2.0$
   (b) to the right of $Z = 2.94$
   (c) to the left of $Z = 1.75$
   (d) to the left of $Z = 0.33$
   (e) to the left of $Z = -0.89$
   (f) to the left of $Z = -1.96$
   (g) to the right of $Z = -2.61$
   (h) to the right of $Z = -0.1$
   (i) between $Z = +1.37$ and $Z = +1.95$
   (j) between $Z = +1.00$ and $Z = +2.00$
   (k) between $Z = -1.55$ and $Z = -0.55$
   (l) between $Z = -3.1$ and $Z = -0.99$
   (m) between $Z = -2.1$ and $Z = +1.31$
   (n) between $Z = -2.58$ and $Z = +2.58$

3. Find the Z value, such that the standard normal curve area:

   (a) to the right of Z is 0.0307
   (b) to the left of Z is 0.1539
   (c) to the right of Z is 0.2005
   (d) to the right of Z is 0.8907
   (e) to the left of Z is 0.9901
   (f) to the left of Z is 0.001 35
   (g) between $-Z$ and $+Z$ is 0.9010
   (h) between $-Z$ and $+Z$ is 0.9500

4. Invoices at a particular depot have amounts which follow a normal distribution with a mean of £103.60 and a standard deviation of £8.75.

   (a) What percentage of invoices will be over £120.05?
   (b) What percentage of invoices will be below £92.75?
   (c) What percentage of invoices will be between £83.65 and £117.60?
   (d) What will be the invoice amount such that approximately 25% of invoices are for greater amounts?
   (e) Above what amount will 90% of invoices lie?

5. Items coming from the end of a production line are measured for their diameter. The measurements have a mean of 1450 mm and a variance of 0.25 mm^2.

   (a) To meet quality control checks, the items must be between 1448.5 mm and 1451.5 mm. What proportion will meet these standards?
   (b) At a later stage in the production process, this item has to fit into a hole with a diameter which has a normal distribution with a mean of 1451 mm and a standard deviation of 1 mm. What proportion of these holes will have diameters over 1448.5?
   (c) What proportion of holes will have diameters above 1451.5 mm?

11.3 NORMAL APPROXIMATION TO THE BINOMIAL

Although the binomial distribution is a discrete probability distribution, and the normal distribution is continuous, it will be possible to use the normal distribution, as an approximation to the binomial if n is large, and $p > 0.1$. (As we saw in the last chapter if $p < 0.1$ we would use the Poisson approximation to the binomial.) To see why this will work, consider a binomial distribution with a probability, p, of 0.2. For various values of n, we have distributions as shown in Fig. 11.4.

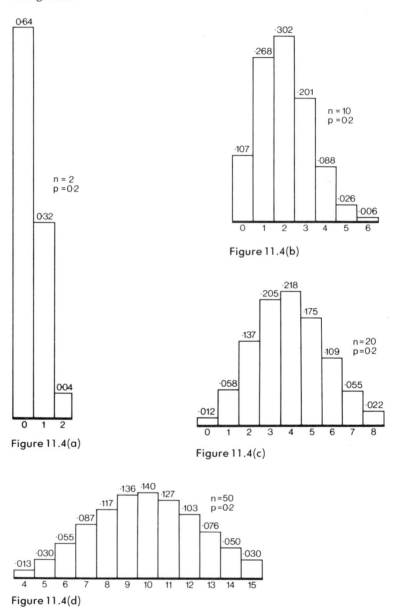

Figure 11.4(a)

Figure 11.4(b)

Figure 11.4(c)

Figure 11.4(d)

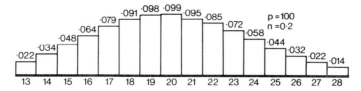

Figure 11.4(e)

Looking at the various parts of Fig. 11.4, we see that with $n = 2$, we have a highly skewed distribution; the mean will be $np = 0.4$. As n increases, the amount of skewness decreases: in Fig. 11.4b, the mean is 2 and in Fig. 11.4c, the mean is 4, and even at this stage, we are beginning to see the typical 'bell shape' of the normal distribution curve. In Fig. 11.4e, the mean is 20, and although the shape of the histogram is not exactly that of the normal curve, it is very close.

If we wish to use the normal distribution as an approximation to the binomial distribution, we must develop a method of moving from a discrete distribution to a continuous one. To do this, look at Fig. 11.5 where a curve has been superimposed on the histogram.

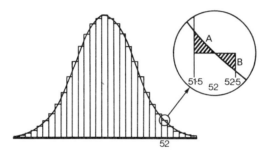

Figure 11.5

Here we see that as the curve cuts through the **midpoints** of the blocks of the histogram, small areas such as B are **excluded**, while other areas, such as A, are **included** under the curve but not in the histogram. These areas will tend to cancel each other out. Since each block represents a whole number, often the number of successes, it can be considered as extending from 0.5 below that integer to 0.5 above. Thus in the example above, the block representing 52 successes extends from 51.5 to 52.5. In order to find the area and hence the probability for a series of outcomes, it will thus be necessary to go from 0.5 below the lowest integer to 0.5 above the highest integer. If from Fig. 11.5 we wanted to find the probability of 49, 50, 51 and 52 successes, then we would need to find the area under the normal curve from $X = 48.5$ to $X = 52.5$, or if we wanted to find the probability of 52 or more successes, we should require the area to the right of $X = 51.5$.

To find areas, we must convert the X values into Z values, on the standard normal distribution. From the previous chapter, we know that for a binomial distribution, the mean $= np$ and the standard deviation $= \sqrt{[np(1 - p)]}$; and these values can be used to obtain the Z value:

$$Z = \frac{X - np}{\sqrt{[np(1 - p)]}}$$

Example   Enquiries at a travel agents lead only sometimes to a holiday booking being made. The agent needs to take 35 bookings per week to break even. If during a week he has 100 enquiries and the probability of a booking in each case is 0.4, find the probability that he will at least break even in this particular week.

This is a binomial situation since p is fixed (at 0.4) and each enquiry either leads to a booking or does not.

$n = 100$ $p = 0.4$ mean $= np = 40$
standard deviation $= \sqrt{[np(1 - p)]} = \sqrt{[(100(0.4)(0.6)]} = 4.899$

He will at least break even if he takes 35 or more bookings, and thus we need the area under the normal curve to the right of $X = 34.5$.

$$Z = \frac{34.5 - 40}{4.899} = -1.12$$

Area to the left of $Z = -1.12$: 0.1314.
Therefore, area to the right of $Z = -1.12$: $1 - 0.1314 = 0.8686$.
The probability he will at least break even is 0.8686, using the normal approximation to the binomial distribution.
If the binomial probability had been computed directly as

P(at least break even) $= P(35) + P(36) + \ldots + P(100)$

we have $= 0.8697$
As you can see, there is very little difference in the two answers.

11.4   NORMAL APPROXIMATION TO THE POISSON

In a similar way to the binomial distribution, as the mean, $\lambda = np$, gets larger and larger, the amount of skewness in the Poisson distribution decreases, until it is possible to use the normal distribution. To convert values from the original distribution into Z values, we will now use:

$$Z = \frac{X - \lambda}{\sqrt{\lambda}}$$

(Note that it is usual to use the normal approximation if $\lambda > 30$. Again, we should allow for the fact that we are going from a discrete to a continuous distribution.)

Example   The average number of broken eggs per lorry load is known to be 50. What is the probability that there will be more than 70 broken eggs on a particular lorry load?

Mean $= \lambda = 50$; standard deviation $= \sqrt{\lambda} = \sqrt{50} = 7.071$
Area required is that above $X = 70.5$

$$Z = \frac{70.5 - 50}{7.071} = 2.90$$

Area to right of $Z = 2.9 = 0.001\ 87$
Therefore, P(more than 70 broken eggs) $= 0.001\ 87$

11.5 COMBINATIONS OF VARIABLES

It is often useful to combine variables by either adding or subtracting values. An assembled product, for example, could be made from a number of different components, each individually described by a mean and a standard deviation. To consider the characteristics of this assembled product we will need to **combine** the means and standard deviations from the consituent parts. In assessing the results of a survey (see Sections 13.2.1 and 13.2.2 for examples) we may need to combine **results** with several sources of variation. We may wish to compare the difference in annual income by region or by sex, for example.

If X and Y are two **independent, normally distributed** random variables with means of μ_1 and μ_2 and variances of σ_1^2 and σ_2^2 respectively, then for X + Y:

mean   = $\mu_1 + \mu_2$
variance = $\sigma_1^2 + \sigma_2^2$

for X − Y

mean   = $\mu_1 - \mu_2$
variance = $\sigma_1^2 + \sigma_2^2$

We can note that if we are adding variables, the mean of the sum is the sum of the means and the variance of the sum is the sum of the variances. We add variances and not standard deviations. Standard deviation is calculated from the square root of variance

$$\text{standard deviation} = \sqrt{(\sigma_1^2 + \sigma_2^2)}$$

Example   An assembled product is made from two parts. The weight of each part is normally distributed with mean and standard deviation as follows:

Part	Mean	Standard deviation
1	15	4
2	20	2

What percentage of these assembled products weighs more than 36 kilograms?

Consider the assembled product as an addition of weights. We obtain

mean $= \mu = 15 + 20 = 35$
standard deviation $= \sigma = \sqrt{(4^2 + 2^2)} = 4.4721$

The corresponding Z-value is

$$Z = \frac{X - \mu}{\sigma} = \frac{36 - 35}{4.4721} = 0.22$$

The area to the right of $Z = 0.22$ is 0.4129 so that the percentage we would expect to weigh more than 36 kilograms is 41.29%.

11.6 CENTRAL LIMIT THEOREM

If the normal distribution only applied to the situations given above, it would be a very useful statistical distribution for modelling behaviour. It also applies to a whole range of sampling situations which permits an even wider range of use. The interpretation of sample results will be dealt with in Part V, but in this chapter we will indicate **why** the **sampling distributions** come about.

We will not attempt to derive this idea mathematically but rather will consider what will happen in a specific case, and then state the general theorem. Consider a population that has a normal distribution with a mean μ and a variance σ^2 as shown in Fig. 11.6. If we took every possible sample of one from this distribution then we would just obtain the original population, and the diagram would be **exactly** as in Fig. 11.6. However, if we increase the sample size to two, and calculate the mean, there will be a change in the distribution obtained. From the use of the probability tables, we know that we are much more likely to get a sample value from somewhere near the mean rather than from a point on the distribution which is a long way away from the mean. Thus the probability that both values in our sample of two will be close to the mean will be considerably higher than the probability that both values will be a long way below the mean, or a long way above the mean. Again, considering every possible sample of two from the distribution, and calculating the mean, there will be more sample means close to the population mean than there were original population values, since one small value and one large value will give a mean close to the centre of the distribution.

Figure 11.6

This situation is illustrated in Fig. 11.7 where we also see that the average of all of the sample averages will be the population mean μ. As we increase the sample size, the probability of getting all of the sample values, and hence the sample average in an extreme tail of the original population distribution, becomes extremely small, while the probability of the sample mean being close to the original population mean increases.

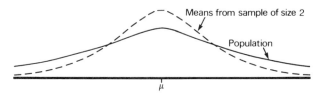

Figure 11.7

The illustration in Fig. 11.8 shows that as the sample size increases, the distribution of sample means remains a normal distribution with μ as its mean; however, the variance of the distribution decreases as the sample size increases. It can be shown that the sample mean has the following distribution:

$$\overline{X} \sim N\left(\mu, \ \frac{\sigma^2}{n}\right)$$

where n is the sample size.

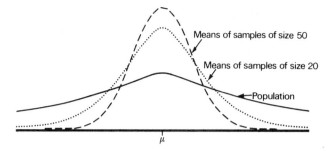

Figure 11.8

More generally, the central limit theorem states that for any population distribution, whether it is discrete or continuous, skewed, rectangular or even multimodal, the distribution of the sample means will be approximately normal if the sample size is sufficiently large.

In the case of a proportion of a sample, we are effectively considering a binomial situation, and, as we saw above in Section 11.2, as n becomes large, the binomial distribution can be approximated by the normal distribution.

Thus the sampling distribution of a proportion will also be a normal distribution. For a distribution with a population proportion π we have the distribution of the sample proportion, P, as:

$$P \sim N\left(\pi, \frac{\pi(1 - \pi)}{n}\right)$$

It is not being suggested that in any situation all possible samples would be selected, but if we know the **theoretical distribution** of sample means or sample proportions, then we can compare this with the one, particular sample that we have taken.

11.7 PROBLEMS

1. (a) In a very large population there are 40% of the people who support a change in government policy on regional aid. If a sample of 1000 people is chosen at random, what is the probability that this sample will contain over 425 people who support a change in policy?

   (b) What is the probability that less than 390 people support a change in policy?

2. The average number of customers in a shop per week is 256. What is the probability of there being

   (a) more than 240 customers in a week?
   (b) less then 280 customers in a week?
   (c) 234 to 290 customers in a week?

3. A process yields 15% defective items. If 180 items are randomly selected from the process, what is the probability that the number of defectives is 30 or more?

4. If the probability of a smoker is 0.3, determine the probability of more than 20 smokers

   (a) in a randomly selected sample of 80,
   (b) at a conference of 70 doctors.

   State any assumptions made.

5. In a certain manufacturing process, 25% of the items produced are classified as seconds. If 5000 items have been produced, what is the probability that at least 1300 items will be available as seconds for a sale?

6. A switchboard receives 42 calls per minute on average. Estimate the probability that there will be at least

   (a) 40 calls in the next minute,
   (b) 50 calls in the next minute.

7. The average demand for a particular item from stock is found to be 45 per week. Estimate the probability of a demand for 50 or more

   (a) in the next week,
   (b) in the next 2 weeks.

8. The times taken, in minutes, to complete three tasks, machining, assembly and packaging, have been recorded as follows:

	Mean	Standard deviation
Machining	25	7.5
Assembly	15	5.5
Packaging	15	4.5

   If a particular job requires all three tasks, what is the probability that the job will take no more than 1 hour?

9. It has been estimated that the average weekly wage in a particular industry is £172 and that the standard deviation is £9.

   (a) What is the probability that a random sample of 10 employees will have an average weekly wage of £180 or more?
   (b) What is the probability that an individual will have an average weekly wage of £180 or more if it can be assumed that wages follow a normal distribution?

Part IV
CONCLUDING EXERCISE

Draw a floor plan of a work place or meeting place that you are familiar with. It could look something like this:

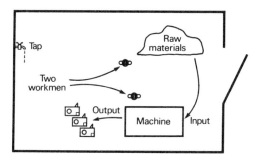

Then note all the events you consider could affect this place of activity, the outcomes of which you believe are subject to chance.

For each of these events (e.g. loss of water supply, delivery of a new machine, sickness, machine breakdown) suggest an appropriate model (or distribution) and hypothetical parameters. Determine the probability of an event-free day.

Part V
STATISTICAL INFERENCE

Once measurement has been achieved and the data collated we need to quantify our findings. These chapters are concerned with what meaning we can give to the data: the answers the data can provide. We may need to say how reliable our results are, whether the data provide evidence to support our views, or whether certain relationships exist.

If, for example, we had estimated the value of stock to be £15 000 000 from a sample, it would give more meaning to our result if we could say the figure was within £1000, or £5000, or £10 000, or more of the exact value. A political party may estimate its share of the vote to be 52% from a random sample but before predicting victory it would need to know whether this estimate was likely to be within 1%, 2%, 5% or 10% of the true figure. A brand manager may wish to know whether there is evidence to suggest a relationship between the sales of a particular product and the packaging used on the basis of survey data. All these are examples of statistical inference: the use of survey data to infer something about a population.

Survey or sample data provide **estimates** of true population parameters. If we want to know exact values for these parameters we will need census or complete data. It is worth noting though that a complete census will only provide complete data for a certain point in time.

Exercise   Give examples of where estimated values are used to provide business, political and social information.

12 Confidence intervals for means, percentages and medians

In general, sampling is concerned with the collection of data from some defined population. The usefulness of these data will depend on the sample design, method of measurement and the sampling error.

Sample design refers to the method of selecting people, items or institutions. We have already considered how a sample can be selected and improved by the use of appropriate stratification factors (see Chapter 1). In terms of sampling theory, it is important that the method of selection is in accordance with random or probability sampling.

The method of measurement could be a personal interview, postal questionnaire or an observation. The results of the survey will only be as meaningful as the measurement achieved. If the questions asked, for example, are misunderstood, no statistical analysis, however detailed, is going to give the answers meaning. Sociology and psychology are two disciplines particularly concerned with the useful measurement of complex phenomena in human populations.

In this chapter we shall consider only an assessment of the sample statistics rather than sample design; a sample statistic being any summary figure we calculate from the survey data. These sample statistics are likely to vary from sample to sample. Suppose that you are one of a group of 30 students and that 5 students are to be randomly selected to estimate the average time spent each week reading statistics books. The sample, by chance, could include the 5 students who are the most conscientious or the least conscientious. Sampling theory is concerned with how the sample results represent the population.

12.1 STATISTICAL INFERENCE

If we want to be certain about our results, then we need to include all members of the population in our sample. To calculate exactly the average time a group of students spend each week reading statistics books would require a complete enumeration or census. To test the market response to a new product with certainty or predict the outcome of the next election almost exactly, would also require a census. However, a census is unnecessary for most purposes. Censuses are costly, time-consuming and likely to give an accuracy not required. Could you possibly imagine a situation where a marketing manager would fund interviews with all people who had purchased baked beans in the last two weeks? The findings of social, economic or marketing research are generally based on survey results.

Statistical inference is concerned with the ways we use sample results to estimate or infer values for the population. A sample mean $\bar{x}$ is used to estimate the population average, μ. A sample percentage, p, is used to estimate the population percentage, π. In assessing the sample results we write probability statements of the following form:

$$\mu = \bar{x} \pm \text{sampling error}$$
$$\pi = p \pm \text{sampling error}$$

The **sampling error** is our measurement of how close to the population value we expect the sample result to be.

12.2 CONFIDENCE INTERVAL FOR THE MEAN

The sample mean $\bar{x}$ is used as an estimate for the fixed population parameter μ. The value of $\bar{x}$ will **vary** from sample to sample as illustrated in Fig. 12.1.

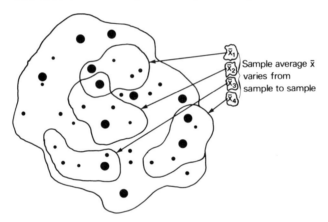

Sample average $\bar{x}$ varies from sample to sample

Figure 12.1 A population of different sized 'dots'

The variation of the sample means is described by the sampling distribution (see Chapter 11). This follows a normal distribution, for large samples, in accordance with the central limit theorem.

The **central limit theorem** (for means) states that if a simple random sample of size n $(n > 30)$ is taken from a population with mean μ and standard deviation σ, the sampling distribution of the sample mean $\bar{x}$ is approximately normal with mean μ and standard error $\sigma/\sqrt{n}$.

One characteristic of the normal distribution is that 95% of sample means will be within the range $\mu \pm 1.96\ \sigma/\sqrt{n}$ as shown in Fig. 12.2. As we have already seen, a z-value of 1.96 will exclude $2\frac{1}{2}\%$ in the right-hand tail area and, owing to the symmetry of the normal distribution, a z-value of -1.96 will exclude $2\frac{1}{2}\%$ in the left-hand tail area. As a probability statement we could write:

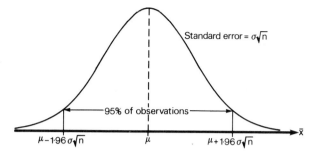

Figure 12.2   The distribution of sample means

$$P\left(\mu - 1.96\frac{\sigma}{\sqrt{n}} \leqslant \bar{x} \leqslant \mu + 1.96\frac{\sigma}{\sqrt{n}}\right) = 0.95$$

Some algebraic manipulation will produce the more familiar form of a 95% confidence interval:

$$\mu = \bar{x} \pm 1.96\frac{\sigma}{\sqrt{n}}$$

The 95% confidence interval gives a range which will include the true population parameter 19 times out of 20. It must be remembered that μ, the population parameter, remains fixed, and generally unknown, and that it is the sample mean, $\bar{x}$, and the corresponding error term that are subject to variation. It can be seen in Fig. 12.3, for example, that sample 3 is one of those 5% of samples which produces an interval estimate not including μ.

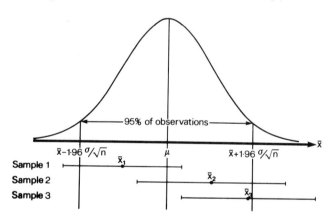

Figure 12.3   Confidence interval from different samples

Example

A sample of 100 invoices is randomly selected from a large file and the sample mean calculated to be £86. If the population standard deviation is known to be £6, calculate the 95% confidence interval of the mean.

The sample size is $n = 100$, the sample mean = £86 and the standard deviation $\sigma = $ £6. By substitution, the 95% confidence interval is:

$$\mu = 86 \pm 1.96 \times \frac{6}{\sqrt{100}}$$

$$= £86 \pm £1.176$$

or, we could write

$$£84.824 \leqslant \mu \leqslant £87.176$$

The confidence interval shows how closely a sample result is likely to estimate a true value.

The above calculations assume that the true standard deviation σ is known. In most cases, σ is unknown and we need to substitute a sample estimate s. This sample estimate of standard deviation s, will differ slightly from that used as a descriptive statistic (see Chapter 3) in that a divisor of $(n - 1)$ rather than n is used (see Section 12.1.2). The structure of the confidence interval is still valid provided the sample size is reasonably large. In general we shall use a 95% confidence interval of the form

$$\mu = \bar{x} \pm 1.96 \frac{s}{\sqrt{n}}$$

Examples

1. A sample of 80 housewives was selected from a large population. If the average amount spent weekly on a particular product was found to be £1.40 and the sample standard deviation was £0.15, calculate the 95% confidence interval of the mean.
   The sample size $n = 80$, and the sample statistics are $\bar{x} = £1.40$ and $s = £0.15$. By substitution, the 95% confidence interval is:

$$\mu = 1.40 \pm 1.96 \times \frac{0.15}{\sqrt{80}}$$

$$= £1.40 \pm £0.033$$

or we could write

$$£1.367 \leqslant \mu \leqslant £1.433$$

2. A sample of 200 components was selected from a production process to estimate the expected length of life. The sample mean was 300 hours and the sample standard deviation 8 hours. Calculate the 95% and the 99% confidence intervals.
   The sample statistics are $n = 200$, $\bar{x} = 300$ hours and $s = 8$ hours. By substitution, the 95% confidence interval is

$$\mu = 300 \pm 1.96 \times \frac{8}{\sqrt{200}}$$

$$= 300 \text{ hours} \pm 1.1 \text{ hours}$$

To calculate the 99% confidence interval we use a z-value of 2.576, which excludes $\frac{1}{2}$% in each tail area, rather than a z-value of 1.96. By substitution, the 99% confidence interval is

$$\mu = 300 \pm 2.576 \times \frac{8}{\sqrt{200}}$$

$$= 300 \text{ hours} \pm 1.5 \text{ hours}$$

We would expect to be correct 99 times out of 100 in making a statement of the kind 'the mean is 300 hours $\pm$ 1.5 hours'. You will notice that as we become more certain about the statement we are making, that is by moving from a 95% to a 99% confidence interval, the sampling error becomes larger. Sampling error depends on the probability excluded (or observations excluded) in the extremes of the normal distribution.

This example provides yet another justification for sampling. Measurement itself can be destructive, e.g. estimating the length of life of a light bulb or measuring the power of an H-bomb.

12.2.1 The calculation of confidence intervals using survey data

Suppose the results of an incomes survey were given as in Table 12.1. We can calculate the mean and sample standard deviation using

$$\bar{x} = \frac{\Sigma fx}{n}$$

$$s = \sqrt{\left[\frac{\Sigma f(x - \bar{x})^2}{n - 1}\right]} \quad \text{or} \quad s = \sqrt{\left[\frac{\Sigma fx^2}{n - 1} - \frac{(\Sigma fx)^2}{n(n - 1)}\right]}$$

Table 12.1

Weekly income	Frequency
£100 but less than £200	10
£200 but less than £300	28
£300 but less than £400	42
£400 but less than £600	50
£600 but less than £1000	20
	150

The sample standard deviation, s, sometimes denoted by $\hat{\sigma}$, is being used as an **estimator** of the population standard deviation σ. The sample standard deviation will vary from sample to sample in the same way that the sample mean, $\bar{x}$, varies from sample to sample. The sample mean will sometimes be too high or too low, but on average will equal the population mean μ. You will notice that the distribution of sample means $\bar{x}$ in Fig. 12.2 is symmetrical about the population mean μ. In contrast, if we use the divisor n, the sample standard deviation will on average be less than σ. To ensure that the sample standard deviation is large enough to estimate the population standard deviation σ reasonably, we use the divisor $(n - 1)$. The calculations are shown in Tables 12.2 and 12.3.

Table 12.2

Weekly income	Frequency	x	fx	$f(x - \bar{x})^2$
£100 but less than £200	10	150	1 500	772 840
£200 but less than £300	28	250	7 000	887 152
£300 but less than £400	42	350	14 700	255 528
£400 but less than £600	50	500	25 000	259 200
£600 but less than £1000	20	800	16 000	2 767 680
	150		64 200	4 942 400

$$\bar{x} = \frac{\Sigma fx}{n} = \frac{64\ 200}{150} = £428$$

$$s = \sqrt{\left[\frac{\Sigma f(x - \bar{x})^2}{n - 1}\right]} = \sqrt{\frac{4\ 942\ 400}{149}} = £182.13$$

Table 12.3

Weekly income	Frequency	fx	fx²
£100 but less than £200	10	1 500	225 000
£200 but less than £300	28	7 000	1 750 000
£300 but less than £400	42	14 700	5 145 000
£400 but less than £600	50	25 000	12 500 000
£600 but less than £1000	20	16 000	12 800 000
	150	64 200	32 420 000

$$\bar{x} = \frac{\Sigma fx}{n} = \frac{64\ 200}{150} = £428$$

$$s = \sqrt{\left[\frac{\Sigma fx^2}{n-1} - \frac{(\Sigma fx)^2}{n(n-1)}\right]} = \sqrt{\left[\frac{32\ 420\ 000}{149} - \frac{(64\ 200)^2}{150 \times 149}\right]} = \underline{£182.13}$$

Confidence intervals are obtained by the substitution of sample statistics, e.g. using the results from Tables 12.2 or 12.3, by substitution the 95% confidence interval is:

$$\mu = \bar{x} \pm 1.96\ \frac{s}{\sqrt{n}}$$

$$= £428 \pm 1.96 \times \frac{182.13}{\sqrt{150}}$$

$$= £428 \pm £29.147$$

12.2.2 The determination of sample size for a mean

In general, we would not wait for the completion of a survey before assessing the likely value of the information. An important feature of sample design is the determination of sample size (see Section 1.2.3). The accuracy achieved is measured by the sampling error. Assuming simple random sampling from a large population, this error term, e, depends on the choice of confidence interval, variability within the population and sample size:

$$e = z\frac{s}{\sqrt{n}} \quad \text{or} \quad z\frac{\sigma}{\sqrt{n}}$$

if the population standard deviation is known, where $z = \pm 1.96$ for a 95% confidence interval.

The error term is increased if the standard deviation or the critical value from the normal distribution increases. The error term decreases as the sample size increases. In terms of sample design, the sample size n is one of the factors we can control:

$$n = \left(\frac{zs}{e}\right)^2$$

Example   What sample size would be required to estimate the population mean for a large file of invoices to within $\pm£0.50$ with 95% confidence if the population standard deviation is known to be £6?

To determine sample size for a 95% confidence interval, let $z = 1.96$ and, in this case, $e = 0.50$ and $\sigma = 6$. By substitution:

$$n = \left(\frac{1.96 \times 6}{0.50}\right)^2 = 553.19$$

As we are trying to achieve a minimum accuracy of $\pm £0.50$ we would round-up and specify a sample size of at least 554.

In general, the standard deviation is **unknown** and we substitute the best available estimate. This may come from a previous survey of a similar nature or from a pilot survey.

12.2.3 The finite population correction factor

It is generally assumed in sampling theory that the sample is drawn from a large population, and that the sampling error will depend only on z, σ and n. If, however, the sample is drawn from a small population, the size of the error term will also depend on the proportion of the population included. As this proportion increases, the size of the error decreases, as might be expected. An allowance is made by multiplying the standard error by the finite population correction factor:

$$\sqrt{\left(1 - \frac{n}{N}\right)}$$

where n is the sample size and N is the population size.

The 95% confidence interval becomes:

$$\mu = \bar{x} \pm 1.96 \sqrt{\left(1 - \frac{n}{N}\right)} \frac{s}{\sqrt{n}}$$

If we take a census, the sample size, n, will equal the population size, N. As a result, the finite population correction factor will be zero and the sampling error will be zero. Census results have no sampling error. In contrast, if the sample represents a small proportion of the population, the finite population correction factor will have little impact on the sampling error.

Example

Suppose a random sample of 20 students is selected from a class of 30 to estimate the average amount spent each term on books. Given that the sample mean was £12 and sample standard deviation £3, determine the 95% confidence interval.

By substitution we obtain the 95% confidence interval:

$$\mu = £12 \pm 1.96 \sqrt{\left(1 - \frac{20}{30}\right)} \frac{3}{\sqrt{20}}$$

$$= £12 \pm £0.76$$

If no allowance had been made for the proportion of the population selected (the finite population correction factor ignored) the sampling error would have been calculated as

$$1.96 \frac{s}{\sqrt{n}} = 1.96 \times \frac{3}{\sqrt{20}} = £1.31$$

In the same way that we have used a multiplication factor to allow for the proportion of the population selected, we can also use multiplication factors to allow for the effects of other aspects of the sample design.

---

1. A sample of 50 employees was randomly selected from a workforce to estimate the average travel time to work each morning. If the sample mean was 55 minutes and the sample standard deviation 13 minutes, calculate the 95% and the 99% confidence intervals.

   (Answer: 95% confidence interval μ = 55 minutes $\pm$ 3.6 minutes
   99% confidence interval μ = 55 minutes $\pm$ 4.7 minutes.)

2. A sample of 50 employees was randomly selected from a workforce to estimate the average cost of travel to work each week. Calculate the 95% confidence interval for the population mean from the survey data tabulated as follows:

Weekly travel cost (£s)	Number of employees
0 but under 5	8
5 but under 10	24
10 but under 15	14
15 but under 20	4
	50

   (Answer: $\bar{x}$ = £8.90, s = £4.17
   95% confidence travel μ = £8.90 $\pm$ £1.16.)

3. Suppose a random sample of 50 employees was selected from a workforce of 100 to estimate the average travel time to work each morning. If the sample mean was 55 minutes and the sample standard deviation 13 minutes, calculate the 95% confidence interval.

   (Answer: 95% confidence interval μ = 55 minutes $\pm$ 2.55 minutes.)

12.3 CONFIDENCE INTERVAL FOR PERCENTAGES

In the same way that the sample mean $\bar{x}$ is used to estimate the population mean μ, the sample percentage p can be used to estimate the population percentage π. The sample percentage will vary from sample to sample and follow a normal distribution, for large samples, in accordance with the central limit theorem.

The **central limit theorem** (for percentages) states that, if a simple random sample of size n ($n \geqslant 30$) is taken from a population with a percentage π having a particular characteristic, then the sampling distribution of the sample percentage p is approximated by a normal distribution with a mean of π and a standard error of

$$\sqrt{\left(\frac{\pi(100 - \pi)}{n} \right)}$$

Using an already noted characteristic of the normal distribution, we know that 95% of observations will lie within the range

$$\pi \pm 1.96 \sqrt{\left(\frac{\pi(100 - \pi)}{n} \right)}$$

as shown in Fig. 12.4.

As a probability statement we could write:

$$P\left(\pi - 1.96 \sqrt{\left[\frac{\pi(100 - \pi)}{n} \right]} \leqslant p \leqslant \pi + 1.96 \sqrt{\left[\frac{\pi(100 - \pi)}{n} \right]} \right) = 0.95$$

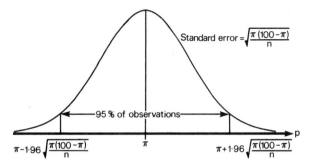

Figure 12.4   The distribution of sample percentages

but generally prefer the form:

$$\pi = p \pm 1.96 \sqrt{\left[\frac{\pi(100 - \pi)}{n} \right]}$$

As π is unknown, we substitute the value p for the estimation of standard error. The 95% confidence interval is calculated using:

$$\pi = p \pm 1.96 \sqrt{\left[\frac{p(100 - p)}{n} \right]}$$

Example   A sample of 100 invoices is randomly selected from a large file. If 12 are found to be incorrect, calculate the 95% confidence interval for the true percentage of invoices that are incorrect.

The sample percentage of invoices incorrect was $p = 12\%$. This sample statistic is used to estimate the percentage incorrect, π, for the whole file. By substitution, the 95% confidence interval is:

$$\pi = 12\% \pm 1.96 \sqrt{\left(\frac{12 \times 88}{100} \right)}$$

$$= 12\% \pm 6.4\%$$

or we could write

$$5.6\% \leqslant \pi \leqslant 18.4\%$$

12.3.1   The determination of sample size for a percentage

When estimating percentages from sample data, the size of the error term, e, will depend on the choice of confidence interval and the sample percentage, p:

$$e = z \sqrt{\left[\frac{p(100 - p)}{n} \right]}$$

where z is a critical value from the normal distribution corresponding to a particular confidence interval.

In terms of sample size:

$$n = \left(\frac{z}{e} \right)^2 \times p \times (100 - p)$$

In calculating a value for n, we need to assume either a reasonable approximation for p or that $p = 50\%$.

An approximation for p

It may be that a previous survey of similar nature or a pilot study provides a reasonable approximation for p to substitute into the above equation for n.

Example

In a pilot survey of 100 invoices, randomly selected from a large file, 12 were found to be incorrect. What sample size would be required to produce an estimate of the percentage incorrect for the whole file to within $\pm 3\%$ with 95% confidence.

In this case, the sample percentage p is 12% and the value for z is 1.96. By substitution:

$$n = \left(\frac{1.96}{3}\right)^2 \times 12 \times 88$$
$$= 450.75$$

To achieve a minimum accuracy of $\pm 3\%$ we would specify a minimum sample size of 451.

p equals 50%

If no information is available regarding the value of p we substitute 50%. Consider Table 12.4. It can be seen that 50% produces the largest possible standard error, and hence sampling error for a given sample size.

Table 12.4   The size of standard error

p	$(100-p)$	$\sqrt{\left(\dfrac{p(100-p)}{n}\right)}$
10	90	$\sqrt{(900/n)}$
20	80	$\sqrt{(1600/n)}$
30	70	$\sqrt{(2100/n)}$
40	60	$\sqrt{(2400/n)}$
50	50	$\sqrt{(2500/n)}$

Example

What sample size would be required to produce an estimate to within $\pm 3\%$ with 95% confidence if no prior information were available?

In this case let $p = 50\%$ and assume the 'worst' possible case. By substitution:

$$n = \left(\frac{1.96}{3}\right)^2 \times 50 \times 50$$
$$= 1067.11$$

To achieve a minimum accuracy of $\pm 3\%$ we would specify a sample size of 1068.

If we contrast the sample sizes calculated using the approximate value, 12%, and the assumed value, 50%, we gain some insight of the cost of no prior information. A small, investigative pilot survey is not only used to test questionnaire and analysis procedures but also to provide basic quantitative information.

As an alternative to a pilot survey followed by the main survey, a **sequential sampling procedure** can be adopted. This involves a relatively small sample to start with, to which we add numbers as better and better estimates of the parameters become available. In practice, sequential sampling requires continuation of interviewing until results with sufficient accuracy have been achieved.

Exercises

1. A sample of 50 employees was randomly selected from a workforce to estimate the percentage satisfied with existing working arrangements. If 22 of those interviewed were found to be satisfied, calculate the 95% confidence interval.
   (Answer: $\pi = 44\% \pm 13.8\%$.)

2. It has been decided to estimate the percentage of a workforce satisfied with existing working arrangements to within $\pm 5\%$ with a 95% confidence interval. What sample size would you recommend if:

   (a) a pilot study had shown that 44% were satisfied;
   (b) no prior information was available.
   (Answer: (a) 379; (b) 385.)

12.4 CONFIDENCE INTERVAL FOR THE MEDIAN: A LARGE SAMPLE APPROXIMATION

The median is a particularly useful order statistic that describes what is typical for a population when the mean is not appropriate for the measurement achieved (see Chapter 3). If the distribution is particularly skewed, as with wealth data, or lacks calibration, as with the ranking of consumer preferences, we would use the sample median as an estimate of the population median. The variation in the results that we could attribute to sampling can be expressed in terms of a confidence interval.

Since the median is determined by ranking all the observations and then counting to locate the ordered value, the probability distribution is discrete (the confidence interval for a median can be determined directly using the binomial distribution). If the sample is reasonably large ($n > 30$), however, a large sample approximation will give adequate results (see Chapter 11). Consider the ordering of observations by value, as shown below.

$$X_1, X_2, X_3, \ldots, X_n$$

where $X_i \leqslant X_{i+1}$

The median is the middle value of this ordered list, corresponding to the $(n + 1)/2$ observation. The confidence interval is defined by an upper and a lower ordered value. For a 95% confidence interval these values are located using

$$u = \frac{n}{2} \pm 1.96 \frac{\sqrt{n}}{2}$$

$$l = \frac{n}{2} - 1.96 \frac{\sqrt{n}}{2} + 1$$

where u is the location of the upper value, l is the location of the lower value, n is the sample size and 1.96 is the critical value from the normal distribution.

Example

Suppose a sample of 30 housewives was selected at random to determine the median amount spent on groceries in the last 7 days and the results listed as follows:

£3.50	£4.90	£5.30	£6.12	£7.40	£8.90
£9.67	£10.18	£10.58	£11.07	£11.28	£11.98
£12.48	£12.56	£12.83	£13.17	£13.61	£14.19
£14.85	£15.10	£15.99	£16.18	£17.41	£18.92
£20.20	£24.40	£29.80	£33.21	£38.80	£42.79

The median would correspond to the $(30 + 1)/2 = 15\frac{1}{2}$th observation. Its value would be found by averaging the 15th and 16th observations:

$$\text{median} = \frac{12.83 + 13.17}{2} = £13.00$$

The sample median provides a **point estimate** of the population median. A 95% confidence interval is determined by locating the upper and lower boundaries.

$$u = \frac{30}{2} + 1.96 \frac{\sqrt{30}}{2} = 20.37$$

$$l = \frac{30}{2} - 1.96 \frac{\sqrt{30}}{2} + 1 = 10.63$$

The upper boundary is defined by the 21st value (rounding-up) and the lower boundary by the 10th value (rounding-down). By counting values from the left, the 95% confidence interval is:

$$£11.07 \leqslant \text{median} \leqslant £15.99$$

A confidence interval provides an **interval estimate** of the population parameter.

Exercise

1. The number of faults in a sample of new cars have been listed as follows:

0	0	1	3	1	0	0	2	3
1	1	0	1	0	0	4	4	1
1	2	3	0	0	1	1	4	3
0	4	2	2	1	0	0	0	3

Determine the 95% confidence interval for the median.
(Answer: $0 \leqslant \text{median} \leqslant 2$.)

12.5 PROBLEMS

1. A sample of 50 second-hand cars was selected to estimate the average selling price. The sample mean was £2400 and sample standard deviation £800. Calculate the 95% confidence interval of the mean. Describe how you could reduce the sampling error in this case.
2. The mileages recorded for a sample of company vehicles during a given week yielded the following data:

138	164	150	132	144	125	149	157
146	158	140	147	136	148	152	144
168	126	138	176	163	119	154	165
146	173	142	147	135	153	140	135
161	145	135	142	150	156	145	128

(a) Calculate the mean and standard deviation, and construct a 95% confidence interval.

(b) What sample size would be required to estimate the average mileage to within ± 3 miles with 95% confidence? State any assumptions made.

3. The numer of breakdowns each day on a section of road were recorded for a sample of 250 days as follows:

Number of breakdowns	Number of days
0	100
1	70
2	45
3	20
4	10
5	5
	250

Calculate the 95% and the 99% confidence intervals. Explain your results.

4. The average weekly overtime earnings from a sample of workers from a particular service industry were recorded as follows:

Average weekly overtime earnings (£)	Number of workers
under 1	19
1 but under 2	29
2 but under 5	17
5 but under 10	12
10 or more	3
	80

(a) Calculate the mean, standard deviation and the 95% confidence interval for the mean.

(b) What sample size would be required to estimate the average mileage to within ± £0.50 with a 95% confidence interval?

5. In a survey of 1000 electors, 20% were found to favour party X.
  (a) Construct a 95% confidence interval for the percentage in favour of party X.
  (b) What sample size would be required to estimate the percentage in favour of party X to within ± 1% with a 95% confidence interval?

6. What sample size would be required if you wanted to estimate the percentage of homes with gas central heating to within ± 5% with a 95% confidence interval if:
  (a) a previous survey had shown the percentage to be approximately 42%;
  (b) no prior information were available?

7. Describe how you would design a survey to estimate the percentage of homes in the UK in need of major repairs.

8. A sample of 35 workers was randomly selected from a workforce of 110 to estimate the average amount spent weekly at the canteen. The sample mean was £5.40 and the sample standard deviation £2.24.

    (a) Calculate a 95% confidence interval for the mean.

    (b) What sample size would be required to estimate the mean to within ± £0.50 with a 95% confidence interval?

9. Using the data from Exercise 3 determine the median and a 95% confidence interval for the median.

10. Using the data from Exercise 4 determine the median and a 95% confidence interval for the median. Explain your results.

13 Confidence intervals: further developments

As we have seen in Chapter 12, confidence intervals generally take the form

population parameter = sample statistic ± a sampling error

The sample statistic could be a mean, a percentage or some other calculated value, and will vary from sample to sample. This variation is described by a sampling distribution and measured by a standard error. If the sampling distribution follows the normal distribution, in accordance with the central limit theorem, the sampling error for a two-sided, 95% confidence interval is ± 1.96 standard errors.

The notation and standard errors for means, percentages and their differences are summarized in Table 13.1.

Table 13.1   Notation and standard errors

Sample statistic	Population parameter	Sample estimate of standard error
$\bar{x}$	μ	$\dfrac{s}{\sqrt{n}}$
p	π	$\sqrt{\left[\dfrac{p(100-p)}{n}\right]}$
$\bar{x}_1 - \bar{x}_2$	$\mu_1 - \mu_2$	$\sqrt{\left[\dfrac{s_1^2}{n_1} + \dfrac{s_2^2}{n_2}\right]}$

(for independent samples)

13.1   ONE-SIDED CONFIDENCE INTERVAL FOR PERCENTAGES

The one-sided, 95% confidence intervals for a percentage take the form

$$\pi > p - 1.645\sqrt{\left[\frac{p(100-p)}{n}\right]}$$

or

$$\pi < p + 1.645\sqrt{\left[\frac{p(100-p)}{n}\right]}$$

Example

A sample of 40 components is randomly selected from those available for production, and 5 are found to be defective. In response to comments that the percentage of defectives is too high, construct an appropriate 95% confidence interval.

The sample size $n = 40$ and the percentage $p = (5/40) \times 100 = 12.5\%$. We can establish an upper boundary by substitution, 95% confidence interval:

$$\pi < 12.5 + 1.645 \sqrt{\left(\frac{12.5 \times 87.5}{40} \right)}$$

$$< 21.10\%$$

In contrast, the two-sided, 95% confidence interval would be:

$$\pi = 12.5 \pm 10.25$$

or $\qquad 2.25\% \leqslant \pi \leqslant 22.75\%$

The one-sided confidence interval, in this case, has allowed a more precise statement about how **high** the true percentage defective is likely to be.

Exercises

1. An operator of fleet vehicles wishes to estimate the largest number of days he can expect to lose through maintenance and repair each year. A sample of 40 service records is randomly selected. If the sample mean is 8 days, and the standard deviation 5 days, construct an appropriate 95% confidence interval. (Answer 95% confidence interval $\mu < 9.3$ days.)
2. In a survey of 600 electors, 315 claimed they would vote for party X. Construct a 95% confidence interval to show the minimum support party X can expect. (Answer: 95% confidence interval $p > 49.15\%$.)

One-sided confidence intervals for the mean can be calculated in a similar way.

13.2 THE DIFFERENCE OF MEANS AND PERCENTAGES

So far, we have considered only estimating a single population parameter from survey data, the measurement being quantified by a confidence interval. This is one important aspect of survey research, but there are others. A survey enquiry is often designed to compare changes over time or differences between two distinct groups. The comparison can be facilitated by calculating the difference of means or percentages. It shall be assumed that the samples are **independent** (see Section 11.4) and **large enough** to make any of the implicit assumptions valid.

13.2.1 The difference of means

The 95% confidence interval for the difference of means takes the form

$$\mu_1 - \mu_2 = \bar{x}_1 - \bar{x}_2 \pm 1.96 \sqrt{\left(\frac{s_1^2}{n_1} + \frac{s_2^2}{n_2} \right)}$$

where the subscripts denote sample 1 and sample 2.

Example

A sample of 75 packets of cereals was randomly selected from the production process and found to have a mean of 500 g and standard deviation of 20 g. A week later a second sample of 50 packets of cereal was selected, using the same procedure and found to have a mean of 505 g and standard deviation of 16 g. Construct a 95% confidence interval for the change in the average weight of cereal packets.

The summary statistics are as follows:

Sample 1	Sample 2
$n_1 = 75$	$n_2 = 50$
$\bar{x}_1 = 500$	$\bar{x}_2 = 505$
$s_1 = 20$	$s_2 = 16$

By substitution, the 95% confidence interval is:

$$\mu_1 - \mu_2 = (500 - 505) \pm 1.96 \sqrt{\left[\frac{(20)^2}{75} + \frac{(16)^2}{50}\right]}$$

$$= -5\,g \pm 6.34\,g$$

or

$$-11.34 \leqslant \mu_1 - \mu_2 \leqslant 1.34\,g$$

As this range includes zero, we cannot be 95% confident that there has been a decrease or increase. The observed change in the average weight could be explained by inherent variation in the sample results. In this example, a confidence interval is being used to describe the measurement or measurements achieved. A related approach is significance testing (see Chapter 14) which provides a method of deciding only whether there has been an increase, decrease or no change.

13.2.2 The difference of percentages

The 95% confidence interval for the difference of percentages takes the form

$$\pi_1 - \pi_2 = p_1 - p_2 \pm 1.96 \sqrt{\left[\frac{p_1(100 - p_1)}{n_1} + \frac{p_2(100 - p_2)}{n_2}\right]}$$

where the subscripts denote sample 1 and sample 2.

Example A sample of 120 housewives was randomly selected from those reading a particular magazine, and 18 were found to have purchased a new household product. Another sample of 150 housewives was randomly selected from those not reading the particular magazine, and only 6 were found to have purchased the product. Construct a 95% confidence interval for the difference in the purchasing behaviour.

The summary statistics are as follows:

Sample 1	Sample 2
$n_1 = 120$	$n_2 = 150$
$p_1 = \dfrac{18}{120} \times 100$	$p_2 = \dfrac{6}{150} \times 100$
$= 15\%$	$= 4\%$

By substitution, the 95% confidence interval is:

$$\pi_1 - \pi_2 = (15\% - 4\%) \pm 1.96 \sqrt{\left(\frac{15 \times 85}{120} + \frac{4 \times 96}{150}\right)}$$

$$= 11\% \pm 7.1\%$$

or

$$3.9\% \leqslant \pi_1 - \pi_2 \leqslant 18.1\%$$

The range does not include any negative value or zero, suggesting that the readership of this particular magazine has made a **statistically significant** impact on purchasing behaviour. The significance of results will reflect the survey design. The width of the confidence interval (or the chance of including zero) will decrease as:

(a) the size of sample or samples is increased; and
(b) the percentage becomes larger or smaller than 50% (see Table 12.4).

Exercises

1. An operator of fleet vehicles wishes to compare the service costs at two different garages. Records from one garage show that for the 70 vehicles serviced the mean cost was £55 and the standard deviation £9. Records from the other garage show that for the 50 vehicles serviced the mean cost was £52 and the standard deviation £12. Construct a 95% confidence interval for the difference in servicing costs.
(Answer: 95% confidence interval, $\mu_1 - \mu_2 = £3 \pm £3.94$.)

2. In a survey of 600 electors, 315 claimed they would vote for party X. A month later, in another survey of 500 electors, 290 claimed they would vote for party X. Construct a 95% confidence interval for the difference in voting.
(Answer: 95% confidence interval, $\pi_1 - \pi_2 = -5.5\% \pm 5.89\%$.)

13.3 THE t-DISTRIBUTION

In constructing confidence intervals we have previously assumed either that the population standard deviation σ was known or that the sample size was sufficiently large so that the sample standard deviation s provided a good estimate (see Section 12.1.1). If the sample size is small and the population standard deviation σ unknown, the sampling distribution can no longer be assumed to follow the normal distribution. The estimation of standard deviation from sample data (see Section 12.1.2), for small samples, introduces **more variability** and, as a result, confidence intervals should be **wider**.

If the standard deviation σ is known or can be reasonably approximated from a large sample, confidence intervals can be constructed as follows:

$$\mu = \bar{x} \pm z \; \frac{\sigma}{\sqrt{n}}$$

where z is a critical value from the normal distribution.

If the sample size is small and the standard deviation σ unknown, confidence intervals are constructed using the t-distribution:

$$\mu = \bar{x} \pm t \; \frac{s}{\sqrt{n}}$$

where t is a critical value from the t-distribution.

The t-distribution, as we would expect, has a wider spread than the normal distribution. This spread **increases** as the sample size **decreases**. The t-distribution, however, is not tabulated by sample size but by degrees of freedom. In this case the degrees of freedom, ν (pronounced nu), equal $n - 1$. The distribution of t is compared to z in Fig. 13.1.

We can note that it is only when the sample size is small that the t-distribution differs substantially from the normal distribution. As the sample size gets smaller, the degrees of freedom will also get smaller and the t-value required to

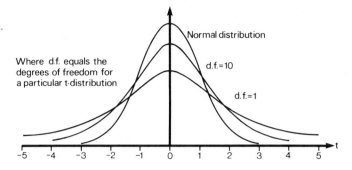

Figure 13.1 The standard normal distribution (z) and the t-distribution

exclude a given percentage of possible observations will get larger. The t-distribution is tabulated in Appendix 4.

Consider the extract from the t-distribution given in Table 13.2. We can see that as the degrees of freedom approach infinity, the t-distribution begins to give the same result as the normal distribution.

Table 13.2 Percentage points of the t-distribution

ν	Percentage excluded in right-hand tail area $2\frac{1}{2}\%$
1	12.706
2	4.303
5	2.571
10	2.228
30	2.042
∞	1.960

Before using the t-distribution, let us consider an intuitive explanation of degrees of freedom. If a sample were to consist of one observation we could estimate the mean (take the average to be that value) but could make no estimate of the variation. If the sample were to consist of two observations, we would have only one measure of difference or one degree of freedom. Degrees of freedom can be described as the number of independent pieces of information. In estimating variation around a single mean the degrees of freedom will be $n - 1$. If we were estimating the variation around a line on a graph (see section 16.5) the degrees of freedom would be $n - 2$ since two parameters have been estimated to position the line.

The 95% confidence interval for the mean from sample data when σ is unknown takes the form

$$\mu = \bar{x} \pm t_{0.025} \frac{s}{\sqrt{n}}$$

where $t_{0.025}$ excludes $2\frac{1}{2}\%$ of observations in the extreme right-hand tail area.

Example

A sample of six company vehicles was selected from a large fleet to estimate the average annual maintenance cost. The sample mean was £340 and the standard deviation £60. Calculate the 95% confidence interval for the population (fleet) mean.

The summary statistics are: $n = 6$, $\bar{x} = £340$ and $s = £60$.

In this case, the degrees of freedom are $v = n - 1 = 6 - 1 = 5$, and the critical value from the t-distribution 2.571 (see Table 13.2 or Appendix 4). By substitution 95% confidence interval:

$$\mu = £340 \pm 2.571 \times \frac{60}{\sqrt{6}}$$

$$= £340 \pm £62.98$$

or

$$£277.02 \leqslant \mu \leqslant £402.98$$

If the sampling error is unacceptably large we would need to increase the size of the sample.

Exercises

1. A sample of 15 employees was randomly selected from a workforce to estimate the average travel time to work. If the sample mean was 55 minutes and the standard deviation 13 minutes calculate the 95% and the 99% confidence intervals.
   (Answer: 95% confidence interval, $\mu = 55 \pm 7.20$;
   99% confidence interval, $\mu = 55 \pm 9.99$.)

2. The sales of a particular product in one week were recorded at five randomly selected shops as 16, 82, 29, 31 and 54. Calculate the sample mean, standard deviation (using a divisor of $n - 1$) and 95% confidence interval.
   (Answer: $\bar{x} = 42.4$, $s = 26.02$;
   95% confidence interval, $\mu = 42.4 \pm 32.30$.)

13.4 PROBLEMS

1. A contractor supplies sand to the building industry by the cubic yard. It is accepted that the amount delivered in each lorry load is going to vary for a number of reasons, but to check that sufficient quantities are forthcoming, the contractor has agreed that the weight should be recorded for a sample of 50 lorry loads. It was found that the sample mean was 20 cubic yards and the sample standard deviation was 1.5 cubic yards. Construct an appropriate 95% confidence interval.

2. A store manager is concerned about the amount owing by customers in the store's credit scheme. In a sample of 60 customers it was found that the average amount owing was £12.43 and the standard deviation was £6.50. Construct an appropriate 95% confidence interval.

3. Following the promotion of a new product, a brand manager would like to know how much a potential customer is now spending each week on a competing product. In a survey of 450 potential customers the mean was calculated to be £0.80 and the standard deviation to be £0.28. Construct a 95% confidence interval to show 'at least' how much is being spent on average.

4. Following the promotion of a new product, a brand manager would like to know what percentage of potential customers are now aware of this product. In a survey of 450 potential customers, 432 were found to be aware of this new product. Construct a 95% confidence interval to show the minimum level of awareness.

5. It has been claimed that party Y can expect no more than 10% of the vote. If 13 out of a sample of 150 electors say they will vote for party Y is there evidence to support the claim?

6. The average weekly overtime earning from a sample of workers this year and last year were recorded as follows:

Sample statistics	Average weekly overtime earnings (£)	
	Last year	This year
Number	80	90
Mean	3.00	3.50
Standard deviation	2.98	3.06

Construct a 95% confidence interval for the increase in average weekly overtime earnings.

7. The number of breakdowns each day on two sections of road, section A and section B were recorded independently for a sample of 250 days as follows:

Number of breakdowns	Number of days	
	Section A	Section B
0	100	80
1	70	65
2	45	57
3	20	31
4	10	11
5	5	6
	250	250

Construct a 95% confidence interval for the difference in the average number of breakdowns on the two sections of road and comment on the structure of the test.

8. In a survey of 1000 electors, 600 in the North and 400 in the South, 22% were found to favour party X in the North and 18% to favour party X in the South. Construct a 95% confidence interval to show the regional difference.

9. In a sample of 200 cars produced by company A, 42 were found to have faults whilst in a sample of 230 cars produced by company B, 46 were found to have faults. Is there any evidence to suggest a significant difference in the percentage of cars with faults produced by company A and company B?

10. To estimate the average cost of window replacement, 11 quotes were obtained for a typical semi-detached house. The mean was £1259 and the standard deviation £153. Construct a 95% confidence interval for the mean.

11. The time taken to complete the same task was recorded for seven participants in a training exercise as follows:

Participant	1	2	3	4	5	6	7
Time taken (in minutes)	8	7	8	9	7	7	9

Construct a 95% confidence interval for the average time taken to complete the task.

14 Significance testing

Significance testing closely resembles the construction of confidence intervals. Both are concerned with sample data, both depend on the validity of sample statistics and both require the same assumptions about an underlying sampling distribution. So what is the difference?

The difference (if any) is a matter of emphasis. Confidence intervals are a statement about the measurement achieved by a particular sample statistic. The most probable values for the population parameter or parameters are included within an interval. In contrast, a test is constructed to provide an answer to a question of the yes/no variety. We may wish to test, for example, whether an average was significantly different from zero or whether there had been any significant change in voting behaviour over time. Significance in both cases refers to statistical evidence that suggests a difference or a change exists. A test provides no measure of this difference or change and does not necessarily imply something of practical importance.

14.1 SIGNIFICANCE TESTING USING CONFIDENCE INTERVALS

Significance testing is concerned with accepting or rejecting ideas. These ideas are known as **hypotheses**. If we wish to test one in particular, we refer to it as the **null hypothesis**. The term 'null' can be thought of as meaning 'no change' or 'no difference.'

As a procedure, we would first state a null hypothesis; something we wish to judge as true or false on the basis of statistical evidence. We would then check whether or not the null hypothesis was consistent with the confidence interval. If the null hypothesis was contained within the confidence interval it would be accepted, otherwise, it would be rejected. A confidence interval can be regarded as a set of acceptable hypotheses.

To illustrate significance testing consider an example from Chapter 12.

Example

A sample of 80 housewives was randomly selected from a large population to estimate the average amount spent weekly on a particular product. The sample mean was found to be £1.40 and the standard deviation £0.15.

Assuming the sample size is large enough to justify an assumption of normality, the 95% confidence interval can be constructed as follows:

$$\mu = 1.40 \pm 1.96 \times \frac{0.15}{\sqrt{80}} = £1.40 \pm £0.033$$

or $£1.367 \leqslant \mu \leqslant £1.433$

Now suppose that the purpose of the survey was to test a store manager's view that the average amount spent on this product was £1.50. If the confidence interval can be regarded as the set of acceptable hypotheses, then the null hypothesis (denoted by H_0) that

$$H_0: \quad \mu = £1.50$$

must be rejected.

The values of the null hypothesis that we can accept or reject are shown in Fig. 14.1. In rejecting the store manager's view that the average could be £1.50 we must also accept that our decision could be wrong. There is a 5% chance that the average is greater than £1.433 or less than £1.367. As we shall see (Section 14.3) there is a probability of making a wrong decision and that the acceptance or rejection of a null hypothesis is a matter of balancing risks.

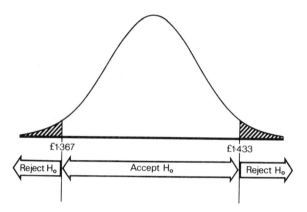

Figure 14.1   Acceptance and rejection regions

14.2   TEST STATISTICS

Once the data have been collected, some hypotheses are acceptable and some are not. As an alternative to confidence intervals, and as a method we can develop for more advanced statistical work, a test statistic can be calculated and compared to values from the sampling distribution. The central limit theorem (see Section 11.5) describes the sampling distribution for sample means and sample percentages as being normal, provided the sample size is reasonably large. If the sample size were small, then the sampling distribution can be shown to follow the t-distribution. It is these distributions that provide the necessary test statistics. You may recall, that the use of the normal distribution tables (Appendix 3) required the calculation of a z-value. The larger the z-value, the more extreme or less likely the observation. It is the z-value that will provide a test statistic for large samples and a t-value (Appendix 4) that will provide a corresponding test statistic for small samples.

14.2.1   A test statistic for a population mean

As with all tests we are concerned with establishing whether something is true or false. In the case of a population mean, we need to decide whether a sample mean provides evidence to support or reject the view that a population mean has a specified value. This view we state as a null hypothesis (H_0):

$$H_0: \quad \mu = \mu_0$$

The null hypothesis challenges us with the view that the true mean, μ, is equal to a specified value μ_0. This is a view we can only reject on the basis of **significant** statistical evidence. The rejection of this view necessarily implies the acceptance of another. An **alternative hypothesis** (denoted by H_1) is a statement of the view we are prepared to accept if we reject H_0. If the test were concerned only with the view that the population mean were equal to a certain value ($\mu = \mu_0$) or different ($\mu \neq \mu_0$), then the alternative hypothesis would take the form

$$H_1: \quad \mu \neq \mu_0$$

The above is consistent with a two-sided confidence interval; we either accept that the population mean, μ, is as specified or accept the alternative that the true mean is larger or smaller. The test is therefore two-sided. If we wish to test the null hypothesis against the view that the population mean is less than the specified value ($H_1: \mu < \mu_0$) or that the population mean is greater than the specified value ($H_1: \mu > \mu_0$), the test would be one-sided (see Section 14.3).

The test-statistic, for large samples, is derived from the central limit theorem (see Section 12.1.2) to take the form:

$$z = \frac{\bar{x} - \mu}{\sigma/\sqrt{n}}$$

If σ is unknown we substitute the sample estimate as follows:

$$z = \frac{\bar{x} - \mu}{s/\sqrt{n}}$$

This test statistic, z, is a measure of the difference between the sample result, $\bar{x}$, and the hypothesized value for the true mean, μ. To be able to make probability statements about this difference, it is quantified in terms of the number of standard errors. Once a z-value is calculated, it can be compared with critical values from the normal distribution. If, for example, the test is two-sided, and

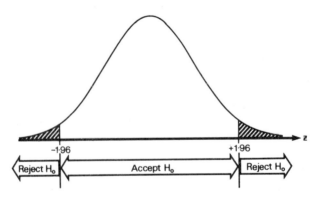

Figure 14.2 Acceptance and rejection regions

the **level of significance** (the chance of rejecting H_0) is set at 5% the critical values will be ± 1.96. The acceptance and rejection regions are shown in Fig. 14.2.

Example

A sample of 80 housewives was randomly selected from a large population to test a store manager's view that the average amount spent on a particular product was £1.50. The sample mean was found to be £1.40 and the standard deviation £0.15.

The null hypothesis, in this case, is the store manager's view which we can state as follows

H_0: $\mu = £1.50$

At this point, we assume the null hypothesis to be **correct** and use the hypothesized value of the population parameter, μ, in the calculation of z. It is also necessary to substitute the sample estimate of standard deviation.

$$z = \frac{\bar{x} - \mu}{s/\sqrt{n}} = \frac{1.40 - 1.50}{0.15/\sqrt{80}} = -5.96$$

Although there is only a difference of 10 pence between the sample mean and what the store manager believes to be true, the test statistic is highly significant. The sample mean is 5.96 standard errors below the value for μ (hence the negative sign). If the significance level chosen for this test is 5% then we must reject the null hypothesis, H_0, as the test statistic, z, lies outside the range defined by the critical values -1.96 and $+1.96$. We would conclude that the average amount spent on this product is **significantly different** from the £1.50 suggested by the store manager.

14.2.2 A test statistic for a population percentage

We can test whether a population percentage is of a specified value or not, on the basis of sample data, in the same way we did for a population mean (see Section 14.2.1). A null hypothesis states that the population percentage, π, is equal to a specified percentage, π_0, and it is this that we accept or reject:

H_0: $\pi = \pi_0$

If we were concerned only with the view that the population percentage were equal to that value ($\pi = \pi_0$) or different, then the alternative hypothesis would take the form:

H_1: $\pi \neq \pi_0$

The test statistic, for large samples, is again defined by the central limit theorem (see Section 12.1.5) and takes the form

$$z = \frac{p - \pi}{\sqrt{\left[\dfrac{\pi(100 - \pi)}{n}\right]}}$$

where p is the sample percentage. If the significance level for the test is to be 5% then we compare the calculated z-value to the critical values -1.96 and $+1.96$.

Example

An auditor claims that 10% of invoices are incorrect. To check this claim, a sample of 100 invoices was randomly selected and 12 found to be incorrect.

We need to compare the sample percentage of 12% with the hypothesized percentage of 10% and on the basis of a test statistic decide whether or not to accept the claim. The null hypothesis and alternative hypothesis can be stated thus:

H_0: $\pi = 10\%$
H_1: $\pi \neq 10\%$

Assuming the null hypothesis to be correct we can calculate a value for z:

$$z = \frac{p - \pi}{\sqrt{\left[\dfrac{\pi(100 - \pi)}{n}\right]}} = \frac{12 - 10}{\sqrt{\left[\dfrac{10 \times 90}{100}\right]}} = 0.67$$

The value of the test statistic lies within the acceptance region for the test (see Fig. 14.2). We are therefore unable to reject the view of the auditor on the basis of the sample evidence.

There is one conceptual difference to be noted between a confidence interval for a percentage (see Section 12.1.5) and a test for a percentage and that is in the treatment of the standard error. In the construction of a confidence interval it is usually assumed that the true percentage, π, is estimated by the substitution of p. Hence, standard error is taken to equal

$$\sqrt{\left[\frac{p(100 - p)}{n}\right]}$$

In contrast, a test of a hypothesis assumes a value for the population percentage (H_0: $\pi = \pi_0$) and it is this value that we use in the calculation of the standard error

$$\sqrt{\left[\frac{\pi_0(100 - \pi_0)}{n}\right]}$$

In practice, the difference between the two calculated values for standard error may be small, but it is good practice to remain consistent with the null hypothesis when carrying out this test. We assume that the null hypothesis is correct throughout the calculations and only reject the statement if the test statistic produces an extreme value (a large number of standard errors from the estimate).

14.3 TYPES OF ERROR

In significance testing there are two types of error, type I and type II. Type I error is that probability, referred to as significance level, used to define the rejection region. It is the probability of rejecting the null hypothesis when it is correct. When the test statistic (z-value) takes an extreme value, we argue that although there is a small probability of such an observation when the null hypothesis is correct it is far more likely that the null hypothesis is incorrect. A 5% significance level can be taken to mean that we reject the null hypothesis when it is correct, 1 in 20 times. **Type II error is the probability of accepting the null hypothesis when it is incorrect.** The two types of error are shown in Table 14.1. In constructing a test of a hypothesis, we choose a significance level for the test, usually 5% or 1% and define the rejection region so as to **minimize the type II error.**

Table 14.1   Possible results of a hypothesis test

	Accept H_0	Reject H_0
If H_0 is correct	Correct decision	Type I error
If H_0 is not correct	Type II error	Correct decision

Consider the sampling distribution of z, consistent with the null hypothesis, $H_0: \mu = \mu_0$, illustrated as Fig. 14.3. The two values for the test-statistic, A and B, are both possible, with B being less likely than A. The construction of this test, with a 5% significance level, would mean the acceptance of the null hypothesis when A was obtained and its rejection when B was obtained. Both values could be attributed to an alternative hypothesis, $H_1: \mu = \mu_1$, which we accept in the case of B and reject for A. It is worth noting that if the test statistic follows a sampling distribution we can never be certain about the correctness of our decision. What we can do, having fixed a significance level (type I error) is construct the rejection region to minimize type II error. Suppose the alternative hypothesis was that the mean for the population, μ, was not μ_0 but a larger value μ_1. This we would state as:

$$H_1: \quad \mu = \mu_1 \quad \text{where } \mu_1 > \mu_0$$

or, in the more general form:

$$H_1: \quad \mu > \mu_0$$

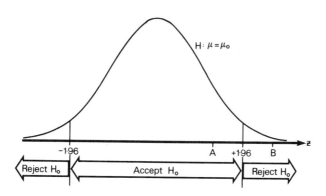

Figure 14.3   The sampling distribution assuming the null hypothesis to be correct

If we keep the same acceptance and rejection regions as before (Fig. 14.3), the type II error is as shown in Fig. 14.4. As we can see, the probability of accepting H_0 when H_1 is correct can be relatively large. If we test the null hypothesis $H_0: \mu = \mu_0$ against an alternative hypothesis of the form $H_1: \mu < \mu_0$ or $H_1: \mu > \mu_0$, we can reduce the size of the type II error by careful definition of the rejection region. If the alternative hypothesis is of the form $H_1: \mu < \mu_0$, a critical value of $z = -1.645$ will define a 5% rejection region in the left-hand tail, and if the alternative hypothesis is of the form $H_1: \mu > \mu_0$, a critical value of $z = 1.645$

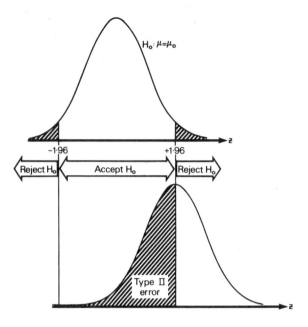

Figure 14.4　The type II error resulting from a two-tailed test

will define a 5% rejection region in the right-hand tail. The reduction in type II error is illustrated in Fig. 14.5.

It can be seen from Fig. 14.5 that the test statistic now rejects the null hypothesis in the range 1.645 to 1.96 as well as values greater than 1.96. If we

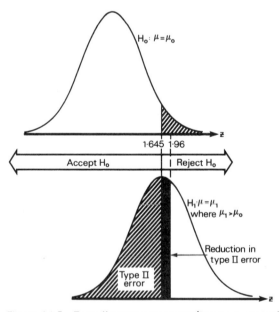

Figure 14.5　Type II error corresponding to a one-sided test

construct one-sided tests, there is more chance that we will reject the null hypothesis in favour of a 'more radical' alternative that the parameter has a larger value (or has a smaller value) than specified when that alternative is true. Note that if the alternative hypothesis was of the form $H_1: \mu < \mu_0$, the rejection region would be defined by the critical value $z = -1.645$ and we would reject the null hypothesis if the test statistic took this value or less.

14.3.1 A one-sided test for a population mean

The test statistic for a population mean (see Section 14.2.1) is

$$z = \frac{\bar{x} - \mu}{\sigma / \sqrt{n}}$$

where the sample standard deviation, s, is substituted for the population standard deviation, σ, providing the sample size is reasonably large. The null hypothesis takes the form

$$H_0: \quad \mu = \mu_0$$

and the alternative, for a one-sided test,

$$H_1: \quad \mu < \mu_0 \text{ or } H_1: \quad \mu > \mu_0$$

It is the direction of the alternative hypothesis that determines the rejection region.

Examples

1. A manufacturer has for many years produced components with an expected length of life of 299 hours. As a result of recent changes to the production process, the manufacturer now wishes to test whether the expected length of life has increased. A sample of 200 components is randomly selected and the sample mean found to be 300 hours and the standard deviation 8 hours. In keeping with previous practice, it has been decided to use a significance level of 5%.

   The null hypothesis is generally a statement of the status quo giving the existing value to the population parameter. Assuming no change, the null hypothesis can be stated thus:

$$H_0: \quad \mu = 299$$

The alternative hypothesis, which is often the claim you wish to prove, can be stated as:

$$H_1: \quad \mu > 299$$

Given the nature of the alternative hypothesis, the critical value, $z = 1.645$, defines a rejection region for H_0 in the right-hand tail of the sampling distribution.

The test statistic, z, is calculated by substitution:

$$z = \frac{\bar{x} - \mu}{s / \sqrt{n}} = \frac{300 - 299}{8 / \sqrt{200}} = 1.77$$

We have again made the large sample assumption that the sample standard deviation reasonably approximates the population standard deviation. Implicit assumptions of this kind are sometimes referred to as **background** hypotheses. These assumptions are not the subject of the test but are required for the construction of the test.

In this example, the test statistic, $z = 1.77$, is greater than the critical value 1.645. We would conclude that the result is significant at the 5% level and as a consequence we must reject H_0. If the test were two-sided (a larger type II error), the critical values would have been -1.96 and $+1.96$, and the null hypothesis accepted.

2. The management of a company claim that the average weekly income of their employees is £450. The trade unions dispute this figure, believing that it is rather less. An independent survey of 150 randomly selected employees estimated the average to be £428 and the standard deviation to be £182.13. Formulate a test using a 5% significance level.

A null hypothesis and an alternative hypothesis can be stated thus:

$$H_0: \quad \mu = £450$$
$$H_1: \quad \mu < £450$$

The rejection region corresponding to the 5% significance level is defined by $z = -1.645$ or less.

The test statistic is calculated by substitution:

$$z = \frac{\bar{x} - \mu}{s/\sqrt{n}} = \frac{428 - 450}{182.13/\sqrt{150}} = -1.48$$

On the basis of this test statistic we would accept H_0. This result could be explained by saying that there is insufficient statistical evidence to reject the view of management, even though there is a difference of £22.

14.3.2 A one-sided test for a population percentage

The test statistic for a population percentage (see Section 14.2.2) is

$$z = \frac{p - \pi}{\sqrt{\left[\dfrac{\pi(100 - \pi)}{n}\right]}}$$

The null hypothesis takes the form

$$H_0: \quad \pi = \pi_0$$

and the alternative, for a one-sided test,

$$H_1: \quad \pi < \pi_0 \text{ or } H_1: \quad \pi > \pi_0$$

The nature of the alternative hypothesis again determines the rejection region.

Examples

1. A small political party expects to gain, on average, 20% of the vote. One of the party's candidates believes that he can do rather better, and has commissioned a survey of 200 randomly selected electors within his constituency. Test the claim of this candidate, at the 5% significance level, if he can expect the vote of 44 of those interviewed.

A test can be formulated in terms of the following null hypothesis and alternative hypothesis:

$$H_0: \quad \pi = 20\%$$
$$H_1: \quad \pi > 20\%$$

The rejection region is defined by a critical value of $z = 1.645$. The sample percentage is:

$$p = \frac{44}{200} \times 100 = 22\%$$

The test statistic is found by substitution

$$z = \frac{p - \pi}{\sqrt{\left[\dfrac{\pi(100 - \pi)}{n}\right]}} = \frac{22 - 20}{\sqrt{\left[\dfrac{20 \times 80}{200}\right]}} = 0.7071$$

In this case, we would accept the null hypothesis (the hypothesis of no change or no difference) that the candidate is likely to do no better than the national average. In other words, there is insufficient statistical evidence to demonstrate that the candidate is doing better than average. We can note that, for a difference of 2% to be significant, we would need a considerably larger sample (see Section 12.1.6).

2. A company claims that 4% of the components it uses are defective. The supplier believes that the percentage of defectives is less than this. To test the company's claim, a sample of 500 components was randomly selected and 12 found to be defective. Would you accept the claim using a significance level of 1%?

The test can be formulated as follows:

H_0: $\pi = 4\%$
H_1: $\pi < 4\%$

The rejection region is defined by $z = -2.326$, which excludes 1% of observations in the left-hand tail area. The sample percentage is:

$$p = \frac{12}{500} \times 100 = 2.4\%$$

The test statistic is calculated by substitution:

$$z = \frac{p - \pi}{\sqrt{\left[\dfrac{\pi(100 - \pi)}{n}\right]}} = \frac{2.4 - 4}{\sqrt{\left[\dfrac{4 \times 96}{500}\right]}} = -1.8257$$

In this case, we accept H_0, although the sample evidence does cast doubt upon this claim. This is yet another example of the conservative nature of hypothesis testing; we accept the claim or present position unless there is sufficient statistical evidence to suggest otherwise.

14.4 TESTING THE DIFFERENCE OF MEANS AND PERCENTAGES

Tests for the difference of means and the difference of percentages can be developed in the same way as confidence intervals for the difference of means and the difference of percentages (see Section 13.2). We would first calculate the difference between the sample estimates and the values given by the null hypothesis, transform this difference to a number of standard errors, and then compare with a critical value consistent with the alternative hypothesis. We can test, for example, whether two sample means or two sample percentages come from the same population:

H_0: $\mu_1 = \mu_2$
H_0: $\pi_1 = \pi_2$

or, as this would more usually be written,

H_0: $\mu_1 - \mu_2 = 0$
H_0: $\pi_1 - \pi_2 = 0$

The alternative hypothesis can take the forms

$$H_1: \mu_1 \neq \mu_2 \text{ (or } H_1: \mu_1 - \mu_2 \neq 0)$$
$$H_1: \pi_1 \neq \pi_2 \text{ (or } H_1: \pi_1 - \pi_2 \neq 0)$$
} a two-sided test

or

$$H_1: \mu_1 > \mu_2 \text{ (or } H_1: \mu_1 - \mu_2 > 0)$$
$$H_1: \pi_1 > \pi_2 \text{ (or } H_1: \pi_1 - \pi_2 > 0)$$
} a one-sided test

or

$$H_1: \mu_1 < \mu_2 \text{ (or } H_1: \mu_1 - \mu_2 < 0)$$
$$H_1: \pi_1 < \pi_2 \text{ (or } H_1: \pi_1 - \pi_2 < 0)$$
} a one-sided test

We could also test whether the difference between means or percentages could be assigned a specified value. We could argue, for example, that the average earnings of one group of workers was £15 higher than for another group of workers ($H_0: \mu_1 - \mu_2 = 15$).

The methods involved are illustrated in the following examples.

Examples

1. A sample of 75 packets of cereal was randomly selected from the production process and found to have a mean of 500 g and a standard deviation of 20 g. After a technical change in the production process, a second sample of 50 packets of cereal was selected, using the same procedure and found to have a mean of 505 g and a standard deviation of 16 g. Has there been a significant change in the average weight of packets of cereal at the 1% level?

The null hypothesis of no change can be written thus:

$$H_0: \mu_1 - \mu_0 = 0$$

As we are only interested in whether there has been a change, rather than an increase or decrease in average weight, we can formulate the null hypothesis as

$$H_1: \mu_1 - \mu_2 \neq 0$$

The alternative hypothesis has described a two-tailed test with a rejection region defined by the critical values of -2.576 and $+2.576$, assuming the large sample approximation to be valid.

The standard error for the difference of means using sample data, is given in Table 13.1 as

$$\sqrt{\left(\frac{s_1^2}{n_1} + \frac{s_2^2}{n_2}\right)}$$

The test statistic for this large sample test is

$$z = \frac{(\bar{x}_1 - \bar{x}_2) - (\mu_1 - \mu_2)}{\sqrt{\left(\frac{s_1^2}{n_1} + \frac{s_2^2}{n_2}\right)}}$$

Assuming H_0 to be correct, this simplifies to

$$z = \frac{(\bar{x}_1 - \bar{x}_2)}{\sqrt{\left(\frac{s_1^2}{n_1} + \frac{s_2^2}{n_2}\right)}}$$

By substitution

$$z = \frac{500 - 505}{\sqrt{\left(\frac{20^2}{75} + \frac{16^2}{50}\right)}} = -1.546$$

In this case we would accept the null hypothesis that there is no difference in the average weight as a result of the technical change in the production process.

2. A small political party believes it has increased its percentage of the vote by 5% over the previous 12 months. A survey of 500 electors 1 year ago showed them to have 20% of the vote and a recent survey of 400 electors to have 24%. Would you accept the view of a 5% increase using a 5% significance level?

The null hypothesis and alternative hypothesis can be stated thus:

$$H_0: \quad \pi_2 - \pi_1 = 5\% \text{ (or } H_0: \pi_1 - \pi_2 = -5\%)$$
$$H_1: \quad \pi_2 - \pi_1 < 5\% \text{ (or } H_1: \pi_1 - \pi_2 > -5\%)$$

In this case, we are interested in whether a 5% improvement could have been achieved. An appropriate test statistic is as follows

$$z = \frac{(p_2 - p_1) - (\pi_2 - \pi_1)}{\sqrt{\left(\dfrac{\pi_2(100 - \pi_2)}{n_2} + \dfrac{\pi_1(100 - \pi_1)}{n_1} \right)}}$$

If the null hypothesis had assumed actual values π_1 and π_2, these values could have been inserted into the term for standard error (see Section 14.2.2). However, as we only have a hypothesized difference for the percentages, in this example, we will do the next best thing and substitute the sample estimates into the standard error term. The test statistic then becomes:

$$z = \frac{(24 - 20) - 5}{\sqrt{\left(\dfrac{24 \times 76}{400} + \dfrac{20 \times 80}{500} \right)}} = -0.3590$$

To test whether an increase in the order of 5% could have been achieved we would compare this test statistic with the critical value of $z = -1.645$. In this case we would accept the null hypothesis of a 5% increase.

14.5 SIGNIFICANCE TESTING USING THE *t*-DISTRIBUTION

As with confidence intervals (see Section 13.3) the assumption that sample statistics follow a normal distribution is only valid if the population standard deviation, σ, is known or that the sample size is sufficiently large so that the sample standard deviation, s, provides a good estimate (see Section 12.1.1). By analogy to the test statistic, z, for large samples, we can use for small samples:

$$t = \frac{\bar{x} - \mu}{s/\sqrt{n}}$$

The critical values of the *t*-distribution are tabulated by degrees of freedom, ν (see Appendix 4). In the case of single sample tests, the degrees of freedom are:

$$\nu = n - 1$$

For the difference of means or percentages (see Section 14.4), the degrees of freedom would be $n_1 + n_2 - 2$, where n_1, n_2 are the respective numbers in the two samples.

The methods involved are illustrated in the following examples.

Examples
1. It is claimed that the average annual maintenance cost for company vehicles is £300. The maintenance department believes it to be higher and randomly selects a

sample of six vehicles. The sample mean was calculated to be £340 and the standard deviation £60. Formulate an appropriate test using a 5% significance level.

The null hypothesis and alternative hypothesis can be stated thus

H_0: $\mu = £300$
H_1: $\mu > £300$

In this case, degrees of freedom are $\nu = n - 1 = 6 - 1 = 5$, and the critical value which excludes 5% of extreme observations is the right-hand tail area, $t = 2.015$.

The test statistic is found by substitution:

$$t = \frac{\bar{x} - \mu}{s/\sqrt{n}} = \frac{340 - 300}{60/\sqrt{6}} = 1.6330$$

We therefore accept the null hypothesis.

2. Seven applicants for a post were interviewed by two different personnel officers. The two interviewers gave marks 1 to 10 for the appearance of each of the applicants. Is there any evidence from the marks recorded below that the interviewers have applied different standards? Carry out an appropriate test using a 5% significance level.

| | Marks for applicant: | | | | | | |
	I	II	III	IV	V	VI	VII
Interviewer A	8	7	6	9	7	5	8
Interviewer B	7	4	6	8	5	6	7

In this particular example, where we have **matched** or **paired samples**, we first find the differences between the paired observations. If there were no differences in the standards applied by the personnel officers the mean of these differences should be zero. We can therefore state the null hypothesis as

H_0: $\mu = 0$

where μ is the mean for all possible differences. As we are just testing for a difference, in no specific direction, the alternative hypothesis is

H_1: $\mu \neq 0$

In this case, degrees of freedom are $\nu = n - 1 = 7 - 1 = 6$, and the critical values $t = -2.447$ and $t = 2.447$.

The calculations of difference, mean of differences and standard deviation of differences (see Section 12.1.2) are shown in Table 14.2.

Table 14.2   The calculation of summary statistics for recorded differences of marks

Interviewer A	Interviewer B	Difference (x)	$(x - \bar{x})^2$
8	7	1	0
7	4	3	1
6	6	0	1
9	8	1	0
7	5	2	1
5	6	−1	4
8	7	1	0
		7	10

$$\bar{x} = \frac{\Sigma x}{n} = \frac{7}{7} = 1$$

$$s = \sqrt{\left[\frac{\Sigma(x - \bar{x})^2}{n - 1}\right]} = \sqrt{\frac{10}{6}} = 1.2910$$

The test statistic is found by substitution:

$$t = \frac{\bar{x} - \mu}{s/\sqrt{n}} = \frac{1 - 0}{1.2910/\sqrt{7}} = 2.0494$$

We therefore accept the null hypothesis.

The use of matched or paired samples is common in market research and psychology. If, for reasons of time and cost, we need to work with small samples, results can be improved if we reduce the between-sample variation. In this example, both interviewers worked with the same group of seven applicants. If they had worked with two independent groups of seven applicants the standard error would have been greater and the test, therefore, less sensitive. The procedure outlined is only valid if observations are **paired**. If two samples are selected and are independent, we would test for the difference of means or the different of percentages (see Section 14.4).

14.6 PROBLEMS

1. A machine is supposed to be adjusted to produce components to a dimension of 2.000 inches. In a sample of 50 components the mean was found to be 2.001 inches and the standard deviation to be 0.003 inches. Is there evidence to suggest that the machine is set too high?

2. A production manager believes that 100 hours are required to complete a particular task. The accountant, however, disagrees and believes that the task takes less time. To test the view of the accountant, the time taken to complete the task was recorded on 60 occasions by an independent observer. The mean was found to be 96 hours and the standard deviation to be 2.5 hours. Formulate and perform an appropriate test at the 5% significance level.

3. A manufacturer claims that only 2% of the items produced are defective. If 7 defective items were found in a sample of 200 would you accept or reject the manufacturer's claim?

4. A photocopying machine produces copies, 18% of which are faulty. The supplier of the machine claims that by using a different type of paper the percentage of faulty copies will be reduced. If 45 are found to be faulty from a sample of 300 using the new paper, would you accept the claim of the supplier?

5. A dispute exists between workers on two production lines. The workers on production line A claim that they are paid less than those on production line B. The company investigates the claim by examining the pay of 70 workers from each production line. The results were as follows:

Sample statistics	Production line A	B
Mean	£193	£194.50
Standard deviation	£6	£7.50

Formulate and perform an appropriate test.

6. Two models of washing machine, the Washit and the Supervat, were tested for a specified range of faults. In a sample of 200 Washit washing machines, 60 were found to have such faults and in a sample of 250 Supervat washing machines, 52 were found to have such faults. Do you consider the two models of washing machine to be equally prone to such faults?

7. A sample of 10 job applicants were asked to complete a mathematics test. The average time taken was 28 minutes and the standard deviation was 7 minutes. If the test had previously taken job applicants on average 30 minutes, is there any evidence to suggest that the job applicants are now able to complete the test more quickly?

8. Records were kept for 7 cars to test whether they could achieve a fuel consumption of 56 miles to a gallon of petrol. The results obtained were 52, 49, 57, 53, 54, 55 and 53 miles to the gallon. Formulate and perform an appropriate test at the 5% significance level.

9. The times taken to complete a task of a particular type were recorded for a sample of eight employees before and after a period of training as follows:

| Employee | Time to complete task (minutes) | |
	Before training	After training
1	15	13
2	14	15
3	18	15
4	14	13
5	15	13
6	17	16
7	13	14
8	12	12

Test whether the training is effective.

10. The hypothesis $H_0: \mu = 20$ is to be tested against the hypothesis $H_1: \mu = 21$. The test is based on a sample of 100 at the 5% significance level and the sample standard deviation is 4. What is the type II error if the rejection region is (a) both tails of the normal distribution, and (b) only the right tail of the normal distribution?

15 Chi-square tests

There are a number of tests designed to answer specific questions about the parameters of a population, and these are referred to as **parametric tests**. They may be concerned, for example, with whether a population mean has a certain value or whether there is any difference between two population percentages. Whatever the parametric test, in general, they all have a common structure. Having specified a null hypothesis, which is initially assumed to be true, a test statistic is constructed in terms of a number of standard errors. The test statistic is then compared with its known distribution; usually the normal distribution or the t-distribution. All these tests involve a number of implicit and explicit assumptions; each of which can cast doubt on the validity of the results. In particular, parametric tests require that all of the following conditions are satisfied:

(a) that a null hypothesis can be stated in terms of parameters; we are not always interested in means, percentages, difference of means or difference in percentages;

(b) that a level of measurement has been achieved that gives validity to differences; they are many examples of where a standard error cannot be calculated in many meaningful way;

(c) that the test statistic follows a known distribution.

If one or more of these conditions cannot be satisfied we need to consider other test procedures. The chi-square test, denoted by χ^2, offers an alternative to the parametric tests described in Chapter 14. It is **non-parametric**, which means that it does not require the same assumptions about parameters or the distributions. As we shall see, it is concerned only with counts and not numerical scores. However, we can if necessary arrange numerical scores into ranges (see Section 2.1) and obtain a classification of data in the form of a frequency table.

We shall consider two applications of the chi-square statistic. Firstly, as a measure of association in tables and secondly, as a measure of the way theoretical distributions (Poisson, binomial, normal) fit the data.

15.1 CONTINGENCY TABLES

If survey data can be classified according to a number of factors then the results can be presented in the form of a table. We might then be concerned with whether a relationship exists between these factors. As an example, consider the classification of data given in Table 15.1.

Table 15.1 Sales of four types of industrial trolley by region during the last financial year

Model	North	South	Region East	West	Total
Tug	675	60	35	20	790
Conveyor	30	490	30	20	570
Lifter	150	180	235	15	580
Mover	5	20	0	35	60
	860	750	300	90	2000

This **cross-tabulation** is designed to show the regional differences in sales. In terms of presenting the data, any differences would be clearer if we could compare the percentage sales of each model by region. However, we may need to decide whether any differences observed could be explained by sampling variations or explained by different regional sales patterns. In this example, we wish to decide whether or not there is evidence of an association between regions and model sold. A test can be specified in terms of a null hypothesis (H_0) and an alternative hypothesis (H_1):

H_0: there is no association between region and model sold,
H_1: there is an association between region and model sold.

In this particular example we may expect an association between the two factors and therefore expect to reject the null hypothesis. Any table that allows us to make a test of this kind, a test of dependence, we refer to as a **contingency table**.

As with all tests of hypotheses (see Chapter 14), we initially assume the null hypothesis to be correct. On this basis we can construct the chi-square test. The frequencies observed (the counts recorded in each cell of the table) are compared with those frequencies we would expect if the null hypothesis were correct. In this example, the null hypothesis implies that the same percentage of each model would be sold in each of the regions. In other words, what is true for the total market should also be true for each of the regions. The percentage of overall sales accounted for by each of the models is shown in Table 15.2.

Table 15.2 Percentage sales of industrial trolley by model

Model	Sales	Proportion of total	Percentage of total
Tug	790	0.395	39.5
Conveyor	570	0.285	28.5
Lifter	580	0.290	29.0
Mover	60	0.030	3.0
	2000	1.000	100.0

We calculate the expected frequencies, assuming the null hypothesis to be correct, by multiplying the regional totals (860, 750, 300, 90) by the proportion of sales we would expect each model to account for (0.395, 0.285, 0.290, 0.030). For example, the conveyor accounts for 28.5% of sales overall, so we would expect $750 \times 0.285 = 213.75$ to be sold in the South, if there were no regional difference. The expected frequencies are shown in Table 15.3.

Table 15.3 Expected sales of industrial trolley by region (assuming H_0 to be correct)

Model	North	South	Regions East	West	Total
Tug	339.7	296.25	118.5	35.55	790
Conveyor	245.1	213.75	85.5	25.65	570
Lifter	249.4	217.50	87.0	26.10	580
Mover	25.8	22.50	9.0	2.70	60
	860.0	750.00	300.0	90.00	2000

It has been assumed that each region has the same distribution of sales by model. Alternatively, the same null hypothesis implies that each model has the same regional distribution. The percentage of overall sales accounted for by each region is shown in Table 15.4. We could calculate the expected frequencies by multiplying the sales totals (790, 570, 580, 60) by the regional proportions expected (0.43, 0.375, 0.15, 0.45). The expected frequency for the Conveyor in the South, for example, would be calculated as $570 \times 0.375 = 213.75$. If we proceed in this way we can produce Table 15.3. Essentially, we calculate expected frequency, one way or another, by assuming **no interaction** between the factors. The convention is to present the observed and expected frequencies, as in Table 15.5 where the expected frequencies are shown in brackets. The difference between the observed frequencies and expected frequencies is a measure of the interaction between the factors.

Table 15.4 Percentage sales of industrial trolley by region

	North	South	Regions East	West	Total
Sales	860	750	300	90	2000
Proportion of sales	0.43	0.375	0.15	0.045	1.000
Percentage of sales	43	37.5	15	4.5	100

Table 15.5 Observed and expected sales of industrial trolley

Model	North	South	East	West
Tug	675 (339.7)	60 (296.25)	35 (118.5)	20 (35.55)
Conveyor	30 (245.1)	490 (213.75)	30 (85.5)	20 (25.65)
Lifter	150 (249.4)	180 (217.5)	235 (87)	15 (26.1)
Mover	5 (25.8)	20 (22.5)	0 (9)	35 (2.7)

We only proceed with the chi-square test if all the expected frequencies are equal to 5 or more. If this is not the case, we need to combine adjacent groups (see Section 15.2.1).

In this example, the sales of Mover in the West are expected to be 2.7. To achieve expected frequencies of 5 or more, we can either add the sales in the West to those in an adjacent region or add the sales of Mover to another model of industrial trolley. Either approach makes sense statistically but they may not make sense in the business context. The choice is yours! If we are concerned with regional differences and the regions are geographically distinct we may choose to add cell frequencies for two models as shown in table 15.6.

Table 15.6 Observed and expected sales when adjacent groups are combined

Model	North	South	East	West
Tug	675 (339.7)	60 (296.25)	35 (118.5)	20 (35.55)
Conveyor	30 (245.1)	490 (213.75)	30 (85.5)	20 (25.65)
Lifter and Mover	155 (275.2)	200 (240)	235 (96)	50 (28.8)

15.1.1 The chi-square test for contingency tables

The chi-square test-statistic is as follows:

$$\chi^2 = \sum_{\substack{\text{all} \\ \text{cells}}} \frac{(O - E)^2}{E}$$

where O is the observed cell frequency
and E is the corresponding expected cell frequency.

It is worth noting the following characteristics of the test statistic:

(a) χ^2 is a symbol only. The square root of χ^2 has no meaning.
(b) χ^2 can never be less than zero. The squared term ensures zero or positive values.
(c) χ^2 is concerned with a comparison of observed and expected frequencies (or counts). We therefore only need a classification of data to allow such counts and not the more stringent requirements of measurement.
(d) If there is a close correspondence between the observed and expected frequencies, χ^2 will tend to a low value attributable to sampling error, suggesting the correctness of the null hypothesis.
(e) If the observed and expected frequencies are very different we would expect a large positive value for χ^2 not explicable by sampling errors alone, which would suggest that we reject the null hypothesis.

The value of the test statistic for Table 15.6 is

$$\chi^2 = \frac{(675 - 339.7)^2}{339.7} + \frac{(60 - 296.25)^2}{296.25} + \frac{(35 - 118.5)^2}{118.5} + \frac{(20 - 35.55)^2}{35.55}$$
$$+ \frac{(30 - 245.1)^2}{245.1} + \frac{(490 - 213.75)^2}{213.75} + \frac{(30 - 85.5)^2}{85.5} + \frac{(20 - 25.65)^2}{25.65}$$
$$+ \frac{(155 - 275.2)^2}{275.2} + \frac{(200 - 240)^2}{240} + \frac{(235 - 96)^2}{96} + \frac{(50 - 28.8)^2}{28.8}$$
$$= 1444.0987$$

You may wish to check this calculation or write a computer program to undertake such a task. To decide whether or not to accept the null hypothesis we compare the calculated value of the test statistic with its known distribution. The chi-square distribution, like the t-distribution, is tabulated according to degrees of freedom, ν. For a contingency table having r rows and c columns, the degrees of freedom are

$$\nu = (r - 1)(c - 1)$$

In our example, with three rows and four columns, the degrees of freedom are ν = 6. If the significance level chosen for the test is 5%, the critical value is 12.6 (see Appendix 5). Our calculated value of χ^2 = 1444.0987 is highly significant and we can as a result reject the null hypothesis of no association. There is very clearly a relationship between sales region and models sold.

Exercise

What does inspection of the observed and expected frequencies in Table 15.6 suggest are the main features of this relationship?

15.1.2 The determination of expected frequencies: a more mathematical approach

Consider the results of a survey (see Chapter 9) as shown in Table 15.7. We can use the chi-square statistic to test whether or not there is an association between the classifications of sex and salary. The null hypothesis could be written as:

H_0: there is no association between sex and salary,

or, in terms of probability,

H_0: there is independence between sex and salary.

Table 15.7   Observed frequencies

Sex	Less than £6000	Salary £6000 and less than £10 000	£10 000 or more	Total
Men	30	50	80	160
Women	50	50	40	140
	80	100	120	300

To calculate the expected frequencies we require two ideas previously developed:

(a) **Independence:** if events are independent, as stated in the null hypothesis, we can determine a joint probability by multiplying corresponding probabilities, e.g. $P(A \text{ and } B) = P(A) \times P(B)$.

(b) **Expectation:** an expected frequency is found by multiplying a total by the corresponding probability.

Consider our example. There are 160 men and 140 women in the sample, so:

$$P(\text{man}) = \frac{160}{300} , P(\text{woman}) = \frac{140}{300}$$

In the same way we can find

$$P(\text{less than } £6000) = \frac{80}{300}$$

$$P(£6000 \text{ and less than } £10\,000) = \frac{100}{300}$$

$$P(£10\,000 \text{ or more}) = \frac{120}{300}$$

The joint probabilities (those corresponding to a cell) are found by multiplication if we can assume independence. For example

$$P(\text{of being a woman and having a salary of } £10\,000 \text{ or more}) = \frac{140}{300} \times \frac{120}{300}$$

The expected number of women that have a salary of £10 000 or more

$$= 300 \times \frac{140}{300} \times \frac{120}{300} = \frac{140 \times 120}{300} = 56$$

In this case the observed frequency was 40 and the expected frequency 56. What, at this stage, is important to note is the procedure: the expected frequency for any cell is the product of its row total and its column total, divided by the overall total. As a second illustration, using our understanding of probability, the expected number of men with a salary of '£6000 and less than £10 000,' assuming independence is:

$$\frac{160 \times 100}{300} = 53.33$$

We can continue in this way to calculate all the expected values as shown in Table 15.8.

Table 15.8 Expected frequencies

Sex	Less than £6000	Salary £6000 and less than £10 000	£10 000 or more
Men	42.67	53.33	64
Women	37.33	46.67	56

The chi-squared statistic is calculated thus:

$$\chi^2 = \frac{(30 - 42.67)^2}{42.67} + \frac{(50 - 53.33)^2}{53.33} + \frac{(80 - 64)^2}{64} + \frac{(50 - 37.33)^2}{37.33}$$
$$+ \frac{(50 - 46.67)^2}{46.67} + \frac{(40 - 56)^2}{56}$$
$$= 17.0793$$

The degrees of freedom are

$$\nu = (r - 1)(c - 1)$$
$$= 1 \times 2$$
$$= 2$$

If the significance level chosen for the test is 5%, the critical value is 5.99. As the test statistic exceeds this value we would reject the null hypothesis at the 5% significance level.

15.2 GOODNESS OF FIT TESTS

The chi-square statistic provides a measure of the difference between observed frequencies and expected frequencies. As such, it is particularly suitable for testing whether collected data follow one of the known distributions. We may, for example, want to know whether the sales of gin follow a Poisson distribution, the number of defective components in a finished product follows a binomial distribution, or the time taken to complete a task follows a normal distribution. Expected frequencies can be derived from theoretical distribution as specified by a null hypothesis, and these can be compared with the frequencies actually observed.

The chi-squared statistic retains the same structure:

$$\chi^2 = \sum_{\substack{\text{all} \\ \text{cells}}} \frac{(O - E)^2}{E}$$

where O is the observed cell frequency and E is the corresponding expected cell frequency.

This test statistic follows the chi-square distribution, assuming the null hypothesis to be correct, with v degrees of freedom, where

v = number of cells (or classes) **minus** the number of estimated parameters required for the calculation of expected frequency **minus** 1

Suppose, for example, the number of tasks completed satisfactorily in a working week by five machine operators was recorded as Table 15.9.

Table 15.9   Tasks completed in a working week by five machine operators

Machine operator	Number of tasks
A	27
B	31
C	29
D	27
E	26
	140

The total number of tasks satisfactorily completed in the chosen working week was 140. It is not surprising to see some differences between the machine operators, as a number of random factors are likely to exist that affect the number of tasks completed, but what we may wish to decide is can these differences be explained completely in this way (sampling variation) or is there a 'real' differences between machine operators? In terms of a null hypothesis and an alternative hypothesis we would state:

H_0:   no difference exists between machine operators,
H_1:   a difference does exist between machine operators.

If no difference were to exist, we would **expect** each machine operator to complete the same number of tasks. In effect we are testing whether a uniform distribution (see Section 10.1) fits the data. Expected frequency (total multiplied by cell probability) is

$$140 \times \frac{1}{5} = 28$$

By substitution, the chi-squared statistic is

$$\chi^2 = \frac{(27 - 28)^2}{28} + \frac{(31 - 28)^2}{28} + \frac{(29 - 28)^2}{28} + \frac{(27 - 28)^2}{28} + \frac{(26 - 28)^2}{28}$$

$$= 0.5714$$

The chi-squared test statistic has four degrees of freedom in this case. There are five cells, no estimated parameters required for the calculation of the expected frequencies (we knew the number of machine operators and the total) and finally the $- 1$.

$$\nu = 5 - 0 - 1 = 4$$

If the significance level chosen for the test is 5%, the critical value is 9.49. We therefore accept the null hypothesis.

15.2.1 Test for a Poisson or binomial distribution

The same procedure is used to test whether the data are from a Poisson or a binomial distribution. In each case the expected frequencies are calculated by multiplying the total by the probabilities derived from the theoretical distribution. The derivation of these probabilities, and hence expected frequency requires the estimation of **one** parameter; the Poisson distribution being defined by a mean (see Section 10.3) and the binomial distribution described by a probability (see Section 10.2). The degrees of freedom corresponding to the test statistic in each case are

$$\nu = \text{number of cells} - 1 - 1$$
$$= \text{number of cells} - 2$$

Examples

1. The number of items required from stock in the last 100 days has been recorded as following:

Number of items	Number of days
0	7
1	17
2	26
3	22
4	17
5	9 ⎱ 11
6	2 ⎰
	100

Is it reasonable to assume demand follows a Poisson distribution?

It is first necessary to estimate the one required parameter (λ) by the sample mean.

$$\bar{x} = \frac{(0 \times 7) + (1 \times 17) + (2 \times 26) + (3 \times 22) + (4 \times 17) + (5 \times 9) + (6 \times 2)}{100}$$

$$= \frac{260}{100} = 2.6$$

The expected values, assuming a Poisson distribution ($\lambda = 2.6$), are derived from cumulative Poisson probabilities as follows:

r	$P(r$ or more$)$	$P(r)$	Expected frequency $= 100 \times P(r)$
0	1.0000	0.0743	7.43
1	0.9257	0.1931	19.31
2	0.7326	0.2510	25.10
3	0.4816	0.2176	21.76
4	0.2640	0.1414	14.14
5	0.1226	0.0736	7.36 ⎱ 12.26
6 or more	0.0490	0.0490	4.90 ⎰
		1.0000	100.00

The final groups have been combined so that all expected frequencies are equal to 5 or more. This is a basic condition of the chi-square test.

By substitution, the chi-square statistic is:

$$\chi^2 = \frac{(7 - 7.43)^2}{7.43} + \frac{(17 - 19.31)^2}{19.31} + \frac{(26 - 25.10)^2}{25.10} + \frac{(22 - 21.76)^2}{21.76}$$
$$+ \frac{(17 - 14.14)^2}{14.14} + \frac{(11 - 12.26)^2}{12.26}$$
$$= 1.04411$$

The degrees of freedom, in this example, are

$$\nu = 6 - 2 = 4$$

and the critical value at the 5% significance level is 9.49. We therefore accept the null hypothesis.

2. A finished product is assembled from five components of a particular type. The distribution below shows the number of defective components from a sample of 96 finished products.

Number of defective components	0	1	2	3	4	5
Number of finished products	15	20	20	18	13	10

Test at the 1% significance level whether the observations agree with an appropriate binomial distribution.

The binomial distribution is fully described by two parameters; the sample size ($n = 5$) and the probability of a characteristic (unknown p). To estimate p we first need to calculate the mean.

$$\bar{x} = \frac{(0 \times 15) + (1 \times 20) + (2 \times 20) + (3 \times 18) + (4 \times 13) + (5 \times 10)}{96}$$

$$= \frac{216}{96} = 2.25$$

The mean of a binomial distribution is equal to np (see Sectin 10.2) hence

$$p = \frac{\bar{x}}{n}$$

An intuitive way to reason this formula is as follows: if on average we observed 30 heads in 60 tosses of a coin we would argue that the probability of a head is 0.5. In the same way, if this finished product averaged 2.25 defectives, then we would infer that the probability of a defective was

$$p = \frac{2.25}{5} = 0.45$$

The expected values, assuming a binomial distribution ($p = 0.45$, $n = 5$), are as follows:

r	$P(r$ or more$)$	$P(r)$	Expected frequency $96 \times P(r)$	
0	1.0000	0.0503	4.83	} 24.6
1	0.9497	0.2059	19.77	
2	0.7438	0.3369	32.34	
3	0.4069	0.2757	26.47	
4	0.1312	0.1127	10.82	} 12.59
5	0.0185	0.0185	1.77	
		1.0000	96.00	

In this particular example, two categories have expected frequencies of less than 5 and have thus been combined with adjacent groups.

By substitution, the chi-square statistic is

$$\chi^2 = \frac{(35 - 24.6)^2}{24.6} + \frac{(20 - 32.34)^2}{32.34} + \frac{(18 - 26.47)^2}{26.47} + \frac{(23 - 12.59)^2}{12.59}$$

$$= 20.4231$$

The degrees of freedom are

$$\nu = 4 - 2 = 2$$

and the critical value at the 1% significance level is 9.21. We therefore reject the null hypothesis and conclude that it is most unlikely that the distribution is binomial.

As an additional note, we only lose degrees of freedom by estimating parameters. If we were asked to fit a specified Poisson or binomial distribution (parameters given) to a set of data, the degrees of freedom would be ν = number of cells − 1.

15.2.2 Test for a normal distribution

In testing whether or not a normal distribution describes a set of data, we must first tabulate the data into intervals or ranges. We can then calculate expected frequencies within these intervals by the estimation of two parameters: the mean and standard deviation. The associated degrees of freedom are

$$\nu = \text{number of cells} - 2_{\prime} - 1 = \text{number of cells} = 3$$

Example

The results of an incomes survey are as follows:

Weekly income	Frequency
less than £200	10
£200 but less than £300	28
£300 but less than £400	42
£400 but less than £600	50
£600 or more	20
	150

Test at the 5% significance level whether this incomes' distribution follows the normal distribution.

The mean and standard deviation for the data (see Section 12.1.2) are

$$\bar{x} = £428$$
and $s = £182.13$

These summary statistics $\bar{x}$ and s are estimators of the population parameters μ and σ. The area (probability) excluded in the extreme right-hand tail of the normal distribution is tabulated according to z-values (see Section 11.1) where

$$z = \frac{x - \mu}{\sigma}$$

The expected values, assuming a normal distribution ($\mu = £428$ and $\sigma = £182.13$) are calculated as follows:

Weekly income	z	Probability	Expected frequency 150 × probability
less than £200	−1.25	0.1056	15.84
£200 but less than £300	−0.70	0.1364	20.46
£300 but less than £400	−0.15	0.1984	29.76
£400 but less than £600	0.94	0.3860	57.90
£600 or more		0.1736	26.04
		1.0000	150.00

All the expected frequencies are equal to 5 or more, so we can proceed to the chi-square test. By substitution:

$$\chi^2 = \frac{(10 - 15.84)^2}{15.84} + \frac{(28 - 20.46)^2}{20.46} + \frac{(42 - 29.76)^2}{29.76} + \frac{(50 - 57.90)^2}{57.90}$$
$$+ \frac{(20 - 26.04)^2}{26.04}$$
$$= 12.4449$$

The degrees of freedom, in this example, are

$$\nu = 5 - 2 - 1 = 2$$

and the critical value at the 5% significance level is 5.99. We therefore reject the null hypothesis and conclude that it is most unlikely that the distribution is normal.

15.3 PROBLEMS

1. The respondents of a survey were classified by magazine read and income as follows:

Magazine read	under 10 000	Annual income (£) 10 000 and under 15 000	15 000 and over
A	28	60	57
B	12	40	53

Test the hypothesis that magazine choice is independent of the level of income using a 5% level of significance.

2. In a survey concerned with changes in working procedures the following table was produced:

	Opinion on changes in working procedures		
	In favour	Opposed	Undecided
Skilled workers	21	36	30
Unskilled workers	48	26	19

Test the hypothesis that the opinion on working procedures is independent of whether workers are classified as skilled or unskilled.

3. The table below gives the number of claims made in the last year by the 9650 motorists insured with a particular insurance company:

Number of claims	Insurance groups			
	I	II	III	IV
0	900	2800	2100	800
1	200	950	750	450
2 or more	50	300	200	150

Is there an association between the number of claims and the insurance group?

4. A production process uses four machines in its three-shift operation. A random sample of breakdowns was classified according to machine and the shift in which the breakdown occurred:

	Machine			
Shift	A	B	C	D
1	10	11	8	9
2	16	9	13	11
3	12	9	14	9

Is there reason to doubt the independence of shift and machine breakdown?

5. A random sample of 500 units is taken from each day's production and inspected for defective units. The number of defectives recorded in the last working week were as follows:

Day	Number of defectives
Monday	15
Tuesday	8
Wednesday	5
Thursday	5
Friday	12

Test the hypothesis that the difference between the days is due to chance.

6. The number of breakdowns each day on a section of road were recorded for a sample of 250 days as follows:

Number of breakdowns	Number of days
0	100
1	70
2	45
3	20
4	10
5	5
	250

Test whether a Poisson distribution describes the data.

7. The number of car repairs completed each month in the last year were recorded as follows:

Month	Number of repairs
January	95
February	98
March	92
April	90
May	83
June	102
July	108
August	95
September	94
October	92
November	97
December	94

Is there reason to believe that the number of car repairs does not follow a uniform distribution?

8. The demand for hire cars from a specialist company has been tabulated for the last 100 working weeks.

Demand for hire cars	Number of weeks
0	39
1	32
2	19
3	10

Does demand follow a known distribution?

9. The average weekly overtime earnings from a sample of workers from a particular service industry were recorded as follows:

Average weekly overtime earnings (£)	Number of workers
under 1	19
1 but under 2	29
2 but under 5	17
5 but under 10	12
10 or more	3
	80

Do average weekly overtime earnings follow a normal distribution?

10. Eggs are packed into cartons of six. A sample of 90 cartons is randomly selected and the number of damaged eggs in each carton counted.

Number of damaged eggs	Number of cartons
0	52
1	15
2	8
3	5
4	4
5	3
6	3

Does the number of damaged eggs in a carton follow a binomial distribution?

Part V
CONCLUDING EXERCISE

The data collected in a pilot survey of 30 randomly selected individuals were recorded as follows:

Code No.	Sex	Region	Whether working	Weekly amount (£) spent on		
				fruit & vegetables	frozen foods	tinned foods
01	0	1	1	1.10	1.99	2.42
02	0	1	0	2.58	4.04	2.78
03	1	1	1	1.20	2.30	2.61
04	1	1	0	2.08	3.18	2.96
05	1	0	1	2.52	3.05	1.88
06	0	0	1	1.93	3.05	1.89
07	0	0	0	2.50	3.68	2.06
08	0	0	0	1.88	2.93	1.90
09	0	1	1	2.43	3.44	1.68
10	0	1	0	2.05	3.15	3.23
11	1	1	0	2.50	2.40	2.58
12	1	0	1	2.61	4.10	2.30
13	0	1	1	2.51	3.58	2.76
14	1	0	1	2.68	3.78	2.40
15	0	1	0	2.57	3.56	3.20
16	0	0	0	2.53	3.48	1.68
17	1	0	0	2.79	3.61	2.09
18	1	0	0	2.80	2.98	2.40
19	0	1	0	1.98	2.71	3.40
20	1	1	0	2.61	2.52	2.69
21	0	0	1	2.55	3.47	1.30
22	1	0	1	2.13	3.41	1.14
23	1	1	1	1.98	2.72	2.18
24	0	0	1	1.68	2.52	2.15
25	0	1	0	2.40	3.36	1.98
26	1	0	0	2.93	3.58	2.36
27	1	1	1	2.55	3.53	2.14

Code No.	Sex	Region	Whether working	Weekly amount (£) spent on		
				fruit & vegetables	frozen foods	tinned foods
28	0	1	1	1.88	2.76	3.05
29	0	0	1	1.88	2.97	2.31
30	0	0	1	2.48	3.47	1.40

where the codings used were:

Sex: male 0; female 1.
Region: North 0; South 1.
Whether working: working 0; not working 1.

(a) Discuss the importance of survey design when assessing results such as these.
(b) Describe the data using charts and diagrams when appropriate.
(c) Identify possible relationships within the data and test when appropriate.
(d) On the basis of this pilot survey, what minimum sample size would you recommend for the main survey? Describe the factors you consider important for the determination of sample size.
(e) Describe the methods you would use to collate and analyse the data from the main survey.

Part VI
RELATING TWO OR MORE VARIABLES

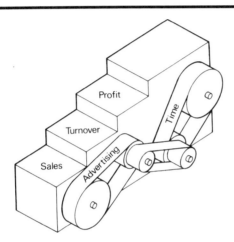

Many of the statistics that have been discussed in earlier parts of this book have been concerned with just a single variable, but business activities are governed by a large number of interrelated factors. If we can show that there are relationships between some of these factors we may be able to affect the outcome of one variable by acting on one or a series of other variables, or we may be able to predict what will happen to a particular variable in the future.

Exercise For each of the following variables state the most important single factor which you think determines its value:

(a) the balance of payments figure;
(b) new car registrations;
(c) deaths from heart disease;
(d) your income in 10 years' time.

List other factors which will affect these variables and in each case state whether or not it might be possible to collect quantitative data on these factors.

Some national statistics are presented as seasonally adjusted, for example the unemployment figures, and we need to consider the analysis of time series to understand the meaning of government statements such as the seasonally adjusted figure has declined but the trend is still upwards.

Exercises

1. Find examples of two series from government publications (e.g. *Economic Trends* or the *Monthly Digest of Statistics*) which are presented in a seasonally adjusted format.
2. Suggest two things that you do which vary depending on the time of year.

16 Correlation

Businesses and governments, as we have seen, collect large amounts of information both in depth at a particular point in time and over long periods of time. This chapter is concerned with trying to find out if there is a relationship of some sort between two sets of data (we will look briefly at more complex relationships in Chapter 18). If we do discover some apparent relationship, we need to find out things like 'how strong is it?'; 'where does it work?'; 'when doesn't it work?'; 'is it better than some other relationship?'.

16.1 SCATTER DIAGRAMS

We noted earlier (Chapter 2) that visual presentation of information allows us to appreciate what is happening to a particular variable. A scatter diagram allows us to show two variables together, one on each axis, each pair being represented by 'X'. If there are only a few 'pairs' of data available then there is little that can be inferred from the scatter diagram, but normally there will be a large number of observations and thus a pattern, or lack of pattern, can be used to infer something about the relationship between the two variables.

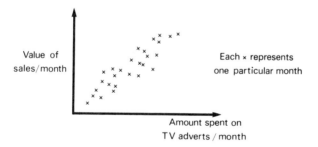

Figure 16.1

Looking at Figure 16.1 we can see that, in general, the larger the amount spent on TV advertising the larger the sales value. This is by no means a deterministic relationship and does not imply a necessary cause and effect: it just means that in months with high sales value, there is usually a large amount spent on TV advertising.

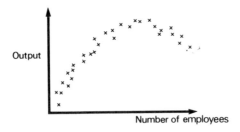

Output

Number of employees

Figure 16.2

Figure 16.2 shows the relationship between the number of employees employed with a fixed capital investment and the total output of the plant: here we see that there is somewhat more of a relationship than in the previous example, since the points lie within a much narrower band. This type of result is expected if the law of diminishing returns is true. The law says that as more and more of one factor of production is used, there will come a point when total output will fall.

Having established that some relationships can be seen from scatter diagrams, we now need to find some 'extreme' relationships so that we may compare future diagrams with given standards.

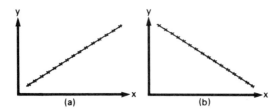

Figure 16.3

Each part of Fig. 16.3 shows a perfect or deterministic linear relationship, since all of the points of the scatter lie on a straight line: (a) is a positive relationship, b is a negative relationship. The opposite extreme is represented in Fig. 16.4 which shows a typical diagram if there is no relationship between X and Y.

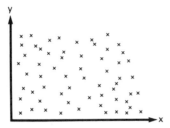

Figure 16.4

Comparison of the scatter diagram for a particular two-variable problem with these three cases may suggest how the variables are related. If they are related, the relationship may be either linear (Fig. 16.3) or non-linear (Fig. 16.2) and it is important to distinguish which of these types applies before analysing the data further. Calculations which are appropriate to a linear relationship could show only a weak relationship when applied to non-linear data.

16.2 CAUSE AND EFFECT

It is very tempting, having plotted a scatter diagram such as Fig. 16.5 which suggests a strong linear relationship, then to go on to say that wage rises cause rises in prices, i.e. inflation. Others, however would argue from this diagram that it is price rises that cause wage rises.

Figure 16.5

Exercise   Is either assertion correct? Are they both correct?

Whilst it is unlikely that there will ever be an answer to these questions that everyone can agree with, some consideration of cause and effect will help in understanding the relationship.

Only one of the variables can be a cause at a particular point in time, but they could both be effects of a common cause! If you increase the standard of maternity care in a particular region, you will, in general, increase the survival rate of babies: it is easy to identify the direction of the relationship as it is extremely unlikely that an increasing survival rate would encourage health authorities to increase spending and improve standards! But would you agree on the direction of causation in Fig. 16.6?

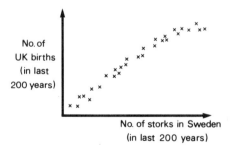

Figure 16.6

Here there appears to be a correlation, but it is spurious as **both** variables are changing over **time**. Time itself cannot be a cause, except perhaps in the ageing process, but where a situation of this type occurs, or where we have two effects of a **common cause**, there will be no way of controlling, or predicting, the behaviour of one variable by taking action on the other variable. An example of two effects of a common cause would be ice-cream sales and the grain harvest, both being affected by the weather.

Whilst it cannot be the intention of this chapter to look deeply into the philosophy of cause and effect it will help to pick out a few conclusions from that subject. David Hume, in the eighteenth century, suggested that 'all reasonings concerning matters of fact seem to be founded on the relation of cause and effect': he then went on to prove that this is not rationally justified. Which matters are justified in using cause and effect has interested many philosophers.

Conditions, or variables, can be divided into two types, stable and differential, and it is the second type which is most likely to be identified as a cause. New roadworks on the M1 at Watford Gap will be cited as a cause of traffic jams tailing back to Coventry, since the roadworks are seen as a changed situation from the normally open three lane road. Drug abuse will be cited as a cause of death or illness, since only taking the recommended dosage is seen as normal (in some cases this will be a nil intake e.g. heroin), and thus the alteration of normal behaviour is seen as causing the illness or death. There is also the temporal ordering of events; an 'effect should not precede a cause' and usually the events should be close together in time. A long time interval leads us to think of chains of causality. It is important to note the timing of events, since their recording must take place at the same time; for example, the studies by Doll and Hill of smoking and deaths from lung cancer conducted in the UK in the 1950s, which asked how many cigarettes per day people had smoked in the past and not just how many they were currently smoking. Some events may at first sight appear to be the 'wrong' way around. If most newspapers and commentators are predicting a sharp rise in VAT at a forthcoming budget in, say, 6 weeks' time, then many people will go out to buy fridges, washing machines and video recorders before budget day. If asked, they will say that the reason for their purchase is the rise in VAT in the budget in 6 weeks' time; however, if we look a little more closely, we see that it is their expectation of a VAT rise, and not the rise itself, which has caused them to go out and buy consumer durables. This however, leads us to a further problem: it is extremely difficult to measure expectations!

A final, but fundamental question that must be answered is 'does the relationship make sense?'

Returning now to the problem in Fig. 16.5, we could perhaps get nearer to cause and effect if we were to lag one of the variables, so that we relate wage rises in one month to price rises in the previous month: this would give some evidence of prices as a cause. The exercise could be repeated with wage rises lagged one month behind price increases — giving some evidence of wages as a cause. In a British context of the 1970s and 1980s both lagged relationships will give evidence of a strong association. This is because the wage–price–wage spiral is quite mature and likely to continue, partly through cause and effect, partly through expectations and partly through institutionalized factors.

Exercises
1. Give two other examples of variables between which there is a spurious correlation apart from those mentioned in the text.
2. What are the stable and differential conditions in relation to a forest fire?

Scatter diagrams, as we have seen, give some initial insight into the relationship between two variables, but it is also important to be able to measure the strength of that relationship. To do this we may calculate a statistic known as a **correlation coefficient**. If we deal first of all with linear relationships, then we have seen in Fig. 16.3 that an extreme form is where all of the points of the scatter diagram lie on a straight line: this is known as **perfect correlation**. When the correlation coefficient is calculated for a set of data such as Fig. 16.3a, the answer will be $+1$; and for the data from Fig. 16.3b, the answer will be -1. The extreme shown in Fig. 16.4 where there is no relationship will give a correlation coefficient of 0. Thus we see that the correlation value will vary from 0 to 1 depending on how close the points are to a straight line, and the sign will be positive if the general direction of the points is upward to the right (positive correlation), and negative if the points are in a band that slopes downward to the right (negative correlation).

Calculating a correlation coefficient will depend upon identifying the type of data we are using. If the data are **ordinal** (i.e. defined by position in an ordered series), we will calculate Spearman's coefficient of rank correlation; but if the data are **cardinal** (i.e. defined quantitatively), we will find Pearson's coefficient of correlation.

16.3.1   Rank correlation

Whilst this statistic will allow us to find the strength of the relationship in ordering between two sets of data, we should be careful in interpreting the answer, since when the ordering is subjective, there is no way of measuring how much better first is than second.

Table 16.1   Ranking of relative importance of various areas of government policy

	Country A	Country B
Defence	1	9
Health	5	1
Social services	8	4
Education	7	2
Provision for elderly	9	5
Transport	6	8
Foreign affairs	2	6
Monetary policy	3	7
Fiscal policy	4	3

The rankings in Table 16.1 show how the governments of two different countries view various policy areas. The question we are setting out to answer is 'is there an association between these rankings?' To do this, we need to find the difference in the rankings (Table 16.2) for each area of policy ($d = A - B$). This gives us a series of positive and negative numbers which sum to 0. To overcome this, we square each of the numbers, and then add them up (Σd^2). Spearman's coefficient of rank correlation, r_s, relates this summation to the number of pairs of numbers, n, using the formula:

$$r_s = 1 - \frac{6 \, \Sigma d^2}{n(n^2 - 1)}$$

Using the data below, we have:

$$r_s = 1 - \frac{6 \times 174}{9 \times (81 - 1)}$$

$$= 1 - \frac{1044}{720}$$

$$= 1 - 1.45$$

$$= -0.45$$

This answer indicates that there is very little correlation (since the answer is not near -1) and that, because of the minus sign, the two governments tend to fairly opposing policy profiles.

Table 16.2

A	B	d	d^2
1	9	-8	64
5	1	4	16
8	4	4	16
7	2	5	25
9	5	4	16
6	8	-2	4
2	6	-4	16
3	7	-4	16
4	3	1	1
			$\overline{174} = \Sigma d^2$

16.3.2 Correlation for cardinal data

Using cardinal data, we **do** have quantitative measures of the variables which are not subjective and thus may be able to rely more on the statistic when drawing conclusions. Again we wish to measure the strength of the relationship and also its sign. To do this, we use a statistic developed by Pearson, r, often referred to as the product-moment correlation coefficient.

Our formula will be:

$$r = \frac{n\Sigma XY - \Sigma X \Sigma Y}{\sqrt{\{[n\Sigma X^2 - (\Sigma X)^2][n\Sigma Y^2 - (\Sigma Y)^2]\}}}$$

This can be shown to be variation together (or covariance) divided by the product of individual variation (or standard deviation of X and standard deviation of Y). See Section 16.8.

Again this statistic will give numerical answers in the range -1 to $+1$, and will be interpreted, as discussed above.

Example Taking a simple example from the records of individual sales representatives, we have the figures given in Table 16.3.

Table 16.3

No. of months as a representative (X)	No. of regular contacts (Y)	X^2	Y^2	XY
10	48	100	2 304	480
20	60	400	3 600	1 200
30	63	900	3 969	1 890
40	71	1 600	5 041	2 840
50	72	2 500	5 184	3 600
60	84	3 600	7 056	5 040
70	89	4 900	7 921	6 230
80	90	6 400	8 100	7 200
360	577	20 400	43 175	28 480

Thus $\Sigma X = 360, \Sigma X^2 = 20\ 400, \Sigma Y = 577, \Sigma Y^2 = 43\ 175, \Sigma XY = 28\ 480, n = 8$.

$$r = \frac{(8)(28\ 480) - (360)(577)}{\sqrt{\{[(8)(20\ 400) - 360^2][(8)(43\ 175) - 577^2]\}}}$$

$$= \frac{227\ 840 - 207\ 720}{\sqrt{\{[163\ 200 - 129\ 600][345\ 400 - 332\ 929]\}}}$$

$$= \frac{20\ 120}{\sqrt{\{(33\ 600)(12\ 471)\}}} = \frac{20\ 120}{\sqrt{419\ 025\ 600}} = \frac{20\ 120}{20\ 470.115}$$

$$= 0.9829$$

The fact that r is close to 1 here shows that there is a high degree of association between the number of months as a representative and the number of regular contacts, and further, that this is a positive relationship.

Exercise Draw a scatter diagram for the data to see how closely the points follow a straight line. Whilst there are too little data from which to draw firm conclusions, there does appear to be a significant relationship here!

16.4 MEASURING ASSOCIATION: NON-LINEAR

So far we have been limited to simple linear relationships, but many inter-connections in business and economics (and elsewhere) are not linear. In order to measure association, we will still use Pearson's correlation coefficient, but will adjust it to allow for the non-linearity of the data. We must return to the scatter diagram in order to decide upon the type of non-linearity present. (It is beyond the scope of this book to look at every type of non-linearity, but a few of the most commonly met types are given below.)

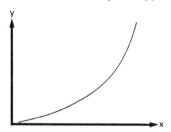

Figure 16.7

If the scatter diagram shows the relationship in Fig. 16.7, then we will find that by taking the log of Y, we get a linear function as in Fig. 16.8. When performing the calculations, we will take the log of Y and then use this value exclusively, as in Table 16.4. (Note that we could use either natural logs or logs to base 10. Here logs to base 10 are used, to two decimal places.)

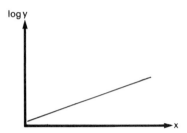

Figure 16.8

Table 16.4

X	Y	$\log_{10}Y$	X^2	$(\log_{10}Y)^2$	$X(\log_{10}Y)$
1	20	1.30	1	1.6900	1.30
2	30	1.48	4	2.1904	2.96
3	50	1.70	9	2.8900	5.10
7	100	2.00	49	4.0000	14.00
10	150	2.18	100	4.7524	21.80
11	200	2.30	121	5.2900	25.30
14	260	2.42	196	5.8564	33.88
14	400	2.60	196	6.7600	36.40
16	400	2.60	256	6.7600	41.60
17	700	2.85	289	8.1225	48.45
95		21.43	1221	48.3117	230.79

$$r = \frac{(10)(230.79) - (95)(21.43)}{\sqrt{[\{(10)(1221) - 95^2][(10)(48.3117) - 21.43^2]\}}} = \frac{272.05}{\sqrt{\{3185 \times 23.8721\}}}$$

$$= 0.9866 \qquad \text{(With } X \text{ and } Y, r = 0.884)$$

We have carried out a **transformation to linearity**.

Figure 16.9 illustrates some other common transformations which yield linear correlation when the untransformed data have the forms shown in these scatter diagrams.

These scatter diagrams are only given as guidance in selecting a transformation for a particular problem on which you are working. If there is high correlation, it will usually be easy to select the most appropriate transformation, but when there is a low correlation, signified by a high scatter of points, it may be necessary to use trial and error to find the 'best' transformation. This is considerably less difficult than it appears at first, since most computer systems have a regression and correlation package available, which will also transform the data in many different ways.

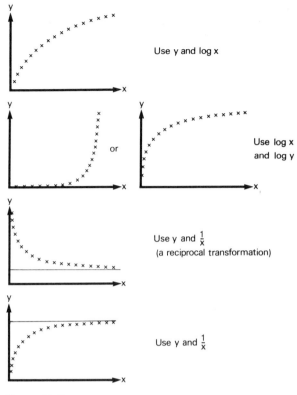

Use y and log x

Use log x
and log y

or

Use y and $\frac{1}{x}$
(a reciprocal transformation)

Use y and $\frac{1}{x}$

Figure 16.9

16.5 SIGNIFICANCE OF THE CORRELATION

We have talked above about 'high' and 'low' correlations, but the statistical significance of a particular numerical value will vary with the number of pairs of observations available to us. The smaller the number of observations, the higher must be the value of the correlation coefficient to establish association between the two sets of data, and thus, more generally, between the two variables under consideration. Showing that there is a significant correlation will still not be conclusive evidence for cause and effect but it will be a necessary condition before we propound a theory of this type.

As we have seen in Chapter 14, the values obtained from sample observations, r, form a distribution about the population (or true) value, ρ, of the statistic we are estimating. In the case of the correlation coefficient, this distribution is symetrical, but is narrower than the normal distribution. It is known as the t-distribution (or Student's t distribution), and it gradually changes its shape as the number of observations varies. To test the significance of a correlation coefficient, we will use the same procedure as that adopted in Chapter 14: setting up hypotheses, selecting a significance level, finding the critical value or values associated with this level, calculating a testing statistic, and drawing a conclusion based on a comparison between the critical values and the calculated statistic:

(a) Hypotheses: normally the null hypothesis will be that there is no correlation between the two sets of observations, i.e. $H_0: \rho = 0$. The alternative hypothesis may be either one-tailed or two-tailed; however, in this context it is preferable to use a one-tailed test, since if H_0 is rejected, then we may conclude not only that there is a significant correlation, but also that the sign of that coefficient is either $H_1: \rho > 0$ or $H_1: \rho < 0$.

(b) Significance level: the level selected depends upon the type of data being used and the way in which they were collected. There is no point in using a significance level of 0.5% if the data are thought to be slightly unreliable. For most business and economic applications the levels of 5% and 1% will be sufficient.

(c) Critical value: having chosen a one-tailed test and a particular significance level, there will only be one critical value, and this will cut off a given percentage of the distribution at one end. As stated above, the distribution changes as the number of observations changes, and thus we shall need to know both the significance level and n (the number of pairs of observations in the sample) before we can determine the critical value, $t_{\delta, \alpha}$ (δ is the number of degrees of freedom, and is equal to $n-2$, α is the significance level). The critical value of t is then found from tables (see Appendix).

(d) The testing statistic: the formula for converting the sample correlation coefficient into a t-statistic value is:

$$t_\delta = \frac{r\sqrt{(n-2)}}{\sqrt{(1-r^2)}}$$

(e) If the calculated value of t falls into an unshaded region in Fig. 16.10, then we are unable to reject H_0, but if it is numerically larger than the critical value, and falls into a shaded region, then we may reject H_0, that there is no significant correlation.

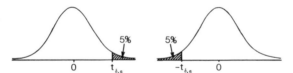

Figure 16.10

In Section 16.3.2 we found a correlation coefficient of $r = 0.9829$ from eight observations. To test this, we have:

(a) $H_0: \rho = 0$
$H_A: \rho > 0$
H_0 suggests that there is no correlation between the two variables.

(b) Significance level (α) = 5% (say).

(c) Critical value $t_{6, 5\%}$ = 1.94 (from tables, use a one-tailed test).

(d) $t_\delta = \dfrac{0.9829\sqrt{(8-2)}}{\sqrt{(1-0.9829^2)}} = \dfrac{0.9829 \times 2.4495}{\sqrt{0.033\ 907\ 6}}$

$= \dfrac{2.4076}{0.184\ 14} = 13.075$

Since $13.075 > 1.943$ we may reject H_0. It would be reasonable to conclude that there **is** a significant positive correlation between the number of months as a representative and the number of regular contacts.

16.6 COEFFICIENT OF DETERMINATION

Having established if the correlation coefficient is significant or not, we often need to go on to describe more about the relationship, and the **coefficient of determination** is a useful statistic for this purpose. It is defined to be:

$$\frac{\text{variation of variable explained by the association}}{\text{total variation of variable}}$$

and by some algebraic manipulation, can be shown to be the value of the correlation coefficient squared, r^2. It is usual to multiply the result by 100 and thus express the answer as a percentage. Thus from the example in Section 16.4, where $r = 0.9866$, $r^2 = 0.9734$ and 97.34% of the variation in the data is 'explained' by an association (in this case non-linear) between X and Y. Even where we have shown that the correlation is not significant, we may still want to use the coefficient of determination to emphasize the point. If $r = 0.3$, then only 9% ($r^2 = 0.09$) of the variation in the data is explained by an association. This type of result may lead us to look for various transformations to achieve a higher coefficient, or may lead us to abandon the relationship that we were attempting to establish. Even an extremely high value for r^2 does not give evidence of cause and effect.

Exercises
1. Why is it important to know the number of observations when interpreting a correlation coefficient?
2. If a firm has studied the relationship between its sales and the price which it charges for its product over a number of years and finds that $r^2 = 0.75$, how would you interpret this result? Is there enough evidence to suggest a cause and effect relationship?

16.7 PROBLEMS

Calculate the coefficient of rank correlation (Spearman's) for each of the following data sets:

1.
X	4	1	2	5	6	3		
Y	1	3	2	4	5	6		

2.
A	5	2	8	1	4	6	3	7
B	4	5	7	3	2	8	1	6

3.
X	1	2	3	4	5	6
Y	6	5	4	3	2	1

4. A group of students were ranked on their ability when they entered college, and again after one term. Calculate the correlation between their positions in the two rankings.

Student	Position at entry	Position after one term
Alf	1	3
Bernice	2	2
Chuck	3	1
Dave	4	6
Emma	5	5
Frances	6	8
Graham	7	4
Helen	8	10
Ian	9	7
Jennifer	10	9

5. Give examples for two different characteristics which would be likely to receive (a) similar and (b) very different rankings from two individuals.

Calculate the value of Pearson's correlation coefficient and the coefficient of determination for each of the following data sets. Draw a scatter diagram for each data set.

6.
X	1	2	3	4	5
Y	2	4	8	10	14

7.
X	1	2	3	4	6	8	10
Y	3	4	6	9	20	28	40

8.
X	8	10	12	4	9	17	14
Y	20	14	6	25	18	4	10

9.
X	15	16	17	18	19	20	21	22
Y	10	10	10	10	10	10	10	10

10.
X	100	110	121	132	143	155	168	180	199
Y	40	20	35	17	52	58	19	40	21

11. (a) Calculate the value of Pearson's correlation coefficient and the coefficient of determination for the following data:

X	1	2	3	4	5	6	7	8	9	10	11	12	13	14	15
Y	10	12	14	17	21	25	30	36	43	51	62	74	89	107	129

(b) Draw a scatter diagram for the data.
(c) Calculate the value of Pearson's correlation coefficient and the coefficient of determination between X and log Y.

12. Costs of production have been monitored for some time within a company and the following data found:

Production level (000)	Average total cost (£000)
1	70
2	65
3	50
4	40
5	30
6	25
7	20
8	21
9	20
10	19
11	17
12	18
13	18
14	19
15	20

(a) Construct a scatter diagram for the data.
(b) Calculate the coefficient of determination and explain its significance for the company.
(c) Is there a better model than the simple linear relationship which would increase the value of the coefficient of determination? If your answer is 'yes', calculate the new coefficient of determination.
(d) What factors would affect the average total cost other than the production level?

16.8 APPENDIX

Pearson's correlation coefficient is

$$\frac{\text{covariance of } X \text{ and } Y}{\sqrt{[(\text{standard deviation of } X)(\text{standard deviation of } Y)]}}$$

$$= \frac{\frac{1}{n}\Sigma(X-\bar{X})(Y-\bar{Y})}{\sqrt{\left[\frac{1}{n}\Sigma(X-\bar{X})^2 \; \frac{1}{n}\Sigma(Y-\bar{Y})^2\right]}}$$

$$= \frac{\frac{1}{n}[\Sigma(XY-X\bar{Y}-\bar{X}Y+\bar{X}\bar{Y})]}{\frac{1}{n}\sqrt{[\Sigma(X^2-2X\bar{X}+\bar{X}^2)\,\Sigma(Y^2-2Y\bar{Y}+\bar{Y}^2)}}$$

$$= \frac{\Sigma XY - \frac{1}{n}\Sigma X\Sigma Y - \frac{1}{n}\Sigma X\Sigma Y + \frac{n}{n^2}\Sigma X\Sigma Y}{\sqrt{\left\{\left[\Sigma X^2 - \frac{2}{n}(\Sigma X)^2 + \frac{n}{n^2}(\Sigma X)^2\right]\left[\Sigma Y^2 - \frac{2}{n}(\Sigma Y)^2 + \frac{n}{n^2}(\Sigma Y)^2\right]\right\}}}$$

$$= \frac{\Sigma XY - \frac{1}{n}(\Sigma X)(\Sigma Y)}{\sqrt{\left\{\left[\Sigma X^2 - \frac{1}{n}(\Sigma X)^2\right]\left[\Sigma Y^2 - \frac{1}{n}(\Sigma Y)^2\right]\right\}}}$$

or if we multiply top and bottom by n, we have:

$$r = \frac{n\,\Sigma XY - \Sigma X \Sigma Y}{\Sigma\{[n\Sigma X^2 - (\Sigma X)^2][n\Sigma Y^2 - (\Sigma Y)^2]\}}$$

17 Regression

It is not usually sufficient to conclude that there is **some** association between two variables, since a business needs to know **what** the relationship is. The previous chapter has allowed us to find the correlation between two variables and to test if this value is significant: now we wish to specify the relationship as a function, so that we may **predict** what will happen to one of the variables if the other is changed. This functional relationship is known as regression.

Three factors should be borne in mind before a regression relationship is calculated. Firstly, that it will only be appropriate with cardinal data since for ordinal data there is no way of telling how much better first is than second. Next, that even though it is possible to find a regression relationship when the correlation coefficient is very small, the result will be meaningless. Finally, that the existence of a regression relationship does not imply a cause and effect (see Section 16.2).

17.1 A LINEAR FUNCTION

A straight line is very powerful relationship and will be found to approximate to a wide variety of situations. If we have a scatter diagram where all of the points are within a fairly narrow linear band, thus giving a relatively high correlation between the two variables, then it will be worth while to find a linear function through these points. A first attempt might be to just draw a line through the points with a ruler, so that it looks about right, but a major problem would be that different people would draw different lines; we need to find a function such that anyone analysing the data will agree on the answer (although there is still likely to be some argument about the implications of the relationship that has been located!). We need to find the **best** line.

How can we define 'best' in these circumstances? One objective of finding a relationship is to predict as accurately as possible the behaviour of one of the variables, say Y, from the behaviour of the other, X; and we may use this as the criterion for deciding upon the best line.

If you consider Fig. 17.1, which shows part of a scatter diagram, you will see that a straight line has been superimposed on to the scatter of points and the **vertical** distance, d, has been marked between one of the points and the line. This shows the difference, at one particular value x, between what actually happened to the other variable, y, and what would be predicted to happen if we use the linear function, $\hat{y}$ (pronounced y hat). This is the error that would be made in using the line for prediction. To get the best line for **predicting** Y we

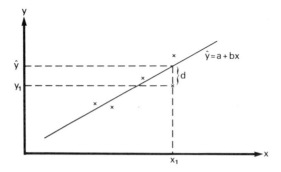

Figure 17.1

want to make all of these errors as small as possible and, as we have seen in Chapter 7, to minimize something we can use calculus (see Section 17.8 for complete derivation of formulae). Working through this process will give values for a and b and thus we will have identified a specific linear function through the data. The line we have identified may be called by a number of names, the line of best fit, the least squares line (since it minimizes the sum of squared differences of observed values from the regression line; see Section 17.8), or the regression line of y on x (since it is the line which was derived from a desire to predict y values from x values).

The formulae for estimating a and b are:

$$b = \frac{n\,\Sigma XY - \Sigma X\,\Sigma Y}{n\,\Sigma X^2 - (\Sigma X)^2}$$

and $a = \bar{Y} - b\bar{X}$

giving the regression line: $\hat{y} = a + bx$.

If we compare the formula for b with the correlation formula for cardinal data given in Chapter 16:

$$r = \frac{n\,\Sigma XY - \Sigma X\,\Sigma Y}{\sqrt{\{[n\,\Sigma X^2 - (\Sigma X)^2][n\,\Sigma Y^2 - (\Sigma Y)^2]\}}}$$

then we see that their numerators are identical, and the denominator of b is equal to the first bracket of the denominator for r. Thus the calculation of b, after having calculated the correlation coefficient, will be a simple matter.

Example

From the example in Section 16.3.2 we have:

$\Sigma X = 360$ $\Sigma Y = 577$ $n = 8$
$\Sigma X^2 = 20\ 400$ $\Sigma XY = 28\ 480$

and $r = \dfrac{20\ 120}{\sqrt{(33\ 600 \times 12\ 471)}} = 0.9829$

thus $b = \dfrac{20\ 120}{33\ 600} = 0.5988$

This is the slope of the regression line.

$a = \bar{Y} - b\bar{X}$

$$\bar{X} = \frac{\Sigma X}{n} = \frac{360}{8} = 45$$

$$\bar{Y} = \frac{\Sigma Y}{n} = \frac{577}{8} = 72.125$$

$$
\begin{aligned}
a &= 72.125 - (0.5988)(45) \\
&= 72.125 - 26.946 \\
&= 45.179
\end{aligned}
$$

and the regression line of y on x is:

$$\hat{y} = 45.179 + 0.5988x$$

17.2   GRAPH OF THE REGRESSION LINE

Having identified the specific regression line that applies to a particular set of points, it is usual to place this on the scatter diagram. Since we are dealing with a linear function, we only need **two points** on the line, and these may then be joined using a ruler. The two points could be found by substituting values of x into the regression equation and working out the values of $\hat{y}$, but there is an easier way. For a straight line, $y = a + bx$, the value of a is the intercept on the y-axis, so this value may be plotted. From the formula for calculating a (or from the proof in Section 17.8) we see that the line goes through the point $(\bar{X}, \bar{Y})$, which has already been calculated, so that this may be plotted. The two points are then joined together (Fig. 17.2).

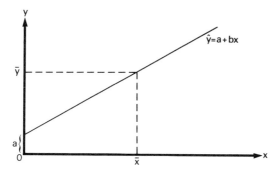

Figure 17.2

Exercise   Plot the regression line on the scatter diagram that you drew for the exercise in Section 16.3.2.

17.3   PREDICTION

The regression line that has been derived above may be used to make predictions about the behaviour of the Y variable from the behaviour of the X variable. For the basic prediction, just substitute the value of X into the equation. For example:

if $x = 65$
and $\hat{y} = 45.179 + 5988x$
then $\hat{y} = 45.179 + 0.5988(65) = 45.179 + 38.922 = 84.101$

From this we predict that someone who has spent 65 months as a representative for their company will have approximately 84 regular contacts.

How good this prediction will be depends upon two factors, the value of the correlation coefficient and the value of X used. If the correlation coefficient is close to 1 (or -1), then all of the points on the scatter diagram are close to the regression line and thus we would expect the prediction to be fairly accurate. However, with a low correlation coefficient, the points will be widely scattered away from the regression line, and thus we will have less faith in the prediction. For this reason it may not be worth calculating a regression line if the correlation coefficient is small.

The value of X used to make the prediction will also affect the accuracy of that prediction. If the value is close to the average value of X, then the prediction is likely to be more accurate than if the value used is remote from $\bar{X}$. In Chapter 12 we looked at confidence intervals for certain statistics, and the same idea can be applied to the regression line when we consider prediction. Note that we will have to calculate the confidence interval for **each value** of X that we use in prediction since the width of the interval depends upon a standard deviation for the prediction which itself varies. At first sight these formulae look extremely daunting, but they use numbers that have already been calculated!

The 95% confidence interval will be:

$$\hat{y}_0 \pm t_{\delta,\, 2\frac{1}{2}\%}\, \hat{\sigma}_p$$

where $\hat{y}_0$ is the value of y obtained by putting X_0 into the regression equation, $\hat{\sigma}_p$ is the standard deviation of the prediction (see below) and $t_{\delta,\, 2\frac{1}{2}\%}$ is a value from the t-distribution, obtained from tables and using both tails of the distribution with $\delta = n - 2$, the number of degrees of freedom.

To find the standard deviation of the prediction, $\hat{\sigma}_p$, we will use the following formulae:

$$\hat{\sigma}^2 = \frac{1}{n(n-2)} \left\{ \frac{[n\Sigma X^2 - (\Sigma X)^2][n\Sigma Y^2 - (\Sigma Y)^2] - (n\Sigma XY - \Sigma X\Sigma Y)^2}{n\Sigma X^2 - (\Sigma X)^2} \right\}$$

$$\text{and} \quad \hat{\sigma}_p = \hat{\sigma} \cdot \sqrt{\left[\frac{1}{n} + \frac{n(X_0 - \bar{X})^2}{n\Sigma X^2 - (\Sigma X)^2} \right]}$$

These formulae can be simplified if we look back to the formula for correlation:

$$r = \frac{n\Sigma XY - \Sigma X\Sigma Y}{\sqrt{\{[n\Sigma X^2 - (\Sigma X)^2][n\Sigma Y^2 - (\Sigma Y)^2]\}}}$$

let A equal the numerator, B equal the first bracket of the denominator and C equal the second bracket of the denominator. Then:

$$r = \frac{A}{\sqrt{(B \cdot C)}}$$

Using the same notation, we have:

$$\hat{\sigma}^2 = \frac{1}{n(n-2)} \left(\frac{B \cdot C - A^2}{B} \right)$$

$$\hat{\sigma}_p = \hat{\sigma} \cdot \sqrt{\left[\frac{1}{n} + \frac{n(X_0 - \overline{X})^2}{B}\right]}$$

Before going on to look at an example which uses these formulae, consider the bracket $(X_0 - \overline{X})$ which is used in the second formula. X_0 is the value of X that we are using to make the prediction, and thus the value of this bracket gets larger the further we are away from the mean value of X; this in turn will change the value of $\hat{\sigma}_p$ which explains why the confidence intervals will vary in width, with the value of X used.

Example

From the previous example (on the data in Section 16.3.2), if we wish to predict the number of contacts of a representative with 65 months' service, we have:

$$r = \frac{20\ 120}{\sqrt{(33\ 600 \times 12\ 471)}}$$

so, $A = 20\ 120$, $B = 33\ 600$, $C = 12471$, $n = 8$ and $X_0 = 65$.

$$\hat{\sigma}^2 = \frac{1}{8(8 - 2)}\left[\frac{(33\ 600)(12\ 471) - (20\ 120)^2}{33\ 600}\right]$$

$$= \frac{1}{48}\left[\frac{419\ 025\ 600 - 404\ 814\ 400}{33\ 600}\right]$$

$$= \frac{1}{48}\left[\frac{14\ 211\ 200}{33\ 600}\right] = \frac{1}{48}(422.9524)$$

$$= 8.8115$$

$$\hat{\sigma} = 2.968$$

$$\hat{\sigma}_p = 2.5614\ \sqrt{\left[\frac{1}{8} + \frac{8(65 - 45)^2}{33\ 600}\right]}$$

$$= 2.5614\ \sqrt{[0.125 + 0.095238]}$$

$$= 2.5614\ \sqrt{0.220238}$$

$$= 2.5614 \times 0.4692953$$

$$= 1.3929$$

This is the standard deviation of the prediction from $X_0 = 65$. To find the confidence interval, we will need a value from tables for $t_{\delta,\ 2\frac{1}{2}\%}$ where $\delta = n - 2$ (here $\delta = 6$).
From tables: $t_{6,\ 2\frac{1}{2}\%} = 2.447$.

The prediction from the regression line was $\hat{y} = 84.155$ when $X_0 = 65$. Thus the 95% confidence interval is:

$$84.101 \pm 2.447 \times 1.3929$$

i.e. 84.10 ± 3.408

80.69 to 87.51

We are 95% confident that a salesman with 65 months' service as a representative for his company will have between 80.7 and 87.5 regular contacts.

If the confidence intervals are calculated for a series of values of X and these are plotted together with the regression line, the result will be as shown in Fig. 17.3.

Prediction is often broken down into two sections: predictions from x-values that are within the original range of X-values are called **interpolation**, and predictions from values outside this range are called **extrapolation**.

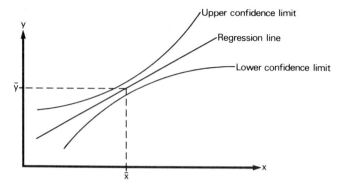

Figure 17.3

17.4 ANOTHER REGRESSION LINE

When we were trying to decide how to define the best line through the scatter diagram we used the vertical distances between the points and the linear function. What would happen if we had used **horizontal** distances? Doing this would mean that we were trying to predict X-values from a series of Y-values, but again we would want to minimize the errors in prediction. Following through a similar line of logic using horizontal distances gives:

$$\text{if} \quad \hat{x} = c + my$$

$$\text{then} \quad m = \frac{n\,\Sigma XY - \Sigma X \Sigma Y}{n\,\Sigma Y^2 - (\Sigma Y)^2}$$

$$\text{and} \quad c = \bar{X} - m\bar{Y}$$

The result of this calculation is called the regression line of x on y. Note that this also goes through the point $(\bar{X}, \bar{Y})$, but in most circumstances, the line will be different from the regression line of y on x. The only exception is when the correlation coefficient is equal to $+1$ or -1, since there we have a completely deterministic relationship and all of the points on the scatter diagram are on a **single straight line**. Figure 17.4 shows two regression lines superimposed on to a scatter diagram.

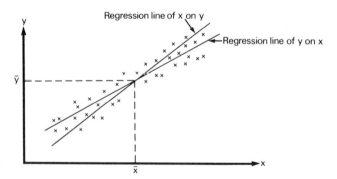

Figure 17.4

For many sets of data it is only necessary to calculate one of the regression lines, since it will only make sense to predict one of the two variables. If we are using data on advertising expenditure and sales of a product, then we wish to be able to predict sales for a particular level of advertising expenditure.

17.5 INTERPRETATION

As stated above, the major reason for wishing to identify a regression relationship is to make predictions about what will happen to one of the variables (the endogenous variable) at some value of the other variable (often called the exogenous variable). However, it is also possible to interpret the parts of the regression equation. According to the simple Keynesian model of the economy, consumption expenditure depends upon the level of disposable income. If data are collected on each of these variables over a period of time, then a regression relationship can be calculated. For example:

consumption expenditure $= 2000 + 0.85$(disposable income)

From this we see that even if there is no disposable income, then consumption expenditure is 2000 to meet basic needs, this being financed from savings or from government transfer payments. Also, we can see that consumption expenditure increases by 0.85 for every increase in disposable income of 1. If the units used were pounds, then 85 pence of each pound of disposable income is spent on consumption and 15 pence is saved. Thus 0.85 is the average propensity to consume (APC). This type of relationship will work well for fairly narrow ranges of disposable income, but the correlation coefficient is likely to be small if all households within an economy are considered together, since those on low disposable incomes will tend to spend a higher proportion of that income on consumption than those on very high disposable incomes.

17.6 NON-LINEAR RELATIONSHIPS

As we saw in Section 16.4, some relationships are non-linear, and thus we will need to be able to calculate a regression relationship that will allow prediction from a non-linear function. If the correlation coefficient has already been calculated, then little additional calculation is needed to obtain the regression equation.

Extending the example in Section 16.4, we continue to use the log of Y instead of Y:

$$r = \frac{272.05}{\sqrt{(3185 \times 23.8721)}} = 0.9866$$

For log Y on X

$$b = \frac{272.05}{3185} = 0.085\,42$$

and $\quad a = \frac{\Sigma(\log_{10} Y)}{n} - b\bar{X}$

$$= \frac{21.43}{10} - 0.085\,42(9.5)$$
$$= 2.143 - 0.811\,49$$
$$= 1.331\,51$$

So the log-linear regression relationship is:

$$\log_{10} y = 1.331\,51 + 0.085\,42x$$

Note: although this is a linear relationship, if you wish to plot it on a scatter diagram, you will have to work out several individual values of $\hat{y}$ and join these together to form a curve.

To predict from this relationship, if $X = 9$

then
$$\log_{10} \hat{y} = 1.331\,51 + 0.085\,42(9)$$
$$= 1.331\,51 + 0.768\,78$$
$$= 2.100\,29$$

and
$$\hat{y} = 125.98 \quad \text{(by taking the antilog)}$$

Finding the regression line for other non-linear transformations will follow a similar pattern.

17.7 PROBLEMS

1. (a)–(e) Calculate the regression line of Y on X and place this on your scatter diagram for each of Exercises 6, 7, 8, 9 and 10 from Chapter 16.
2. (a) Calculate the regression line of Y on X for the data from Exercise 11 in Chapter 16 and place this on your scatter diagram.
    (b) Calculate the regression line of Y on X for the same data, and place this line on your scatter diagram.
    (c) Which of these relationships would you choose to predict values of y?
3. (a) Using the data from Exercise 12 of Chapter 16, find the regression line of average total cost (£000) on production level (000).
    (b) Place this line on your scatter diagram.
    (c) Predict average total cost if the production level were:
       (i)   8500 units;
       (ii) 16000 units;
       (iii) 20000 units;
    (d) Predict average total cost at these levels using the alternative model produced in part (c) of your answer to Exercise 12 in Chapter 16.
4. Using the data from Exercise 6 in Chapter 16, calculate the regression line of X on Y and place on your scatter diagram, together with the regression line of Y on X already calculated in Exercise 1 above.
5. Repeat the above exercise for the data from Exercise 9 of Chapter 16.
6. Repeat the exercise for the data from Exercise 10 of Chapter 16.

17.8 APPENDIX

Equation of the straight line to predict Y values is:

$$\hat{y} = a + bx$$

Thus for a value x_1, we have

$$\hat{y}_1 = a + bx_1$$
$$\text{and} \quad d_1 = y_1 - \hat{y}_1 = y_1 - (a + bx) = y_1 - a - bx_1$$

where d is the difference between an observed Y and its value predicted by the regression equation.

This vertical distance may be defined, and calculated as above, for each point on the scatter diagram. To minimize the prediction error, we may sum these vertical distances; however, if the observed Y values deviate from the regression line in a random manner, then:

$$\Sigma d = 0$$

To overcome this problem, we may square each value of d, and then minimize the sum of these squares:

$$d_1 = y_1 - a - bx_1$$
$$d_1^2 = (y_1 - a - bx_1)^2$$

$$S = \sum_{i=1}^{i=n} d_i{}^2 = \sum_{i=1}^{i=n} (y_i - a - bx_i)^2$$

To minimize S we need to differentiate the function with respect to a and b (since the values of X and Y are fixed by the problem we are trying to solve). Thus:

$$\frac{\partial S}{\partial a} = -2 \sum_{i=1}^{i=n} (y - a - bx) = 0$$

$$\frac{\partial S}{\partial b} = -2 \sum_{i=1}^{i=n} x(y - a - bx) = 0$$

These are **the first order conditions**, and if they are rearranged, we have the normal equations

$$\Sigma y = na + b\Sigma x \qquad \qquad 17.1$$
$$\Sigma xy = a\Sigma x + b\Sigma x^2 \qquad \qquad 17.2$$

These equations could be used as a pair of simultaneous equations each time that we wanted to identify the values of a and b, but it is usually more convenient to find the general solution for a and b to give the following formulae.

Multiply eqn 17.1 by $\dfrac{\Sigma x}{n}$

$$\frac{\Sigma x \Sigma y}{n} = a\Sigma x + \frac{b}{n}(\Sigma x)^2 \qquad \qquad 17.3$$
$$\Sigma xy = a\Sigma x + b\Sigma x^2 \qquad \qquad 17.2$$

Subtracting eqn 17.3 from eqn 17.2:

$$\Sigma xy - \frac{\Sigma x \Sigma y}{n} = b\Sigma x^2 - \frac{b}{n}(\Sigma x)^2$$

$$= b\left[\Sigma x^2 - \frac{(\Sigma x)^2}{n}\right]$$

$$n\Sigma xy - \Sigma x\Sigma y = b\left[n\Sigma x^2 - (\Sigma x)^2\right]$$

or
$$b = \frac{n\Sigma xy - \Sigma x\Sigma y}{n\Sigma x^2 - (\Sigma x)^2}$$

Rearranging eqn 17.1 gives:

$$a = \frac{\Sigma y - b\,\Sigma x}{n} \qquad \text{or} \qquad a = \bar{y} - b\bar{x}$$

18 Multiple regression and correlation

In the previous two chapters we have developed a regression model which is capable of identifying a relationship between two variables and measuring the strength of the association between them. This relationship has also allowed the prediction of one variable (usually y) from the other variable. If we were now to take an extra variable into account we may get a higher correlation and better predictions of Y. Now, if two variables give better results than one, should we consider three, four, five or even more? Many relationships from economics and business suggest that the answer to this question is yes, since there is rarely a single factor which overwhelmingly determines the behaviour of a particular variable. For example, the sales of a company's product will depend upon its price, the availability of close substitutes and their prices, the level of advertising expenditure by the company and its competitors, and perhaps on the level of economic activity in the economy as a whole. Much of the data is easily available, but other factors, such as consumers' tastes and preferences, are much more difficult to measure.

While it is possible to calculate these multiple regression relationships by hand, it is a very time-consuming process, and in general we will be interested in the output from computer programs such as the Statistical Package for the Social Sciences (SPSS). A detailed analysis of the multiple regression model is beyond most first year courses, but a few of the things to look for may help those who are going on to study marketing or econometrics.

18.1 COEFFICIENT OF MULTIPLE DETERMINATION

The coefficient of multiple determination (R^2) is the equivalent of r^2 in the simple two-variable model and is interpreted in a similar way. It shows the overall explanatory power of all of the variables on the right-hand side of the equation, taken together, in explaining the behaviour of the one variable on the left-hand side (Y). Again, as with the two-variable case, it is usually multiplied by 100 and expressed as a percentage.

Many computer programs (including SPSS) will normally add the variables into the relationship one at a time, starting with the one that 'explains' most on its own. They then produce a table which gives not only the R^2 values, but also the changes in R^2 as extra variables are included.

Table 18.1

	R^2	R^2 change
X_4	0.6051	0.6051
X_2	0.7234	0.1183
X_1	0.8014	0.0780
X_3	0.8114	0.0100

In Table 18.1 four variables have been used in a multiple regression relationship. The most important variable was X_4, 'explaining' 60.51% of the variation in Y. By adding in the variable X_2 a further 11.83% of the variation is explained; X_1 adds another 7.8% whilst X_3 only adds 1% to the explanatory power of the model. The overall explanatory power of the model is 81.14%.

Each of the values in the 'R^2 change' column is the extra explanation obtained by including that variable: if, say, X_1 were used on its own with Y the value of the coefficient of determination (r^2) would be much larger than 7.8%.

From a table such as 18.1 we may decide that the extra benefit of using X_3 is so small that it is not worth the trouble of collecting the data and so use a model with only X_1, X_2 and X_4.

18.2 COEFFICIENTS

The multiple regression relationship with three explanatory variables will be of the following form:

$$Y = \beta_0 + \beta_1 X_1 + \beta_2 X_2 + \beta_3 X_3$$

where the various β-values are the coefficients.

When interpreting a relationship of this type it is useful to look at the sizes and signs of these coefficients. This will give an indication of the way in which each of the variables affects the Y-value.

For example, if:

$$\text{sales} = 200 + 0.03(X_2) - 0.01(X_3) + 0.5(X_4) - 0.1(X_5)$$

where X_2 is the advertising expenditure on the product, X_3 is the level of advertising by other companies, X_4 is the quality rating of the product and X_5 is the quality rating of the nearest competitor, it can be seen that the company would sell 200 units if there were no advertising or quality rating and that its sales are increased by its own advertising and the quality of its product. However, sales are also adversely affected by the behaviour of other companies in terms of their advertising expenditure (X_3) and their quality (X_5) as shown by the negative signs of the coefficients of these variables.

18.3 PREDICTION

It is not possible to draw scatter diagrams and superimpose regression lines for the multiple regression case, but it is possible to make predictions about the behaviour of Y by substituting a **series of values** for the variables on the right-hand side into the final equation.

From the previous example, if

$X_2 = £20\,000$
$X_3 = £50\,000$
$X_4 = 105$ ⎫ derived from an agreed quality rating by customers
$X_5 = 99$ ⎭

then: sales $= 200 + 0.03(20\,000) - 0.01(50\,000) + 0.5(105) - 0.1(99)$
$= 200 + 600 - 500 + 52.5 - 9.9$
$= 342.6$

The prediction is that sales will be 342.6 units, but note that this could be affected by a change in any one, or any combination, of the variables on the right-hand side.

Confidence intervals may also be calculated for multiple regression relationships, but this does not usually form part of a first year course.

19 Time series

Most things that interest businessmen and economists can be seen to vary over time. This variability may take the form of a gradual movement continually in the same direction, or, more usually, as a series of apparently haphazard oscillations. A few of the haphazard movements seem to move and change direction purely in relation to things that are happening at the present time, for example the *Financial Times* 30 share index. Others seem to be proceeding in some general direction when viewed over fairly lengthy time periods, even though short-term fluctuations are frequent. Still other variables tend to behave in a particular way at certain points in time, perhaps every spring, or once every 9 years. These observations, while interesting in themselves for a particular variable that affects a company, are purely descriptive of what has happened in the past.

Can we use these observations for more general situations? For these series which react immediately to current events only, it is unlikely that much can be done but record the history of the variation. However, many business and economic variables exhibit a combination of the other factors noted above and we shall aim to draw these ideas together to try to **explain** the behaviour of these series over time. Whilst this explanation may be very useful in helping to show what has happened in the past, for business, a more fundamental aim of analysing a time series is to try to **predict** what will happen in the future by projecting the patterns identified in the past. This involves a **fundamental assumption** that these patterns will still be relevant in the future. For the near future, this assumption is likely to be true, but for the distant future there are so many things that could, and will, change to affect the particular variable in which we are interested that the assumption can only be viewed as a rough guide to likely events.

An example of this problem may be drawn from population studies: we need to project population figures into the future in order to plan the provision of housing, schools, hospitals, roads and other public utilities. How far ahead do we need to project the figures? For schools we need to plan 5–6 years ahead, to allow time to design the buildings, acquire the land and train teachers in the case of expansion of provision. For contraction, the planning horizon is somewhat shorter. In the case of other social service needs, for example the increasing number of elderly in the UK over the next 30–40 years, advance warning will allow consideration of how these needs are to be met, and who is to finance the provision. Population projections have been made over many years for the UK population in the year 1990. The projection from 1951 was for 53.1 million, from 1965 it was 66.6 million and from 1971, 60 million. The most accurate predictions will only be made in 1989!

If we are willing to accept the assumption above of a continuing pattern, plus the restriction of only limited prediction, then we may build models of the behaviour of a variable over time and use them to project into the future.

19.1 THE TREND

It was suggested above that a series may show a movement in some general direction, and this broad underlying movement is called a **trend**. The first step in trying to identify this trend is to draw a graph of the data. Conventionally, time is represented on the horizontal axis, and values of the variable on the vertical axis, as in Fig. 19.1. Here we can see that while there are fluctuations from week to week in the production level, over the whole period the general level of production has increased. For some purposes this conclusion will be sufficient; for instance, if we are interested only in whether or not some new working practice has been successful in stimulating production. If, however, our aim is to go on to predict the level of production in the future, we need to quantify this trend in the behaviour of the figures.

How can we do this? We need to take into account the shape of the trend — is it linear or non-linear, regular or erratic — and then find some averaging procedure that will identify the underlying pattern.

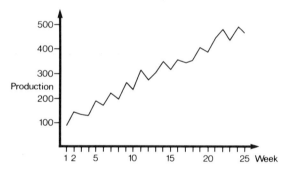

Figure 19.1   (Note that points are joined by straight lines)

19.1.1   A linear trend

To find a linear trend we can return to the ideas of regression presented in Chapter 17, since there we were trying to fit a straight line through a series of points. (In this case there can be no query about which to use as X and which to use as Y, since it is the variable that we will eventually want to predict, and the passage of time that we will use to predict from.) The variable will form the Y values, and X will represent time. Thus X will be a dummy variable, with 1 representing the earliest time period, 2 the next time period, and so on up until the final time period (often the present day). Having established the values for the X and Y variables, we may now use the formulae derived in Chapter 17 to identify a linear trend through the data. These were:

$$\hat{y} = a + bx$$

$$\text{where} \quad b = \frac{n\Sigma XY - \Sigma X \Sigma Y}{n\Sigma X^2 - (\Sigma X)^2}$$

$$\text{and} \quad a = \bar{Y} - b\bar{X}$$

For example, consider the figures given in Table 19.1. Thus,

$$n = 16, \ \Sigma X = 136, \ \Sigma Y = 245, \ \Sigma XY = 2193, \ \Sigma X^2 = 1496$$

$$b = \frac{16 \times 2193 - 136 \times 245}{16 \times 1496 - (136)^2}$$

$$= \frac{35\ 088 - 33\ 320}{23\ 936 - 18\ 496}$$

$$= \frac{1768}{5440}$$

$$= 0.325$$

$$\bar{y} = \frac{245}{16} = 15.3125, \qquad \bar{x} = \frac{136}{16} = 8.5$$

$$a = 15.3125 - 0.325(8.5) = 12.55$$

Thus the trend line is:

$$\hat{y} = 12.55 + 0.325x$$

This may now be placed on the graph of the data in the usual way (Fig. 19.2).

Table 19.1   Sales of shirts

Date	Sales (000) Y	X	XY	X^2
1982 Q_1	10	1	10	1
Q_2	14	2	28	4
Q_3	11	3	33	9
Q_4	21	4	84	16
1983 Q_1	11	5	55	25
Q_2	16	6	96	36
Q_3	10	7	70	49
Q_4	22	8	176	64
1984 Q_1	14	9	126	81
Q_2	18	10	180	100
Q_3	13	11	143	121
Q_4	22	12	264	144
1985 Q_1	13	13	169	169
Q_2	16	14	224	196
Q_3	9	15	135	225
Q_4	25	16	400	256
	245	136	2193	1496

Numerical values for the trend may be found by substituting the values of X back into the trend equation.

For $X = 1$, we have $\hat{y} = 12.55 + 0.325(1) = 12.875$
For $X = 2$, we have $\hat{y} = 12.55 + 0.325(2) = 13.2$
etc.

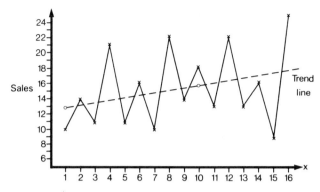

Figure 19.2

Results are given in Table 19.2.

Table 19.2

Date	Sales	Trend
1982 Q_1	10	12.875
Q_2	14	13.200
Q_3	11	13.525
Q_4	21	13.850
1983 Q_1	11	14.175
Q_2	16	14.500
Q_3	10	14.825
Q_4	22	15.150
1984 Q_1	14	15.475
Q_2	18	15.800
Q_3	13	16.125
Q_4	22	16.450
1985 Q_1	13	16.775
Q_2	16	
Q_3	9	
Q_4	25	

Exercise

Work out the final three values of the trend.
(Answer: 17.1, 17.425, 17.75.)

This type of trend will be very easy to predict from, since the next time period will be represented by $X = 17$, and this can be substituted into the trend equation:

$\hat{y} = 12.55 + 0.325(17) = 18.075$

Exercises

1. Work out the trend for the subsequent three time periods (1986 quarters 2, 3 and 4).
2. What would be the effect of using the method given above for data with a non-linear trend? How could this problem be overcome?
   (Hint: look back to Chapter 16.)

19.1.2 A moving-average trend

This type of trend tries to smooth out the fluctuations in the original series by looking at relatively small sections, finding an average, and then moving on to another section. The size of the small section will often be related to the type of data that we are looking at; if it is quarterly data, we would use subsets of 4; if monthly data, subsets of 12; if daily data, subsets of 5 or 7.

Table 19.3   Breakdowns on a complex production line

Week	Day	No. of breakdowns	Σ5 days	Average
1	Monday	3		
	Tuesday	4		
	Wednesday	7	32	6.4
	Thursday	8	34	6.8
	Friday	10	34	6.8
2	Monday	5	34	6.8
	Tuesday	4	36	7.2
	Wednesday	7	38	7.6
	Thursday	10	39	
	Friday	12		
3	Monday	6		
	Tuesday	4		
	Wednesday	5		
	Thursday	8		
	Friday	9		
4	Monday	5		

In Table 19.3 we have daily data, and the appropriate subset size is 5, representing one complete cycle, which here is 1 week. Taking the first 5 days' breakdowns, we find that the total number of breakdowns is 32; dividing by 5 (the number of days involved) gives an average number of breakdowns of 6.4. Since both of these figures relate to the first 5 days, it will be appropriate to record them opposite the middle day (i.e. Wednesday). If we now move the subset forward in line by 1 day, we will have another subset of 5 days (from week 1, Tuesday, Wednesday, Thursday, Friday, from week 2, Monday). For this group, the total number of breakdowns is 34, giving an average of 6.8. These two results will be recorded in the middle of this subset (i.e. opposite Thursday of week 1). This process is continued until we reach the last group of 5 days.

Exercise   Calculate the total number of breakdowns for each of the subsets of 5 days, and hence the averages for each subset.
(Answer: the averages will be 6.4, 6.8, 6.8, 6.8, 7.2, 7.6, 7.8, 7.8, 7.4, 7.0, 6.4, 6.2.)

Once each of the averages is recorded opposite the middle day of the subset to which it relates, we have found the moving-average trend. Two points should be noted about this trend, firstly that there are no trend figures for the **first** two data points, nor for the **last** two data points. Secondly, that the extension of this trend into the future to make predictions will be more difficult than from the linear trend calculated above: however, the trend is not limited to a small group of functional shapes and will thus be able to follow data where the trend does change direction.

A feature of using a subset with an odd number of data points is that there will be a middle item opposite which to record the answers; if we use subsets with an even number of data points, there will be no middle item. Does this matter? If the only thing that we want to do is to identify the trend then the answer is no! However, we usually want to go on and look at other aspects of the time series, and in this case we will want trend values to be associated with a particular data point. To do this we need to use an extra step in the calculations to centre the average we are finding.

Table 19.4

		Sales	$\Sigma 4$ qtrs	$\Sigma 8$ qtrs	Average
Year 1	Q_1	100			
	Q_2	120			
	Q_3	150	460	930	116.25
	Q_4	90	470	930	116.25
Year 2	Q_1	110	460	910	113.75
	Q_2	110	450	890	111.25
	Q_3	140	440	870	108.75
	Q_4	80	430	850	106.25
Year 3	Q_1	100	420	830	
	Q_2	100	410	820	
	Q_3	130	410	810	
	Q_4	80	400	800	
Year 4	Q_1	90	400	790	
	Q_2	100	390	770	
	Q_3	120	380		
	Q_4	70			

The data in Table 19.4 are quarterly sales, and the appropriate subset size will be 4 (or 1 year). Summing sales for the first four quarters gives a total of 460 which is again recorded in the middle of the subset (here, between quarters 2 and 3 of year 1). Moving the subset forward by one quarter, and summing gives a total of 470 sales, recorded between quarter 3 and quarter 4 of year one. As above, this process continues up to and including the final subset of 4. None of these sums of four numbers is directly opposite any of the original data points. To bring a total number of sales (and hence the average too) opposite a data point, we may now add the first column of totals in **pairs**, putting the new total between them, and hence opposite a particular time period. (In the first case this will be opposite quarter 3 of year 1.) Each of these new totals is the sum of two sums of four numbers, i.e. a sum of 8 numbers, so we need to divide by 8 to obtain the average.

Exercise

Complete the final column of Table 19.4.
(Answer: the averages will be 103.75, 102.5, 101.25, 100, 98.75, 96.25.)

This set of figures is a centred four point moving-average trend. To graph this trend, we plot each of the trend values at the time period where it appears in our calculations, as in Fig. 19.3. As with the previous example, there are no trend values for the first two data points, nor the last two. If the size of the subset had been larger, say 12s for monthly data, we would again need to add the $\Sigma 12$s in pairs to give a sum of 24 and then divide by 24 to get the centred moving average trend.

Exercise

How many data points would not have an associated trend value in this case?

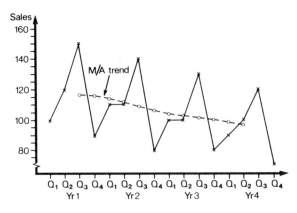

Figure 19.3

19.2 TIME SERIES MODELS

When we are only interested in looking at the overall direction of change in the data, then location of the trend will be all that is necessary. However, if a time series has several of the features noted in the introduction to this chapter, then we need to consider how they are related to each other and how we can combine them to explain the past behaviour of the data and to predict its future pattern.

We wish to combine the following features.

(a) The trend (T) — already identified by one of the methods outlined above.

(b) The seasonal factors (S) — these are regular fluctuations which take place within one complete period. If the data are quarterly, then they are fluctuations specifically associated with each quarter; if the data are daily, then fluctuations associated with each day. An example would be the demand for electronic games. If we have quarterly data for sales, then there will usually be the highest level of sales in the fourth quarter each year (because of Christmas), with perhaps the lowest levels in the third quarter each year (because families are on holiday).

(c) The cyclical factor (C) — this is a longer term regular fluctuation which may take several years to complete. The most famous example of a cycle is the trade cycle in economic activity in the UK that was observed in the late nineteenth century. Whilst this cycle, which lasted approximately 9 years, does not exist at the end of the twentieth century, there are other cycles which do affect businesses and the economy in general.

(d) The random factor (R) — many other factors affect a time series, and their overall effect is usually small. However, from time to time, they do have a significant, but unpredictable, effect on the data. For example, if we are interested in new house starts, then occasionally there will be a particularly low figure due to a more than usually severe winter. Despite advances in weather forecasting, these are not yet predictable. The effects of these non-predictable factors will be gathered together in this random, or residual, factor.

There are two basic models for combining these factors: the additive model and the multiplicative model.

19.2.1 The additive model

In the additive model all of the elements are added together to give the original or actual data (A).

$$A = T + S + C + R$$

For many models there will not be sufficient data to identify the cyclical element, and thus the model will be reduced to:

$$A = T + S + R$$

Since the random element is unpredictable, we shall make a **working assumption** that its overall value, or average value, is 0.

The additive model will be most appropriate where the variations about the trend are of similar magnitude in the same period of each year or week, as in Fig. 19.4.

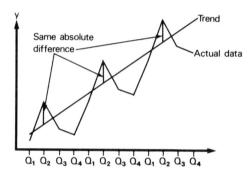

Figure 19.4

19.2.2 The multiplicative model

In the multiplicative model the main, or predictable elements of the model are multiplied together; the random element may be either multiplied together with this product:

$$A = T \cdot S \cdot C \cdot R \text{ (here } A \text{ and } T \text{ are actual quantities while } S, C \text{ and } R \text{ are ratios)}$$

or may be added to the product:

$$A = T \cdot S \cdot C + R \text{ (here } A, T \text{ and } R \text{ are actual quantities while } S \text{ and } C \text{ are ratios)}$$

In the second case, the random element is still assumed to have an average value of 0, but in the former case the assumption is that this average value is 1. Again, the lack of data will often mean that the cyclical element cannot be identified, and thus the models will become:

$$A = T \cdot S \cdot R$$
$$\text{and} \quad A = T \cdot S + R$$

The multiplicative model will be most appropriate for situations where the variations about the trend are the same proportionate size (or percentage) of the trend in the same period of each year or week, as in Fig. 19.5.

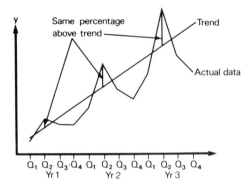

Figure 19.5

Note that the illustrations to this section have used linear trends for clarity, but the arguments apply equally to non-linear trends. In the case where the trend is a horizontal line, then the same absolute deviation from the trend in a particular quarter will be identical to looking at the percentage change from the trend in that quarter; i.e. with a constant (or stationary) trend, both models will give the same result, as illustrated in Fig. 19.6.

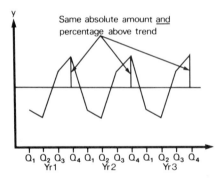

Figure 19.6

19.3 THE SEASONAL FACTOR

These regular fluctuations show effects which are very familiar to most businessmen, that at certain times of the year they can expect higher than average sales, and at other times, lower than average sales. The pattern is repeated for other variables; the price of strawberries is relatively low in early summer, but in December or February the price may be 10 or 20 times as much — a seasonal variation. In the sales example, it will be useful to be able to identify **when** the high sales will take place so that stocks may be built up. It is important to identify the **magnitude** of the increase so that the **size** of these increased stocks can be planned.

These seasonal factors can be identified by additive and multiplicative means.

19.3.1   The additive model

Looking first at an additive model, for a short run of data, we have:

$$A = T + S + R$$

A is known, T has been isolated by using either the linear regression trend or the moving-average trend and R may be assumed to be zero. Therefore:

$$A = T + S$$
or $\quad S = A - T$

This subtraction may be applied to each data point for which we have a trend value and an actual value.

Table 19.5   Sales of shirts

		Sales (000) (A)	Trend (T)	S = A − T
1982	Q_1	10	12.875	−2.875
	Q_2	14	13.200	0.800
	Q_3	11	13.525	−2.525
	Q_4	21	13.850	7.150
1983	Q_1	11	14.175	−3.175
	Q_2	16	14.500	1.500
	Q_3	10	14.825	−4.825
	Q_4	22	15.150	6.850
1984	Q_1	14	15.475	−1.475
	Q_2	18	15.800	2.200
	Q_3	13	16.125	−3.125
	Q_4	22	16.450	5.550
1985	Q_1	13	16.775	−3.775
	Q_2	16	17.100	−1.100
	Q_3	9	17.425	−8.425
	Q_4	25	17.75	7.250

Having completed this process we now have a considerable number of 'seasonal factors', but if we examine them a little more closely, we see that there are **four different figures** associated with quarter 1. A similar observation may be made for each of the other quarters. Each figure may be treated as an estimate of the seasonal factor for that particular quarter, and the average of these four estimates provides a single representative estimate of the seasonal variation for that quarter. The easiest approach to this procedure is to rewrite the final column of Table 19.5, the estimates, into a working table (Table 19.6) that gathers together the various estimates for each quarter.

Table 19.6

	Q_1	Q_2	Q_3	Q_4
1982	−2.875	0.800	−2.525	7.150
1983	−3.175	1.500	−4.825	6.850
1984	−1.475	2.200	−3.125	5.550
1985	−3.775	−1.100	−8.425	7.250
	−11.300	3.400	−18.900	26.800
Average (/4)	−2.825	0.850	−4.725	6.700

The averages will be the additive seasonal factors.

Exercise Work out the $S = A - T$ column from Table 19.3
(Answer: Table 19.7a).

Table 19.7a

Week	Monday	Tuesday	Wednesday	Thursday	Friday
1	—	—	0.6	1.2	3.2
2	−1.8	−3.2	−0.6	2.2	4.2
3	−1.4	−3.0	−1.4	1.8	—
	−3.2	−6.2	−1.4	5.2	7.4
Average	−1.6	−3.1	−0.467	1.733	3.7

(Note that in some cases we divided by 2 and in other cases by 3 since for this example we have used a moving-average trend which does not give a trend value for the first and last two values; we thus cannot calculate S for these observations.)

Above, we have specified that the seasonal factors are fluctuations **within** a year or a week; thus the effect over the whole period should be zero. The effects should cancel out over the year or week. Looking at the results of Table 19.7a we find that this is not the case! The sum of the averages is 0.266. To overcome this problem we may distribute this excess equally amongst the seasonal factors; i.e. **subtract** $(0.266/5) = 0.0532$ from each estimate so that the sum of the averages is zero.

Table 19.7b

Averages	−1.6000	−3.1000	−0.4670	1.7330	3.7000
Correction	−0.0532	−0.0532	−0.0532	−0.0532	−0.0532
	−1.6532	−3.1532	−0.5202	1.6798	3.6468

Note that if the sum of the averages had been negative, we would have **added** a fifth to each estimate: with quarterly data, you divide the sum of averages by four before redistribution. For most practical purposes, this adjustment is not necessary!

Exercise Why do the seasonal factors sum to zero in Table 19.6 so that no corrections are necessary?

19.3.2 The multiplicative model

For short runs of data using the multiplicative model, we have:

$$A = T \cdot S \cdot R$$

As before, A and T are known and R may be assumed to be equal to 1. Therefore:

$$A = T \cdot S$$
or $\quad S = A/T$

Taking the data from Table 19.1, we have Table 19.8.

Table 19.8

		Sales (A)	Trend (T)	S = A/T
1982	Q_1	10	12.875	0.777
	Q_2	14	13.200	1.061
	Q_3	11	13.525	0.813
	Q_4	21	13.850	1.516
1983	Q_1	11	14.175	0.776
	Q_2	16	14.500	1.103
	Q_3	10	14.825	0.675
	Q_4	22	15.150	1.452
1984	Q_1	14	15.475	0.905
	Q_2	18	15.800	1.139
	Q_3	13	16.125	0.806
	Q_4	22	16.450	1.337
1985	Q_1	13	16.775	0.775
	Q_2	16	17.100	0.936
	Q_3	9	17.425	0.517
	Q_4	25	17.750	1.408

Table 19.9   Seasonals table

	Q_1	Q_2	Q_3	Q_4
1982	0.777	1.061	0.813	1.516
1983	0.776	1.103	0.675	1.452
1984	0.905	1.139	0.806	1.337
1985	0.775	0.936	0.517	1.408
	3.233	4.239	2.811	5.713
Average (/4)	0.808 25	1.059 75	0.702 75	1.428 25

Since there are four quarters in Table 19.9, the sum of these factors should be four (it is 3.999). These seasonal factors are often expressed as percentage figures or seasonal indices:

| 80.825 | 105.975 | 70.275 | 142.825 |

19.4 THE CYCLICAL FACTOR

Although we can talk about there being a cyclical factor in time series data and can try to identify it by using *annual* data, these cycles are rarely of consistent lengths. A further problem is that we would need six or seven full cycles of data to be sure that the cycle were there, and for some proposed cycles this would mean obtaining 140 years of data!

Several cycles have been proposed and a brief outline of a few of these is given below.

(a) Kondratieff Long Wave: 1920s, a 40–60 year cycle, there seems to be very little evidence to support the existence of this cycle.
(b) Kuznets Long Wave: a 20 year cycle, there seems to be evidence to support this from studies of GNP and migration.
(c) Building cycle: a 15–20 year cycle, some agreement that it exists in various countries.
(d) Major and minor cycles: Hansen 6–11 year major cycles, 2–4 years minor cycles; cf. Schumpeter inventory cycles. Schumpeter: change in rate of innovations leads to changes in the system.
(e) Business cycles: recurrent but not periodic, 1–12 years, cf. minor cycles, trade cycle.

19.5 THE RESIDUAL OR RANDOM FACTOR

We have made a series of assumptions about this element of a time series. These assumptions may be checked by now looking at the **actual values** (Table 19.10) for R at each data point; i.e.

$$R = A - T - S$$

where S is the average seasonal variation (Table 19.6)

or $R = A/T \cdot S$

where S is the average seasonal index (Table 19.9)

Table 19.10

		Sales (A)	$R = A - T - S$ (additive)	$R = A/TS$ (multiplicative)
1982	Q_1	10	-0.05	0.961
	Q_2	14	-0.05	1.001
	Q_3	11	2.20	1.157
	Q_4	21	0.45	1.061
1983	Q_1	11	-0.35	0.960
	Q_2	16	0.65	1.041
	Q_3	10	-0.10	0.961
	Q_4	22	0.15	1.017
1984	Q_1	14	1.35	1.120
	Q_2	18	1.35	1.075
	Q_3	13	1.60	1.147
	Q_4	22	-1.15	0.936
1985	Q_1	13	-0.95	0.959
	Q_2	16	-0.25	0.883
	Q_3	9	-3.70	0.736
	Q_4	25	0.55	0.986

In the additive case, the average value of R was assumed to be 0 — here the average is 0.106 25 which is not particularly dissimilar. For this type of model, we should also look for long runs of positive or negative values, as this may be evidence of a cyclical effect. With a multiplicative model, R was assumed to be 1 — here the total is 16.001 giving an average of 1; a long run of values above or below 1 may again give evidence of a cyclical effect in the model.

19.6   PREDICTIONS

To make a prediction, we will recombine the time series elements that have been identified above. The first step is to extend the trend into the future. For a linear trend we have seen (Section 19.1.1) that extension of the trend is achieved by substituting appropriate values for X; however, the problem is somewhat more difficult from a moving-average trend. Predictions of the trend are done by extending its graph in an appropriate direction, consistent with its past behaviour. There are two problems here: there is a considerable amount of judgement (or assumption) used in the process and, since the first few predictions are the best (being closest to the data), these are being used to find a trend for past data. (This is because the moving-average trend **ends before** the end of the data, Section 19.1.2.)

Having obtained the appropriate number of trend values, the average seasonal factors (for the predicted quarter or day) are added to, or multiplied by, the trend value to give a prediction. Extending the sales of shirts example, using a linear trend purely for convenience, we have the results given in Table 19.11.

Table 19.11a   Additive

	Trend (T)	Seasonal (S)	Prediction = $T + S$
1986 Q$_1$	18.075	−2.825	15.25
Q$_2$	18.400	+0.850	19.25
Q$_3$	18.725	−4.725	14.00
Q$_4$	19.050	+6.700	25.75
1987 Q$_1$	19.375	−2.825	16.55

Table 19.11b   Multiplicative

	Trend (T)	Seasonal (S)	Prediction = $T \cdot S$
1986 Q$_1$	18.075	0.808 25	14.609
Q$_2$	18.400	1.059 75	19.499
Q$_3$	18.725	0.702 75	13.159
Q$_4$	19.050	1.428 25	27.208
1987 Q$_1$	19.375	0.808 25	15.660

Exercise   Make sure that you can get the answers in Table 19.11.

Time series models are often judged on the accuracy of the predictions.

Seasonal or other factors are often removed from past or present time series data in order to highlight salient features. For example:

deseasonalized data = $A - S$ (for appropriate period)
detrended data   = $A - T$

This has been a rather long chapter and deserves some concluding thoughts. The results from time series analysis may be used in two ways: firstly by using the identified seasonal factors to help in production planning so that stocks may be built up in advance of peaks of demand, and be run down before troughs. Secondly, the overall predictions, but especially the prediction of the trend, may be used for longer term planning in terms of the size of the market in the future and the consequent effects upon the company.

Figures relating to the national economy in the second half of the twentieth century are affected by government intervention, either national or foreign, and there are a few periods without massive residual effects. Among factors influencing inflation data for the UK are:

early	1950s	rationing and effects of its end
	1956	Suez crisis
	1964	change of government
	1966	price freeze
	1967	devaluation of £
	1970	change of government
	1973	threshold agreements on pay
	1974	two elections, 3 day week, oil crisis
	1977	minority government
	1978/9	'winter of discontent'
	1979	oil crisis, change of government, VAT change
	1983/4	trade union legislation on strikes

It may thus be an oversimplification to use a mathematical trend equation by itself for making predictions, and special factors such as the above should be borne in mind when interpreting such equations.

19.8 PROBLEMS

1. Sales within an industry have a seasonal pattern, and in order to identify this pattern you are provided with the following data:

	Sales			
Year	Quarter 1	Quarter 2	Quarter 3	Quarter 4
1	40	60	80	35
2	30	50	60	30
3	35	60	80	40
4	50	70	100	50

    (a) Calculate a centred four point moving-average trend.
    (b) Find the additive seasonal components for each quarter.
    (c) Graph the data and the trend.
    (d) Use your model to predict the sales of each quarter of years 5 and 6.
    (e) How would you explain your predictions to the company?
2. Calculate the linear regression trend for the data in Exercise 1. Does this represent an improvement over the previous model?
3. A company's advertising expenditure has been monitored for 3 years, giving the following information:

Year	Advertising expenditure			
	Q_1	Q_2	Q_3	Q_4
1	10	15	18	20
2	14	16	19	23
3	16	18	20	25

(a) Calculate a linear regression trend for this data.
(b) Graph the data and the trend.
(c) Find the additive seasonal components for each quarter.
(d) Predict the level of advertising expenditure for each quarter of year 4.

4. Calculate the multiplicative seasonal components for each quarter, using the data in Exercise 3. Does this represent an improvement on the previous model?

5. Using the additive model and the data in Exercise 3, calculate the average value of the residual component.

6. The level of economic activity in a county of England have been recorded for 15 years as follows:

Year	Activity rate
1	52.7
2	54.4
3	54.7
4	55.4
5	53.8
6	53.5
7	53.4
8	52.6
9	50.7
10	49.8
11	48.3
12	43.8
13	40.3
14	37.8
15	35.1

(a) Graph the data.
(b) Find a linear regression trend through this data and place it on your graph.
(c) Predict the activity rate for year 25.
(d) How confident are you of your prediction?

Part VI
CONCLUDING EXERCISE

Collect data on the quarterly consumption of energy for the last 10 years (from *Economic Trends Annual Supplement*) and analyse this by:

(a) drawing a time series graph;
(b) finding an appropriate trend line and seasonal factors;
(c) predicting energy consumption for 1 year ahead. Now:
(d) select a variable and collect data which you think will explain energy consumption, and carry out a regression and correlation analysis;
(e) select further variables and collect data to produce a multiple regression relationship if you have access to a suitable computer package;
(f) consider if it would be appropriate to lag some or all of the explanatory variables in order to improve the relationship you have found.

Part VII
MATHEMATICAL MODELS

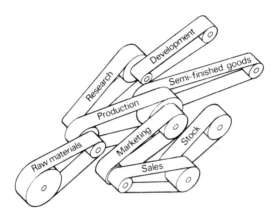

In Part III we developed the mathematical methods and in Part IV the probability theory which allow the analysis of a number of business situations. Every business is engaged in a range of activities which consume scarce resources, such as managerial time, and will attempt to achieve certain objectives subject to its own working environment. In this part we are concerned with the ways we can model three important aspects of business operation: the allocation of scarce resources to achieve company objectives, the schedule of work and the procedures for stock control.

Exercises

1. Consider one aspect of one type of business and list the events which are certain to happen, and list the events which could possibly happen.
2. List a number of business situations which could be modelled mathematically or statistically.
3. List a number of factors which might limit the expansion of a business.

20 Linear programming

Linear programming describes graphical and mathematical procedures that seek the optimum allocation of scarce or limited resources to competing products or activities. It is one of the most powerful techniques available to the decision-maker and has found a range of applications in business, government and industry. The determination of an optimum production mix, media selection and portfolio selection are just a few possible examples. They all require definition and, for a numerical solution, mathematical formulation. Typically, the objective is either to maximize the benefits while using limited resources or to minimize costs while meeting certain requirements.

20.1 DEFINITION OF A FEASIBLE AREA

If a company needs to decide what to produce, as a matter of good management practice it would want to know all the possible options. In mathematical terms, it would want a definition of a **feasible space**. Suppose that the company were involved with the production of two products, X and Y, and that X required 1 hour or labour and Y required 2 hours of labour. Labour hours, in this case, are resource requirements, X and Y the competing products. If all the labour required were available at **no** cost, there would be **no** scarcity and **no** production problem. However, if only 40 hours of labour were available each week then there would be an allocation problem. A decision would have to be taken as to whether only X, or only Y or some combination of the two be produced. In mathematical terms the allocation problem could be written as an inequality:

$1X + 2Y \leqslant 40$

where $\leqslant$ is read as 'less than or equal to'.

As we have already seen (Chapter 6) an equation can be represented graphically by a straight line. All the points on this line would provide a solution to the equation. If we were dealing only with the equation $1X + 2Y = 40$, we would first find two sets of points that provide solutions, plot these points on a graph and finally join these two points with a straight line. Two possible solutions are:

(a) $X = 0, Y = 20$
(b) $X = 40, Y = 0$

An interpretation of these two solutions would be that if only Y is to be produced then 20 units can be made and if only X is to be produced then 40 units can be made. Another possible solution would be to produce 10 units of X and 15 units of Y. All three solutions are shown in Fig. 20.1.

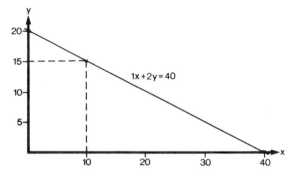

Figure 20.1   The definition of a line

In the same way that an equation can be represented by a line, an inequality can be represented by an **area**. If we consider the example $1X + 2Y \leqslant 40$, the three points

  (a) $X = 0$, $Y = 20$
  (b) $X = 40$, $Y = 0$
  (c) $X = 10$, $Y = 15$

still provide solutions. In addition to these points, others that give an answer of less than 40 are also acceptable. The point $X = 20$, $Y = 5$ (answer 30) is acceptable whereas the point $X = 20$, $Y = 15$ (answer 50) is not. The 'less than or equal to' inequality defines an area that lies to the left of the line as shown in Fig. 20.2.

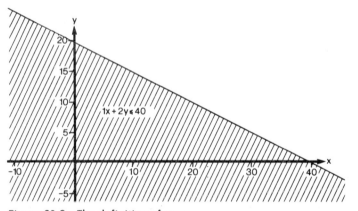

Figure 20.2   The definition of area

Inequalities can also take the form

$X \leqslant 20$
$Y \leqslant 15$

The area **jointly** defined by these two inequalities is shown in Fig. 20.3.

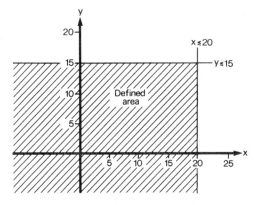

Figure 20.3 Area defined by two inequalities

The definition of what is possible can be represented mathematically by a number of inequalities and together they can define a feasible area.

Exercises

1. Show graphically the following inequalities:

(a) $5X + 2Y \leqslant 80$;
(b) $X + Y \geqslant 30$;
(c) $X \leqslant 10$;
(d) $Y \geqslant 12$.

2. Show graphically a feasible area defined jointly by:

$$2Y + 5X \geqslant 140$$
$$X + Y \leqslant 40$$

20.2 THE SOLUTION OF A LINEAR PROGRAMMING PROBLEM

All linear programming problems have three common characteristics:

(a) a linear objective function;
(b) a set of linear structural constraints;
(c) a set of non-negativity constraints.

The objective function is a mathematical statement of what management wishes to achieve. It could be the maximization of profit, minimization of cost or some other measurable objective. Linearity implies that the parameters of the objective function are **fixed**; for example, a constant cost per unit or constant contribution to profit per unit. The structural constraints are the physical limitations on the objective function. They could be constraints in terms of budgets, labour, raw materials, markets, social acceptability, legal requirements or contracts. Linearity means that all these constraints have fixed coefficients and can be represented by straight lines on a graph. Finally, the non-negativity constraints limit the solution to positive (and meaningful) answers only.

20.2.1 The maximization problem

Consider the following example were the objective is to maximize one function (profit).

Example　　A small company produces two products, X and Y. Suppose that each unit of product X requires 1 hour of labour and 6 tons of raw materials, whereas each unit of product Y requires 2 hours of labour and 5 tons of raw materials. Suppose also that the number of labour hours available each week is 40 and the available raw materials each week is 150 tons. If the contribution to profit is £2 per unit of X and £3 per unit of Y, determine the weekly production mix that will maximize profits.

This linear programming problem can be formulated mathematically as:

Maximize

$$z = 2X + 3Y \qquad \textbf{the linear objective function}$$

subject to the constraints

$$\left. \begin{array}{l} 1X + 2Y \leqslant 40 \\ 6X + 5Y \leqslant 150 \end{array} \right\} \textbf{the linear structural constraints}$$

and

$$X \geqslant 0, \; Y \geqslant 0 \qquad \textbf{the non-negativity constraints}$$

The objective function is the sum of the profit contributions from each product. If we were to decide to produce 5 units of X and 7 units of Y then the total contribution to profit would be $z = 2 \times 5 + 4 \times 7 = £38$. Linear programming provides a method to find what combination of X and Y will maximize the value of z subject to the given constraints.

In this example there are two structural constraints, one in terms of available labour and the other in terms of available raw materials. The usefulness of the solutions will depend on how realistically the constraints model the decision problem. If, for example, marketing considerations were ignored the optimum solution may suggest production levels that are the incompatible with sales opportunities. Mathematically, we need a structural constraint to correspond to each limitation on the objective function. If we consider the labour constraint as an example, the coefficients represent the labour requirements of 1 hour for product X and 2 hours for product Y. A product mix of 5 units of X and 7 units of Y will require only 19 hours of labour ($1 \times 5 + 2 \times 7$), does not exceed the available labour time of 40 hours and satisfies the first constraint. A production mix of 18 units of X and 13 units of Y exceeds the available labour time, does not satisfy the constraint and therefore could not provide a possible solution. The product mix of 5 units of X and 7 units of Y also satisfies the remaining structural constraint, $6 \times 5 + 5 \times 7 \leqslant 150$, and is one of the possible or feasible solutions. Jointly the structural constraints define the feasible area. In this example, the feasible area is defined by the labour and raw material constraints. No account is taken of the many other factors that could affect the optimum production mix.

The feasible area is found graphically by treating each constraint as an equation, plotting the corresponding straight lines and defining an area bounded by the straight lines which satisfies all the inequalities. We proceed as follows.

The **labour constraint**: if we were to use all the labour time available then

$$1X + 2Y = 40$$
$$(X = 0, \; Y = 20) \, (X = 40, \; Y = 0)$$

The two points shown in brackets are the 'one-product' solutions; we can use the 40 hours of labour to make 20 units of Y each week or 40 units of X. A line joining the two points will show combinations of X and Y that will require 40 hours of labour.

The **raw materials constraint**: if we were to use all the raw material available then

$$6X + 5Y = 150$$
$$(X = 0, \; Y = 30) \, (X = 25, \; Y = 0)$$

A line joining two possible solutions shown in brackets will show the combinations of X and Y that will require 150 tons of raw materials.

The **non-negativity constraints**: the constraints $X \geqslant 0$ and $Y \geqslant 0$ exclude any possibility of negative production levels which have no physical counterpart. Together they include the X-axis and the Y-axis as possible boundaries of the feasible area.

The feasible area defined by the two structural constraints and the two non-negativity constraints is shown in Fig. 20.4. The feasible area is contained within the boundaries of $OABC$. It is now a matter of deciding which of the points in this area provides an optimum solution. The choice is determined by the objective function. In this example, the choice of whether to produce just X, or just Y or some combination of the two will depend on the **relative profitability** of the two products.

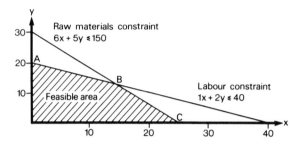

Figure 20.4   The definition of the feasible area

Profit has been expressed as a mathematical function $z = 2X + 3Y$, where z is the profit level. If we were to fix the level of profits, z, the necessary combination of X and Y could be shown graphically as a straight line. This is referred to as a **trial profit** line. If we let $z = £30$ then:

$$30 = 2X + 3Y$$
$$(X = 0, Y = 10)\ (X = 15, Y = 0)$$

A profit of £30 can be made by producing 15 units of X, or 10 units of Y or some combination of the two. This trial profit is shown in Fig. 20.5. All the points on the trial profit line will produce a profit of £30. The gradient gives the 'trade-off' between the two products. In this case, to maintain a profit level you would need to trade 2 units of Y against 3 units of X (a loss of £6 against a gain of £6). The trial profit line shown violates none of the constraints so profit can be increased from £30. Consider a second trial profit line where the profit level is fixed at £60.

If we let $z = £60$ then

$$60 = 2X + 3Y$$
$$(X = 0, Y = 20)\ (X = 30, Y = 0)$$

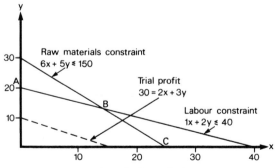

Figure 20.5   A trial profit ($z = £30$)

This trial profit line is shown in Fig. 20.6.

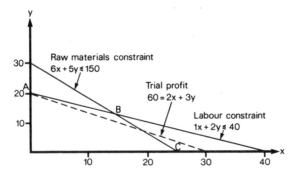

Figure 20.6   Trial profit fixed at £60

This second trial profit line is higher than and parallel to the first. It can be seen that a profit of £60 can be achieved at point A, and that some points on the trial profit line violate the raw materials constraint. To operate at point A would exhaust all the available labour hours but leave surplus raw materials. This solution can be improved upon by trading-off the more labour intensive product Y against the more raw material intensive product X. In terms of the graphical approach, we can note that any line that is **higher and parallel** to the existing trial profit line represents an improvement. By inspection we can see from Fig. 20.6 that higher trial profit lines will eventually lead to the optimum point B. This point B ($X = 14\frac{2}{7}$, $Y = 12\frac{6}{7}$) can be determined directly from the graph, or by simultaneously solving the two equations that define lines crossing at point B. The resultant profit is found by substitution into the objective function:

$$z = 2 \times 14\frac{2}{7} + 3 \times 12\frac{6}{7} = £67\frac{1}{7} \text{ per week}$$

Exercise

A manufacturer of fitted kitchens produces two units, a base unit and a cabinet unit. The base unit requires 90 minutes in the production department and 30 minutes in the assembly department. The cabinet unit requires 30 minutes and 60 minutes respectively in these departments. Each day 21 hours are available in the production department and 18 hours are available in the assembly department. It has already been agreed that not more than 15 cabinet units are produced each day. If base units make a contribution to profit of £2 per unit and cabinet units £5 per unit, what product mix will maximize the contribution to profit and what is this maximum?
(Answer: 6 base units, 15 cabinet units, contribution to profit = £87.)

20.2.2   The minimization problem

Consider the following example where the objective is to minimize one function (cost).

Example

A company operates two types of aircraft, the RS101 and the JC111. The RS101 is capable of carrying 40 passengers and 30 tons of cargo, whereas the JC111 is capable of carrying 60 passengers and 15 tons of cargo. The company is contracted to carry at least 480 passengers and 180 tons of cargo each day. If the cost per journey is £500 for a RS101 and £600 for a JC111, what choice of aircraft will minimize cost?
    This linear programming problem can be formulated mathematically as:

Minimize $z = 500X + 600Y$ **the linear objective function**

where X is the number of RS101 and Y is the number of JC111 subject to the constraints

$$40X + 60Y \geqslant 480$$
$$30X + 15Y \geqslant 180$$

the linear structural constraints

and

$$X \geqslant 0, \ Y \geqslant 0$$ the non-negativity constraints

In this case we are attempting to minimize the cost of a service subject to the operational constraints. These structural constraints, the requirement to carry so many passengers and so many tons of cargo, are expressed as 'greater than or equal to'. The inequalities are again used to define the feasible area.

The **passenger constraint**: if we were to carry the minimum number of passengers then

$$40X + 60Y = 480$$
$$(X = 0, \ Y = 8) \ (X = 12, \ Y = 0)$$

We could use 8 JC111s to carry 480 passengers or 12 RS101s or some combination of the two as given by the above equation.

The **cargo constraint**: if were to carry the minimum amount of cargo then

$$30X + 15Y = 180$$
$$(X = 0, \ Y = 12) \ (X = 6, \ Y = 0)$$

We could use 12 JC111s to carry 180 tons of cargo or 6 RS101s or some combination of the two as given by the above equation.

The **non-negativity constraints**: to ensure that the solution excludes negative numbers of aircraft, $X \geqslant 0$ and $Y \geqslant 0$ are included as possible boundaries of the feasible area.

The resultant feasible area is shown in Fig. 20.7. The objective is to locate the point of minimum cost within the feasible area. We proceed as before, by giving a convenient value of z which defines a trial cost line, but in this case attempting to make the line as near to the origin as possible, while retaining at least one point within the feasible area so as to minimize cost. If we let $z = £6000$ then

$$6000 = 500X + 600Y$$
$$(X = 0, \ Y = 10) \ (X = 12, \ Y = 0)$$

Figure 20.7   The definition of the feasible area

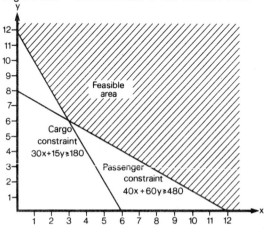

A cost of £6000 will be incurred by operating 12 RS101s, or 10 JC111s or a combination of the two as defined by the above equation, including combinations which are non-feasible. This trial cost line is shown in Fig. 20.8.

All lines lower than and parallel to the trial cost line show aircraft combinations that produce lower costs. By inspection we can see that point B is the point of lowest cost (X = 3, Y = 6). The level of cost corresponding to the use of 3 RS101s and 6 JC111s can be determined from the objective function:

$$z = 500 \times 3 + 600 \times 6 = £5100 \text{ per day}$$

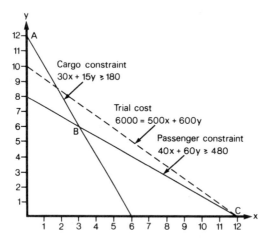

Figure 20.8   The trial cost line (z = £6000)

Exercise

Suppose you have been given the job of providing adequate transport to a new exhibition hall and it is possible to use existing railway connections and bus routes.

Each bus will cost £30 000 and carry 40 passengers. Each railway train will cost £45 000 and carry 50 passengers. A bus can make 15 trips a day and a railway train 12 trips a day.

The system has a number of financial and design constraints. It must carry at least 48 000 passengers a day and cost no more than £2 700 000. There is also an agreement to use at least 10 trains, while no more than 60 buses are available.

Formulate as a linear programming model for the minimization of costs and solve using the graphical method.

(Answer: 60 buses, 20 trains.)

20.3 SPECIAL CASES

Linear programming problems do not always yield a unique optimal solution. There are a number of special cases and we shall consider just two of them, no feasible solution and multiple optimum solutions.

20.3.1   No feasible solution

If the constraints are mutually exclusive, no feasible area can be defined and no optimum solution can exist. Consider again the maximization problem.

Maximize $z = 2X + 3Y$ **the linear objective function**

subject to the constraints

$$\left. \begin{array}{l} 1X + 2Y \leqslant 40 \\ 6X + 5Y \leqslant 150 \end{array} \right\}$$ **the linear structural constraints**

and

$$X \geqslant 0, Y \geqslant 0$$ **the non-negativity constraints**

The feasible area has been defined by the constraints as shown in Fig. 20.4. Suppose that in addition to the existing constraints the company is contracted to produce at least 30 units each week. This additional constraint can be written as:

$$X + Y \geqslant 30$$

As a boundary solution the constraint would be:

$$X + Y = 30$$
$$(X = 0, Y = 30)\,(X = 30, Y = 0)$$

The three structural constraints are shown in Fig. 20.9.

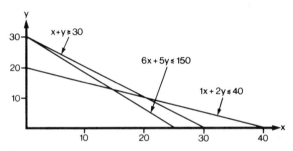

Figure 20.9   No feasible solution

The no feasible area case presents the manager with demands which cannot **simultaneously** be satisfied.

20.3.2   Multiple optimum solutions

A multiple optimum solution results when the objective function is **parallel** to one of the boundary constraints. Consider the following problem.

Minimize $z = 600X + 900Y$ **the linear objective function**

subject to the constraints

$$\left. \begin{array}{l} 40X + 60Y \geqslant 480 \\ 30X + 15Y \geqslant 180 \end{array} \right\}$$ **the linear structural constraints**

and

$$X \geqslant 0, Y \geqslant 0$$ **the non-negativity constraints**

This is the aircraft scheduling problem from Section 20.2.2 with different cost parameters in the objective function. If we let $z = £8100$ then

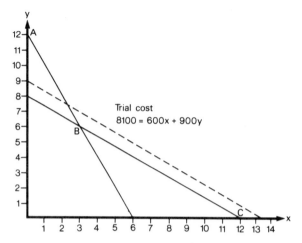

Figure 20.10   Multiple optimum solutions

$$8100 = 600X + 900Y$$
$$(X = 0, Y = 9)\ (X = 13.5, Y = 0)$$

The resultant trial cost line is shown in Fig. 20.10. This line is parallel to the boundary line BC. The lowest acceptable cost solution will be coincidental with the line BC making point B, point C and any other points on the line BC optimal. Multiple optimum solutions present the manager with choice and hence some flexibility.

Exercise

A textile firm makes two types of cloth, a Sutton Tweed and a Moseley Mohair. Each yard of tweed requires 3 oz of shoddy, 12 oz of mungo and 2 oz of flock, whilst the mohair requires 2 oz of shoddy, 5 oz of mungo and 7 oz of flock.

An agreement with the Dudley Mungo Manufacturers limits the amount of mungo available each day to 3000 oz. The transport restrictions only enable 800 oz of shoddy to be delivered each day, while conservation restrictions on the hunting of flock limits this to 1500 oz per day.

It has been estimated that the profit on tweed will be 20p per yard, and on mohair 15p per yard.

(a) How many yards of each cloth should be produced and what is the maximum profit?
(b) If a further constraint is added, that at least 300 yards of tweed be produced, what should the production mix be?

(Answer: (a) 170.6 yards of mohair, 152.9 yards of tweed, profit = £56.17; (b) constraints do not define a feasible area so no optimum solution exists.)

20.4 CONCLUSIONS

Linear programming provides the decision-maker with a means of formulating and solving a wide range of problems. If these problems are defined in terms of two variables, then the solution can be found by graphical methods as shown. However, in practice, decision problems are likely to have three or more variables, one or more objective functions and a number of complex constraints. To solve these problems a number of methods have developed, such as the Simplex Method, but these are generally beyond the scope of this book.

There are a number of computer programs available for the solution of linear programming problems. Many are easy to use and their successful application will depend on your skills at formulating a realistic mathematical model.

20.5 PROBLEMS

1. (a) Maximize $z = 10x_1 + 10x_2$

   subject to
   $$6x_1 + 10x_2 \leqslant 90$$
   $$15x_1 + 10x_2 \leqslant 120$$
   $$-8x_1 + 8x_2 \leqslant 40$$
   $$x_1 \leqslant 7$$
   $$x_2 \geqslant 2$$
   $$x_1, x_2 \geqslant 0$$

   (b) If the objective function were changed to
   $$z = 20x_1 + 10x_2$$
   find the new maximum value of z.

2. Minimize $z = x_1 + x_2$

   subject to
   $$5x_1 + 4x_2 \geqslant 40$$
   $$x_1 + 2x_2 \geqslant 14$$
   $$x_1 + 3x_2 \geqslant 18$$
   $$x_1, x_2 \geqslant 0$$

3. A company sells two products A and B which it prices at £200 and £100 respectively. From a long term contract it must produce at least 1 unit of A per week, and its plant capacity limits production of B to 11 per week. There are two raw materials used in production: a unit of A requires 28 units of raw material X and 12 units of raw material Y; a unit of B requires 24 units of X and 25 units of Y. There are 336 units of X available and 300 units of Y. A further constraint within the factory is that the number of units of A minus twice the number of units of B must be less than 4.

   (a) Formulate this problem into a linear programming format and hence find the maximum revenue that can be achieved if all units are sold.
   (b) If the amount of raw material X were increased to 420 units, what would be the new maximum revenue?

21 Networks

For any large project there are a host of smaller jobs that will need to be completed along the way. Some will have to await the completion of earlier tasks, while others can be started together. A **network** is a way of illustrating the various tasks, and the order in which they must be done, so that planning for the whole project may take place. It will also highlight those tasks which must not be delayed if the whole project is to be completed on time. These tasks collectively are known as the **critical path**. The technique of drawing up networks was developed during World War II and in the late 1950s in both the UK and the USA. In the UK it was developed by the Central Electricity Generating Board where its application reduced the overhaul time at a power station to 32% of the previous average. The US Navy independently developed the Programme Evaluation and Review Technique (PERT), whilst the Du Pont company developed the Critical Path Method, said to have saved the company $1 million in 1 year. All of these techniques are similar and have been applied in the building industry, in accountancy, and in the study of organizations, as well as their original uses.

Since for most projects only some of the tasks, or **activities**, will be critical to the overall timing of the project, the other activities can be seen as having **slack time**. This means that there will be some flexibility in when they need to be started or the length of time they may take. The objectives of the network analysis are:

(a) to locate the critical activities;
(b) to allocate the timing of other activities to obtain the most efficient use of manpower and other resources;
(c) to look for ways to reduce the total project time by speeding up the activities on the critical path, while monitoring the other activities to ensure that they do not, themselves, become critical.

21.1 NOTATION AND CONSTRUCTION

A network consists of a series of **nodes** linked together by **arrows**. There are two ways of representing the activities within the project; these are 'activity between nodes' and 'activity on nodes': we shall be using the first of these alternatives, so that each arrow will represent an activity. Nodes are drawn with three sections, as shown in Fig. 21.1.

Earliest starting time ——— 21 | 30 ——— Latest starting time
6 ——— Node number

Figure 21.1

The **node number** will allow us to discuss with others where on the network we are, the **earliest starting time** will be the soonest that the next activity, or activities, can begin, while the **latest starting time** also relates to the next activity. Each arrow which joins a node to a later node will represent an activity, for example, selecting a sample of invoices in an audit check. **Dummy activities**, represented by dotted lines, are often used in networks where one activity can begin immediately a previous one is complete, but another activity has to await the completion of a second previous activity. These activities take no time.

To meet the objective of locating the critical activities, we must:

(a) find the duration of the various activities and any activities which must be completed before a particular one may commence;
(b) arrange these into a network;
(c) find the earliest starting time by a forward pass through the network;
(d) find the latest starting time by a backward pass through the network;
(e) identify the critical path as consisting of those activities which have the same earliest and latest starting times.

21.1.1 Duration

Information about duration will often be available from previous projects, for example, the company will know how long it takes to obtain copies of plans from their head office. If the activity has not been undertaken before, then estimates can be obtained from those who have conducted this activity, or those most qualified to estimate the time needed. Activities which must be completed before a particular one may commence are usually a matter of technical information or common sense; for example, if you were constructing a new house, you would be unlikely to fit the carpets before you built the walls!

If we consider the example given in Table 21.1, we can develop the method of analysing networks.

Table 21.1

Activity	Duration	Any previous activites
A	10	—
B	3	A
C	4	A
D	4	A
E	2	B
F	1	B
G	2	C
H	3	D
I	2	E, F
J	2	I
K	3	G, H

21.1.2 Construction

The speedy construction of a network is a matter of practice and experience, and, especially with large and complex projects, there may need to be several versions before a neat, legible network is drawn. Every effort should be made to avoid having arrows which cross each other, although this is sometimes inevitable.

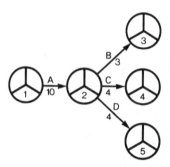

Figure 21.2

In Fig. 21.2 we see the beginnings of the network to represent the project set out in Table 21.1. Activity *A* is the only activity which may begin immediately, since it has no prerequisites, and it is represented by the arrow between node 1 and node 2. Once this activity is completed, activities *B*, *C* and *D* may begin, and these are shown going to nodes 3, 4 and 5 respectively. Note that each arrow is labelled with its activity and duration at this stage, to avoid confusion at a later stage. Each branch of the network will eventually end at a common node.

Exercise

Draw up the whole network for the project represented in Table 21.1.
  Your network should be similar to that shown in Fig. 21.3. (Note the use of dummy activities *F* → *E* and *G* → *H*.)

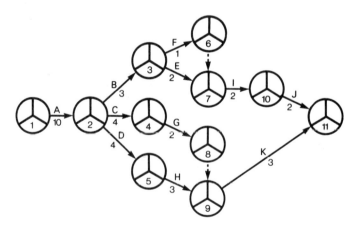

Figure 21.3

21.1.3 Earliest starting times

To find the earliest starting times, place a zero in the EST section of node 1 and follow the arrows **forwards** through the network. The EST at node 2 will be 10, at 3 it will be 13, at 6 it will be 14 and so on.

Note that activitiy *I* can only begin when both *E* and *F* are complete; thus if your network has a dummy activity from node 6 to node 7 (as in Fig. 21.4a), *I* starts at time 15. If the dummy activity goes from node 7 to node 6, then the EST at node 6 is now 15, since activity *E* must be completed before *I* can begin (as shown in Fig. 21.4b). It is possible to construct this network without using dummy activities, by making both *E* and *F* terminate at the **same** node. In this case the EST is the **highest number** of (EST at node 3 + duration of E) and (EST at node 3 + duration of F). This is illustrated in Fig. 21.4c). The total project time at node 11 will be 20.

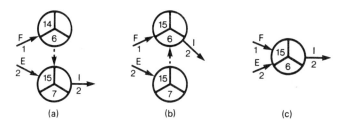

Figure 21.4

21.1.4 Latest starting times

To find the latest starting times, the total project time is inserted in the LST section of the final node, and we go **backwards** through the network, **subtracting** the activity times at each stage. If two routes lead back to the same node, the **lowest value** is put into LST. This will eventually give 0 in the LST section of note 1 (Fig. 21.5).

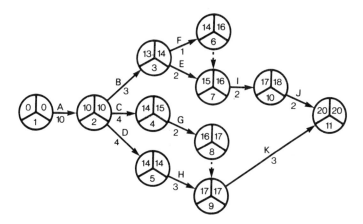

Figure 21.5

21.1.5 Critical path

The critical path consists of those activities which have the same earliest starting time and latest starting time; here *A, D, H* and *K*, and any delay in these activities will extend the total project time. There could be a delay of **one time period** elsewhere in the project without the total project time being increased.

21.2 PROBLEMS

For each of the following projects, determine the earliest starting times and latest starting times of each activity, identify the critical path, and determine the total project time.

1.

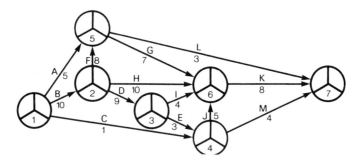

2.

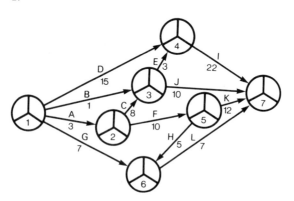

For each of the following projects, construct a network, identify the critical path, and determine the total project time.

3.	Activity	Duration	Preceding activities
	A	6	—
	B	8	—
	C	5	—
	D	4	A
	E	7	A
	F	3	C

3.

Activity	Duration	Preceding activities
G	2	D
H	8	D
I	10	D
J	5	B, E, F
K	6	F
L	7	I, K

4.

Activity	Duration	Preceding activities
A	4	—
B	3	—
C	2	—
D	3	—
E	4	—
F	5	—
G	6	A
H	6	A
I	5	B
J	4	B
K	6	C
L	7	C
M	7	C
N	12	D
O	14	D
P	7	E
Q	8	F
R	4	H, I, K
S	6	J, L, N
T	8	J, L, N
U	5	J, L, N
V	6	M, P, Q
W	7	G, R, S
X	7	O, U, V

21.3 PROJECT TIME REDUCTION

In the introduction to this chapter we specified three objectives for network analysis, the third of which was to look for ways to reduce the overall project time. Where an activity involves some chemical process it may be impossible successfully to reduce the time taken, but in most other activities the duration can be reduced **at some cost**. Time reductions may be achieved by using a (different) machine, adopting a new method of working, allocating extra personnel to the task or buying-in a part or a service. The minimum possible duration for an activity is known as the **crash duration**. Considerable care must be taken when reducing the times of activities on the network to make sure that the activity time is not reduced by so much that it is no longer critical. New critical paths will often arise as this time reduction exercise continues.

Table 21.2

Activity	Duration	Preceding activities	Cost	Crash duration	Crash cost
A	8	—	100	6	200
B	4	—	150	2	350
C	2	A	50	1	90
D	10	A	100	5	400
E	5	B	100	1	200
F	3	C, E	80	1	100

The project given in Table 21.2 will have a critical path consisting of activities *A* and *D*, a project time of 18 and a cost of 580 if the normal activity durations are used. This is illustrated in Fig. 21.6.

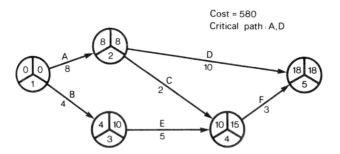

Figure 21.6

Since cost is likely to be of prime importance in deciding whether or not to take advantage of any feasible time reductions, the first step is to calculate the cost increase per time period saved for each activity. This is known as the **slope** for each activity. For activity *A*, this would be:

$$\frac{\text{increase in Cost}}{\text{decrease in Time}} = \frac{100}{2} = 50$$

The slopes for each activity are shown in Table 21.3.

Table 21.3

Activity	A	B	C	D	E	F
Slope	50	100	40	60	25	10

A second step is to find the **free float time** for each **non-critical activity**. This is the difference between the earliest time that the activity can finish and the earliest starting time of the next activity. By definition, activities on the critical path will have zero free float time. The initial free float times are shown in Table 21.4.

Table 21.4

Activity	EST	EFT	EST of next activity	Free float time
B	0	4	4	0
C	8	10	10	0
E	4	9	10	1
F	10	13	18	5

To reduce the project time, select that activity on the critical path with the lowest slope (here A) and note the difference between its normal duration and its crash duration (here, $8 - 6 = 2$). Look for the **smallest** (non-zero) free float time (here 1 for activity E), select the **minimum** of these two numbers and reduce the chosen activity by this amount (here A now has a duration of 7). Costs will increase by the time reduction multiplied by the slope (1×50). It is now necessary to reconstruct the network (Fig. 21.7).

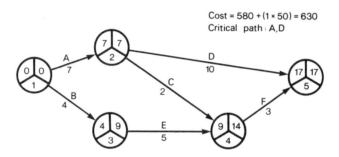

Cost = 580 + (1 × 50) = 630
Critical path : A,D

Figure 21.7

Table 21.5

Activity	EST	EFT	EST next activity	Free float time
B	0	4	4	0
C	7	9	9	0
E	4	9	9	0
F	9	12	17	5

The procedure may now be repeated. The activity on the critical path with the lowest slope is still A, but it can only be reduced by one time period. If this is done, we have the situation illustrated in Fig. 21.8. Any further reduction in the project time must involve activity D, since A is now at the crash duration; the minimum non-zero free float time is 1, but if this is used, we find that the free float time is reduced.

Exercise   Construct the network with activity D having a duration of 9 and recalculate the free float times for each non-critical activity.

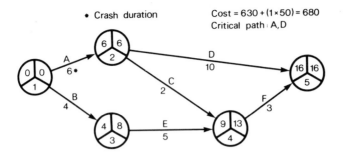

Figure 21.8

Table 21.6

Activity	EST	EFT	EST next activity	Free float time
B	0	4	4	0
C	6	8	9	1
E	4	9	9	0
F	9	12	16	4

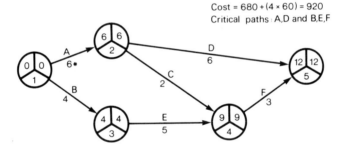

Figure 21.9

Table 21.7

Activity	EST	EFT	EST next activity	Free float time
C	6	8	9	1

Reducing activity D to a duration of 6 (i.e. $10 - 4$) we have the situation given in Fig. 21.9. There are now two critical paths through the network and thus for any further reduction in the project time it will be necessary to reduce **both** of these by the same amount. On the original critical path, only activity D can be reduced, and only by 1 time period at a cost of 60. For the second critical path, the activity with the lowest slope is F, at a cost of 10. If this is done, we have the situation in Fig. 21.10.

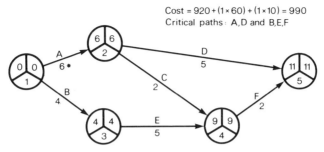

Cost = 920 + (1 × 60) + (1 × 10) = 990
Critical paths : A,D and B,E,F

Figure 21.10

Since both activities on the original critical path are now at their crash durations, it will not be possible to reduce the total project time further.

21.4 UNCERTAINTY

In all of the calculation so far in this chapter we have assumed that the time
taken for an activity will be the projected time as assessed at the planning stage,
or some given reduced time due to the diversion of extra resources into that
activity. In practice this may well not be true. Time may be saved if conditions
are particularly favourable or the activity may take longer due to unforeseen
difficulties. In general, delay is more likely than time saving, and thus if we
wish to estimate the time for the whole project and produce a confidence
interval, we cannot use the normal distribution (since that was symmetric, see
Chapter 12). It has been found that the beta distribution gives a good representation of the situation proposed above, and we shall use this to produce a
confidence interval for the total project time. To produce this interval we shall
need further information about the duration of the various activities, especially
those on the critical path. The estimates needed are for the shortest duration
and the longest duration of each activity, whilst the initial estimate of duration,
which we have used in the earlier parts of this chapter, is seen as the most likely
duration.

For the beta distribution, the mean and variance of the ith activity time are:

$$\text{mean} = \mu_i = \left(\frac{a + 4b + c}{6} \right)$$

$$\text{variance} = \sigma_i^2 = \left(\frac{c - a}{6} \right)^2$$

where a = shortest time, b = most likely time and c = longest time.

The 95% confidence interval for the total project time will be:

$$\mu \pm 1.96\sigma \quad \text{where } \mu = \Sigma\mu_i \quad \text{and } \sigma = \sqrt{\Sigma\sigma_i^2}$$

(since we assume the sum of beta variables has approximately a normal
distribution).

If a network has been constructed for a particular project and the critical
activities have been found to be A, D, H and K, then we may calculate the confidence interval as in Table 21.8.

Table 21.8

Activity	Shortest (a)	Most likely (b)	Longest (c)	Mean	Variance
A	8	10	14	10.333	1.000
D	3	4	6	4.167	0.250
H	2	3	6	3.333	0.444
K	1	3	7	3.333	1.000
				21.166	2.694

Therefore, $\mu = 21.666$, $\sigma^2 = 2.694$, $\sigma = 1.641$

Therefore, confidence interval is $21.166 \pm 1.96(1.641)$, i.e. 17.95 to 24.38.

Where the time taken for the critical activities is longer than the initial estimate, there need be no effect on the other activities, but if this time is shorter than the initial estimate it may be found that other activities become critical. Similarly, even if the activities on the critical path take their most likely durations, if some of the non-critical activities take their longest duration this may well extend the total project time. This is a further reason for calculating the free float time available on the non-critical activities.

21.5 CONCLUSIONS

The use of networks is a valuable aid to project planning and may result in considerable time-saving through the identification of those activities which are critical to the overall completion of the project within some target time. It will also help with resource planning and the phasing of activities, but it should be an ongoing process, especially where the project is large and complex. By monitoring the project in relation to the network, it is possible to identify where delays over the expected duration of an activity are occurring and what the implications will be for subsequent activities. Thus, if a non-critical activity is delayed through unforeseen circumstances, a new critical path may emerge through the network and the phasing of resource allocations, or the delivery of materials can be changed to meet the new timing of activities.

21.6 PROBLEMS

1. Construct a network for the project outlined below and calculate the free float times on the non-critical activities and the critical path time. Find the cost and shortest possible duration for the whole project.

Activity	Preceding activities	Duration	Cost	Crash duration	Crash cost
A	—	4	10	2	60
B	—	6	20	3	110
C	A	5	15	4	50
D	B, C	4	25	3	70
E	B	3	15	1	55
F	E	5	25	1	65
G	D, F	10	20	4	50

2. (a) Construct a network for the project outlined below and calculate the free float time and slope for each activity.
   (b) Identify the critical path and find the duration of the project using normal duration for each activity.
   (c) Find the cost of reducing the duration for the whole project to 54 days.
   (d) If there is a penalty of £500 per day over the contract time of 59 days and a bonus of £200 per day for each day less than the contract time, what will be the duration and cost of the project?

Activity	Preceding activities	Duration	Cost (£)	Crash duration	Crash cost (£)
A	—	5	200	4	300
B	A	7	500	3	1000
C	A	6	800	4	1400
D	—	6	500	5	700
E	D	6	700	3	850
F	D	8	900	5	1050
G	D	9	1000	5	1240
H	—	8	1000	4	1320
I	H	7	600	4	900
J	H	7	800	6	1000
K	—	5	1000	4	1200
L	K	9	500	5	700
M	K	10	1200	8	1240
N	B	8	600	4	760
O	N, Q, S	14	1500	10	1780
P	R, U	15	2000	10	2500
Q	C, E, Y	10	2000	8	2400
R	C, E, Y	15	1500	7	1900
S	F, I	20	3000	15	3750
T	V, W	10	2000	7	3200
U	G, J, L	14	1800	9	2250
V	G, J, L	22	5000	13	7700
W	M	18	4000	10	5280
X	O, P, T	11	3000	9	4000
Y	H	3	300	2	350

22 Stock control models

Stocks, or inventories as they are often called, can represent a significant asset to any business, organization or individual. They can consist of raw materials, production supplies, partially completed goods or finished goods. If we consider a car manufacturer, for example, decisions need to be made as to what stocks are required in response to anticipated demand and what should constitute the stock. Stock could be held as sheet metal, components, car bodies, engines or completed cars! In organizations such as hospitals or government departments, stocks of supportive materials are required to maintain the necessary service. As individuals, we could consider our own stock control policies for comparison: whether it be for the garage, garden or larder.

Stock can be defined as usable but idle resources. Associated with any stock policy are a number of costs and these give a numerical value to the consequences of our policy decisions. In this chapter we shall be concerned with describing the costs of holding stock mathematically and the ways in which cost can be minimized. A mathematical representation of a problem of this kind is referred to as a mathematical model. It must be remembered, though, that a mathematical model will generally exclude social, environmental and business 'costs' (pollution, loss of goodwill) that cannot be given a numerical value.

22.1 THE ECONOMIC ORDER QUANTITY MODEL

The economic order quantity (EOQ) model, or the economic batch quantity (EBQ) model as it is often called, is one mathematical representation of the costs involved in stock control. It is one of the simplest mathematical stock control models, but has been found to provide reasonable solutions to a number of practical problems.

The derivation of this model involves two simplifying assumptions:

(a) there is **no uncertainty** — demand is assumed to be known and constant;
(b) the **lead time** is zero — the lead time is the time between placing an order and receiving the goods.

The economic order quantity model is developed from two types of cost associated with stock control: **ordering costs** and **holding costs**. Ordering costs are those costs incurred each time an order is placed. They can involve administrative work, telephone calls, postage, travel or a combination of two or more of these. Holding costs are the costs of keeping an item in stock. These can

---

include the cost of capital, handling, storage, insurance, taxes, depreciation, deterioration and obsolescence.

1. A retailer, A to Z Limited, has a constant demand for 300 items each year. The cost of each item to the retailer is £20. The cost of ordering, handling and delivering is £18 per order regardless of the size of the order. The cost of holding items in stock amounts to 15% of the value of the stock held. If the lead time is zero, determine the order quantity that minimizes total inventory cost.

If Q is the quantity ordered on each occasion and D is the constant annual demand then the stock level as a function of time appears as in Fig. 22.1.

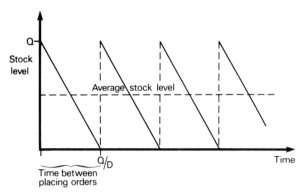

Figure 22.1   Stock level as a function of time

We can start with an order of Q and since the lead time is zero the inventory rises from 0 units to Q units. Thereafter, the stock level falls at the constant rate of D units per year. The time taken for the stock level to reach 0 is Q/D years. If we consider the annual demand of 300 items per year as given in our example, the stock level would fall to 0 in 2 years if we placed orders for 600 and would fall to 0 in 3 months ($\frac{1}{4}$ of a year) if we placed orders for 75.

It follows that the **number of orders** per year is D/Q. If orders of 75 units are placed to meet an annual demand of 300 then four deliveries are required each year. It also follows that the **average stock level** is $Q/2$ units, since the stock level varies uniformly between 0 and Q units. On this basis we are able to determine ordering costs and holding costs for this particular stock control model. Consider again the example given.

Total ordering costs (TOC) = cost per order × number of orders

$$= 18 \times \frac{D}{Q}$$

Total holding cost (THC)

= cost of holding per item × average number of items in stock

(15% of £20) $\times \dfrac{Q}{2}$ =

$3 \times \dfrac{Q}{2}$ =

We can note that actual holding cost will vary directly with the stock level from (15% of £20) × Q to 0 and that the above is an average. We can also note that it is typical for holding costs to be expressed as a percentage of value.

In seeking a stock control policy we need to consider **total variable cost** (TVC) and **total annual cost** (TAC), where

Total variable cost = total ordering costs + total holding costs

and

Total annual cost = total ordering costs + total holding costs + purchase cost (PC)

We can locate an order quantity that will minimize the costs of a stock control policy for our example by 'trial and error' as shown in table 22.1.

Table 22.1   The costs of stock

Ordering frequency p.a. f	Order size Q	Total ordering cost p.a. $18 \times f$	Average stock $Q/2$	Holding costs $3 \times Q/2$	TVC (TOC + THC)	TAC (TVC + PC) TVC + 6000
1	300	18	150.0	450.0	468.0	6468.0
2	150	36	75.0	225.0	261.0	6261.0
3	100	54	50.0	150.0	204.0	6204.0
4	75	72	37.5	112.5	184.5	6184.5
5	60	90	30.0	90.0	180.0	6180.0
6	50	108	25.0	75.0	183.0	6183.0
10	30	180	15.0	45.0	225.0	6225.0
12	25	216	12.5	37.5	253.5	6253.5

In this example both total variable cost and total annual cost are minimized if we place orders for 60 items, 5 times each year.

The structure of the table is as follows:

(a) Demand is uniform at 300 items each year. It can be statisfied by one order of 300 each year, two orders of 150 every 6 months, three orders of 100 every four months and so on.

(b) The cost of ordering remains fixed at £18 per order regardless of the size of an order. The total annual ordering cost is the ordering cost (C_0) multiplied by the ordering frequency. As the size of the order increases, the total annual order cost decreases.

(c) Total annual holding cost is the cost of keeping an item in stock for a year (often expressed as a percentage of value) multiplied by the average stock level. At the time an order is received, holding cost will be high but will

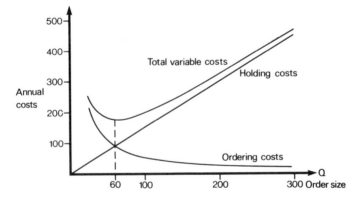

Figure 22.2   The costs of stock control

decrease to zero as the stock level falls to zero. Total annual holding cost is derived from the averaging process. As the size of the order increases the total annual holding cost increases.

(d) Total variable cost is the sum of one cost that decreases with order quantity (TOC) and one cost that increases with order quantity (THC). These cost functions are shown in Fig. 22.2.

(e) Total annual cost includes the annual purchase cost which in this case is £6000 (£20 × 300). The order quantity that minimizes the total variable cost need not minimize the more important total annual cost. It is the total annual cost of the inventory that the retailer will need to pay and it is this cost which can be affected by such factors as price discounts.

The order quantity that minimizes the total variable cost could have been determined by substitution into the following equation:

$$Q = \sqrt{\left(\frac{2 \times C_0 \times D}{C_H}\right)}$$

where Q is the economic order quantity, D is the annual demand, C_0 is the ordering cost and C_H is the holding cost per item per annum.

By substitution we are able to obtain the solution found by 'trial and error'.

$$Q = \sqrt{\left(\frac{2 \times 18 \times 300}{3.00}\right)} = 60$$

The derivation of this formula is given in Section 22.4.

2. A company uses components at the rate of 500 a month which are bought at the cost of £1.20 each from the supplier. It costs £20 each time to place an order, regardless of the quantity ordered.

The total holding cost is made up of the capital cost of 10% per annum of the value of stock plus 3p per item per annum for insurance plus 6p per item per annum for storage plus 3p per item for deterioration.

If the lead time is zero, determine the number of components the company should order, the frequency of ordering and the total annual cost of the inventory.

Annual demand = 500 × 12 = 6000
Ordering cost = £20
Holding cost = 1.20 × 0.10 + 0.03 + 0.06 + 0.03 = 0.24

By substitution,

$$Q = \sqrt{\left(\frac{2 \times 20 \times 6000}{0.24}\right)} = 1000$$

To minimize total variable cost, and in this case also total annual cost, we would place an order for 1000 components when the stock level is zero. The number of orders (or ordering frequency) is

$$\frac{D}{Q} = \frac{6000}{1000} = 6$$

We would therefore expect to place orders every 2 months.

$$
\begin{aligned}
\text{TAC} &= \text{TOC} + \text{THC} + \text{PC} \\
&= C_0 \times \frac{D}{Q} + C_H \times \frac{Q}{2} + \text{price} \times \text{quantity} \\
&= 20 \times \frac{6000}{1000} + 0.24 \times \frac{1000}{2} + 1.20 \times 6000 \\
&= 120 + 120 + 7200 \\
&= £7440
\end{aligned}
$$

22.2 QUANTITY DISCOUNTS

In practice it is common for a supplier to offer discounts on items purchased in larger quantities. This reduces the purchase cost. The ordering cost is also reduced since fewer orders need to be placed each year. However, holding costs are increased with the larger average stock level. The economic order quantity formula cannot be used directly since unit cost and hence purchase cost is no longer fixed.

Example

Suppose the retailer, A to Z Limited (see Section 22.1), is offered a discount in price of $2\frac{1}{2}\%$ on purchases of 100 or more. If the lead time remains zero, determine the order that minimizes total inventory cost.

The total annual cost function, as shown in the last column of table 22.1, now becomes discontinuous at the point where the discount is effective. Not only is the purchase cost reduced, but also the holding cost if expressed as a percentage of value (15% of the value of the stock level).

If $Q = 100$, the minimum order quantity to qualify for the discount, then:

$$\text{TOC} = £18 \times \frac{D}{Q} = £18 \times \frac{300}{100} = £54$$

purchase price (with $2\frac{1}{2}\%$ discount) $= £20 \times 0.975 = £19.50$
holding cost per item (15% of value) $= £19.50 \times 0.15 = £2.925$

$$\text{total holding cost} = £2.925 \times \frac{Q}{2} = £2.925 \times \frac{100}{2} = £146.25$$

total variable cost $= £54 + £146.25 = £200.25$
total annual cost $=$ total variable cost $+$ purchase cost
$\qquad\qquad\qquad = £200.25 + £19.50 \times 300 = £6050.25$

The discount on price of $2\frac{1}{2}\%$ will give the retailer (refer to Table 22.1) an annual saving of

$$£6204 - £6050.25 = £153.75$$

if he places orders of 100.

The effects on costs of the discount are shown in Table 22.2.

Table 22.2   The costs of stock taking into account a price discount

Ordering frequency p.a. f	Order size Q	Total ordering cost p.a. 18 × f	Average stock Q/2	Holding costs	TVC (TOC + THC)	TAC (TVC + PC)
1	300	18	150.0	438.750	456.750	6306.750
2	150	36	75.0	219.375	255.375	6105.375
3	100	54	50.0	146.250	200.250	6050.250
4	75	72	37.5	112.500	184.500	6184.500
5	60	90	30.0	90.000	180.000	6180.000
6	50	108	25.0	75.000	183.000	6183.000
10	30	180	15.0	45.000	225.000	6225.000
12	25	216	12.5	37.500	253.500	6253.500

By inspection of total annual cost we can see that a minimum is achieved with an order size of 100. This function is shown as Fig. 22.3.

The formula for the economic order quantity can be used within a price range to obtain a local minimum (up to 100 for example) but needs to be used with caution.

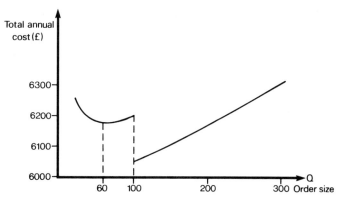

Figure 22.3 Total annual cost taking into account a price discount

22.3 NON-ZERO LEAD TIME

One of the assumptions of the basic economic order quantity model (see Section 22.1) was a lead time of zero. The model can be made more realistic if we allow a time lag between placing an order and receiving it. The calculation of the economic batch quantity does not change; it is the time at which the order is placed that changes. A **reorder point** must be calculated.

22.3.1 Non-zero lead time and constant demand

Suppose the retailer, A to Z Limited, retains a constant demand of 300 items each year but has a lead time of 1 month between placing an order and receiving the goods. The monthly demand for the items will be

$$300 \times \frac{1}{12} = 25$$

When the stock level falls to 25, the retailer will need to place his order (60 items in this case) to be able to meet demand in 1 month's time. Stock levels are shown in Fig. 22.4.

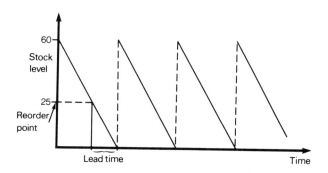

Figure 22.4 Stock levels with non-zero lead time

22.3.2 Non-zero lead time and probabilistic demand

If demand is probabilistic, as shown in Fig. 22.5, a reorder level cannot be specified that will guarantee the existing stock level reaching zero at the time the new order is received.

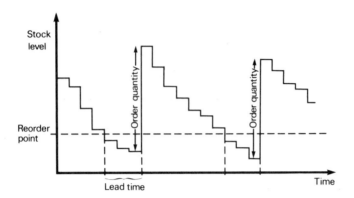

Figure 22.5 Stocks levels with non-zero lead time and probabilistic demand

To determine the reorder point we need to know the lead time (assumed constant), the risk a retailer or producer is willing to take of not being able to meet demand and the probabilistic demand function. The number of items held in stock when an order is placed will depend on the risk the stockholder is prepared to take in not being able to meet demand during the lead time. The probability distribution of demand is often described by the Poisson or normal distributions.

Examples
1. Suppose the retailer, A to Z Limited, now finds that the lead time is 1 month and that demand for items follows a Poisson distribution with a mean of 25 items per month. What should the reorder level be if the retailer is willing to take a risk of 5% of not being able to meet demand?

   To determine the reorder level we need to refer to cumulative Poisson probabilities as shown in Table 22.3.

Table 22.3 Cumulative Poisson probabilities for $\lambda = 25$

r	$P(r \text{ or more})$
32	0.1001
33	0.0715
34	0.0498
35	0.0338

If the reorder level were 32, then

P(not being able to meet demand) $= P$(33 or more items in 1 month)
$= 0.0715$ or 7.15%

If the reorder level were 33, then

P(not being able to meet demand) $= P$(34 or more items in 1 month)
$= 0.0498$ or 4.98%

Given that the risk the retailer is willing to take of not being able to meet demand is at most 5%, the reorder level would be set at 33 items. Once stock falls to this level a new order is placed.

2. You have been asked to develop a stock control policy for a company which sells office typewriters.

The cost to the company of each machine is £250 and the cost of placing an order is £50. The cost of holding stock has been estimated to be 10% per annum of the value of the stock held. If the company runs out of stock then the demand is met by special delivery, but the company is willing to take only a 5% risk of this service being required. From past records it has been found that demand is normally distributed with a mean of 12 machines per week and a standard deviation of 2 machines.

If there is an interval of a week between the time of placing an order and receiving it, advise the company on how many machines it should order at one time and what its reorder level should be.

By substitution, we are able to calculate the economic order quantity.

$$Q = \sqrt{\left(\frac{2 \times C_0 \times D}{C_H} \right)}$$

where D is annual demand.

Let $C_0 = £50$
$C_H = £250 \times 0.10 = £25$
and $D = 12 \times 52 = 624$

We have assumed that demand can exist for 52 weeks each year although production is not likely to take place for all 52 weeks:

$$Q = \sqrt{\left(\frac{2 \times 50 \times 624}{25} \right)} = .50$$

To minimize costs, assuming no quantity discounts, orders for 50 office typewriters would be made at any one time. Given a lead time of a week, we need now to calculate a reorder level such that the probability of not being able to meet demand is no more than 5%.

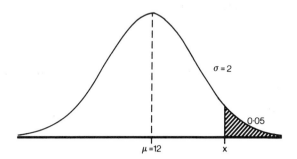

Figure 22.6   Weekly demand for office typewriters

Consider Fig. 22.6. With reference to tables for the normal distribution, a z-value of 1.645 will exclude 5% in the extreme right-hand tail area. By substitution, we are able to determine x:

$$z = \frac{x - \mu}{\sigma}$$

$$1.645 = \frac{x - 12}{2}$$

$$x = 12 + 1.645 \times 2$$
$$= 15.29$$

To ensure that the probability of not being able to meet demand is no more than 5%, a reorder level of 16 would need to be specified. It should be noted that any increase in the reorder level will increase the average stock level and as a result will increase holding costs. As we include more factors, the model becomes more and more complex. The inclusion of uncertainty, for example, makes the stock control model more realistic in most circumstances. As we have seen, the economic order quantity model can describe some stock control situations and can be developed to describe a number of others.

22.4 PROBLEMS

1. A company has decided to review its policy for the ordering of raw materials.
   After investigation, it has been estimated that the annual holding cost of stock is £0.10 per unit. Each raw material order incurs a procurement cost of £20 which includes invoicing and transportation. Annual demand can be assumed constant at 1 000 000 units. Production is steady throughout the year, there are no delivery problems with suppliers, so safety stocks need not be held. It is therefore the practice to time purchases to be received just as the stocks of raw materials reach zero.
   Determine the economic order quantity and the frequency of ordering.

2. A small business requires 200 boxes of paper each year. The cost of purchase is £12 per box. The cost to place an order with the supplier is £20 which includes telephone calls, clerical work and management time. The holding costs are estimated to be 12% of the value of stock.
   If the lead time is zero, determine the number of boxes the company should order, the frequency of ordering and the total annual cost of the inventory.

3. Suppose that in Exercise 1 there is a lead time of 1 week. Demand during lead time is normally distributed with mean 20 000 units and standard deviation 1000 units. The company wishes to be 99% sure of not running out of stock in any reorder period. Calculate the reorder point and the additional stockholding costs incurred in meeting this target. (Assume that there are 50 working weeks in the year.)

22.5 APPENDIX

This appendix need only concern those interested in the proof of the economic order quantity formula:

$$TVC = THC + TOC$$
$$= C_H \times \frac{Q}{2} + C_0 \times \frac{D}{Q}$$

We can differentiate this function with respect to Q (see Chapter 7) to obtain

$$\frac{d(TVC)}{dQ} = \frac{C_H}{2} - C_0 \frac{D}{Q^2}$$

To find a turning point we set this function for gradient equal to 0:

$$\frac{C_H}{2} - C_0 \frac{D}{Q^2} = 0$$

$$Q^2 = \frac{2 \times C_0 \times D}{C_H}$$

$$Q = \pm \sqrt{\left(\frac{2 \times C_0 \times D}{C_H} \right)}$$

To identify a maximum or a minimum we can differentiate a second time to obtain

$$\frac{d^2(TVC)}{dQ^2} = \frac{2 \times C_0 \times D}{Q^3}$$

This second derivative is only positive (identifies a turning point which is a minimum) when Q is positive. Hence the order quantity that minimizes total variable cost is

$$Q = + \sqrt{\left(\frac{2 \times C_0 \times D}{C_H} \right)}$$

Part VII
CONCLUDING EXERCISE

Draw a floor plan of a work place with at least two workers, two machines or two desks engaged in at least one activity with which you are familiar. It could look something like this:

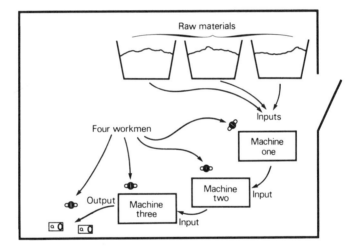

(a) Identify the work processes and organization at this work place.
(b) Identify where it would be appropriate to use mathematical models and the most realistic type of model in each case with special reference to any formulae and parameters needed.

Appendix 1 Cumulative binomial probabilities

		$p = 0.01$	0.05	0.10	0.20	0.30	0.40	0.45	0.50
$n = 5$	$r = 0$	1.0000	1.0000	1.0000	1.0000	1.0000	1.0000	1.0000	1.0000
	1	0.0490	0.2262	0.4095	0.6723	0.8319	0.9222	0.9497	0.9688
	2	0.0010	0.0226	0.0815	0.2627	0.4718	0.6630	0.7438	0.8125
	3		0.0012	0.0086	0.0579	0.1631	0.3174	0.4069	0.5000
	4			0.0005	0.0067	0.0308	0.0870	0.1312	0.1875
	5				0.0003	0.0024	0.0102	0.0185	0.0313
$n = 10$	$r = 0$	1.0000	1.0000	1.0000	1.0000	1.0000	1.0000	1.0000	1.0000
	1	0.0956	0.4013	0.6513	0.8926	0.9718	0.9940	0.9975	0.9990
	2	0.0043	0.0861	0.2639	0.6242	0.8507	0.9536	0.9767	0.9893
	3	0.0001	0.0115	0.0702	0.3222	0.6172	0.8327	0.9004	0.9453
	4		0.0010	0.0128	0.1209	0.3504	0.6177	0.7430	0.8281
	5		0.0001	0.0016	0.0328	0.1503	0.3669	0.4956	0.6230
	6			0.0001	0.0064	0.0473	0.1662	0.2616	0.3770
	7				0.0009	0.0106	0.0548	0.1020	0.1719
	8				0.0001	0.0016	0.0123	0.0274	0.0547
	9					0.0001	0.0017	0.0045	0.0107
	10						0.0001	0.0003	0.0010

where p is the probability of a characteristic (e.g. a defective item), n is the sample size and r is the number with that characteristic.

Appendix 2 Cumulative Poisson probabilities

	$\lambda = 1.0$	2.0	3.0	4.0	5.0	6.0	7.0
$x = 0$	1.0000	1.0000	1.0000	1.0000	1.0000	1.0000	1.0000
1	0.6321	0.8647	0.9502	0.9817	0.9933	0.9975	0.9991
2	0.2642	0.5940	0.8009	0.9084	0.9596	0.9826	0.9927
3	0.0803	0.3233	0.5768	0.7619	0.8753	0.9380	0.9704
4	0.0190	0.1429	0.3528	0.5665	0.7350	0.8488	0.9182
5	0.0037	0.0527	0.1847	0.3712	0.5595	0.7149	0.8270
6	0.0006	0.0166	0.0839	0.2149	0.3840	0.5543	0.6993
7	0.0001	0.0011	0.0335	0.1107	0.2378	0.3937	0.5503
8		0.0002	0.0119	0.0511	0.1334	0.2560	0.4013
9			0.0038	0.0214	0.0681	0.1528	0.2709
10			0.0011	0.0081	0.0318	0.0839	0.1695
11			0.0003	0.0028	0.0137	0.0426	0.0985
12			0.0001	0.0009	0.0055	0.0201	0.0534
13				0.0003	0.0020	0.0088	0.0270
14				0.0001	0.0007	0.0036	0.0128
15					0.0002	0.0014	0.0057
16					0.0001	0.0005	0.0024
17						0.0002	0.0010
18						0.0001	0.0004
19							0.0001

where λ is the average number of times a characteristic occurs and x is the number of occurrences.

Appendix 3 Areas in the right-hand tail of the normal distribution

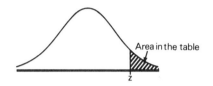

Area in the table

z	.00	.01	.02	.03	.04	.05	.06	.07	.08	.09
0.0	.5000	.4960	.4920	.4880	.4840	.4801	.4761	.4721	.4681	.4641
0.1	.4602	.4562	.4522	.4483	.4443	.4404	.4364	.4325	.4286	.4247
0.2	.4207	.4168	.4129	.4090	.4052	.4013	.3974	.3936	.3897	.3859
0.3	.3821	.3783	.3745	.3707	.3669	.3632	.3594	.3557	.3520	.3483
0.4	.3446	.3409	.3372	.3336	.3300	.3264	.3228	.3192	.3156	.3121
0.5	.3085	.3050	.3015	.2981	.2946	.2912	.2877	.2843	.2810	.2776
0.6	.2743	.2709	.2676	.2643	.2611	.2578	.2546	.2514	.2483	.2451
0.7	.2420	.2389	.2358	.2327	.2296	.2266	.2236	.2206	.2177	.2148
0.8	.2119	.2090	.2061	.2033	.2005	.1977	.1949	.1922	.1894	.1867
0.9	.1841	.1814	.1788	.1762	.1736	.1711	.1685	.1660	.1635	.1611
1.0	.1587	.1562	.1539	.1515	.1492	.1469	.1446	.1423	.1401	.1379
1.1	.1357	.1335	.1314	.1292	.1271	.1251	.1230	.1210	.1190	.1170
1.2	.1151	.1131	.1112	.1093	.1075	.1056	.1038	.1020	.1003	.0985
1.3	.0968	.0951	.0934	.0918	.0901	.0885	.0869	.0853	.0838	.0823
1.4	.0808	.0793	.0778	.0764	.0749	.0735	.0721	.0708	.0694	.0681
1.5	.0668	.0655	.0643	.0630	.0618	.0606	.0594	.0582	.0571	.0559
1.6	.0548	.0537	.0526	.0516	.0505	.0495	.0485	.0475	.0465	.0455
1.7	.0446	.0436	.0427	.0418	.0409	.0401	.0392	.0384	.0375	.0367
1.8	.0359	.0351	.0344	.0336	.0329	.0322	.0314	.0307	.0301	.0294
1.9	.0287	.0281	.0274	.0268	.0262	.0256	.0250	.0244	.0239	.0233
2.0	.02275	.02222	.02169	.02118	.02068	.02018	.01970	.01923	.01876	.01831
2.1	.01786	.01743	.01700	.01659	.01618	.01578	.01539	.01500	.01463	.01426
2.2	.01390	.01355	.01321	.01287	.01255	.01222	.01191	.01160	.01130	.01101
2.3	.01072	.01044	.01017	.00990	.00964	.00939	.00914	.00889	.00866	.00842
2.4	.00820	.00798	.00776	.00755	.00734	.00714	.00695	.00676	.00657	.00639
2.5	.00621	.00604	.00587	.00570	.00554	.00539	.00523	.00508	.00494	.00480
2.6	.00466	.00453	.00440	.00427	.00415	.00402	.00391	.00379	.00368	.00357
2.7	.00347	.00336	.00326	.00317	.00307	.00298	.00289	.00280	.00272	.00264

z	.00	.01	.02	.03	.04	.05	.06	.07	.08	.09
2.8	.00256	.00248	.00240	.00233	.00226	.00219	.00212	.00205	.00199	.00193
2.9	.00187	.00181	.00175	.00169	.00164	.00159	.00154	.00149	.00144	.00139
3.0	.00135									
3.1	.00097									
3.2	.00069									
3.3	.00048									
3.4	.00034									
3.5	.00023									
3.6	.00016									
3.7	.00011									
3.8	.00007									
3.9	.00005									
4.0	.00003									

Appendix 4 Student's *t* critical points

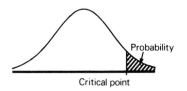

Probability

Critical point

Probability	0.10	0.05	0.025	0.01	0.005
ν = 1	3.078	6.314	12.706	31.821	63.657
2	1.886	2.920	4.303	6.965	9.925
3	1.638	2.353	3.182	4.541	5.841
4	1.533	2.132	2.776	3.747	4.604
5	1.476	2.015	2.571	3.365	4.032
6	1.440	1.943	2.447	3.143	3.707
7	1.415	1.895	2.365	2.998	3.499
8	1.397	1.860	2.306	2.896	3.355
9	1.383	1.833	2.262	2.821	3.250
10	1.372	1.812	2.228	2.764	3.169
11	1.363	1.796	2.201	2.718	3.106
12	1.356	1.782	2.179	2.681	3.055
13	1.350	1.771	2.160	2.650	3.012
14	1.345	1.761	2.145	2.624	2.977
15	1.341	1.753	2.131	2.602	2.947
16	1.337	1.746	2.120	2.583	2.921
17	1.333	1.740	2.110	2.567	2.898
18	1.330	1.734	2.101	2.552	2.878
19	1.328	1.729	2.093	2.539	2.861
20	1.325	1.725	2.086	2.528	2.845
21	1.323	1.721	2.080	2.518	2.831
22	1.321	1.717	2.074	2.508	2.819
23	1.319	1.714	2.069	2.500	2.807
24	1.318	1.711	2.064	2.492	2.797
25	1.316	1.708	2.060	2.485	2.787
26	1.315	1.706	2.056	2.479	2.779
27	1.314	1.703	2.052	2.473	2.771
28	1.313	1.701	2.048	2.467	2.763
29	1.311	1.699	2.045	2.462	2.756
30	1.310	1.697	2.042	2.457	2.750

Probability	0.10	0.05	0.025	0.01	0.005
40	1.303	1.684	2.021	2.423	2.704
60	1.296	1.671	2.000	2.390	2.660
120	1.289	1.658	1.980	2.358	2.617
∞	1.282	1.645	1.960	2.326	2.576

where ν is the number of degrees of freedom.

Appendix 5 χ^2 critical values

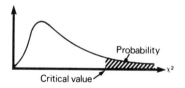

Probability

Critical value

χ^2

Probability	0.250	0.100	0.050	0.025	0.010	0.005	0.001
$\nu = 1$	1.32	2.71	3.84	5.02	6.63	7.88	10.8
2	2.77	4.61	5.99	7.38	9.21	10.6	13.8
3	4.11	6.25	7.81	9.35	11.3	12.8	16.3
4	5.39	7.78	9.49	11.1	13.3	14.9	18.5
5	6.63	9.24	11.1	12.8	15.1	16.7	20.5
6	7.84	10.6	12.6	14.4	16.8	18.5	22.5
7	9.04	12.0	14.1	16.0	18.5	20.3	24.3
8	10.2	13.4	15.5	17.5	20.3	22.0	26.1
9	11.4	14.7	16.9	19.0	21.7	23.6	27.9
10	12.5	16.0	18.3	20.5	23.2	25.2	29.6
11	13.7	17.3	19.7	21.9	24.7	26.8	31.3
12	14.8	18.5	21.0	23.3	26.2	28.3	32.9
13	16.0	19.8	22.4	24.7	27.7	29.8	34.5
14	17.1	21.1	23.7	26.1	29.1	31.3	36.1
15	18.2	22.3	25.0	27.5	30.6	32.8	37.7
16	19.4	23.5	26.3	28.8	32.0	34.3	39.3
17	20.5	24.8	27.6	30.2	33.4	35.7	40.8
18	21.6	26.0	28.9	31.5	34.8	37.2	42.3
19	22.7	27.2	30.1	32.9	36.2	38.6	43.8
20	23.8	28.4	31.4	34.2	37.6	40.0	45.3
21	24.9	29.6	32.7	35.5	38.9	41.4	46.8
22	26.0	30.8	33.9	36.8	40.3	42.8	48.3
23	27.1	32.0	35.2	38.1	41.6	44.2	49.7
24	28.2	33.2	36.4	39.4	43.0	45.6	51.2
25	29.3	34.4	37.7	40.6	44.3	46.9	52.6
26	30.4	35.6	38.9	41.9	45.6	48.3	54.1
27	31.5	36.7	40.1	43.2	47.0	49.6	55.5
28	32.6	37.9	41.3	44.5	48.3	51.0	56.9
29	33.7	39.1	42.6	45.7	49.6	52.3	58.3
30	34.8	40.3	43.8	47.0	50.9	53.7	59.7
40	45.6	51.8	55.8	59.3	63.7	66.8	73.4
50	56.3	63.2	67.5	71.4	76.2	79.5	86.7
60	67.0	74.4	79.1	83.3	88.4	92.0	99.6

Probability	0.250	0.100	0.050	0.025	0.010	0.005	0.001
70	77.6	85.5	90.5	95.0	100	104	112
80	88.1	96.6	102	107	112	116	125
90	98.6	108	113	118	124	128	137
100	109	118	124	130	136	140	149

where ν is the number of degrees of freedom.

Appendix 6 Present value factors

Years	1%	2%	3%	4%	5%	6%	7%	8%	9%	10%
1	.9901	.9804	.9709	.9615	.9524	.9434	.9346	.9259	.9174	.9091
2	.9803	.9612	.9426	.9426	.9070	.8900	.8734	.8573	.8417	.8264
3	.9706	.9423	.9151	.8890	.8638	.8396	.8163	.7938	.7722	.7513
4	.9610	.9238	.8885	.8548	.8227	.7921	.7629	.7350	.7084	.6830
5	.9515	.9057	.8626	.8219	.7835	.7473	.7130	.6806	.6499	.6209
6	.9420	.8880	.8375	.7903	.7462	.7050	.6663	.6302	.5963	.5645
7	.9327	.8706	.8131	.7599	.7107	.6651	.6227	.5835	.5470	.5132
8	.9235	.8535	.7894	.7307	.6768	.6274	.5820	.5403	.5019	.4665
9	.9143	.8368	.7664	.7026	.6446	.5919	.5439	.5002	.4604	.4241
10	.9053	.8203	.7441	.6756	.6139	.5584	.5083	.4632	.4224	.3855
11	.8963	.8043	.7224	.6496	.5847	.5268	.4751	.4289	.3875	.3505
12	.8874	.7885	.7014	.6246	.5568	.4970	.4440	.3971	.3555	.3186
13	.8787	.7730	.6810	.6006	.5303	.4688	.4150	.3677	.3262	.2897
14	.8700	.7579	.6611	.5775	.5051	.4423	.3878	.3405	.2992	.2633
15	.8613	.7430	.6419	.5553	.4810	.4173	.3624	.3152	.2745	.2394
16	.8528	.7284	.6232	.5339	.4581	.3936	.3387	.2919	.2519	.2176
17	.8444	.7142	.6050	.5134	.4363	.3714	.3166	.2703	.2311	.1978
18	.8360	.7002	.5874	.4936	.4155	.3503	.2959	.2502	.2120	.1799
19	.8277	.6864	.5703	.4746	.3957	.3305	.2765	.2317	.1945	.1635
20	.8195	.6730	.5537	.4564	.3769	.3118	.2584	.2145	.1784	.1486
21	.8114	.6598	.5375	.4388	.3589	.2942	.2415	.1987	.1637	.1351
22	.8034	.6468	.5219	.4220	.3418	.2775	.2257	.1839	.1502	.1228
23	.7954	.6342	.5067	.4057	.3256	.2618	.2109	.1703	.1378	.1117
24	.7876	.6217	.4919	.3901	.3101	.2470	.1971	.1577	.1264	.1015
25	.7798	.6095	.4776	.3751	.2953	.2330	.1842	.1460	.1160	.0923

Years	11%	12%	13%	14%	15%	16%	17%	18%	19%	20%
1	.9009	.8929	.8850	.8772	.8696	.8621	.8547	.8475	.8403	.8333
2	.8116	.7972	.7831	.7695	.7561	.7432	.7305	.7182	.7062	.6944
3	.7312	.7118	.6931	.6750	.6575	.6407	.6244	.6086	.5934	.5787
4	.6587	.6355	.6133	.5921	.5718	.5523	.5337	.5158	.4987	.4823
5	.5935	.5674	.5428	.5194	.4972	.4761	.4561	.4371	.4190	.4019
6	.5346	.5066	.4803	.4556	.4323	.4104	.3898	.3704	.3521	.3349
7	.4817	.4523	.4251	.3996	.3759	.3538	.3332	.3139	.2959	.2791
8	.4339	.4039	.3762	.3506	.3269	.3050	.2848	.2660	.2487	.2326
9	.3909	.3606	.3329	.3075	.2843	.2630	.2434	.2255	.2090	.1938
10	.3522	.3220	.2946	.2697	.2472	.2267	.2080	.1911	.1756	.1615
11	.3173	.2875	.2607	.2366	.2149	.1954	.1778	.1619	.1476	.1346
12	.2858	.2567	.2307	.2076	.1869	.1685	.1520	.1372	.1240	.1122
13	.2575	.2292	.2042	.1821	.1625	.1452	.1299	.1163	.1042	.0935
14	.2320	.2046	.1807	.1597	.1413	.1252	.1110	.0985	.0876	.0779
15	.2090	.1827	.1599	.1401	.1229	.1079	.0949	.0835	.0736	.0649
16	.1883	.1631	.1415	.1229	.1069	.0930	.0811	.0708	.0618	.0541
17	.1696	.1456	.1252	.1078	.0929	.0802	.0693	.0600	.0520	.0451
18	.1528	.1300	.1108	.0946	.0808	.0691	.0592	.0508	.0437	.0376
19	.1377	.1161	.0981	.0829	.0703	.0596	.0506	.0431	.0367	.0313
20	.1240	.1037	.0868	.0728	.0611	.0514	.0433	.0365	.0308	.0261
21	.1117	.0926	.0768	.0638	.0531	.0443	.0370	.0309	.0259	.0217
22	.1007	.0826	.0680	.0560	.0462	.0382	.0316	.0262	.0218	.0181
23	.0907	.0738	.0601	.0491	.0402	.0329	.0270	.0222	.0183	.0151
24	.0817	.0659	.0532	.0431	.0349	.0284	.0231	.0188	.0154	.0126
25	.0736	.0588	.0471	.0378	.0304	.0245	.0197	.0160	.0129	.0105

Selected answers to problems

SECTION 3.4

2. mean = 1.3611, median = 1, mode = 0.
4. (a) mean = £9.2365, median = £8.86.
6. mean = £111.93, median = £95.93, mode = £34.
8. mean = 3.174, median = 3, mode = 2 and mean = 2.962, median = 3, mode = 2.
10. mean = £108.264.

SECTION 4.5

2. range = 4, quartile deviation = 1, standard deviation = 1.3775.
4. (a) mean = 9.2365, standard deviation = 2.825.
6. quartile deviation = 49.0635, standard deviation = 74.0944 (assuming a lower boundary of 20 and upper boundary of 400).
8. mean = £0.21, standard deviation = £7.053 (assuming a lower boundary of −20 and upper boundary of 30).

SECTION 5.6

2. (a) 52.63, 63.16, 84.21; (b) 247, 266, 285, 313.5.
4. (a) 100, 150, 375; (b) 100, 66.67, 66.67; (c) 100, 168.75, 431.25; (d) 100, 167, 417; (e) 100, 167, 386; (f) 100, 97, 108; (g) 100, 97, 100.5.

SECTION 6.4

2. $x = -\frac{16}{9}y$.
4. a^{-2}.
6. $a^2 + 2ab$.
8. $a^2 - b^2$.
10. $a + a^2$.
12. $y = 4$.

SECTION 6.6

8. $x = 3, y = 4$.
10. (a) $P = 20 - 2D$; (b) $P = -4 + 2S$; (c) $P = 8, Q = 6$.

---

12. $(x - 9)(x + 4)$.
14. $-14, 2$.
16. $1/2, 3$.
18. $0.4175, 9.5825$.
20. $P = \frac{1}{2}Q^2 - 10Q + 200$.

SECTION 6.8

2. $\begin{bmatrix} 20 \\ 15 \\ 10 \end{bmatrix}$.

4. $\begin{bmatrix} 2 & 5 \\ 5 & 8 \end{bmatrix}$.

6. $\begin{bmatrix} 0 & -1 \\ 1 & 0 \end{bmatrix}$.

8. $\begin{bmatrix} 3 & 6 \\ 9 & 12 \end{bmatrix}$.

10. $\begin{bmatrix} 10 & 14 \\ 14 & 20 \end{bmatrix}$.

12. $\begin{bmatrix} 4 & 3 \\ 8 & 7 \end{bmatrix}$.

14. $\begin{bmatrix} 0.9 \\ 2.0 \\ 1.9 \\ 1.5 \end{bmatrix}$.

16. $\begin{bmatrix} 82 & 52 & 11 \\ 52 & 49 & 7 \\ 56 & 67 & 7 \end{bmatrix}$.

18. $\begin{bmatrix} 1 & 0 & 0 & 0 \\ 0 & 1 & 0 & 0 \\ 0 & 0 & 1 & 0 \\ 0 & 0 & 0 & 1 \end{bmatrix}$.

20. $\begin{bmatrix} 1.75 & -0.75 \\ -2 & 1 \end{bmatrix}$.

22. $\begin{bmatrix} 5 & -3.5 \\ -3.5 & 2.5 \end{bmatrix}$.

24. $\begin{bmatrix} 84 \\ 114 \\ 92 \end{bmatrix}$.

26. impossible.

28. $\dfrac{-1}{46}\begin{bmatrix} 9 & -5 & -4 \\ -2 & -4 & 6 \\ -66 & 52 & -32 \end{bmatrix}$.

30. $(BA)^{-1} = A^{-1}B^{-1}$
    $(AB)^{-1} = B^{-1}A^{-1}$.

SECTION 6.11

2. $x = 3, y = -2$.
4. $x_1 = 3, x_2 = 4, x_3 = 5$.
6. $X = \begin{bmatrix} 260 \\ 310 \end{bmatrix}$.
8. $X = \begin{bmatrix} 9870 \\ 6110 \\ 4510 \end{bmatrix}$.

SECTION 7.3

2. 10.
4. 4.
6. 2.
8. $4x^3 + 6x^2$.
10. $20x^4 + 2x^3 - 3x^2 + 2$.
12. $320x^7 + 30x^2 - 30 - 2x^{-2} + 8x^{-3}$.
14. $AC = \frac{1}{3}x^2 - 4x + 20$, $MC = x^2 - 8x + 20$.
16. (i) (a) $P = 1000 - 5Q$, (b) $P = 1500 - 55Q$; (ii) $MR = 1000 - 10Q$, $MR = 1500 - 110Q$; (iv) (a) $E_D = -19$, (b) $E_D = -1.727$.

SECTION 7.8

2. Max. $x = 5, y = 75$.
4. Min. $x = -1, y = 15$.
6. Max. $x = 3, y = 28$; min. $x = 5, y = 26.67$.
8. Max. $x = 1, y = 31$; min. $x = 4, y = 4$.
10. Min. $x = 2, y = 16$; max. $x = 3.33, y = 19.56$.
12. Max. $x = 10$, profit $= -150$, price $= 5$.
14. (a) $\pi = (-1/30) Q^3 + 5Q^2$, Max. $Q = 100$, profit $= 16\ 666.67$; (b) Max. $Q = 125$, profit $= 13\ 020.83$; (c) 600,500; (d) AC $= 433.33$, MC $= 200$, and AC $= 395.833$, MC $= 312.5$.
16. $9x^2 + 18x + 2$.
18. $-8x^7 + 30x^4 + 80x^3 + 80x - 200$.
20. $\dfrac{1 - 4x - 2x^2}{(2x^2 + 1)^2}$.
22. $16(4x + 10)^3$.
24. $6x^5 + 60x^2$.
26. $5x^3 + 3x^2 + 5x + c$.
28. $20x + c$.
30. 42.5.
32. 154.25.

SECTION 7.12

2. $60x^2z + 8xz^2 + 15z^3 + 80x^3$ and $20x^3 + 8x^2z + 45xz^2 - 6z$.
4. $60xz^2 + 40z$ and $60x^2z + 40x$.
6. Max. $x = 2, z = 6$.
8. Min. $x = 0, z = 0$.

10. Max. $y = 1.5$, $x = 2$.
12. $x = 2$, $y = 2.2$, profit $= 52.6$.
14. Max. $x = 198/76$, $z = 66/76$.
16. Max. $y = 142$, $x = -163$.
18. Min. $y = 1/2$, $x = 1/2$.
20. $L = 250$, $K = 93.75$, $Q = 958.4147$.

SECTION 8.6

2. £641.088.
4. £3519.612.
6. Accept £400 (present value of £520 = £353.912).
8. NPV £4.29756 and £3.96022.
10. £1221.02.
12. £298.31.

SECTION 9.3

2. 1/8.
4. 0.216, 0.144, 0.432.
6. 1/3.
8. Yes, 1/36.
10. 7.
12. 7/12.
14. (a) 0.14793; (b) 0.07692.
16. (a) 0.05; (b) 0.15; (c) 0.02; (d) 0.38.
18. (a) 260; (b) 157.5; (c) 32.5.
20. (a) 0.5222; (b) 0.09212.

SECTION 9.7

2. (a) 0.2; (b) 0.25.
4. (a) 0.387; (b) 0.009 677; (c) 0.1; (d) 0.322 58.
6. $p^2 = \begin{bmatrix} 0.58 & 0.42 \\ 0.42 & 0.58 \end{bmatrix}$ $p^4 = \begin{bmatrix} 0.5128 & 0.4872 \\ 0.4872 & 0.5128 \end{bmatrix}$
   $p^8 = \begin{bmatrix} 0.5003 & 0.4997 \\ 0.4997 & 0.5003 \end{bmatrix}$ $p^{16} = \begin{bmatrix} 0.5 & 0.5 \\ 0.5 & 0.5 \end{bmatrix}$

SECTION 10.3

2. 210, 210.
4. 635, 013, 560, 000.
6. 0.031 25, 0.156 25, 0.312 50, 0.312 50, 0.156 25, 0.031 25.
8. (a) 0.006 046 6; (b) 0.120 932 4; (c) 0.3823.
10. 0.0861.

SECTION 10.6

2. 0.033 257 5.
4. 0.916 625 4; 0.083 374 6.
6. 16.

SECTION 11.2

1. (a) 0.1, (b) 1, (c) −0.6, (d) −1.265, (e) 0.342.
2. (a) 0.022 75; (c) 0.9599; (e) 0.1867; (g) 0.995 47; (i) 0.0597; (k) 0.2306; (m) 0.887 04.
3. (b) −1.02; (d) −1.23; (f) −3; (h) ±1.96.
4. (a) 3.01%; (c) 93.39%; (e) £89.21.

SECTION 11.7

2. (a) 0.834; (b) 0.9292; (c) 0.905 31.
4. (a) 0.8643; (b) cannot assume $p = 0.3$ hence cannot estimate.
6. (a) 0.6480; (b) 0.1230.
8. 0.6844.

SECTION 12.5

2. (a) $\bar{x} = 146.8$, $s = 13.05$, 146.8 ± 4.044; (b) 73.
4. (a) $\bar{x} = 3$, $s = 2.98$, 3 ± 0.65; (b) let $n = 153$ (round-up).
6. (a) 375; (b) 384.
8. (a) £5.40 ± 0.61; (b) 46.
10. $1 \leqslant \text{median} \leqslant 1$.

SECTION 13.4

2. < £13.81.
4. > 94.48%.
6. £0.50 ± 0.91.
8. 4% ± 5%.
10. £1259 ± £102.78.

SECTION 14.6

2. $z = 12.39$, reject H_0.
4. $z = -1.353$, accept H_0.
6. $z = 2.23$, reject H_0.
8. $t = -2.680$, reject H_0.
10. (a) 29.5%, (b) 19.6%.

SECTION 15.3

2. $\chi^2 = 14.46$, reject H_0.
4. $\chi^2 = 2.517$, accept H_0.
6. $\chi^2 = 21.719$, reject H_0.
8. $\chi^2 = 1.281$, accept H_0.
10. $\chi^2 = 50.513$, reject H_0.

SECTION 16.7

2. 0.667.
4. 0.794.
6. 0.993 399, 0.986 84.
8. $-0.940\ 87$, 0.885 24.
10. $-0.053\ 297$, 0.002 84.
12. (b) 0.6898.

SECTION 17.7

2. (b) $7.6345 + 1.6635x$.
4. 10.
6. (a) $-14.6857 + 7.8357x$; (b) $0.9188 + 0.0794x$.
8. $0.5 + 0.3289y$, $-1.52 + 3.04x$.
10. $149.226\ 52 - 0.116\ 022y$.

SECTION 19.8

2. $42.875 + 1.3529x$.
3. (c) -3.346, -1.116, 0.782, 3.68.
4. 0.795, 0.946, 1.057, 1.200.
6. (b) $59.595 - 1.3136x$; (c) 26.756.

SECTION 20.5

1. (b) $x_1 = 6\frac{2}{3}, x_2 = 2, z = 153\frac{1}{3}$.
2. $x_1 = 4, x_2 = 5, z = 9$.

SECTION 21.2

2. Critical path D, I, total time 37.
4. Critical path D, N, S, W, total time 28.

SECTION 21.6

2. (b) H, I, S, O, X, 60 days; (c) £38 170; (d) £35 840 in 58 days.

SECTION 22.4

2. 75, 2.67, £2507.33.

Index